CHELTONIAN SOCIETY

College Echoes:
An Epitaph to the Great War

On behalf of the Cheltonian Society,
this confirms the authenticity of book number:

16

of this signed limited edition of 702 copies.

Patrick Stevens

Patrick Stevens, author

To Seb,

Many thanks for all your help and support with 'Echoes'.

Best wishes,

Paddy

COLLEGE ECHOES

An Epitaph to the Great War

PATRICK STEVENS

SILVERDART PUBLISHING
MMXVIII

COLLEGE ECHOES

Published by Silverdart Ltd
Woodmancote Manor, Cirencester
Gloucestershire GL7 7ED
United Kingdom
www.silverdart.co.uk
+44 (0) 1285 831 789
info@silverdart.co.uk

Copyright © Cheltonian Society 2018

All rights reserved. No part of this publication may be reproduced,
stored in a retrieval system, or transmitted, in any form or by any means,
electronic, mechanical, photocopying, recording or otherwise, without the prior
permission of the publisher and the copyright owner.

ISBN: 978-1-9996776-0-2

In lasting memory of the
702 Old Cheltonians
who fell in the Great War

FOREWORD

by General Sir Michael Rose

As many generations of Cheltonians have done before and no doubt still do, as a young boy I often sat in Cheltenham College Chapel wondering what sort of people they had been whose names were now inscribed on the highly polished brass memorials lining the Chapel walls and where destiny would have taken them had their lives not been so suddenly cut short by war. A century on from the end of the First World War, in which so many Cheltonians were killed or wounded, those thoughts still have great relevance. For behind the impersonal inscriptions, these were ordinary young men who had, without exception, chosen duty and sacrifice over life and material reward. Barely out of school, they had perished fighting for their King and Country and for what they believed in. And, as Sir John Dill, a former Chief of the Imperial General Staff and Old Cheltonian, put it, 'all too rarely does fighting come when men's spirits are high, and their deeds of valour are visible, but rather in the semi-light or the darkness, when courage is at its lowest ebb and when there are few if any witnesses'. Their actions may remain unsung, but they are not forgotten – nor ever should they be. Although almost every family in the country at that time suffered the dreadful loss of loved ones, their deaths were also strongly felt in schools such as Cheltenham College, where both teachers and pupils had only recently said farewell to friends whose names were now inscribed on Chapel memorials.

Patrick Stevens' moving testimony to the fallen of Cheltenham College and his ability to bring the names on these memorials to life not only informs us today of the sort of people they were, but also reminds us of the noble values they held – such as honour, duty and a readiness to sacrifice themselves for others. These are values which have sustained civilised society throughout history and still do so today. They are values which help bring about freedom, justice and peace and which preserve us all from tyranny. If succeeding generations are to flourish and survive then they too need to understand and uphold these values – however difficult this may be in a seemingly confused age of social media, high speed communications and globalisation.

I hope that every Cheltonian now, and in the future, will be encouraged to read and take away from College a copy of this book.

General Sir Michael Rose, KCB, CBE, DSO, QGM,
Commandeur Legion d'Honneur and Old Cheltonian.

ACKNOWLEDGEMENTS

by Patrick Stevens

I am indebted to an army of kind and supportive individuals who have given incredibly generously of their time, advice, encouragement and support during the production of *College Echoes*. The unstinting assistance and wise counsel from my university postgraduate colleagues and true friends, Kevin Dyer and Catherine Long, has been immeasurable, with hours of proofing, scrutiny and historical discussion combining to get the final draft just right. Their personal contributions, as my 'editors-in-chief', have been momentous. Similarly, special mention must be made of Jo Doidge-Harrison, the Head of History at Cheltenham College. Jo's infectious enthusiasm for the task, and her organisation of the various battlefield tours over the centenary period allowed a current cohort of Cheltonians to visualise the circumstances of the fighting in the Dardanelles and on the Western Front. The collation and inclusion of current student contributions has been pivotal in providing that crucial link between contemporary Cheltonians and their Great War forbears. Under Jo's tutelage, the personal accounts from battlefield visits by the current cohort of Cheltonians, especially Noni Stuckey, Sam Hamilton, Tommy and Charlotte Maddinson, Felix Watson-Smyth, Charlie Meecham-Jones, Angus Thomson, Caitlin Brister, Victoria Brain, Charles Hellens and Freya Haddon, have been most welcome and have all added a significant dimension to the final narrative. Rachael Merrison, the College Archivist and Data Manager, has been a pillar of strength in unearthing information, primary sources and photographic illustrations from the deeper recesses of the College archives. Despite her increasingly busy primary duties, Rachael has never failed to find key documents and primary sources from the College's archives that have been central in providing real colour to the account. Her contribution and innovative ideas have been greatly aided and abetted by the other recent and current members of the archive team, including Jill Barlow, Danielle Joyce, Deborah Beames and Katie Barrett. I must also thank Jo Millar, the Head of Art at College, whose First World War theme inspired the production of several beautiful pieces of work by her students, one of which is the commemorative vase on the back of the book's cover. This beautiful and poignant work was made by Rebecca Cook, one of Jo's pottery protégées, and was inspired by Rebecca's great grandfather, a tank driver in the Great War who was Mentioned in Despatches. Rebecca created the sculpture using predominantly the colours grey, white and red to reflect the colours on the battlefield.

    This book would have been even more of a challenge to complete without the initial groundwork of research diligently set out by three key people. Christine Leighton, the College's former archivist, rightly identified that the number of Great War Old Cheltonian fatalities greatly exceeded the 675 originally recorded. From her primary work, and with my detailed follow-on research at the National Archives and elsewhere, the final figure of 702 was reached. Her database of Great War Old Cheltonians was significantly added to by the work of Richard Moore, who taught History and Politics at College between 2008 and 2016. Richard supported the early battlefields visits with Jo Doidge-Harrison, which helped initiate the series of centenary commemorative events. I must also acknowledge the willingness and help of Clive Loebenstein-Peckham, OC, who helped to lay the database groundwork and the first level spreadsheet that helped to structure much of my later research.

There are, of course, many other individuals who have also played their part during the gestation and development of *College Echoes*. All in the Cheltenham College development team, especially Sebastian Bullock, Christiane Dickens, and Malcolm Sloan, the Old Cheltonian Administrator, have provided tremendous help with the administration of the book and its marketing. So too has Andy Banks, the College photographer, who has provided many of the charming photographic illustrations. Also, I must pass my warm thanks to Robin Badham-Thornhill OC (a team-mate in the College cricket and hockey XIs during our school days) and his Cheltonian Society Committee whose whole-hearted support was instrumental in securing the financial backing for the publishing of the book. In that regard, I am also most appreciative of the support and encouragement of Paul Arengo-Jones OC and the members of the Cheltonian Endowment Trust. The book cover illustration is based on the beautiful 'In Memory' design by Bella Janson which was made specifically to mark the start of the Great War centenary commemorations at College four years ago. I am indebted to Bella for allowing us to use the same design, gently adjusted, for the book cover; a more suitable image to help close the series of commemoration events is inconceivable. All in all, producing this book about the remarkable stories of Old Cheltonians in the Great War has been largely, and most appropriately, a Cheltonian endeavour. To 'full stop' this perception, nothing captures this spirit more than the moving foreword composed by General Sir Michael Rose OC, to whom I am, of course, extremely grateful for agreeing to provide the words which so elegantly capture the mood of the script.

However, I also owe tremendous thanks to many others, especially for the support and advice of Patrick Francis, the former Head of History and Housemaster of Lyon House at Sherborne School, and Rachel Hassel, the school's archivist, whose beautiful book *Vivat Shirbirnia* of similar intent set a very high standard for *College Echoes* to emulate. My thanks also go to Sir Hew Strachan, a doyen of First World War historians, who kindly agreed with his publishers (Simon & Schuster UK Ltd) to the reproduction of various map illustrations from his brilliant 2003 book, *The First World War*. I also express my gratitude to Matthew Bell who allowed me to include key letters from Cheltonians in his lovely volume about those commemorated on the Great War Memorial in Sevenoaks, and to Vicki Hopson at the Soldiers of Gloucestershire Museum whose kind permission enabled the inclusion of material from the *Fifth Glo'ster Gazette*. I must also thank collectively the members of staff at the National Archives and the

Imperial War Museum who supported and enabled my research and illustrative inclusions.

I also owe thanks to Dr Julian Summerfield and Dr Marianne Dyer for providing their expertise to help contextualise the individual cases involving 'shell shock' (or PTSD) and the Spanish Flu pandemic respectively. To Sue Van Poppel, Margaret Jones, Sarah Cole, Jenny Robbins and Jeremy Robbins, I pass my full appreciation for their patience and kindness while acting as my token sample readership as the various Acts (chapters) came off the assembly line.

I would also like to record my appreciation of the academic guidance and historian insight to British First World War Studies I was fortunate enough to experience from my tutors at the University of Birmingham's School of History and Cultures. Doctor Jonathan Boff, ably assisted by Doctors Jonathan Gumz, Dan Whittingham and Peter Gray, provided an intriguing course which sharpened my postgraduate appetite for further research, study and writing. I would also like to extend my thanks to the sparkling series of lectures, given by several iconic figures within First Word War academia, especially Professor Peter Simkins, Professor John Bourne and Doctor Aimee Fox-Godden, whose tremendous knowledge and thoughtful context provided a profound grasp of the total effect of industrialised warfare, and the monumental consequences that the events of the First World War perpetrated.

Last, but by no means least, it would be totally remiss of me if I did not record the debt of gratitude I owe to the one person who has kept body and soul together over the last two years; my wife, Pam, whose love, support and gentle forbearance, notwithstanding the endless cups of tea and coffee in the small hours, sustained my entire effort.

CONTENTS

Foreword by General Sir Michael Rose		iv
Acknowledgements by Patrick Stevens		v
Contents		viii
Cheltenham, a poem by Sir John Betjeman		1
PROLOGUE		3
ACTS ONE:	1914 – THE YEAR OF OPTIMISTIC PATRIOTISM	11
Scenes One:	Precautionary Measures	12
Scenes Two:	Optimism and Patriotism	14
Scenes Three:	Mobilisation	16
Scenes Four:	Rush to the Colours	18
Scenes Five:	Initial Casualties	22
List of Fallen Old Cheltonians – 1914		37
ACTS TWO:	1915 – THE YEAR OF FALSE HOPE	45
Scenes One:	Painful Apprenticeships	47
Scenes Two:	The Dardanelles	69
Scenes Three:	Mesopotamia	82
Scenes Four:	West Africa	87
Scenes Five:	The Home Front	88
Scenes Six:	The Mediterranean	91
Scenes Seven:	Year's End	91
List of Fallen Old Cheltonians – 1915		95
ACTS THREE:	1916 – THE YEAR OF ENDLESS SHADOW	109
Scenes One:	Heartaches	111
Scenes Two:	Missing in Action	117
Scenes Three:	Personal Effects	120
Scenes Four:	Forgotten Fronts – Mesopotamia and Salonika	124
Scenes Five:	Endless Shadow – The Somme	127
Scenes Six:	Amphibians	144
Scenes Seven:	Somme Aviators	147
Scenes Eight:	Chaplains	150
Scenes Nine:	Dinner Time	152
List of Fallen Old Cheltonians – 1916		155

ACTS FOUR:	1917 – THE YEAR OF STOIC RESOLVE	165
Scenes One:	Brief Interlude	168
Scenes Two:	Bloody April	176
Scenes Three:	Flying Officers	182
Scenes Four:	Music Masters	191
Scenes Five:	Mediterranean Menace	194
Scenes Six:	Summer's Solstice	198
Scenes Seven:	Autumn Agony	200
Scenes Eight:	Memorial Plans	208
List of Fallen Old Cheltonians – 1917		211
ACTS FIVE:	1918 – THE YEAR OF TURNING TIDES	219
Scenes One:	Spring Tide	226
Scenes Two:	Following Waves	237
Scenes Three:	Wings	244
Scenes Four:	Changing Tide	250
Scenes Five:	Deadly Virus and Last Posts	260
List of Fallen Old Cheltonians – 1918		265
ACTS SIX:	ARMISTICE AND BEYOND	273
Scenes One:	Aftermath	273
Scenes Two:	Brothers in Arms	283
Scenes Three:	Legacy	286
List of Fallen Old Cheltonians – After Armistice		293
EPILOGUE		297
Memorialisation by Catherine Long		297
Remembrance		302
Cheltenham Too, a poem by Patrick Stevens		311
BIBLIOGRAPHY		312
IMAGE SOURCES		318
INDEX		321

COLLEGE ECHOES

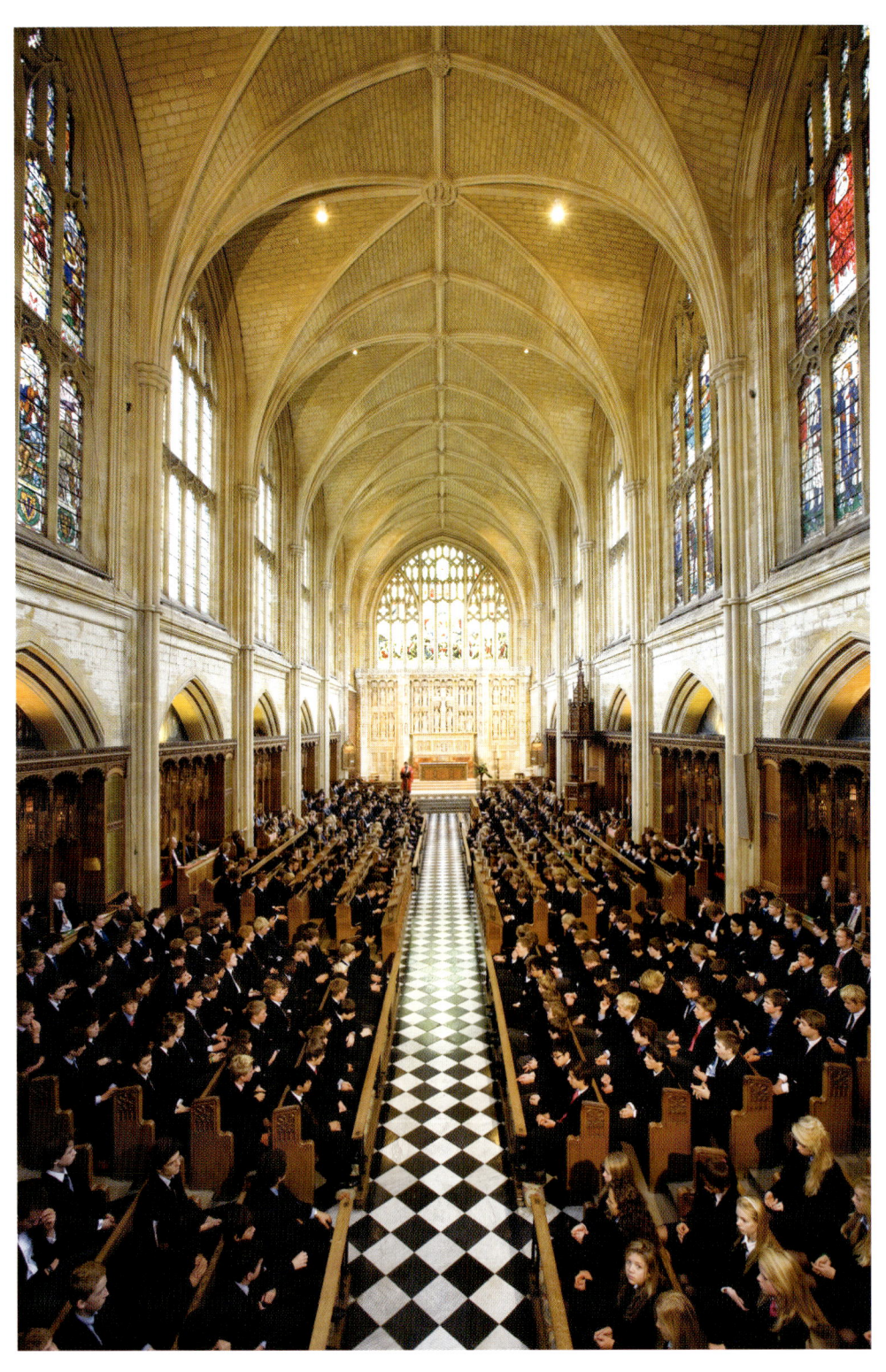

COLLEGE ECHOES

CHELTENHAM

by Sir John Betjeman

Floruit, Floret, Floreat! Cheltonia's children cry.
I composed those lines when a summer wind
Was blowing the elm leaves dry,
And we were seventy-six for seven and they had C.B. Fry.

Shall I forget the warm marquee, and the general's wife so soon,
When my son's colleger* acted as tray
For an ice and a macaroon.
And distant carriages jingled through the stuccoed afternoon?

Floruit. Yes, the Empire Map. Cheltonia's sons have starred.
Floret. Still the stream goes on, of soldier, brasher** and bard.
Floreat. While behind the limes lengthens the Promenade.

* Mortar Board
** Schoolmaster

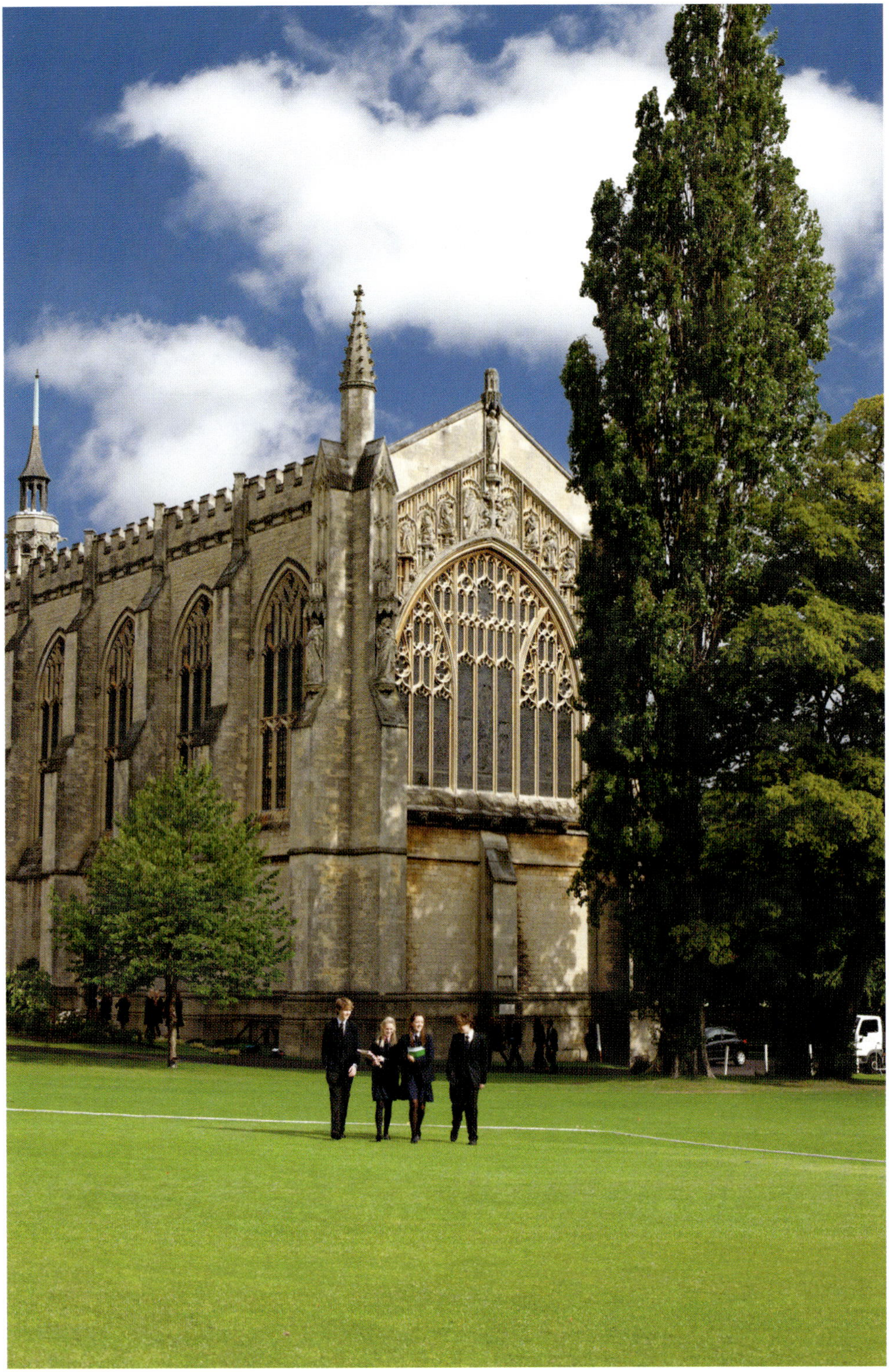

PROLOGUE

On the evening of Saturday, 11th July 1914, as shadows began to lengthen, the final wicket was taken in a close two-day cricket match against Clifton and the stumps were drawn on College Field. Cheltenham College had won by the slender margin of 25 runs, and the players walked off to a gentle round of applause which rippled off the Chapel walls in the atmospheric tranquillity of an idyllic English summer evening. Even now College Field, with its quintessentially English backdrop, exudes the history and ethos of a public school whose old boys, and latterly old girls, have been serving sovereign, country, and empire since 1841.

College Cricket, circa 1914

As one of the four original rugby playing schools, generations of its alumni, collectively the Old Cheltonians, have embraced the school's traditions and heritage, and spent many happy hours of their formative years playing sport within this beautiful setting. Even the immortal 'WG' had graced the cricket square on several occasions playing for Gloucestershire.[1] More importantly for the 1914 XI, this final match marked the end of

---

[1] Doctor William Gilbert (WG) Grace took 17 for 89 for Gloucestershire against Nottinghamshire and scored the first ever triple hundred, 318 not out, on College Field during the annual county cricket festival which started in 1876.

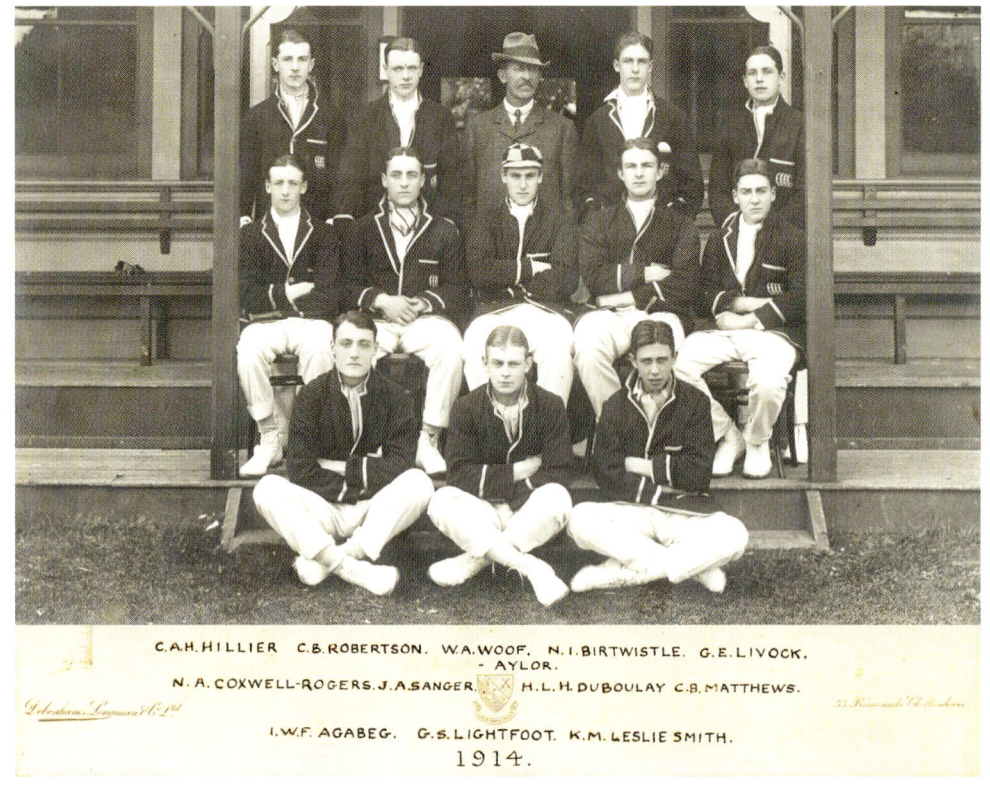

College Cricket XI, July 1914

both the summer term and the school year, and, for most of the team, the end of their days at College and the start of the next chapter in their young lives. Little did they know, however, that in just three weeks this next chapter would take a dramatic turn for the worse. Personal qualities, such as sense of duty, service and loyalty, had been inculcated in them throughout their years of education from preparatory school onwards. Other attributes, including teamwork, initiative, competitiveness and physical fitness had been honed during many hours of sporting endeavour on College Field. All would be tested to the full in the ensuing four and half years as a different and much darker shadow began to emerge.

So, on that balmy evening in July 1914, the cricketers from both schools were barely aware that international events would overtake them all and dictate a markedly different future to the one they had planned for and were eagerly anticipating.

Of that Cheltenham XI, captained by the talented Geoffrey Brooke-Taylor (Christowe, 1914), all would enlist and serve as officers during the First World War.[2] Three went directly to the Royal Military College at Sandhurst to be infantry and cavalry officers, and

---

[2] Geoffrey Brooke-Taylor played for the College cricket XI for three seasons, captaining the XI in his last year. He was also in the College football XV for two years, and was the school's senior prefect.

two to the Royal Military Academy Woolwich to gain artillery and engineering commissions. Geoffrey ended the War as a captain in the Royal Field Artillery with a Military Cross to his name, before resuming his academic activity and cricketing prowess at Cambridge University. Gerald Livock (Boyne House, 1914), the wicket-keeper and batsman, finished the War as a squadron leader in the fledgling Royal Air Force having been decorated with one of the early Distinguished Flying Crosses to be awarded.[3] Three of the team were wounded; John Sanger (Christowe, 1914), who had scored a total of 87 runs in both innings, and Norman Coxwell-Rogers and Kenneth Leslie-Smith (both Leconfield, 1914), who between them had claimed eight of the Cliftonian wickets. But sadly, three of the team were killed. The young and enthusiastic Cyril Hillier (Hazelwell, 1914), who had played cricket for two years in the XI, died from his wounds in February 1915 aged just 17. He was the youngest army officer to die from the effects of enemy action on the Western Front.[4] Hubert du Boulay (Day Boy, 1915), the Senior Prefect and member of the rugby XV in his last year at College, was killed on the Somme leading his platoon in the first wave of an attack against the German line on 3rd September 1916. Finally, Norman Birtwistle (Christowe, 1914), who had undertaken the lion's share of the bowling during the match, died just a month before the Armistice during one of the last cavalry charges of the conflict near Brancourt-le-Grand on 8th October 1918. These three young men became part of the tragic statistics of the world's first experience of total and industrialised warfare, alongside over a million of their fellows from across the British Empire, and many more millions of soldiers from the other countries involved in the fighting.

Few illustrations epitomise the futility of the First World War more than a very short stretch of road in Belgium. As one drives on the road from Mons to Soignies, two easily-missed but historically significant memorials are passed. On the right-hand side of the road, attached to the wall of a large building near the Soignies to Saint Denis crossroads, is a plaque which shows where the Allies stopped on Armistice Day 1918. It reads; 'The outpost

Cyril Hillier

H. L. H. DU BOULAY.
Sec. Lieut., 3rd Batt. Wiltshire Regt.
Killed at Battle of the Somme, France,
3rd September, 1916. Age 19.

Hubert du Boulay

Norman Birtwistle

---

[3] Gerald Livock was also awarded the Air Force Cross in 1929 for his pioneering work in developing the potential of long range flying boat operations. He also played first class cricket for Middlesex, the Royal Air Force, and the MCC. His younger brother Arthur (Junior, 1917) served in the Royal Navy during the war and later transferred to the Royal Air Force.

[4] J. Lewis-Stempel,: *Six Weeks. The Short and Gallant Life of the British Officer in the First World War*, Orion Books, London, (2011), page 279.

of the 116th Canadian Infantry Battalion stopped at this very point upon the cease-fire on 11 November 1918'. Yet on the left-hand side of the road, just 200 metres further on, and on the brow of the gentle slope down to the village of Casteau, is a white obelisk which records the position where Drummer Edward Thomas, of the 4th Dragoon Guards, fired the first British shot of the War on the Western Front in the early morning of 22nd August 1914. Though just a short difference of 200 metres in distance, it represents 51 long months, or 13 school terms, of pain and misery across the world, and an eternity that casts an endless shadow over the estimated 18 million lives lost, nearly half of them being civilians.

So why is yet another book of the First World War needed, and why is such an epitaph needed now? Following the signing of the Treaty of Versailles, that would end 'the war to end all wars', there was a universal clamour to erect lasting memorials to record the dreadful scale of sacrifice, the effects of which had affected almost every household in the nation and most families across the Empire. This was epitomised by the unveiling of the Cenotaph by King George V on 11th November 1920. But, across the length and breadth of the nation's communities, from village greens to town halls, from railway stations to factory premises, from sports clubs to churches, almost every establishment raised monies to sponsor the building of a lasting memorial to the fallen sons of their particular community. Such sentiment was especially prevalent in the nation's public schools and universities. Thus, the three young cricketers from the 1914 XI were commemorated collectively with all the other Old Cheltonians when the Memorial Cloisters were built at the main entrance to the College Chapel. The commemorative Foundation Stone, laid on 4th July 1919 by Lord Lee of Fareham, reads 'In Memory of Six Hundred and Seventy Five Old Cheltonians who gave their lives in the Great War 1914-1919'. But sadly, this statement was a little premature. There were not 675 fallen Old Cheltonians, but 702, all of whom were killed or died as a direct consequence of the War. Even as the mortar was hardening around the Foundation Stone, there was still a small number of Old Cheltonians slowly dying of their wounds and injuries in hospitals, sanatoria, and nursing homes around the country.

Additionally, other fallen Old Cheltonians were perhaps omitted from the registers owing in large part to the social stigmas prevailing during the Victorian and Edwardian eras, but which today's more liberal society accepts. Suicide, for example, was still a criminal offence during the First World War. For an officer it was deemed a dishonourable stain on the reputation of the individual and his family. Recent research has unearthed a number of cases suggesting some Old Cheltonians took this extreme option, and whose names were not included in the Roll of Honour. Similarly, homosexuality was a serious criminal offence of the time and research for this book has discovered one case where the individual's record of death was omitted owing to his sexuality. Such men were just as much war victims as any of the others. Viewing their cases with today's more liberal and egalitarian attitudes provides an important opportunity to set the record straight.

The primary sources and documentary evidence from the many personal files, letters, and battalion war diaries researched for this book will speak loudly and powerfully enough for themselves. Therefore, the book offers perhaps a final testament to all the fallen Old

The Memorial Cloisters

Cheltonians, which was not possible in May 1919 when the first estimates were included in the school's Great War Register. Even by 1921, when the Memorial Cloisters, including the Foundation Stone, were formally dedicated, not all the records had been collated nor the final numbers confirmed.

Besides the students and masters who attended the College and its Junior School being an obvious homogeneity, who were these Old Cheltonians? During the First World War, their family backgrounds were not that dissimilar to those of today's generation, with many coming from the well-established professions: lawyers, doctors, entrepreneurs, the banking and business sectors, the clergy, and the military. But 100 years ago, in an era long before co-educational and multi-racial inclusion, there were several distinct differences. The length and breadth of the British Empire offered huge opportunities to well-connected and privileged families, from Canada to Africa, the Caribbean to Australasia. They emigrated in large numbers, some to farm and others to experience living the colonial lifestyle. Furthermore, and the 'jewel' in the Victorian and Edwardian crowns, there was India. Her management required huge numbers of well-educated professional men, including civil servants, officers for the Indian Army, judges, railway engineers, forestry commissioners, not to mention clergy (to extend the reach of Christianity). Across the empire the colonial diplomatic service was substantial, and Old Cheltonians played an integral part in its administration and development. Some Old Cheltonians came from the minor gentry, and others from land-owning families in Ireland.

In addition, it would be remiss to underplay the part that the College's Junior School played in shaping the attitudes of a generation of schoolboys, the major beneficiary being the College itself, but still a large number of pupils going on to other public schools. Many of the leadership qualities needed for the officers and gentlemen who commanded during the First World War were inculcated in a cohort of very young preparatory school boys over a period stretching from the 1860s up to eve of the conflict, and certainly before they had arrived at College or their other chosen public school. The preparatory school formed an essential start to the wider educational process and social progress of young boys destined to become Britain's military leaders during the First World War. The Cheltenham College Junior School, nowadays referred to as Cheltenham Prep, was no exception. Founded in 1863 as the College's junior department, it formed (and still is) an integral part of the College community, and scores of its alumni flooded the ranks of the armed services as Britain went to war in 1914.

Yet, irrespective of their family backgrounds, education and personal situations, the 3,541 Old Cheltonians that served in the First World War were recorded in alphabetical order, as was the custom of the time, in the Rolls of Honour. However, such rolls provide merely a record of the name, a date or age if one is lucky, and finally (by simple addition) the numbers involved. But, when one transforms, with some simple research, the alphabetical list into chronological order by date of death, with ages, ranks and units included, a completely new picture of the wider social context springs to life. One can immediately see which Old Cheltonians were at school together, fought together, when families lost sets of brothers, and when serving fathers lost serving sons. Without such an approach, for example, it would not have become obvious that two Old Cheltonians, who had been at College together, had died on the same day, were both in the Royal Flying Corps (RFC) on the same squadron and flying from the same aerodrome. But, applying deeper research and focus on their particular personal files and records, it becomes clear that they died in the same aircraft; their story will appear later.

Reviewing the ages of the fallen is also revealing. Of the 702 fatalities, the vast majority, some 64%, were between 15 and 30 years of age. This reflects the fact that most of them were junior officers serving in the front line as platoon, battery and company commanders. For many, their unenviable role, and duty as they saw it, was to lead the men over the top, so enduring the greatest risk while setting an example to the soldiery. With their resolve, steadiness and discipline under fire, where they led, the troops invariably followed. Being the first into the enemy's line of fire and being targeted by enemy snipers and machine gunners from the outset, it is hardly surprising that they suffered the greatest attrition rate of all the ranks in the army. Old Cheltonian fatalities of junior officers were 209 captains, 171 lieutenants, and 152 second lieutenants, equating to 75% of all those killed. Of the senior officers that died, 74 were majors, 39 lieutenant colonels, 11 colonels, and four were brigadier generals. These figures include the equivalent ranks of other Old Cheltonians who fought and served in the other service arms, especially the Royal Navy and, later on, the Royal Air Force. But clearly the younger generation of Old Cheltonians suffered the greatest toll. Some 17% of those that died did not live to see their 21st birthday, including Alan Robertson, a midshipman onboard HMS *Aboukir*, who died early in the morning of 22nd September 1914. He was killed aged just 15, the youngest Old Cheltonian to die during the War.

Another important aspect of this recent research has revealed that 29 of the 'fallen' Old Cheltonians were privates, four were corporals, two were sergeants, and one a company sergeant major, reflecting the fact that many public schoolboys and university undergraduates also fought and died in the ranks of the army, some in the specially formed public school battalions. Furthermore, six civilian Old Cheltonians were also killed as a direct consequence of the War; their stories too are covered in the ensuing chapters. Finally, one Old Cheltonian fatality was a chaplain. Reverend Francis Tuke, the vicar of Holmer near Hereford, had also played cricket on College Field. Having enlisted as a Chaplain 4th Class on 19th July 1915 to 'do his bit', he was killed almost exactly a year to the day later during the Battle of the Somme while bravely carrying water to the troops in action. He was 49 years old.

By adopting a chronological approach, based on the Roll of Honour, key events of the War are given even greater clarity. In a few cases, the associated research has exposed fresh evidence that helps to settle conundrums that, despite the previous attention and scholarship of very many historians, have hitherto remained unresolved. Therefore, this book will explore each year of the First World War in turn through the special experiences and records of the Old Cheltonians themselves, introducing themes which may be new to some readers. For example, the direct involvement of many Old Cheltonians shines a light on the importance of the U-Boat threat in the Mediterranean to the allied war effort, a significant factor to the troop ships and hospital transports plying these waters. Furthermore, the 'fog of war' associated with the nature and extent of fighting on an industrial scale resulted in many Old Cheltonians simply disappearing from the battlefield, their names being amongst the tens of thousands of others on the numerous memorials to the missing. The degree to which comrades, families and military authorities went to determine the whereabouts of their lost 'chums', sons, and soldiers has perhaps been sadly under-documented. This book seeks in part to redress that balance. Therefore, by examining selected individual experiences for each year of the conflict, a clearer and more personal picture appears about all those Old Cheltonians who fought and died in the First World War, and so pays suitable collective tribute and remembrance to them all. Accordingly, the sections and vignettes in this book are referred to as 'acts' and 'scenes', rather than the more traditional 'parts' or 'chapters', to reflect and acknowledge the contributions of the Old Cheltonians themselves and those of their comrades and families. Perhaps this theatrical connotation symbolises the Great War more pertinently as one of the greatest tragedies of modern times. Finally, the book ends with a very fitting epilogue with contributions, most appropriately, from the current cohort of Cheltonians, who offer their thoughts and reflections of *College Echoes* from the lives of their gallant and illustrious forbears who died in the Great War; a communion in spirit which is now 100 years old.

The centenary of the Armistice of the First World War is likely to be the last commemoration of its kind, as the echoes of the Great War slowly fade from human memory away into the annals of statistics. Soon public interest, effort, and attention will naturally and rightly shift to the centenary commemorations of the Second World War, which will start relatively soon in 2039. Now represents, perhaps, the final opportunity to acknowledge our commitment to the memory of all the fallen of the First World War, but especially to all the Old Cheltonians that were either killed in action, or died of wounds, illness or disease. This reflects entirely the original intentions behind the memorialisation efforts of the College, as stated by Sir Arthur Lee, President of the College Council, when he chaired a gathering of Old Cheltonians, parents and friends of the School on 9th January 1918 to discuss a fitting memorial to the fallen:

> Our duty in this time, and our special duty here today, is not merely to report the praises of those whose sacrifices are well known, not merely to those who are nearest to them but to the world at large, but it is our duty, and I venture to say our pious duty, that we owe not merely to our old school but to ourselves, to see that there is no Old Cheltonian who has laid down his life for his country who shall have no memorial and who shall have perished as though he had never been.[5]

The dignified sentiment articulated by Sir Arthur is as valid today as it was 100 years ago. It underpins the purpose of the book, and every page that follows.

---

[5] *The Cheltonian*, January and February 1918, page 25.

ACTS ONE
1914 – THE YEAR OF OPTIMISTIC PATRIOTISM

On that peaceful summer evening of 11th July 1914, the College cricketers unlaced their boots, stowed their pads and bats away, and started to pack their trunks before departing on the special school train, or in the family charabanc, back to their comfortable homes for the summer holidays. Meanwhile, international rhetoric throughout Europe was rising on an increasingly upward thermal of stubborn national belligerence and imperial opportunism. The storm clouds had started to billow just a fortnight before in Sarajevo on 28th June, when a young Serbian nationalist, Gavrilo Princep, assassinated Archduke Ferdinand, the heir to the Austro-Hungarian throne. Emboldened by Germany's tacit support, Austria-Hungary issued an impossible ultimatum to Serbia, a diktat designed to precipitate a third Balkan war that was to be limited to the region and quell Serbian nationalism within Austria-Hungary's empire once and for all. However, the convoluted web of international alliances between the various imperial power blocks, Russia with Serbia, Russia with France, Germany with Austria-Hungary and separately Turkey, Britain with Belgium and latterly with France and Russia, meant that the matter could never be contained to the Balkans. While other states, notably Italy, Bulgaria and Romania were assessing their own national agendas and interests in the region, diplomatic activity and concern throughout the continent grew to fever pitch. Europe's politicians were collectively 'sleep-walking' into catastrophe, through a mêlée of competing political and financial interests, further confused by misunderstanding, misinformation and miscalculation.[6]

The obvious storm warnings and rumblings were underestimated until the thunderclap fell on 4th August. Britain was compelled to uphold her honour and obligations under the first Treaty of London (1839). This treaty had created the Belgian state, independent from the United Kingdom of the Netherlands, and was signed by the major European powers to guarantee Belgium's neutrality and protection against invasion. Cynically, Germany, being a co-guarantor of the treaty, now rejected her associated obligations, and dismissed the treaty as a mere 'scrap of paper'.[7] War against Germany thus seemed imminent, and once declared the associated global tempest raged for the next 1,569 days.

The enormity of the effects of this first global and total war is suitably summarised by the eminent historian, Professor John Bourne, who brings its dimensions into stark reality:

> There are some who dispute the status of the Great War as a 'true' World War. This is perverse. The conflict was global. Major wars were fought not only in western, eastern,

---

[6] C. Clark; *The Sleepwalkers: How Europe went to War in 1914*, (Penguin Books, London, 2012), page xxvii
[7] Attributed to a comment made by German Chancellor Bethmann Hollweg to the British ambassador to Germany, Sir Edward Goschen, on 4th August 1914.

and southern Europe, but also in the Middle East and the Caucasus. A lesser-guerrilla war tied down more than 100,000 British Empire troops in East Africa. Surface fleets and submarines contested naval supremacy on and under the oceans of the world. The insatiable demands of war extended far beyond the battlefields, not least because two of the major belligerents, Great Britain and France, were imperial powers with access to global resources of manpower, raw materials and food. The 'British' Army eventually recruited 1.6 million Indians, 630,000 Canadians, 412,000 Australians, 136,000 South Africans, 130,000 New Zealanders and approximately 50,000 Africans, as well as several hundred thousand Chinese 'coolies'. The 'French' Army recruited 600,000 North and West Africans as combat troops and a further 200,000 as labourers. The ability of the Entente to command the manpower and natural resources of Africa, Asia, Australasia, and North and South America made a major contribution to victory. The political and economic impact of this global mobilisation was also immense.[8]

Many Old Cheltonians served in the military, in the regular forces at home, and in the Indian Army and other colonial services overseas, and many more in civilian businesses and professions of sizeable national and international influence. The corresponding impact of the War on the school's associated communities and families across the globe was equally immense.

Precautionary Measures

Alan Robertson

By the end of July, the mobilisation and forward deployment by rail of large bodies of German troops and artillery suggested the impending calamity. The German Imperial Navy was also reaching operational readiness, undertaking increasing activity in the southern North Sea. Accordingly, the British Government, while seeking diplomatic resolution, took prudent military precautions. At the Royal Naval College at Dartmouth, young Alan Robertson (Junior, 1910) was finishing his summer term before being sent to sea on a warship for his next period of practical training.

On 27th July, the directing staff at Dartmouth received a telegram from the Admiralty ordering the College to stand by for mobilisation. As the cadets were packing their sea chests the following day, the Admiralty ordered the British Fleet secretly to its war bases. All the cadets of Alan's term were allocated to a list of ships, and he, along with eight other cadets of similar age, was assigned to the crew of HMS *Aboukir*, an obsolete armoured cruiser that had been built for the Royal Navy during the Boer War, but had been placed in reserve since 1912.

[8] See P Liddle (Ed), *Passchendaele in Perspective*, Leo Cooper/Pen & Sword, Barnsley, 1997.

HMS *Aboukir* leaving Malta, circa 1912

On 1st August, naval Captain Victor Stanley, the commanding officer at Dartmouth, opened a very short but momentous telegram containing a single written order: 'MOBILISE.' The following day, and a week before his 15th birthday, Alan was appointed as a midshipman and left the Naval College for the war. He, along with some 433 other naval cadets, marched through Dartmouth, encouraged by cheering crowds, to catch trains to their new appointments.[9]

The army too, especially the regulars in the British Expeditionary Force (BEF), was steeling itself. The 1st Battalion, Royal Warwickshire Regiment, based at Shorncliffe just outside Folkestone, had already taken early precautionary measures. Personal telegrams were sent at 12.10pm on 30th July to all officers on leave recalling them back to barracks immediately for duty. By the beginning of the month, the battalion was already assuming a war footing, equipping, drawing in reservists, practising musketry, and undertaking route marches, as war was increasingly anticipated. Lieutenant Cecil Glendower Gilliat (Day Boy, 1903), referred to by his fellow subalterns in the officers' mess as 'Glennie', was busy making preparations for the battalion's deployment as part of the 10th Brigade of the BEF's 4th Division. Glennie had been on leave with his twin brother Reginald (Day Boy, 1903), both of whose careers were following closely parallel paths.[10] They had entered the College's Junior school together in May 1897, and left school in December 1903 just before their 19th birthdays. Both obtained army commissions in militia battalions, before gaining posts in the regular army; Glennie with the 'Warwicks' and Reginald with an attachment to the 1st Battalion, Connaught Rangers. By 1914, both were readying themselves and their

---

[9] Hansard, House of Commons Debate, 16th November 1914, Vol 68, cc 182-4.
[10] Captain Cecil Glendower Gilliat, Royal Warwickshire Regiment, killed by a sniper at Meteren, France, on 14th October 1914.

Glendower 'Glennie' Gilliat

Reginald Gilliat

men for the war; sadly, a war which would claim both of their lives from a sniper's bullet.

Also preparing for war were the four serving Lousada brothers; Charles and William (both Cheltondale, 1898 and 1899 respectively) and their younger twin brothers Edward and Bertie (both Cheltondale, 1907), whose lives had followed almost identical paths to those of the Gilliat brothers. At the beginning of their last term at College, Edward and Bertie had both applied for entry to the Royal Military College at Sandhurst on 13th September 1907. They were going to follow in the footsteps of their elder brother William, who had also been at College playing in the rugby XV on College Field in 1899, and who had then gone into the army through Sandhurst in 1900. As a result of their simultaneous applications, the twins attended the same intake of cadets and completed their training together, both being commissioned as second lieutenants on the same day, 6th February 1909.[11] On 4th August 1914, Edward was stationed in Woking with the 2nd Battalion, Royal Sussex Regiment, and, after a full round of medical inspections for the last of their reservists who had mustered, and final musketry training for the entire battalion, he was preparing to deploy at short notice to France, which he then did with the battalion just eight days later. Bertie, on the other hand, was 4,500 miles away on garrison duties with the 1st Battalion, York and Lancaster Regiment at Jubbelpore in India, but was very aware of unfolding events in Europe.

OPTIMISM AND PATRIOTISM

When Big Ben struck 11pm on the evening of 4th August 1914, the British Government had not received any reply from Germany to the British ultimatum for Germany to withdraw her troops from Belgium. On the contrary, the newspaper presses and the Reuters' telegraph wires were running hot reporting the continued German advance towards Liège. It was war. Two minutes later, Winston Churchill as the First Lord of the Admiralty sent an order by telegram to the Fleet: 'COMMENCE HOSTILITIES AGAINST GERMANY.' Eight minutes after that, King George V went on to the balcony at Buckingham Palace to see the crowds that had assembled along the Mall, and later noted in his diary:

> An enormous crowd collected outside the Palace both before and after dinner. When they heard that war had been declared, the excitement increased, and May and I, with

---

[11] *The London Gazette*, 5th February 1909, pages 948-949.

1914 – THE YEAR OF OPTIMISTIC PATRIOTISM

> David (Prince of Wales), went on to the balcony; the cheering was terrific. Please God it may soon be over.

While the widespread sentiments of enthusiasm and patriotism to defend the national and imperial prestige were laudable, the degree of optimism was sadly misconceived. Most recently etched into the national psyche were the experiences of the Second Boer War, reported by a nationalistic press and then eulogised as another victorious conclusion to one of Britain's most recent major imperial adventures. Yet, these experiences were little more than a mirage to fading glory. They obscured the reality of the new era when the battlefield, in particular the dominance and advantage of the defensive trench system protected by wire and machine gun, and supported with artillery, made attack very costly. Since Britain's early abortive attempts of attacking trenches, as at Magersfontein in December 1899, warfare had now become industrialised. The advent of the machine gun and quick-firing artillery had elevated the lethal nature of warfare. Of the 448,435 British and colonial troops that fought in the three year period of the Second Boer War, some 42,829 soldiers had become battle casualties with 21,942 killed (13,250 of whom died from illness and disease). By the end of 1914, in just five months of fighting, the BEF had lost 86,237 men, killed, wounded or missing, including 3,627 officers. But for the majority of the British public in August 1914, memories of final victory in the Second Boer War, despite some painful setbacks such as Colenso and Spion Kop, were never allowed to fade, and instead were re-energised by a jingoistic press to fuel optimistic patriotism. The pain of the relatively slender fatality rate, some 4.9%, had slowly dissipated collective memory of the Boer War casualties, anaesthetised in part by the passing years. But this war was to be very different, and by an unforeseeable magnitude.

Almost half of the Old Cheltonians serving as regulars in the British and Indian armies in 1914 held either the Queen's Medal or the King's Medal, or sometimes both, for their participation in the South African campaign. These medals and the clasps denoting participation in major actions were well recognised and acknowledged by the general public. Frank Boileau (Day Boy, 1885), for example, was a major in the Royal Engineers during the Boer War, and had six clasps on his Queen's Medal.[12] In addition, public acknowledgement of feats of battlefield bravery, previously unrewarded, was changing and becoming of great popular interest. Petitions to recognise soldierly heroism and posthumous acts of bravery had started to gain traction with the public in 1902, widely reported in the various national magazines, most notably the Boys Own Paper. This weekly edition published adventure stories and unashamedly advocated the British Empire as the pinnacle of human civilisation, becoming a staple part of the intellectual diet for most teenage boys. Accordingly, special cases were celebrated by the pre-war cohort of College students and none more so than the valiant exploits of Lieutenant Teignmouth Melvill. Teignmouth had left College in June 1858, and was a Lieutenant in the 24th Regiment of

---

[12] Colonel Frank Boileau, Royal Engineers, Staff Officer in the 3rd Division deployed to France with the BEF, mortally wounded at Ham, France, and died on 28th August 1914, aged 46. He was the first Old Cheltonian senior officer to be killed in the First World War, just three weeks after its declaration.

Foot during the Anglo-Zulu War. Following the disastrous engagement against the Zulu impis at Isandlwanha on 22nd January 1879, he had been killed while gallantly attempting to save the regiment's Queen's Colour.

Had he survived, he would have been recommended to Queen Victoria for the award of the Victoria Cross, but it was the custom of the day not to make posthumous awards.[13] This changed in 1907, and Teignmouth was one of the first belated recipients when King Edward VII approved his award in the London Gazette on 15th January 1907. The announcement was lauded and celebrated back at College, taking pride of place in *The Cheltonian* edition of the year.

Teignmouth Melvill VC

Within this patriotic and triumphal context embraced by a common national purpose, it is hardly surprising the general public mood was optimistic. After all, the Royal Navy was surely the most powerful navy in the world and, despite the Anglo-German arms race, still outnumbered the German Imperial Navy in battleships by 49 to 29. Furthermore, the British Army, having been reorganised by Lord Haldane in 1907, had a highly trained expeditionary force of just under 250,000 regular soldiers, with a further 270,000 in the part-time Territorial Army, and another 100,000 reservists to call on. Additionally, there were the imperial and colonial forces to call on, including 155,000 in the Indian Army with a high proportion of British officers embedded in each battalion. With powerful allies in Russia, France, and Belgium, and given the justness and honour of the cause in defending 'Little Belgium', public perception was that it would be assuredly over by Christmas.

Mobilisation

With the formal declaration of war at 11pm on 4th August, the Royal Navy immediately began establishing a blockade of Germany in line with strategic plans, developed as early as 1904, to sever maritime trade to and from Germany. This included cargoes carried under neutral flags. The intention of the Grand Fleet's Northern Patrol was to seal access from the Baltic (and German naval port at Kiel) to the North Sea from bases in Scotland, most notably from Scapa Flow in the Orkneys, and, with Rosyth on the Forth not ready in 1914, from Cromarty. Donald Macdonald (Southwood, 1903) was on board HMS *Hawke*, one of eight old Edgar Class cruisers which comprised the 10th Cruiser Squadron and the Northern Patrol. He had left College as a naval scholar in 1903, aged just 14, to join the training ship HMS *Britannia* and begin his career in the Royal Navy. After steady progress in training, where his personal reports record that his general conduct was 'Very good, slow but sound and reliable, with great attention to duties', he was promoted to Lieutenant on 31st December

---

[13] *The London Gazette*, dated 2nd May 1879.

1914 – THE YEAR OF OPTIMISTIC PATRIOTISM

1910.[14] But he found himself unsuited to the quicker pace and more flexible requirements of destroyer duties and requested a transfer to battleships. Thus, he joined the cruiser *Hawke* on 1st August 1914, and within a week he was on watch as the ship conducted operations in the North Sea.

Further south, the task of the Dover Patrol, part of the Channel Fleet based at Dover and Dunkirk, was to cut off entry to the English Channel by the German High Seas Fleet and its submarines from its bases at Wilhelmshaven and Cuxhaven.[15] By the unremitting escort of hundreds of allied merchantmen, hospital and troop ships essential in supporting the BEF with supplies, munitions and reinforcements, the Dover Patrol secured the army's lifeline to the Western Front. Supporting both the Northern and Dover patrols in home waters at the outbreak of the War was the 8th Submarine Flotilla from Harwich, including HM Submarine *D2* with Frederick Coplestone (Southwood, 1897) as a senior member of her crew of 25. Frederick had left College in 1897 aged 15 for a career in the Royal Navy, and notably in the new submariner specialisation. By 1905 he was qualified to command a submarine and in February was appointed to the 8th Submarine Flotilla. But in November 1906 he was retired prematurely, deemed unfit as a result of deafness caused by gunfire and subsequently placed on the Retired List.

Frederick Coplestone

However, with the outbreak of war, he was recalled for submarine duty and appointed to the *D2* and, with mobilisation in full swing and under remit to commence hostilities against Germany, went on patrol almost immediately.

General mobilisation of the Army, especially the BEF, had already been triggered by telegram six hours before the declaration of war, not only all the regular battalions, but also the Territorial Army and reservists. The effect across the army was convulsive and immediate. On 5th August at Shorncliffe, Glennie Gilliat, being a platoon commander, was occupied finding billets and integrating into his platoon some of the 87 reservists, who had arrived late that evening. The battalion swelled to its full strength of some 1,000 by 7th August. Having been sent up by train to Strensall Camp near York for a fortnight of final training,

HM Submarine, *D2*

---

[14] The National Archives, ADM/195/51, pages 267.
[15] Denying German access to the Channel ports was a crucial feature of British strategic policy and underpinned the geography and nature of the fighting on the Western Front, throughout the War, but especially in 1914 during the 'Race to the Sea'.

including route marches and attack exercises, the battalion sailed from Southampton at 10.30am on 22nd August on board the SS *Caledonia*, arriving at Boulogne that evening. But for every ship and battalion that arrived in the various French ports, prior arrangements had to be made with the local authorities. The associated logistical task was immense. Billeting was required, as was onward transport to the battlefront near Mons, not to mention ammunition, rations, and fodder and water for the thousands of horses that were essential to the BEF's cavalry and artillery units. This was the task of the Army Service Corps (ASC). Kenneth Brooke-Murray (Day Boy, 1910) left College having been in the Shooting VIII, and, having gone directly to the Royal Military College at Sandhurst, was commissioned as a second lieutenant in the ASC.

As soon as war was declared, he was one of the initial reconnaissance party sent to France to begin all the logistical arrangements for the deployment and arrival of the BEF. Soon after his disembarkation in France, his father received an official statement from the War Office recording that 'Captain Brooke-Murray was the first man of the British Expeditionary Force to land in France in Aug 1914'. Many other Old Cheltonians were also mobilising and would follow Kenneth to France alongside the tens of thousands of soldiers who were now enlisting.

Kenneth Brooke-Murray

Rush to the Colours

Following the declaration of war late in the evening of 4th August, recruiting offices all over the country opened their doors the next morning at the same time as Lord Kitchener took over the post as Minister for War. He disagreed with the popular press that the war would be over by Christmas, and though an unpopular view, he maintained his more insightful opinion that the war would be long and costly. An initial stream of volunteers who began to arrive on 5th August quickly turned into a torrent of masculinity in the ensuing days. With Kitchener's call to arms resonating across the nation, it had become a tsunami by the end of September with 761,901 men enlisting; over 33,000 volunteered on 3rd September alone.[16] The nation-wide spirit of optimistic patriotism was underpinned by a collective sense of duty to King, Country, and Empire, and by 25th August, the first of Kitchener's new armies (K1) consisting of the initial 100,000 volunteers, had been achieved. The rush to the colours was accompanied by a widespread sense of fair play and honour in defending 'Little Belgium' against the threat of Germany's military aggression. Within this context Old Cheltonians were amongst some of the first to enlist, which they did in their hundreds from four distinct social groupings based on age and occupation.

---

[16] British Government poster, 'Your King and Country need you: a call to arms', with corresponding terms of service, issued by HMG on 11th August 1914. Figures from I. Beckett and K. Simpson, *A Nation in Arms*, Pen and Sword Books Ltd, Barnsley, 2004, page 8.

1914 – THE YEAR OF OPTIMISTIC PATRIOTISM

First, there were those young enthusiastic boys, some still at College and others who had only just left, who applied to the army. Cyril Hillier, for example, could have stayed at College for another year, being only 17 in March 1914, and may well have captained the 1915 cricket XI had he done so. But as soon as war was declared, he sought a commission in the Territorial Army and was quickly appointed as a second lieutenant in the 2nd Battalion, Monmouthshire Regiment on 30th September 1914.[17] He embarked for France on 7th November with the battalion, which, incidentally, was the first of the territorial infantry units to deploy to the Western Front. Hugh Crooke (Day Boy, 1914) was also still at College and a private in the Officer Training Corps (OTC) when he applied for entry to the Royal Military Academy at Woolwich on 13th August 1914 aged 17. Perhaps following his example, John Crawford (Boyne House, 1914) also a cadet private, applied for entry to Woolwich on 21st August 1914; despite being six feet tall, he was only 16 years of age.

Secondly, there were Old Cheltonians who, though employed in civilian occupations and professions, went directly to their local recruiting offices and took the King's shilling. Wilfred Desages (Day Boy, 1898) left College and was a clerk at the Caxton Publishing Company in Egremont, Cheshire when war broke out. He enlisted on 8th August 1914 and attested at Liverpool into the 1/6th Battalion, King's Liverpool Regiment. After training, he embarked from Southampton with the battalion for France on 24th February 1915 on board the SS *City of Edinburgh*, to serve on the Western Front as a rifleman. He was 31 years of age. His younger brother, Owen (Day Boy, 1908), who was a schoolmaster at Parkstone School in Dorset, would enlist the following year as a private in the 18th (Public Schools) Battalion, Royal Fusiliers. There are also a number of cases where brothers volunteered together. Fergus Forbes (Newick, 1908) was living with younger brother, Noel (Newick, 1912), at 51, Wilmslow Gardens in South London when war was declared. Like many young men of the time, both were following in their father's footsteps and were at different stages in their respective careers as engineers. Fergus left College in July 1908 to start his training as a civil engineer at Messrs. Siemens Brothers' Dynamo Works. He served subsequently as an assistant, and in 1913 joined the staff of the Edmundson Electricity Corporation, being employed as a shift engineer at the power station near Hayle in Cornwall until the outbreak of the war. Being an associate member of the Institute of Civil Engineering, he applied for a temporary commission in the Royal Engineers on 17th August 1914. His application was clearly expedited through the system: he was quickly commissioned as a second lieutenant just two weeks later. The colonel who endorsed his application commented: 'He is specially suitable for the Royal Engineers and has been recently supervising large numbers of workers.' Noel, four years his junior, had gone to London University to study for his City and Guilds exams in engineering and was also in the University OTC (an artillery unit) as a private. He had just passed his second year exams (the subjects including maths, mechanics, chemistry for engineers, electrical technology, workshop practice, applied maths, and machine design) at Imperial College when war was declared. Having applied for a post in the Special Reserve of Officers

---

[17] *The London Gazette* 29th September 1914, page 7705.

(Artillery) on 8th August 1914, he was immediately commissioned due to his OTC experience.[18] On 26th August 1914, he too became a second lieutenant, and thereby he gained five days seniority in rank over his older brother. Similarly, Sydney Cooper (Cheltondale, 1900) left College in December 1900, becoming both an accountant and a director of Millington and Sons, a wholesale stationers company in London. He enlisted the day after war was declared and was initially assigned to H Company, of the 5th Battalion, City of London Rifles, as a private. He was 31 years old.

The third group of Old Cheltonians had seen previous military service but had resigned to undertake non-military careers. Some held a reserve status and, therefore, were required or expected to re-enlist. But rather than wait for their orders, they quickly responded to the call for volunteers. Robert Cooper (Hazelwell, 1893, and no relation to namesake Sydney above) had retired from the army in 1902 as a captain in the Royal Fusiliers. Yet he applied to be reinstated to his former regiment on 5th August at the age of 37. He survived the war. Sadly, the three Grieve brothers did not. The two younger brothers, James and William (Cheltondale, 1901 and 1904), had been to preparatory school together at St Andrew's School in Eastbourne, before arriving at College.[19] On leaving in 1901, James immediately gained entry to the Royal Military Academy and was commissioned in the Royal Artillery. William left College three years later and went on to the Royal Military College at Sandhurst. However, both of them decided to leave the military and in 1907 they emigrated to Argentina to become cattle ranchers; William also acting as an overseas agent for Fortune and Douglas, a real estate company in Buenos Aires. But at the outbreak of war they both returned home and enlisted being attested on 25th August at White City, Shepherds Bush. They were both inducted into the II King Edward's Horse as troopers, although both would be appointed to commissions in a matter of weeks, James returning to the Royal Field Artillery and William joining the Middlesex Regiment. They therefore joined their elder brother Charles (Cheltondale, 1899), who was already serving as a captain in the Cameron Highlanders. All three brothers would die from their Great War service. As alluded to earlier, Frederick Coplestone also returned quickly to the colours, despite his poor hearing which had precipitated his premature retirement from the Royal Navy in 1906. He still retained command experience in submarines, a human commodity that was rare and eagerly sought after as more boats rolled down the launching slipways. However, with submarine commanders in such high demand, Frederick was recalled and appointed to HM Submarine *D2* to work alongside less experienced fellow officers.

Finally, there were the overseas contingents of Old Cheltonians, who, having moved abroad, went quickly to the recruiting centres in their newly adopted countries and colonies across the world. For example, in Canada, Frederick Bond (Newick, 1911) was working in the Bank of Montreal when war was declared. Enlisting in September 1914,

---

[18] *The London Gazette*, 25th August 1914, page 6695.
[19] By coincidence, James and William had been with Sydney Cooper at preparatory school at St Andrews in Eastbourne before going on to the College, so they knew each other well. These associations were often perpetuated in the private school system of the Edwardian era.

1914 – THE YEAR OF OPTIMISTIC PATRIOTISM

he was appointed to a commission in the Canadian Field Artillery Militia on the basis of his time on the artillery officers' course at the Royal Military Academy in 1913, from which he had resigned before graduating. However, in order to see action more quickly (presumably as he was expected to complete a similar and lengthy artillery course), he resigned this commission and re-enlisted as a gunner in the Royal Canadian Horse Artillery, the first unit to leave Canada for active service abroad. Following several weeks training in England, and being unable to avoid any longer being given his subaltern's 'pip', he embarked for France as a second lieutenant in the Royal Field Artillery. Meanwhile in Africa, Richard Elwes (Hazelwell, 1910) was working on a farm on the Rhodesian veldt in November 1914. After the fighting had broken out in neighbouring Nyasaland between the colonial forces and the German troops from German East Africa, he decided to enlist. Sadly, on his way to the nearest military unit in Rhodesia he was murdered by his native servant. He was 23 years old.[20] Australian émigré, Charles Maude (Boyne House, 1891) was working as an electrician. He had left College and had fought in the South African War, first as a trooper in the Cape Mounted Rifles, and then, after nomination by the Governor of Cape Colony, as a second lieutenant in the 3rd Battalion, Worcestershire Regiment. He resigned his commission in 1902 after the war and went to live in New South Wales with his brother Maurice. He re-enlisted on 29th October 1914, at Morphettville, South Australia and was quickly made a sergeant in the 9th Australian Light Horse. In New Zealand, Leslie Dighton (Day Boy, 1907) was the company manager for the Neuchatel Asphalt Company in Wellington. Since leaving College in April 1907, he had been in business in Jamaica, Athens, Austria, and West Australia, before settling with his wife, Evelyn. With the mobilisation of the New Zealand Expeditionary Force on the 14th August, he enlisted as a private in the 2nd Battalion, Canterbury Regiment. Also making his way home from Australia to volunteer was John Wills (Leconfield, 1907). Having spent three years undergoing his Bachelor of Arts degree at Emmanuel College, Cambridge, he went out to Australia to continue the practical aspects of his study at the Hawkesbury Agricultural College in New South Wales. John returned to England and was promptly commissioned on 15th October 1914 as a second lieutenant in the Royal Field Artillery. His personal record of the war on the Western Front, held by the Imperial War Museum, provides a gripping personal insight into conditions and the experience of war, a thread that will reappear throughout this narrative. With John's academic studies now on hold, he would have to wait until October 1916 for Cambridge University to award him his Bachelor of Arts degree.

The rush to the colours not only included many Old Cheltonians, it also drew in their schoolmasters, and for College 17 members of the Common Room served in the Great War, all as officers.[21] Sadly, three of the schoolmasters were killed, five were wounded and one suffered from gas poisoning. Between them, they were awarded a Distinguished Service

---

[20] Old Cheltonian Register, 1841-1927, page 587.
[21] The following members of the Common Room served in WW1: Messrs AG Bishop, PE Bodington, JS Bond, BA Bowers, LG Butler, EH Byrde, ST Cross, GH Crump, FG Dyer, G Gray, FRW Hunt, ABL Lloyd-Baker, RF Pearson, CH Pigg, HWT Reed, JG Reid, and CEWV Reynolds.

Order, a Military Cross, an OBE, an MBE, an Italian Croce di Guerra, and three mentions in despatches. Two sets of masters even fought together in the same battalion, Evelyn Byrde and Henry Reed in the 2nd Monmouths, incidentally along with young Cyril Hillier; Charles Pigg and Arthur Bishop serving together in the 10th Worcesters. Not only did the masters at College lead from the front in the classroom and on College Field, they also set a fine example in the armed forces for their young protégés to follow. With the outbreak of war, Old Cheltonians, from all walks of life and occupations, and their teachers were answering the call from across the Empire. Many would not have to wait long before they engaged the enemy.

Initial Casualties

During those first few days of August, nervous refugees on the Franco-German border and British ex-patriots elsewhere in Europe had started a westward exodus seeking safe haven. Consequently, at 1.25pm on the 3rd August, Henry Hadley (Boyne House, 1880) boarded the train to Cologne at Berlin's Friedrichstraße station, accompanied by his English house keeper, Elizabeth Pratley.

Henry had been teaching in Berlin for several years, but, given his British nationality, he decided to move to the relative safety of Paris following Germany's declarations of war against Russia and France. He had left it very late as Germany's ultimatum to Belgium demanding free passage through that country had been issued the day before. Henry also had a military background and was well aware of the implications and extent of Germany's troop deployments. Having left College in July 1880, he had entered the Royal Military College at Sandhurst in 1885 and was commissioned as a second lieutenant, serving in the 1st Battalion, West Indian Regiment until 1890. Seeking a career change, he resigned his commission, and went up to Oxford University as an unattached student in 1892 to become a language teacher and tutor, an occupation that had brought him to Germany. While the train was stopped at Gelsenkirchen station, and with rumours about foreign spies running rife, the German conductor grew suspicious of Henry, and alerted some German officers travelling on the train. Henry became involved in an altercation with these officers who later claimed that he had spoken in several foreign languages, did not appear to know where he was travelling to, and had argued with a waiter in the dining car. After briefly returning to his seat, the arguments continued, which culminated in Henry being shot in the stomach while in the train's corridor by a Prussian military officer, Oberleutnant Nicolay. Henry was taken by ambulance to the Evangelische Krankenhaus in Gelsenkirchen, but died there at 3.15am on 5th August – just over three hours after Britain

Henry Hadley at College

had declared war on Germany. Elizabeth was taken to Münster and interrogated as a potential spy at a military prison, but was eventually released, without charge, to the Clemenshospital in Münster to recover from the ordeal. She was finally allowed to return home in November. Not only was Henry the first of the 702 Old Cheltonians to be killed, he was also, we contend, the first British fatality of the First World War.

Unlike Elizabeth, Maurice Nesbitt (Day Boy, 1898), was not so lucky. After leaving College, he read modern languages at London University achieving a First Class Honours bachelor's degree in 1906. He became a schoolmaster like his father and taught French at the Consett Technical Institute. Having married Catherine in 1908, they both settled down to family life with their two young children; Charles born in 1909 and Marion born in 1911. On 29th July 1914 during the summer holidays, and just before war was declared, Maurice went to Germany to study German philology at Marburg University. His timing proved fatal as the consequences of the international crisis overtook him. Being in Germany when war was declared, he was immediately interned as a prisoner of war with other Englishmen of military age. Though he managed to write to Catherine, smuggling a letter through a friendly German clergyman, he never saw or heard from his young family again as he died quite suddenly in captivity on 5th October. The circumstances of his death were never properly established or explained, and rumours abounded that he had been murdered although his misfortune may well have been made more of at the time by opportunistic British propagandists. Nonetheless, he joined Henry Hadley as the first two Old Cheltonian civilians to become victims of the war, with of course their respective families and friends.

Henry Hadley's death occurred some three weeks before the opening British shot at Casteau in Belgium during the initial skirmish of Britain's war in Europe. After the battle at Mons that immediately followed, and the many subsequent rearguard actions fought during the three-week Anglo-French retirement to the River Marne, deaths of serving Old Cheltonians inevitably and increasingly followed. The first was Robert Sidebottom (Leconfield, 1899). He had left College, having played rugby on College Field for the XV in his last term, before going on to the Royal Military College at Sandhurst and a military career. Following service with the mounted infantry during the Boer War, he subsequently gained a reputation for being a big game hunter. Promoted to captain in July 1914, he joined the 2nd Battalion, Lancashire Fusiliers, based in Dover. When mobilisation was ordered, the battalion was quickly readied and embarked as part of the 4th Division for France on 20th August 1914, landing at Boulogne. Within a week, on 26th August 1914, during the retreat from Mons that had started three days earlier, he was shot in the head and killed instantly at Le Cateau.

Fighting with Robert that day at Le Cateau was Douglas Reynolds (Day Boy, 1896); they had been in the same year together at College. The British defensive action at Le Cateau was essential in stopping the retreat from Mons becoming a rout by slowing the momentum of the following 1st German Army.

Douglas Reynolds VC

For his bravery that day and afterwards, Douglas, a captain in the Royal Field Artillery with the 37th (Howitzer) Battery, was the first Old Cheltonian to win a Victoria Cross in the First World War. His citation was published in the London Gazette on 16th November 1914:

> On 26 August 1914 at Le Cateau, France, Captain Reynolds took up two teams with volunteer drivers, to recapture two British guns and limbered up two guns under heavy artillery and infantry fire. Although the enemy was within 100 yards he managed, with the help of two drivers, to get one gun away safely. On 9 September at Pysloup, he reconnoitered at close range, discovered a battery which was holding up the advance and silenced it.

Having landed at Boulogne the day before the action at Le Cateau, Lieutenant Glennie Gilliat and the 1st Battalion, Royal Warwickshire Regiment were rushed to the fighting by buses and went immediately into action and endured their baptism of fire. Following the battle, the battalion retired further, marching to the Marne and then the Aisne where the German advance was eventually checked. On 12th September, Glennie was elevated, as a field promotion, to his captaincy.[22] A month later the battalion had been redeployed to defend Ypres and was in the front line south of the town facing the village of Meteren occupied in strength by the Germans. On 13th October during the battalion's attack on the village an incident took place which would have unexpected and significant repercussions. The attack on Meteren that day cost many casualties, including Glennie who was killed in action. The circumstances of his death are described as part of a personal biographic entry in *Bond of Sacrifice*:

> A brother officer wrote: 'We were attacking a village called Meteren. My company was next to 'Glennie's' when I fell. He saw at once, and ran to me with two of his men, and started bandaging my wound. It was a very plucky thing to do, as I was lying in a very exposed place, and the Germans were firing at me all the time. Glennie left me after he had put the dressing on, and said he would send some men to carry me back, but was killed himself – shot through the forehead – when he got back to the trench.'[23]

As *Bond of Sacrifice* was published in 1917, the 'fellow officer' survived the action, but who was he? The battalion's war diary entry for the attack on Meteren on 13th October shines considerable light on this mystery, and records the battalion's advance on the village and the nature of the day's fighting:

> 10am   Enemy were reported to be holding high ground along ridge in front of METEREN. A & B Coys were deployed, A on left S, B on right N of road

---

[22] His promotion was not gazetted until 29th October 1914, two weeks after his death in action.
[23] Colonel LA Clutterbuck, *The Bond of Sacrifice, Volume 1*, Anglo-African Publishers, 1917, page 152 (GIL).

	to advance and if possible to cross road. D Coy under Major Christie was sent up behind C Coy in support. Enemy retired into & just outside METEREN occupying trenches and houses.
11am	Regiment ordered to push on & endeavour to drive them out.
1pm	Gained outskirts of village but were held up & great need of supports. C & D Coys again advanced & took several trenches but suffered severely.
1.30pm	GOC ordered regiment to halt & he would attack with X[th] Bde to North of village & 12th Brigade was to attack on S of road.
2pm	12th Brigade commence their attack.
3pm	Seaforths attack on our left through A Coy which withdrew at dusk to PLANEBOON. C & D Coys with Capt Freeman & Major Christie were unable to withdraw till much later owing to heavy fire but about 8pm the Kings OWN came up & passed through them.
10pm	C & D Coys join battalion at PLANEBOON, the regiment becoming RESERVE to brigade. METEREN was taken during the night. Our casualties 42 killed 85 wounded. Major Christie, Lt Gilliat (died of wounds), Lt Montgomery (badly wounded). Lts Brindley, Young, & Thornhill (slightly). Very wet all day.[24]

The two officer fatalities at Meteren were clearly Glennie and Major (William Charles) Christie.[25] The only seriously wounded officer that had required medical evacuation, having been saved by Glennie's prompt first aid and protection during this action, was Lieutenant Montgomery, later to become Field Marshal Montgomery of Alamein.[26]

During the following two weeks, 25 Old Cheltonians were killed. Among them was Edward Lousada, one of the twins, who died on the night of 29/30th October when his battalion was forced to retire under the weight of a German assault towards Ypres. Sadly, his body was never recovered, as the ground was lost in the German advance and not retaken until 1918. Due to the confused nature of the fighting at the time, and the unprecedented number of casualty reports arriving on the officials' desks in the War Office, the British

---

[24] The National Archives, WO 95/1484, War Diary of 1st Royal Warwickshire Regiment, October 1914.
[25] William Christie had played for the Rugby School XV in 1891 in the annual rugby match against Cheltenham College, the game's first and longest-standing school rugby fixture.
[26] Montgomery's description of his wounding and rescue at Meteren from his personal memoirs attributes his survival to an unnamed soldier of his platoon, perhaps in an effort to portray himself as popular with his men. His direct quote in *Bond of Sacrifice* makes clear, however, that Glennie's leadership and swift action secured the life of the future Field Marshal who would be so important to Britain's war efforts in the Second World War 1939-1945. See, *The Memoirs of Field Marshal The Viscount Montgomery of Alamein KG*, (Collins Books, 1958), pages 33-34.

authorities were under immense pressure to discharge by telegram accurate news to families of their loved ones' fate or safety. This was especially difficult in circumstances when soldiers, like Edward, were reported as missing. Given the time needed to determine the facts of such cases of those missing men, in having to resolve the often conflicting detail from subsequent witnesses and field reports, understandable errors appeared in the formally published casualty lists of the day. The time and place of Edward's death is a case in point. His death was officially reported as having occurred on 2nd November. However, since the unit war diary has been declassified and become available to public scrutiny, it is clear that he was killed two days earlier on 29/30th October in a general battalion withdrawal. The unit war diary entry for that date indicates the scale of the fighting, yet importantly states that:

> The casualties of these two days were Lt Col Crispin killed, also Lieuts Lousada, Croft, Marker and Shaw and 394 other ranks. [27]

Despite the intervening 100 years, it is gratifying to correct the record and supplement this small postscript to Edward's narrative and memory.

The following evening, however, two further Old Cheltonians were killed fighting at Messines, south of Ypres. Having been briefly together in the same House at College, both Duncan McGregor (Day Boy, 1913) and William McKay (Day Boy, 1908) were privates in the ranks of the same battalion, the 1st/14th Battalion, London Regiment (London Scottish) and the first territorial army battalion to see active service in the Great War. Duncan left College in July 1913 and, being a scholar and the Silver Medallist for mathematics, won an exhibition scholarship to Corpus Christi College, Cambridge. However, he opted to go to London University where he matriculated in 1914. He was still a student when the war broke out but had been a member of the London Scottish 'territorials' for several months. William had left College in July 1908 and was in the shooting VIII in his last term. Working and living in London, he too was a member of the London Scottish. The speed at which these 'part-timers' made ready for war is impressive. The battalion was mobilised on the outbreak of war in August 1914 at 59, Buckingham Gate, forming part of the 4th London Brigade, 2nd London Division, before moving to Abbotts Langley for final operational training. As a prestige battalion, largely constituted of expatriated Scots, its establishment strength remained remarkably high compared to other Territorial Army units. On 15th September 1914, the battalion deployed to France from Southampton on the SS *Winifredian* landing at Le Havre the following day. Assigned to the 1st Infantry Brigade, 1st Division it became engaged in the brutal fighting south of Ypres in October 1914. While in the line at Wytschaete near Messines on 31st October 1914, the unit undertook a counter-attack on enemy trenches under a terrific German barrage. The battalion was ordered:

> To make a counter attack through the cavalry trenches. This move was carried out under heavy shell fire until reaching dead ground. The cavalry trenches were reached

---

[27] The National Archives, WO 95/1269, Battalion War Diary, 2nd Royal Sussex Regiment, October 1914.

under shrapnel and big gun fire at about 1030am, but as there was no room in the cavalry trenches the best cover obtainable had to be searched for it being impossible to advance further unsupported. The Bn lay under heavy fire until dusk when the firing ceased. From 9pm to 2am the Germans made continuous attacks against our lines, all of which were unsuccessful.[28]

The battalion went into action with 26 officers and 750 men and suffered 321 casualties, of which 185 were posted as missing. One of the fallen was Duncan, and William was among the missing. For some reason, William's death was not recorded in the College Roll of Honour, perhaps because of the commonly experienced difficulties in establishing the precise facts regarding the missing. This was a hard enough task for the officer casualties, but, almost impossible, in reality, for the deaths of the rank and file. This was due not only to the sheer volume of cases of missing soldiers which increasingly overwhelmed the recording authorities, but also to the established practice that afforded a greater degree of administrative effort and priority to officers, a legacy of the Victorian era which today has been thankfully swept away. William's name has now been added to the Roll and his name recorded on the Chapel memorial plaques.

The first death of an Old Cheltonian outside Europe in the war occurred in Nyasaland (now Malawi) on 11th September. Philip Garnett (Boyne House, 1905), though still in his penultimate term but keen to follow a career in the army, applied for entry to the Royal Military College Sandhurst on 10th March 1905. After his officer training, he was commissioned as a second lieutenant in the Royal Berkshire Regiment on 4th May 1907 and promoted to lieutenant four years later in October 1913 and being seconded for service in the 1st Battalion, King's African Rifles. As conflict in the colonies was becoming increasingly likely, he with 57 other ranks of the African Rifles was transferred from Nairobi to Nyasaland on 19th July 1914. The aim of this detachment was to deter, and if necessary counter, any incursion into Nyasaland by imperial German and colonial forces in East Africa. But on 9th September, a German force of 22 officers and 800 armed Askari tribesmen attacked the Nyasaland District Headquarters at Karonga, at the northern end of Lake Nyasa. Although the German force was repulsed with heavy losses, Philip was seriously wounded and died from his injuries two days later. The Germans made no further attempts to advance into Nyasaland.

Some eight weeks later, and on the other side of the continent, Alan Peel (Newick, 1904) was serving with the 2nd Battalion, Nigerian Regiment, a constituent part of the West African Frontier Force (WAFF). Educated at both the Junior School and College from May 1897 to August 1904, Alan also went on to Sandhurst, where he was a year ahead of Philip as he had been at College. Alan was commissioned as a second lieutenant in the South Wales Borderers on 24th January 1906.[29] As the war spread its global tentacles with ever widening and strengthening grip across the colonies, imperial interests and prestige

---
[28] The National Archives, WO 95/1266, 1/14 Battalion London Regiment War Diary 1914.
[29] *The London Gazette*, 23rd January 1906, page 545.

increasingly clashed. Also seconded to the British colonial forces in Africa, Alan was fighting in the German colony of Kamarun. As results and casualties from the various actions and skirmishes took time to be collated, confirmed and disseminated, it was as November drew to a close that a telegram from the Colonial Administrator in Nigeria was received by his parents Herbert and Mary at home in Carmarthen. In simple and stark terms, it stated:

> Regret to inform you that report received from Officer Commanding Maiduguri Column, Lieutenant AR Peel South Wales Borderers was killed by patrol of Germans on 17th November at Geia, just to the north of Marua. [30]

A week later, a further report from the Governor General's office shed more light on the circumstances of Alan's death, describing the action:

> Whilst on the March towards Marua, information was received that the enemy's Mounted Infantry was in the village of Kosseoa. Lt Peel, with 32 of his men, at once proceeded to reconnoitre in that direction. He reached the village, and was informed by the inhabitants, treacherously, that they had seen no Germans. He then proceeded to water and feed his horse. Soon, however, his advanced scouts reported the enemy close by. Handing over the horse to the 'Number 3', Lieutenant Peel advanced on foot with his men towards the southern end of the village, and on coming into touch with the enemy, advanced in by rushes and charged them with the bayonet. He was the first to fall, leading his men.[31]

Alan Peel was buried at 6.30pm on 17th November by supporting French troops after the village had been taken, and is commemorated in the College Chapel and on the War Memorial at Zaria in Northern Nigeria.

As hostilities with Germany intensified, the Royal Navy were not immune to setbacks and significant loss of life similar to those of the BEF in the opening months of the war. Now a midshipman aboard HMS *Aboukir*, Alan Robertson had seen active service during the Battle of Heligoland Bight on 28th August serving alongside the nine other young cadets who had been sent to supplement her crew. Recommissioned from the reserve at the start of the First World War, *Aboukir* was part of Cruiser Force C, a squadron of five obsolete Cressy-class cruisers of the Third Home Fleet. On 22nd September, she and two of her sister cruisers, HMS *Cressy* and HMS *Hogue*, were on patrol together in the southern North Sea, steaming sedately at 10 knots in line astern. They were spotted by Kapitaenleutnant Otto Weddigen, in the German submarine U-9, which submerged, closed the range on the cruisers and fired a single torpedo at the *Aboukir*. The torpedo broke her back and she sank within 25 minutes with the loss of 527 men. The other two cruisers, believing the *Aboukir*

---

[30] The National Archives, WO 339/6429, personal file of Lieutenant AR Peel.
[31] Ibid.

had struck a mine, 'hove to' to pick up survivors. They were both also sunk by the U-9 as they closed to help; an overall cost of 1,459 lives. Alan was both the youngest, and the first Royal Navy Old Cheltonian to be killed in the War.

Sadly, the Navy's misfortune, and a degree of tactical naivety, continued with a further encounter with the German submarine *U-9*. Having transferred from destroyer duties, Donald Macdonald was getting to grips with his new duties on a battleship as a recently arrived lieutenant on board HMS *Hawke*, part of the 10th Cruiser Squadron. On 15th October on patrol off Aberdeen, the squadron's ships were deployed in line abreast some 10 miles from each other and on the limits of visual range. The *Hawke* stopped at 9.30am to pick up mail from her sister ship HMS *Endymion*. Having retrieved her boat which had been sent to collect the mail, she then proceeded at 13 knots without 'zigzagging' to regain her station, but was now out of sight of the rest of the squadron. An hour later, a single torpedo from the German submarine *U-9* struck her amidships, and she quickly capsized. After a separate and unsuccessful submarine attack on another ship, the squadron was ordered to retreat at high speed to the northwest. The lack of response to this order from *Hawke* was the first indication to the squadron that the tragedy had occurred. Some 524 officers and men died, including Donald. There were only 70 survivors. Such operational misfortune was not confined to the Navy's surface units. It also applied to Britain's embryonic submarine force.

Before the start of hostilities, the Royal Navy's long-range submarine force had been active on covert patrols observing the activities of both Germany's High Seas Fleet and her merchant marine. When the headquarters of the 8th Submarine Flotilla, a force of 18 submarines based at Harwich, was established on 31st July, its commander, Commodore Roger Keyes, wrote to the Commander-in-Chief Home Fleet identifying the immediate vulnerabilities to Britain's deployment plans. His primary concern was of 'the German Fleet proceeding to the southward to attack the Expeditionary Force in transit'.[32] From then onwards and in support of the Cruiser Force, the submarines, usually operating in pairs, kept a continuous observation watch in the southern North Sea, especially at the entrance to the River Ems, the entrance to Germany's naval ports between Sylt and Borkum. From her first patrol on 9th August, HM Submarine *D2* enjoyed a mixed fortune. On board as second in command was Frederick Coplestone, the experienced submariner who we encountered previously re-enlisting from the Naval Retired List. Having successfully completed two patrols in the waters near Heligoland, *D2* participated in the sea action there on 28th August, in support of the British surface fleet including HMS *Aboukir*. Stationed near her familiar patrol area of the Ems estuary, she was in position to attack any German vessels venturing out to sea. After conducting four further successful patrols, *D2* left Harwich at 7.30am on 21st November. She took up her station 10 miles to the north east of Heligoland after a transit of some seven and a half hours through minefields, simply using dead reckoning techniques based on a compass, a stop watch and

---

[32] The National Archives, ADM 137/225, 8th Submarine Flotilla, Commodore S, Memoranda and Reports, 1914.

a tide table to navigate. However, throughout her passage the weather steadily worsened and a gale set in. A sister submarine in the area reported that sea state conditions were so rough that waves were breaking continually over the conning tower. Returning on the night of 22nd November in heavy seas, her commander Lieutenant Commander Arthur Jameson was skilfully and bravely guiding the boat back to base in the dark at great personal risk. Precariously perched on the small open conning tower in atrocious weather, he was washed overboard near Harwich. His body was never found. Frederick, as second in command, took control and brought the boat and crew safely back to Harwich. But an urgent replacement as commander was required as *D2* was needed out on patrol, and Lieutenant Commander Clement Head was quickly appointed. Though originally a naval aviator and recently qualified for submarine command, Clement was junior to Frederick by some three years and had less submarine experience. But the pair had the combined benefits of both youth and experience, and good hearing, a sense vital in detecting and interpreting the various acoustics and cavitations within the underwater environment. Three days later, *D2* set off at daybreak for her next, and last, patrol having replenished and being accompanied by the submarine *E15*. She was due back in Harwich on 30th November, but nothing more was heard from her. She was formally reported overdue and lost on 9th December. Without any concrete explanation of her loss, it was surmised that *D2* had struck a mine and sunk on or about 25th November. Of her 25 man crew there were no survivors.

Not all the naval casualties in the early months of the war were as a direct consequence of enemy action. At 7.45am on Thursday 26th November, workers in the Chatham dockyards were arriving for the morning shift as their children finished their breakfasts before going off to school. Moored at buoy number 17 at Kethole Reach on the River Medway, the 15,000 ton battleship HMS *Bulwark* lay undisturbed as she completed the process of rearming. She was part of the 5th Battle Squadron which had recently returned to the Medway from exercise and patrol in the North Sea.

On board as part of the ship's company were two Old Cheltonians; Fleet Surgeon Percy Nix (Leconfield, 1888), the ship's senior medical officer, and Lieutenant Henry Lock (Leconfield, 1904), who was part of the detachment from the Royal Marine Light Infantry allocated to the ship. Percy had left College in July 1888 and gained a place at Pembroke College, Cambridge to read medicine. By 1896 he was a fully qualified surgeon at the London Hospital, but decided to join the Royal Navy Medical Services and was commissioned as a Staff Surgeon on 10th November.[33] By August 1914, he had been appointed to *Bulwark* at the age of 44. Henry had left College in July 1904, having been in the shooting VIII throughout his last three years. Although he passed the entrance exam for the Royal Military College at Sandhurst that year, he elected to join the Royal Marines instead, perhaps to take advantage of accelerated promotion compared with his army counterparts. He was commissioned as a second lieutenant on 1st September 1904 at the Royal Naval College at Greenwich and was promoted to lieutenant on 1st July 1906 and

---

[33] *The London Gazette* 17th November 1896, page 6273.

HMS *Bulwark*, entering Chatham

served on a number of warships.[34] His personal reports showed that his general conduct, ability and professional knowledge were all 'very good'.[35] He joined *Bulwark* when war was declared on 4th August 1914. Just as the Royal Marines were finishing their band practice on the stern of the ship at 7.50am, a violent explosion ripped the ship apart, and she sank in pieces within minutes. Of her complement of 750, only 14 survived, none of them officers. The violence of the explosion shook buildings in Sheerness and Southend, six miles away across the Thames Estuary and contents and pieces from the ship, including burnt and blackened metal and personal effects of the crew, were scattered on both banks of the River Medway. Against standing regulations, 275 6-inch shells were being replaced and had been left close together in the companionways next to the bulkhead of the ship's magazine. It was first believed that one of the shells had been dropped or knocked over which had then set off an immediate and devastating chain reaction. However, the Court of Enquiry accepted the contributory explanation that cordite charges stored alongside a boiler room bulkhead had overheated and set off the shells standing nearby and the ensuing explosion tore the ship apart. It was also noted that the ship was manned in large part by reservists whose application of the necessary safety procedures may not have been up to the same rigour as applied by regular sailors. It was another painful experience for the Royal Navy during the process of getting the Fleet to peak operational efficiency, a process that would not be achieved until the lessons from the Battle of Jutland in 1916 had also been taken into account.

[34] These included HMS *Natal*, HMS *Lancaster*, and HMS *Prince George*.
[35] The National Archives, ADM 196/63/248, page 247.

Yet, the Royal Navy was not alone in having to resolve the many pressures and challenges that the war was imposing on Britain. Across the nation, the immediate necessities of the war touched almost everyone as enlistment and colonial reinforcement required training, equipping and billeting. Hubert Stansfeld (Newick, 1887) retired from the army as a captain in the 3rd Battalion, Yorkshire Regiment on 9th May 1906, although he was granted the rank of honorary Major in September 1907 while supporting the build up of the new volunteer battalion. Although he resigned from these duties on 15th March 1913, he was quickly recommissioned when war was declared becoming the quartermaster general to the 21st Division on 19th September 1914. This position carried great responsibility and pressure for all logistical requirements of the Division as it re-equipped and mobilised for war. Established in September 1914, as part of Kitchener's Third New Army (K3), the Division had to train and equip all its new volunteers. Not least of the pressures placed on the military authorities, and an issue of great urgency, was where to billet this surge of recruits; expediency required many to live in local fields under canvas in temporary tents. As the Division worked up, Hubert supervised the building of huts for a training camp at Codford on Salisbury Plain, work being undertaken by local civilians and reservists while the regular troops were mobilised and deployed. Yet certain social dynamics did not necessarily support his endeavours. During the latter months of 1914 the strength of anti-militaristic socialism had been increasing in Britain with the rise and rumblings of the British Socialist Party, and its effects were even felt in the armed forces. A comment in the war diary of Glennie Gilliat's battalion describes the challenges to attitudes in the front line:

> Discipline. Noticeably worse than in South Africa. Probably due to socialistic ideas imbibed by Reservists.[36]

Given the extent, nature and stress of his work, conducted in ever-worsening weather, Hubert was under immense pressure, not least from superior authorities expecting quick results in unrealistic timescales. While in temporary billets at Boscombe Undercliffe on 8th December 1914, with perhaps no one to turn to, he shot himself in the head. The ensuing Court of Inquiry recorded that he became 'very excitable, more especially after a hard day's work'. He had apparently complained about being unable to concentrate his mind. The Bournemouth coroner returned a verdict of 'suicide during temporary insanity'. For some reason, his death was omitted from the College Roll of Honour.

Cases of suicide were often neglected from official records of the day, perhaps politely overlooked or left unexplained to spare unnecessary embarrassment, as suicide was still a criminal offence in the Edwardian period. Furthermore, many of the associated and contributory psychological issues associated with military service and combat stress were

---

[36] The National Archives, WO 95/1484 (1-20), 1st Battalion, Royal Warwickshire Regiment War Diary, September 1914.

poorly understood as this strand of medical science and expertise was still in its infancy. What was variously diagnosed at the time as neurasthenia, shell shock, cowardice, depression, and, even worse, temporary insanity, would today be viewed as a severe case of post traumatic stress disorder (PTSD). Recognition of this condition in the modern armed forces is now swift and medical support offered immediately with the mental health and well being of the service personnel concerned given top priority. It is therefore quite appropriate that any cases of error or omission from First World War records, such as Hubert's, whether inadvertent or otherwise, should be rectified as every death reflects another victim of the war. Hubert Stansfeld is now suitably remembered and included amongst his fellow Old Cheltonians who died in the Great War.

With the arrival of December, fighting on the Western Front was reaching deadlock, as opposing trench lines stretched for some 470 miles from Nieuport on the Belgian coast to the Swiss border, a feature that few of the 'sleep-walking' politicians, generals and diplomats had anticipated in August. With weather conditions deteriorating markedly, trench warfare took on the mantle of much more limited local raids and counter-attacks involving smaller groups of soldiers, rather than the previous major battles involving many thousands.

Philip Neame (Hazelwell, 1906) left College and spent the next two years training to be a Royal Engineer officer at the Royal Military Academy at Woolwich.

With six years of commissioned service under his belt by 1914, he was an experienced young officer very accustomed to his duties working alongside frontline infantry units. In the very early hours of 19th December, and five days after his 26th birthday, Philip was in charge of a team of sappers who were asked to go forward and consolidate a section of trench that had just been captured in a night raid by the West Yorkshire regiment. As the Germans began to mass for a counter attack, the small group of British defenders were faced with impending disaster as they had run out of fuses for their Mark 1 hand grenades.[37] With some technical knowledge of the fusing mechanism of this type of grenade, Philip rushed forward and improvised an ad hoc method of employing the remaining bombs, and began throwing them very effectively at the advancing Germans. He held his ground single-handedly for some 45 minutes, while being under continuous enemy fire, which allowed the West Yorkshires to retire, with their injured comrades, to the original British front line trench and relative safety. For his bravery and decisive action he was awarded the Victoria Cross, the second to be conferred on an Old Cheltonian during the First World War. His citation read:

Philip Neame VC

---

[37] The Mark 1 grenade was of poor rudimentary design and reliability, as it was prone to explode prematurely. It was therefore highly unpopular with front line soldiers. Nonetheless, the utility of hand grenades by all sides was an essential component during close quarter trench combat.

1914 – THE YEAR OF OPTIMISTIC PATRIOTISM

> For conspicuous bravery on the 19th December, near Neuve Chapelle, when, notwithstanding the very heavy rifle fire and bomb-throwing by the enemy, he succeeded in holding them back and rescuing all the wounded men whom it was possible to move.[38]

Philip survived the war, and went on to have a very successful and highly decorated military career.[39]

As the end of December 1914 drew the first five months of fighting to a close, and as the bitter winter weather became a pervading and common enemy, the realities of the war set in. All of the belligerent armies had suffered appalling casualties, but perhaps none more so in effective terms than the small, highly professional and well equipped BEF. Nearly 90,000 of its number had been killed, wounded or were missing; 3,627 of them officers.[40] But for the arrival of the Indian Corps and the first of the territorial battalions, it would have been very difficult for the BEF to hold its 21 miles of trench line from Messines to Givenchy. From schoolboy cricketer in August to hardened platoon commander by December, Cyril Hillier and the 1/2nd Monmouths were holding trenches just to the west of Frelinghien, rotating with the other brigade battalions and spending four days in the trenches and four days out. After constant rain, conditions in the trenches were atrocious:

> Communication by communication trenches became impossible, owing to the very heavy rains, the sodden state of the country, and the inability to drain trenches owing to flatness of country. Losses became more frequent.[41]

But on Christmas Eve, the noise of fighting died away. It became uncommonly quiet. In contrast to the normal cacophonic percussions of static trench warfare, Cyril heard the softer sound of Christmas carols being sung by the Saxon Regiments on the other side of No Man's Land. Candles were being lit in the evening and Christmas trees could be seen in the trenches opposite. The war diary notes that:

> On Xmas Day practically no firing took place on either side by mutual agreement. The opportunity was made use of to ascertain what German regiment opposed us.[42]

Although no account of fraternisation is referred to in the war diary, one assumes this was achieved by meeting the enemy in No Man's Land. A letter home from a member

---

[38] Supplement to *The London Gazette*, 16th February 1915, page 1700.
[39] Lieutenant General Sir Philip Neame, VC, KBE, CB, DSO, KStJ. He also won an Olympic Gold medal for shooting in the 1924 Paris games; the only person to have been awarded both the VC and an Olympic Gold medal.
[40] See Peter Simkins, *World War 1, 1914-1918, The Western Front*, Colour Library Books Limited, Godalming, 1991, page 45.
[41] The National Archives, WO 95/1506, 1/2nd Battalion, Monmouthshire Regiment, 1914.
[42] Ibid.

Cheltenham College in Winter, E Burrows, 1899

of the battalion confirms this. Having described the welcome quantity of chocolates and Christmas pudding that had been sent from home to the battalion, the letter implies that some of these luxuries were offered to the enemy:

> The Germans don't get looked after like we do. The one to whom we were talking put out his hands the way they hold a rifle and said 'English damned good.[43]

By New Year's Eve, the papers in Britain were widely reporting the personal accounts of the truce from letters sent from the front, under such headings as 'Christmas Time in the Trenches – Greeting the Enemy'.[44] More importantly in practical terms for soldiers holding the line, the lull in the fighting allowed more time to be spent on making the trenches more habitable, bringing up large amounts of brushwood, planks and hand pumps in an effort to keep the trenches, if not dry, at least less wet.

If conditions in the trenches were looking bleak, so too were the prospects for 1915, especially the reconfiguration of the peacetime economy to one fully focused and capable of increasing industrial output to satisfy the military appetite for more shells and military hardware, especially for heavy calibre artillery. The war was far from over by Christmas, and given the deadlock on the Western Front, the strategists would have to reconsider and perhaps look elsewhere for success.

---

[43] *The Birmingham Gazette*, 12th January 1915, letter from Private (No 1250) Arthur Gill, also cited in *The Truce, The Day the War Stopped*, C. Baker, Amberley Publishing, 2014.
[44] *Daily Telegraph*, Thursday, 31st December 1914, page 9.

At the end of 1914, the College community was undoubtedly shocked by the numbers of Old Cheltonians who had been killed in the first five months of the war: the total of 95 almost doubled the losses of three years of fighting in South Africa over a decade before. Ominously, casualty figures would only get worse.

LIST OF FALLEN OLD CHELTONIANS 1914

On the following pages (38 to 43) are the names and service details of Old Cheltonians who died in the first year of the war.

1914 – LIST OF FALLEN OLD CHELTONIANS

	Died (1914)	Name	Rank
1	5 August	Hadley H	Civilian
2	26 August	Sidebottom R	Captain
3	28 August	Boileau E	Colonel
4	1 September	Campbell JD	Lieutenant
5	1 September	Champion de Crestigny C	Lieutenant
6	4 September	White LW	Lieutenant
7	10 September	Collingwood –Thompson E	2nd Lieutenant
8	10 September	White GSA	Lieutenant
9	11 September	Garnett PN	Lieutenant
10	12 September	Tindall EV	2nd Lieutenant
11	13 September	Denroche-Smith AJ	Lieutenant
12	13 September	Owen NM	2nd Lieutenant
13	15 September	Ker CH	Captain
14	16 September	Furse GA	Captain
15	17 September	Girardot PC	2nd Lieutenant
16	17 September	Gordon CG	2nd Lieutenant
17	17 September	Warren D	Lt Colonel
18	18 September	Crane CE	2nd Lieutenant
19	18 September	Vicat HJ	Lieutenant
20	19 September	Brown H	Lieutenant
21	19 September	Foster ACH	Lieutenant
22	20 September	Fenton GR	Lieutenant
23	20 September	MacKenzie CL	Lieutenant
24	20 September	Sarsfield WS	Major
25	20 September	Stanuell CM	2nd Lieutenant
26	22 September	Robertson ADC	Midshipman
27	26 September	Manley JD	2nd Lieutenant
28	26 September	Coker JC	Lieutenant
29	5 October	Nesbit MS	Civilian
30	12 October	Morse GTH	2nd Lieutenant
31	14 October	Gilliatt CGP	Captain
32	14 October	Ker AM	Captain
33	15 October	MacDonald DR	Lieutenant RN
34	18 October	Lyall CG	Captain
35	19 October	Gaitskell CE	Lieutenant
36	19 October	Stainforth RT	Lieutenant
37	20 October	Norton LG	Lieutenant
38	20 October	Tandy AMS	Lieutenant
39	21 October	Elliott PL	2nd Lieutenant

1914 – LIST OF FALLEN OLD CHELTONIANS

Unit	Age	Place
Late 1st West India Regiment	51	Gelsenkirchen, Germany
att 2nd Lancashire Fusiliers	33	Le Cateau
Royal Engineers	46	Ham
Royal Horse Artillery	31	Nery
2nd Dragoon Guards	26	Nery
att 2nd Dragoon Guards	28	Nery
att 2nd Royal Welch Fusiliers	20	La Ferte du Jouarre
2nd South Lancs. Regiment	23	Le Cateau
att 1st King's African Rifles	27	Nyasaland
att 2nd King's Royal Rifle Corps	22	Marne
18th Hussars	23	Aisne
Royal Field Artillery	20	Aisne
1st Bedfordshire Regiment	31	Aisne
Royal Field Artillery	35	Aisne
2nd Oxford and Bucks Light Infantry	18	Aisne
1st Northamptonshire Regiment	20	Aisne
1st Royal West Surrey Regiment	49	Aisne
1st Duke of Cornwall's Light Infantry	22	Aisne
1st Royal West Kent Regiment	29	Aisne
att 1st Nigeria Regiment	24	Cameroons, West Africa
att 1st King's (Uganda) Regiment	28	Tsavo, Kenya, East Aftica
2nd Connaught Rangers	24	Aisne
2nd Highland Light Infantry	22	Aisne
2nd Connaught Rangers	48	Aisne
2nd Durham Light Infantry	20	Aisne, DLI
HMS Aboukir	15	North Sea
Royal Engineers	22	Aisne
1st South Wales Borderers	28	Aisne
Prisoner of War	34	Marburg, Germany
4th Middlesex Regiment	22	La Bassée
1st Royal Warwickshire Regiment	29	Meteren
att 1st Gordon Highlanders	32	Aisne
HMS *Hawke*	26	North Sea
att 1st Lincolnshire Regiment	43	La Bassée
2nd Leinster Regiment	21	Armentières
2nd Royal Warwickshire Regiment	20	Ypres
2nd Durham Light Infantry	24	Ypres
2nd Royal Irish Rifles	23	La Bassée
1st Duke of Cornwall's Light Infantry	18	Cuinchy

1914 – LIST OF FALLEN OLD CHELTONIANS

	Died (1914)	Name	Rank
40	22 October	Ripley CR	Lieutenant
41	23 October	Holmes FL	Lieutenant
42	23 October	Urquhart EFM	Captain
43	24 October	Cowan RC	Lieutenant
44	24 October	Nixon GF	Lieutenant
45	25 October	Hope-Johnstone WGT	Lieutenant
46	26 October	Bayley GB	2nd Lieutenant
47	26 October	Harding JM	2nd Lieutenant
48	27 October	Legard GB	Captain
49	28 October	Rohde JH	Lieutenant
50	30 October	Dunsterville GE	Lieutenant
51	30 October	Woodhouse AJ	Captain
52	30 October	Lousada EA	Lieutenant
53	31 October	Crawshay M	Captain
54	31 October	McGregor DG	Private
55	1 November	Stirling WD	Lieutenant RN
56	1 November	McKay WE	Private
57	2 November	Abbott GD	Lieutenant
58	2 November	Clayhills G	Captain
59	3 November	James GM	Major
60	4 November	Elmslie KW	Lieutenant
61	4 November	Ramsay N	Lieutenant
62	5 November	Phibbs WGB	Major
63	7 November	Geoghegan JR	Captain
64	8 November	Forbes-Robertson K	Captain
65	11 November	Combe BA	Lieutenant
66	11 November	Page RB	Colonel
67	11 November	Tyler AH	Major
68	13 November	McKay HM	Captain
69	13 November	Turnbull HVC	Captain
70	14 November	Evatt GRK	Captain
71	15 November	Stables HR	2nd Lieutenant
72	17 November	Peel AR	Captain
73	18 November	Baillie G	Major
74	18 November	Glenney HQ	Commissioner
75	23 November	Elliot RWS	Major
76	23 November	Reilly RA	Lieutenant
77	24 November	Davidson RIM	Lieutenant
78	24 November	Elwes RHLC	Civilian

1914 – LIST OF FALLEN OLD CHELTONIANS

Unit	Age	Place
2nd York and Lancaster Regiment	25	Armentières
2nd South Staffordshire Regiment	27	Ypres, Zonnebeke
1st Black Watch	37	Ypres, Pilckem
att 2nd Royal Scots	20	Aubers Ridge
Royal Field Artillery	23	Neuve Chapelle
4th Royal Fusiliers	27	Neuve Chapelle
2nd Kings Own Scottish Borderers	20	Ypres
1st Royal West Kent Regiment	20	Neuve Chapelle
1st Royal West Kent Regiment	29	Neuve Chapelle
Royal Engineers	25	Neuve Chapelle
1st Devonshire Regiment	30	Festubert
Royal Field Artillery	28	Ypres
2nd Royal Sussex Regiment	25	Ypres
5th Dragoon Guards	33	Ypres, Messines
1/14th London (Scots) Regiment	20	Ypres, Messines
HMS *Monmouth*	28	Coronel
1/14th London (Scots) Regiment	23	Ypres, Messines
1st Connaught Rangers	23	Laventie
1st East Lancashire Regiment	34	Armentières
1st East Kent (Buffs) Regiment	33	Ypres
4th Dragoon Guards	27	Ypres, Messines
att 4th Dragoon Guards	33	Ypres, Messines
1st Royal Irish Fusiliers	42	London
2nd Royal Inniskilling Fusiliers	28	Ypres, Ploegsteert Wood
att 2nd Seaforth Highlanders	32	Ypres, Ploegsteert Wood
att 4th Royal Fusiliers	25	Ypres
Late 1st Lancashire Fusiliers	57	Le Havre
Royal Engineers	43	Ypres, Nonne Bosschen
Royal Engineers	25	Sailly sur Lys
2nd Kings Own Scottish Borderers	37	Ypres
1st Middlesex Regiment	31	Fromelles
att 1st Cheshire Regiment	28	Ypres
att 1st Nigerian Regiment	28	Cameroons, West Africa
Royal Field Artillery	43	Ypres
att 1st Nigerian Regiment	35	Nigeria, Bakundi
7th Ghurka Rifles IA	40	Festubert
att 58th Vaughan's Rifles IA	25	Festubert, La Bassée
1st Manchester Regiment	25	Festubert, Givenchy
	22	Rhodesia, East Africa

1914 – LIST OF FALLEN OLD CHELTONIANS

	Died (1914)	Name	Rank
79	24 November	Whipple HC	Captain
80	25 November	Coplestone	Lt Commander
81	26 November	Durham E	Captain
82	26 November	Lock HJ	Lieutenant RM
83	26 November	Nix PK	Fleet Surgeon
84	29 November	Annesley WRN	Major
85	30 November	Moores CG	Captain
86	8 December	Stansfeld HA	Captain
87	18 December	Rome HC	Temp Major
88	19 December	Kerr HRG	Lieutenant
89	19 December	Lee HN	Captain
90	20 December	Gore GR	2nd Lieutenant
91	21 December	Pemberton O	Captain
92	21 December	Walters	2nd Lieutenant
93	23 December	Norman SS	Lieutenant
94	23 December	Mansel JL	Captain
95	28 December	Moore JO	Captain

1914 – LIST OF FALLEN OLD CHELTONIANS

Unit	Age	Place
1st Devonshire Regiment	35	Ypres, Messines
HM Submarine D2	32	Southern North Sea, Borkum
2nd Rifle Brigade	24	Festubert, Fauquissart
HMS *Bulwark* Royal Marines Light Infantry	28	Sheerness, Medway
HMS *Bulwark*	44	Sheerness, Medway
late Royal West Kent Regiment	51	London
Royal Engineers	27	Kemmel
19th Yorkshire Regiment	46	Bournemouth
att 129th Baluchis, IA	31	Givenchy
1st Highland Light Infantry	22	Givenchy
59th Scinde Rifles IA	29	La Bassée
att 1st Royal Welsh Fusiliers	21	Armentières
att 2nd Royal Irish Regiment	25	Festubert
att 1st Gloucestershire Regiment	24	Festubert
1st Manchester Regiment	25	Givenchy
7th Dragoon Guards	34	Givenchy, DOW
Royal Engineers	37	Kemmel

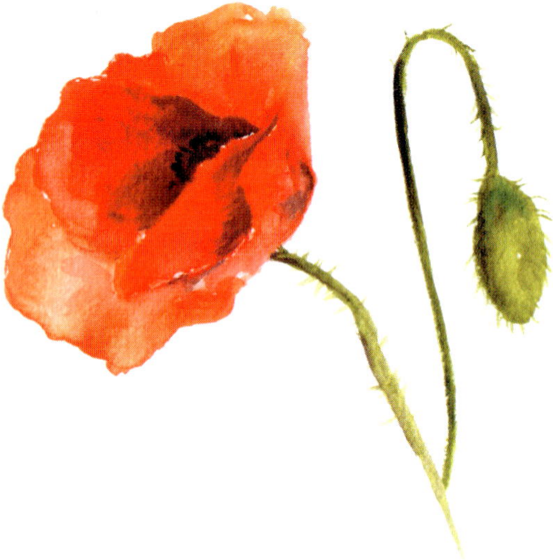

ACTS TWO
1915 – THE YEAR OF FALSE HOPE

Long before the first streaks of dawn appeared on the cold, blustery New Year's Day of 1915, Britain suffered another naval tragedy. Twenty miles south of Portland Bill during a filthy night of worsening weather, HMS *Formidable* was the last in a line of seven battleships steaming slowly in a heavy swell, conditions being deemed by each of the ships' captains to be incompatible with submarine operations. She was steaming without Edward Disney (Day Boy, 1901), her former officer of the watch. Edward had left College, aged 14, as a boy naval cadet, and had progressed well. He gained his gunnery qualification on *Formidable* and was assessed by his superior officer, Commander Pike, as being of *'above average ability, a good officer, reliable and very energetic'*.[45] Accordingly, he was appointed as a gunnery lieutenant on HMS *Arethusa* on 7th December, just three weeks before the New Year. Edward was lucky. At 2.25am, *Formidable* was hit by a torpedo from the German submarine *U-24*, and within two hours she sank with the loss of 547 lives from her complement of 780 officers and ratings. It was a portent of what the year held in store for Britain's fortunes of war.

For western civilisation, however, these first casualties on New Year's Day heralded a year of escalating and unchecked brutality. The war became 'total' and industrialised in nature, with the rules of warfare that had been enshrined in the Le Hague Conventions of 1898 and 1907 being forsaken. Military technology and weaponry would increasingly be brought to bear on the civilian populations, no longer confined solely to the battlefield. By breaking with the accepted conventions and laws of armed conflict, Germany placed herself firmly in the defendant's dock of world opinion. Her devastating release of chlorine gas in the early evening of 22nd April against the French 45th (Algerian) Division, followed by a further gas discharge against the 1st Canadian Division two days later, caused international condemnation of her grand strategy and morality. A fortnight later, the sinking without warning by the German submarine *U-20* of the non-military RMS *Lusitania* with the loss of 1,198 lives, many of them American, caused immediate further worldwide denunciation, none more shrill than that from the United States. With the first bombing raids of London by German Zeppelins at the end of May, the era of psychological and chemical warfare had truly begun. Not only was the sheer brutality of warfare broadening throughout 1915, so was its geographic reach and impact as new theatres of war were opened in the Dardanelles and Salonika, adding to the campaign in Mesopotamia already

---

[45] The National Archives, ADM 196/50/250 and ADM 196/143/807, personal records of Lieutenant Commander EO Disney, RN.

underway. For Old Cheltonians increasingly involved in the fighting, 1915 was the most costly year of the war; a year that was marked by false hopes, miscalculation and unrequited endeavour. The reasons for this were wide and multi-faceted.

As Lord Kitchener noted as he juggled with the myriad of competing military requirements, 'Unfortunately, we must make war as we must, not as we should like to'.[46] His view distilled the many constraints limiting British military effectiveness during 1915. It was a year which marked the start of a steep three-year learning process that the BEF had to embrace to transform into an effective continental-size army capable of competing alongside France, its key ally, and against Germany, its primary foe, in order to keep the hard-pressed Russians in the war on the Eastern Front. As Britain's developing imperial might was brought to bear on enemy forces across the world during the year, victories initially appeared feasible and were anticipated at home. Yet, across the globe, bright starts were quickly dimmed to gloomy failure and costly stalemates. The extent of the BEF's offensive difficulties on Western Front battlefields in 1915 was more generally and pessimistically measured in terms of casualties sustained against the degree of ground, prisoners of war, or guns captured. During 1915 British casualty rates soared, while territorial gains remained meagre at best. In the successive attacks by the BEF at Neuve Chapelle, Aubers Ridge, Festubert and, finally, Loos, opportunities slipped from Britain's grasp. Time after time, battlefield shortcomings were slow to be addressed and overcome. Of particular concern was the coordination and integration of artillery, infantry and the embryonic air services, the magnitude and complexity of which commanders and campaign planners had never experienced. Despite detailed planning and even after initial success in a few cases, the same inabilities reoccurred again and again: the failure to move supporting artillery forward quickly to give effective support to the infantry's second and third objectives; the failure to pinpoint, target and neutralise enemy artillery batteries; and what would prove to be the 'Achilles heel' for all frontline commanders over the next three years, inability to maintain effective tactical communications with the advancing troops.

Furthermore, the failure to make any substantive headway in Gallipoli shattered public optimism. The ever-lengthening casualty list from the Dardanelles merged with the losses to British, Canadian and French divisions that were holding the line by their fingertips in the Ypres salient from Germany's introduction of chemical weapons and second offensive. In Mesopotamia debacle also followed what had appeared a bright start to the campaign in late 1914 against the Turkish troops that threatened the Empire's essential oil resources.

To complete the contextual overview for 1915, the political and strategic difficulties facing the BEF's commanders with regard to shortages in military manpower, materiel, and experience were considerable. Competition for resources between each of the various operational theatres diluted the effectiveness of the overall strategy: supply simply could not match the burgeoning demand. The Shell Scandal in the spring of 1915 encapsulated the problem. Too many shells failed to explode through faulty fuse manufacture, and the

---

[46] Lord Kitchener in August 1915. Cassar, G.H., *Kitchener: Architect of Victory*, London, Kimber, (1977) page 389.

supply of shells to batteries was dwindling. In January, for example, field batteries were rationed to four rounds per day. The British artillery lacked sufficient guns of heavy calibre to provide the necessary destructive power to breach deep enemy dug outs. Similar issues troubled the infantry, as Philip Neame had encountered the year before. The number of effective grenades available to infantry units, so critical a weapon in achieving and maintaining tactical supremacy around the trench lines, was insufficient. No consistent model of grenade was available, nor was there regular supply from trusted manufacturers. All these factors combined to illustrate how industrial inadequacies could be toxic for politicians and army commanders alike, especially as public opinion was encouraged to blame the high combat casualty figures on munitions shortfalls as much as on apparently inept generalship. Consequently, deficiencies in manufacturing output, strategic decisiveness, tactical ability and the need to fight during 1915 for the good of the coalition, all combined greatly to undermine the BEF's ability to develop, adopt and conduct the necessary operational art of attacking entrenched defensive positions. This resulted in painful and costly results.

Painful Apprenticeships

As in the English Channel, where the search for survivors from HMS *Formidable* intensified, the same grey curtains of New Year's dawn slowly opened on the trenches on the Western Front. Cyril Hillier's battalion, the 1/2nd Monmouthshire Regiment, was also wrestling with the filthy weather conditions at Le Bizet:

> Still holding same trenches and being relieved by Essex Regt every 4 days. Since Xmas Day enemies fire has not been nearly so heavy. Communication trench still impassable. Weather cold and wet.[47]

Although January appeared to be the 'calm before the storm', the normal dangers of trench fighting continued, sadly epitomised by the first two deaths of the year. Two school mates, Herbert Chads and Robert Orlebar (both Cheltondale, 1912) had been in the same boarding house and form year on the Military side at College since the start of 1909. Herbert and Robert had served together in the Officers' Training Corps. Leaving College in July 1912, they went directly to the Royal Military College at Sandhurst, part of the same cadet intake. By the time they were both commissioned as second lieutenants (Robert in October 1913 into the Middlesex Regiment and Herbert four months later into the North Staffordshire Regiment), they had been together for the best part of five years. Tragically, they were killed within three days and three miles of each other, both shot in the trenches of Flanders by German snipers. The loss of so many lives to sniper fire was, for the most part, due to the conditions in the trenches which were appallingly wet, and in many places

---

[47] The National Archives, WO 95/1506, 1/2nd Battalion Monmouthshire Regiment, January 1915.

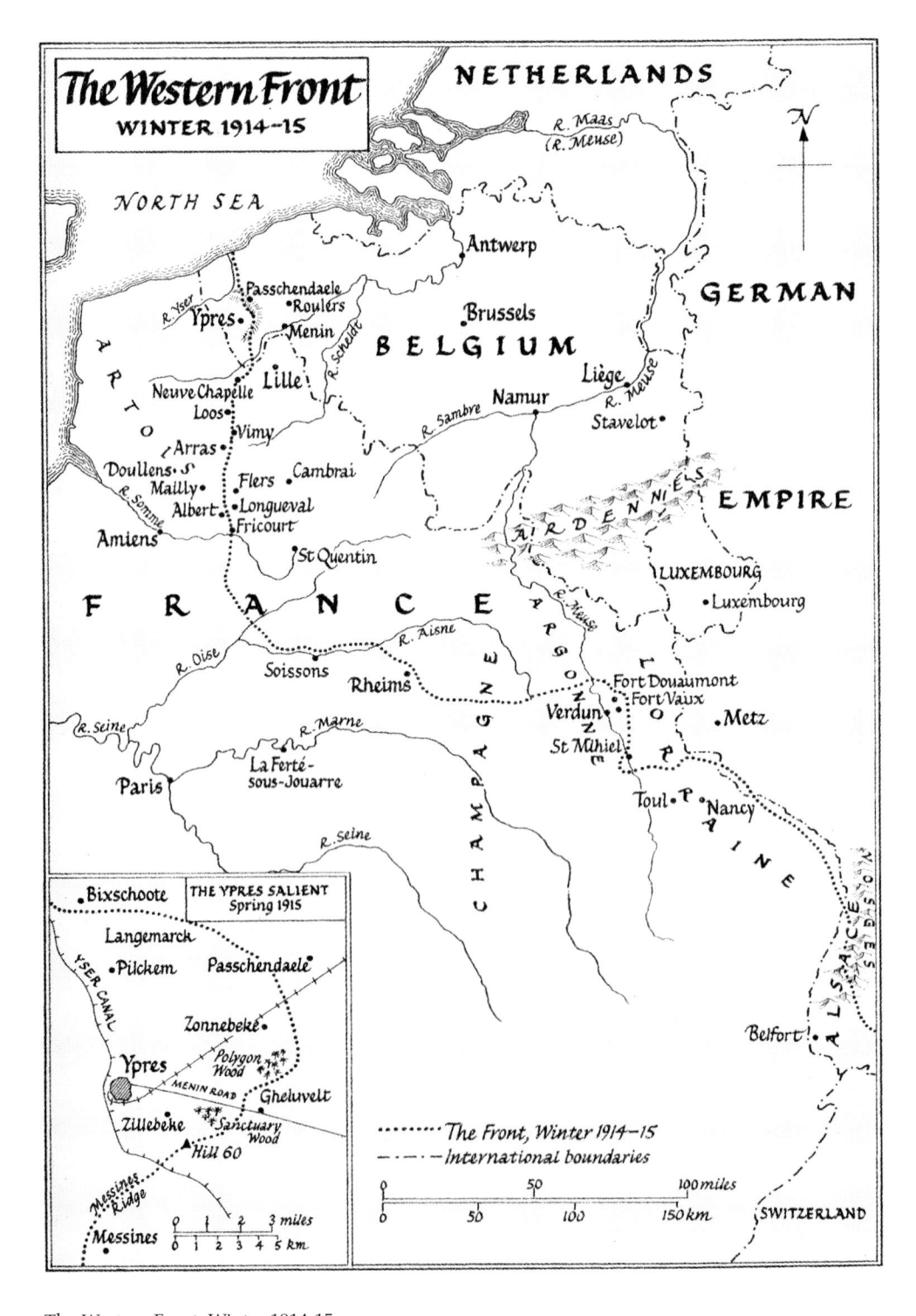

The Western Front, Winter 1914-15

flooded as Cyril Hillier's experience illustrates. By the end of January, he was still highly concerned about the continuous necessity to pump out trenches. Thus, everywhere in the front-line area it was exceedingly difficult to stay concealed from the enemy in the flooded conditions beneath the parapet. On 26th January while moving up to the front line in a waterlogged communications trench, Cyril was shot in the right shoulder and evacuated to England to the Empress Eugenie's Hospital in Farnborough. However, his wound became fatally infected for want of antibiotics. His doctor, Lieutenant Wigmore of the Royal Army Medical Corps, witnessed Cyril's brave fight for life, but noted that he was 'very ill with high fever and recurrent attacks of secondary haemorrhage.'[48] Cyril finally succumbed to his wounds a month later on 27th February, so ending the short life of the youngest British army officer to be killed from fighting on the Western Front and one of the most talented College cricketers of his generation.

As the wounded were brought back home, other troops were readying themselves to take their place on the Western Front. Throughout the year in England, territorial battalions were brought up to strength and prerequisite battle training intensified. Troops from the colonies also arrived from overseas to swell the numbers of the British Army. Ernest Taylor (Newick House, 1902) had arrived with the 2nd Division, Canadian Expeditionary Force from Alberta, Canada. He grew up the youngest of 11 children of James and Emily Taylor at the family home in Bakewell, Derbyshire. After leaving College, Ernest had emigrated to Canada in 1905 with his brother Raymond to take up farming.

Ernest Taylor

Ernest enlisted at Vermilion on 2nd January 1915, joining the 1st Canadian Mounted Rifles (Saskatchewan Regiment) as a trooper. By September 1915, the battalion had reached England and was based at Shorncliffe Barracks, near Folkestone, busy in the process of final training before deploying to the front. His articulate letters home provide a remarkable and stoical insight into the lives of the many young men preparing for battle and, subsequently, fighting in the front line. In a letter to his brother in Canada, he writes:

> My dear old Ray,
>
> I have just finished supper at the soldiers club, and will take advantage of writing you a few lines. I have no facilities for writing at all in Camp and do all my correspondence here. I expect by the time you get this we shall be in France. In fact I think it probable we shall leave this week. We had our emergency medical packet and identification disc served out today, so it begins to look like business. There does not seem to be much doing on the western front now so I don't suppose we shall see much fighting this winter. It seems strange to think that a year ago we used to look with such interest

[48] The National Archives, WO 339/33513, personal record of Second Lieutenant CAH Hillier.

to our war news and the war pictures and soon I shall be seeing it all for myself. It must be nearly three weeks since I last heard from you. I think a letter may have gone astray, but I dare say you are too busy to write much. I shall have many very happy recollections of Folkestone, and though I was rather unlucky in getting such short leave I was very fortunate in seeing so much of the dear ones down here. Every minute of the time at Bakewell was very precious and we made the most of it I can tell you. I forget whether you ever heard that our horses were taken away. We got our infantry equipment a few days ago, and very heavy the pack feels on the march when one is not used to it. If we get in for any long marches right off I think I shall get a sweeny shoulder. Kit bags are done away with now, and all one's outfit including the overcoat has to be put inside the pack on your back. When we leave here we shall also have our blanket and waterproof sheet rolled up under the pack, and 150 rounds of ammunition in the pouches, the whole thing with the rifle weighing about eighty pounds. I hope everything is going well with you. I shall think of you and Lysbeth a great deal and look forward to our next meeting. I hear the crops are heavy this year. I wonder if they would ripen all right. The Dunkerlys and the Freers are all staying here now, and I have seen quite a lot of them lately.

Well, goodbye old chap, I must stop. Best of love and good wishes to you and Lysbeth, and remembrances to Wilson and Liz and the kiddies.[49]

By October, Ernest and the battalion were safely across the Channel and in France, marching up to the line. He wrote to his mother:

My dearest Mother,

I was most delighted to find a parcel awaiting for me this evening. Thank you all so much for it. It was most interesting unpacking all the little parcels. The scarf looks very neat and warm, and I think I shall use it as a body belt when we go to the trenches. Many thanks to Nance for her letter which arrived yesterday. You are all so good in writing, don't have any qualms about your letters being too long as they do not have to be censored. Hearty congratulations to Marjorie on passing her matric. I can well understand how pleased she would feel. We left our last quarters two nights ago at dusk, and had a nine mile march. The transports were to have caught us up and taken our packs, but owing to a mistake we missed them. We were not sorry when about 10 p.m. we reached one of the rest camps behind the firing line. It was a pleasant change to have a dry floor to lie on once more, and I did not need any rocking to sleep. It was very nice the next morning to be wakened by the cry of "Morning Paper." We are able to get the "Express" Mail in these rest camps for 2 1/2d each. There seemed to be no

---

[49] Extracts from the Canadian Letters and Images Project, The Taylor Bury Collection of Letters (online), Dept. of History, Vancouver Island University.

prospect of any breakfast so I wandered to a farm nearby to fill my mess tin with water with a view to making a fire and some tea. I found I could get breakfast there, so had three scrambled eggs, bread and butter and three cups of coffee for ½d. It was a great luxury after cooking my own meals for a week. On the way back to the hut I discovered we were only a few hundred yards from where we were a week ago before moving nearer the firing line. We have not been given the chance of a bath yet. It would not come amiss. The last wash I had was in the sea at Folkestone. The tea tabloids are an excellent idea. I shall be pretty well stocked up for a bit. When you do send another parcel you might put in some coffee tabloids or a tin of café au lait, also a tin of zambuc would be useful. The cake was very nice, but it goes very quickly for the room it takes up. I would propose substituting one of those paper packets of round oatmeal biscuits like I took on the voyage to Canada last time. A few envelopes would be useful too. I posted a letter to Alf two days ago. I hope he got it. Tell Madge I am going to get a tin of fruit to eat with the cream that she sent me when we get paid. I was interested to see all the Standards and have passed them on to the other Vermilion fellows. I think Vermilion has done awfully well in its contribution of men and the machine gun.

Well dearest Mother I will stop for the present

Ever your affectionate son

Ernest.[50]

Throughout 1915, General Joffre and his French army command coerced the BEF under Sir John French to shoulder increasing amounts of the offensive load in support of efforts to expel the German invader. The BEF, though under-prepared in offensive doctrine and tactical training, limited by a shortage of munitions (particularly heavy artillery and high explosive shells), and under potential pressure of having some of its scant manpower resources diverted to the Balkans and the Dardanelles, went on the offensive.

At 7.25am on 10th March, the front line at Neuve Chapelle was relatively quiet save for the stuttering drone of some early observation aircraft. Even the first larks of the day could be heard as they got airborne on their initial forages of the day.[51] Five minutes later to the second, the morning's misty stillness was shattered by a thunder clap from some 530 British guns that signalled the start of the attack on German lines.[52] The artillery roar lasted for 35 minutes, before the British and Indian troops went 'over the top'. One hour later they had taken the German front line and were consolidating their success. The battle of Neuve Chapelle was a milestone event for two reasons: it was the BEF's first planned set piece

---

[50] Extracts from the Canadian Letters and Images Project, The Taylor Bury Collection of Letters (online), Dept. of History, Vancouver Island University.
[51] Personal account of Lieutenant C Tennant in Macdonald. L, *1915; Death of Innocence*, Penguin Books, London (1993), page 93.
[52] Farndale, M.*Western Front 1914–18. History of the Royal Regiment of Artillery*. Royal Artillery Institution, London (1986), page 88.

attack of the war; it also featured the close integration of both British and Indian Army divisions, including their artillery, in offensive operations.[53] The three Old Cheltonians who were killed on the opening day of the battle epitomise this coordinated effort. Ben Sparrow (Hazelwell, 1899) had gained immediate entry to the Royal Military College. By 1914 at the age of 33, he was an experienced captain and company commander in the 39th Garhwal Battalion, 7th (Meerut) Division. He died in the opening attack that morning, leading his company against the German positions as they forced an entry into the enemy trenches. A mile to his left, Alfred Saunders (Christowe, 1910) attacked with the 2nd Battalion, Royal Berkshire Regiment. Despite leaving College over 10 years after Ben, he too followed the well-trodden path from Cheltenham through Sandhurst and into the army. He was killed in the opening minutes of the attack, aged 22. Finally, George Coates (Leconfield, 1912) was deployed with the 33rd Battery, Royal Field Artillery, close to the front line, and killed in action supervising the operation of two of the battery's six 18 pounder field guns. He was just 19 years of age. Having left College in July 1912, he went immediately on to the Royal Military Academy at Woolwich to become a 'gentleman cadet'. As soon as he was commissioned, he was off to war, from which he never returned.[54]

Over the four days of the British attack, which suffered from poor communications, shortage of artillery ammunition and insufficient troops to exploit the capture of enemy positions, seven Old Cheltonians were killed. Due to the confused fighting in the murky weather over the period, when trenches were taken, held, subsequently lost, and then sometimes retaken, trying to command and manage the battalions was exceedingly difficult. Efforts by the military authorities to establish the circumstances of the deaths of individuals for anxious and distraught families waiting for news at home were almost impossible. For example, Charles Wilson (Cheltondale, 1911), after graduating from Sandhurst, was commissioned into the 2nd Border Regiment. He attacked with the battalion on 12th March; the unit war diary captures the day's muddled events:

> The attack was to commence at 8.30am, objective being breastwork and trenches about 600 yards to the NE. The advance at 8.30am was cancelled owing to fog until 10.30am. The attack was ordered to take place at 10.30am precisely. At 10.30 "C" Company moved forward and immediately came under heavy Machine Gun and rifle fire with a Company of Scots Guards on their right. The attack continued for about 15 minutes but the casualties in both Regiments were so heavy that Lieut Colonel L.I. Wood ordered the advance to stop until strong artillery fire or covering fire could be brought to bear.
>
> At this critical time, 20 minutes after the attack had been launched, an order arrived to say the attack would be postponed until 12.30pm. As this order did not arrive till

---

[53] The Lahore and Meerut Divisions reinforced the BEF, especially near Ypres, from late-October 1914, having been transported from India and landed at Marseilles.
[54] Commissioned as a second lieutenant on 17th July 1914, *The London Gazette* dated 7th August 1914, page 6205.

1915 – THE YEAR OF FALSE HOPE

10.50am nothing could be done except wait in the present position for the artillery bombardment. At 12 mid day the artillery commenced their bombardment. At about 12.20 Lieut-Colonel Wood again gave the order to advance, although still enfiladed. The Battalion pushed on and got close up to the enemy's positions and rushed it just as the guns ceased firing. The Germans came out holding up their hands and waving handkerchiefs. Some 200 prisoners were taken and large quantities of rifles, bayonets, and ammunition.

The Battalion then reorganised as quickly as possible and pushed forward in direction of red house on road – but again came under heavy enfilade fire from the right flank and having no battalion on its right had to stop and withdraw into the German trenches which were greatly strengthened at night to provide against a counterattack. The Machine Guns were brought up by hand under 2nd Lt A.V.H. Wood but many were hit – the two guns that did get up doing great execution. Lieut. C.W. Wilson and G.N. Fraser were killed on this day.[55]

However, Charles' mother, Mrs Susan Wilson, was anxiously waiting at her Kendal home for further news of her son. After receiving the official telegram informing her that Charles was missing in action, Susan, herself being widowed, had to contend with the ensuing silence, wait and worry on her own. Her enquiries concerning Charles' whereabouts and fate were investigated and six informants from the battalion, who had survived the day's fighting, were contacted. Cruelly for Susan, their statements differed so markedly that they did nothing to assuage her grave distress. One report suggested that Charles had been killed instantly and buried between the trenches by volunteers. Sergeant Major Jones, himself recovering from wounds at No 16 General Hospital in Le Treport, testified on 23rd June that Charles had died instantly having been shot in three places. A third account suggested that Charles was shot on the Neuve Chapelle to Menin road by a stray bullet while marching up to the line. A fourth stated that he was shot through the head in the trenches while with Sergeant Major Hughes and buried near the trench. The fifth account stated that Charles' body was found three weeks later and had been buried. A subsequent report recorded a sighting of Charles riding a bicycle at Shoeburyness, purportedly recognising the officer as 'he was a very tall man'![56] While one can sympathise with the official channels trying to provide accurate news to next of kin, the emotional turmoil and anguish Charles' mother must have endured, exacerbated by false hope for his safe deliverance, is unimaginable – and affected many families. Neither Charles' body nor his grave was ever found, and he is commemorated on the memorial to the missing at Le Touret; he was just 20 years of age.

The troops that attacked across No Man's Land were extremely exposed to concentrated small arms fire and shrapnel shells as soon as they went 'over the top', and casualty figures

---

[55] The National Archives, WO 95/1665, Unit War Diary, 2nd Battalion Border Regiment, 1915.
[56] The National Archives, WO 339/15793. Personal file, Lieutenant Charles Wyndham Wilson.

rose accordingly. But once offensive action reverted to the more routine defensive posture of holding the line, snipers became another persistent and insidious menace during a battalion's tour of front-line duty. While the trenches, and their defensive structures, wire and parapet, afforded some protection from direct enemy fire, situational awareness regarding the more exposed parts of the front line needed to be assimilated quickly, especially in 1915, before the general issue of the steel helmet. Harry Saward (Day Boy, 1902) and Eric Molson (Hazelwell, 1913) both served in the 2nd Battalion, Royal Scots. Harry, the elder of the two, had left College having been a member of the school's shooting VIII. He gained immediate entry into the Royal Military College, Sandhurst and was commissioned a year later.[57] By the outbreak of war, Harry had been promoted to captain and went to France with his battalion on 14th August 1914. Eric, on the other hand, was still a student. Initially a pupil at Rugby School, Eric came to College in May 1909 where he enjoyed a very successful education. Leaving in April 1913, he was a College prefect and a member of the rugby XV for two years, the last one in 1912 as captain. When war was declared he was an undergraduate at Pembroke College, Cambridge, and, on 6th August 1914, he applied for a commission in the Special Reserve of Officers. His commission came through within six weeks and he joined Harry in the battalion, arriving in France early in the New Year. By late March 1915 they were holding defensive positions in trenches between St Eloi and Vierstraat to the south of Ypres. At 4.30am on 23rd March, heavy rifle fire developed on the battalion's right flank for 10 minutes, and during the exchange of fire Harry was killed by a sniper in a precarious part of their front-line trench designated as M2. The problem facing the battalion was a nasty and notoriously dangerous gap in the line. The two forward companies occupied trenches M1 and M2, between which a soldier had to pass, exposed to fire, to get to the men on the other side. It was a gauntlet that had to be run quite frequently by officers as they supervised their men; dangerous enough at night, but deadly by day. Eric was killed a week later on Good Friday, 1st April at the same spot. The unit war diary records that 'C and D Coys in trenches. Lt EE Molson killed in gap between M1 and M2.'[58]

Reginald Gilliatt (Day Boy, 1903), 'Glennie's' twin brother, was also killed by a sniper, five days later near Neuve Chapelle while attached to the 1st Connaught Rangers from his own battalion, the 5th Leinster Regiment. The battalion war diary notes that on 6th April:

> Captain RHC Gilliatt (5th Leinster Regt) killed in Communication Trench leading to Advanced Post. Loss much regretted by all ranks. This communication trench is in a bad state and a party of pioneers applied for to put it right. Sniping very heavy today.[59]

The circumstances were very similar to the other cases and, in Reginald's case, pitiably ironic. The Leinster's regimental history recorded that:

---

[57] *The London Gazette*, dated 3rd November 1903, page 6697.
[58] The National Archives, WO 95/1423, 2nd Royal Scots War Diary, March and April 1915.
[59] The National Archives, WO 95/3923, 5th Leinster Regiment War Diary, April 1915.

> Captain Gilliatt was an officer brave to the point of recklessness, who simply did not know the meaning of the word fear. He met his death while admonishing his orderly to keep his head down below the level of the parapet – a precaution he scorned to adopt himself.[60]

The regimental history of the Connaught Rangers also paid tribute to Reginald:

> Captain R.H.C. Gilliatt was to the great regret of all in the Rangers, killed during heavy sniping on April 6th. He had brilliantly distinguished himself when with the 2nd battalion of the Rangers in the First Battle of Ypres, in particular on November 11th, 1914, during the attack of the Prussian Guard.[61]

Such accolades would have been ice cold comfort to his parents at home in Cheltenham, having lost the twins killed in action within six months of each other.

The planned attacks at Neuve Chapelle, Aubers Ridge and Festubert came with high hopes and expectation of success. They ended as costly failures. Meanwhile fighting in the Ypres Salient continued. Bertie Lousada (Cheltondale, 1907) had returned to England with his battalion (1st York and Lancaster Regiment) from garrison duty in Jubbelpore in India on 23rd December 1914. After returning their tropical clothing and re-equipping for service in a bitter European winter, they embarked for France and, having landed at Le Havre on 17th January 1915, were immediately deployed to the defence of Ypres. Now in the front-line, Bertie's specific responsibility in the battalion was for the machine gun section, a dangerous task as machine gun teams remained a high priority target for enemy artillery batteries. He was wounded in action near St Jean on 23rd April but stoically remained on duty, appointed battalion Adjutant the following day to replace a wounded colleague. On 29th April Francis Bradshaw-Isherwood (Christowe, 1885) took command of the battalion; the previous commanding officer, Colonel Bart, had been killed in action the week before. Francis had left College in July 1885, and, after going up to Clare College, Cambridge, went on to the Royal Military College, Sandhurst to pursue a career in the army. During the fighting at Frezenberg, the final phase of the Second Battle of Ypres, the battalion had suffered heavy casualties. Consequently, the battalion was relieved on 7th May from the front line to billets near the town and received a draft of some 487 newly trained replacement troops, equivalent to about half the battalion's normal strength. The following evening, however, the battalion was ordered to attack and retake German trenches near Zonnebeke, the same ones that they had occupied only the day before, but which had been quickly lost by their relieving battalion. As they approached the village at 5pm on 8th May, they came under heavy shellfire and had to halt in the support trenches. The war diary records that at 8pm:

---

[60] Whitton, F.E., *The History of the Prince of Wales's Leinster Regiment-Volume 2*, Gale and Polden, Aldershot (1924), page 176.
[61] The National Archives, WO 95/1347/1, War Diary of the 2nd Battalion, Connaught Rangers, November 1914.

> The attack was pushed almost up to the German trenches but owing to the very heavy casualties in officers and men, it did not achieve its effect. All the officers were put out of action with the exception of Lieutenant Briscoe who was able to get together the remnants of the Battalion the next day.[62]

During the evening's attack and the ensuing overnight fighting, the battalion was reduced from over 700 men to just 83, with 125 killed and the remainder wounded or missing. The fatalities included Francis and Bertie. As commanding officer and adjutant of the battalion, they had advanced beside each other and led the attack. Their bodies were never found. During subsequent efforts to establish the circumstances of their deaths, one of the battalion's wounded soldiers, recovering later in hospital, testified that his colonel 'had died like a hero and the last I had seen of him after he fell leading the charge was as he lay bleeding from the head and chest on the field.'[63] The names of these two Old Cheltonians are commemorated on the Menin Gate Memorial to the Missing.

Also fighting nearby on the Frezenberg Ridge was the Leicestershire Yeomanry, including Thomas Brooks (Cheltondale, 1902). Thomas was commissioned in the 11th (Prince Albert's Own) Hussars on 13th August 1904 and transferred into the Imperial Yeomanry in 1907, where he could enjoy the lifestyle of a country gentleman and follow his equestrian orientated interests and activities.[64] Well known in the county's hunting circle, he also took part in local steeplechase meetings with some success. His unique if not bizarre colours, which included a straw jacket and a tartan cap, became quite a familiar and popular feature. Married in April 1910, he settled at The Grange in Queniborough with his wife, Adele. But his way of life was upended when war was declared, as he immediately rejoined the Leicestershire Yeomanry, a territorial army unit attached to the 2nd Cavalry Division.

Thomas was appointed to C Squadron based at Loughborough. Having been mobilised, the Yeomanry began its operational work up, including a training detachment to Diss in Norfolk, before deploying to France on 1st November, leaving Adele to manage the family affairs at Queniborough.

After six months of operations in the Ypres Salient, Thomas and the Yeomanry were defending the line near the Bellewaarde Farm early in the morning of 13th May when they came under a heavy and sustained attack. The unit war diary recorded the day's events and the officer casualties that ensued:

> Position of Regiment at midnight 12th/13th May, 700 yards west of road joining Zonnebeke Road and Ypres – Menin Road, extreme right resting on railway running north east from Ypres, and extending to farm about 300 yards north, north west of railway. The trenches were bad, 5 feet deep and 2½ feet wide at the bottom. Parapets at the front and back slanted very much, and were made of loose soil. There were few

---

[62] The National Archives, WO 95/2275, Battalion War Diary, 1st Yorks and Lancaster Regiment, May 1915.
[63] Letter to the *Stockport Advertiser*, dated 25th June 1915.
[64] *The London Gazette*, dated 10th May 1907, page 3194.

Thomas Brooks (standing far right) with the Leicestershire Yeomanry

sand bags, and no dug-outs or other protection from shell fire. Heavy shell-fire from 03:30 to 06:00, but few casualties. The enemy then began to pour over their parapets, with the evident intention of attacking, but being met by heavy fire from our men, they retired again to their trenches. A second and more violent bombardment began, and was kept up until 07.30. Our losses during this bombardment were much heavier, and the machine guns were knocked out and a trench blown in. At 07:30 the enemy attacked and occupied the advanced trenches vacated by the Regiment on our left, from there they gained part of "B" Squadron trenches. They then advanced to within 200 yards of the Support trenches and dug themselves in, having steel shields as a protection. Those of the enemy who had occupied the "B" Squadron trench advanced along the trench, and Major Bernard Robert Liebert, Lieutenant William Spurrett Fielding-Johnson and Squadron Sergeant Major J. P. SWAIN with what was left of "B" Squadron, retired down the trench and joined "C" Squadron. Here Major William Francis Martin ordered barricades of sand bags to be placed across the trench. Some of the trench party fired over this barricade at the enemy advancing from the flank, others at the enemy advancing from the front. Major Martin, Major Liebert, Lieutenant Colin Peake and 2nd Lieutenant Thomas Edward Brooks were all killed. The casualties were so heavy that Lieutenant Fielding-Johnson, the only surviving officer, decided to retire down the trench, to cross the railway and join the 3rd Dragoon Guards on the other side of it.[65]

---

[65] The National Archives, WO 95/1155/7, Battalion War Diary of the Leicestershire Yeomanry, November 1914 to October 1917.

Although the survivors had to retire, the battalion had clung onto their trenches for almost four hours of bombardment and had also fought off consecutive German infantry assaults for another seven. Thomas was buried at Oosttaverne Wood Cemetery. He left Adele a widow's pension of £100 per annum, a gratuity of £100, and an estate valued at £112,396.[66]

Such loss of life epitomises the intensity and brutality of the fighting during the Second Battle of Ypres. It also indicates the extent and enormity of the shocking impact the losses had to British families at home. For Adele Brooks, the loss of her husband was a single cause of anguish and grief. For the Lousada family, the loss of the second of the twins was the third tragedy to devastate its children. As was quite typical in the Victorian era for the British middle class, Simeon and Charlotte Lousada had a large family; four girls and three boys. Of the three boys, the twins Edward and Bertie were the youngest of the children and were killed in action in 1914 and 1915 respectively. Elder brother William (Cheltondale, 1899) was badly wounded from a bullet graze to his head at Verbrandenmolen near Ypres on 23rd April just two weeks prior to Bertie's death; he would be awarded the Military Cross in 1917 and survive the war.[67] However, their elder sister Emilie lost her husband, coincidentally also an Old Cheltonian. The very day after the twins graduated from Sandhurst, 14th September 1907, Emilie married Oriel Bannerman (Day Boy, 1893) in Mussoorie, Bengal, India. Oriel graduated from Sandhurst in 1896. By August 1914 he was serving in India with 15th Lancers, the divisional cavalry regiment of 3rd (Lahore) Division of the Indian Army. The Division was mobilised on 9th August to reinforce the BEF in France and embarked at Karachi and Bombay for Europe at the end of the month. Oriel and his battalion arrived in Marseille on 26th September, becoming the first British Indian cavalry regiment to land in France. He was seriously wounded in action on 20th December 1914, and immediately evacuated to the military hospital in Boulogne, where, being too badly injured to be evacuated to England, he eventually died on 3rd February. Accordingly, the Lousada family had suffered three shattering blows, and one very near miss, in just over six months.

The suffering and grief of the families at home was acknowledged by those fighting at the front and was a constant consideration despite the many dangerous challenges facing them. The death of Charles Sorby (PBH, 1911) is a typical example, and one which also reflects the close relationship between officer and soldier, a relatively common feature noted throughout the war. The son of the Rector of Darfield and Rural Dean of Wath, near Barnsley, Charles left College when he was 16 to embark on a course of engineering. He was about to enrol as a mining engineer at the collieries in Ebbw Vale when war was declared. Promptly commissioned in September as a second lieutenant in the 3rd Battalion, Monmouths, he distinguished himself during rifle practice and was appointed the battalion's machine gun officer.[68] On 7th May 1915, having spent 21 days in the front line without being relieved, an unusually long exception from the normal four days, he was

---

[66] See edition of *The Morning Post*, dated 11th October 1915.
[67] William Lousada played rugby for the College XV and was in the gymnastics VIII in 1899.
[68] Supplement to *The London Gazette*, dated 14th October 1914, page 8228.

mortally wounded when rescuing his platoon NCO, Sergeant Davies. He was the second soldier from the platoon that Charles had rescued that day.[69] Charles died from his wounds several hours later, and Sergeant Davies wrote to his mother, recording:

> I can only say that I lost my best friend in the Regiment when I lost my Officer. He was the friend of all the men in his Platoon, who simply worshipped him; he was always looking for ways to help them in the hard work they had to do, and not above doing any man's share when he was at all done up. I was wounded through the thigh about six o'clock in the morning, May 6th, and lay in two feet of mud and water in the trench all day; it was too light for stretcher bearers when I got hit, so had to wait for darkness. He came to me many times and asked if he could do anything for me. No stretchers came for that night, (during which Lieut. Sorby had to go to Hd Qrs), so he came back about 5.30am and was in a fine rage that one of his Platoon had been left over, asked for volunteers to carry me out. He could have had dozens, so he picked out four of the strongest, and I was put on a sheet of roofing with two long poles. We had not gone 30 yards, when the Germans opened fire on us, and the men got shattered arms and had to drop me. I was too weak to get back to the trench and lay in the open with bullets dropping all around me, when Lieut Sorby dashed out of the trench, and not only dragged me back, but placed himself between me and the Germans, and so got me back safely. I can assure you it was one of the bravest deeds of the War, but he never thought of anything at all but getting me back. Though he was wounded, he kept asking me if I was alright and never thought of himself.[70]

The battalion's medical officer, who was wounded on the same day, also recorded his views of Charles:

> He came back with a message to Headquarters, missed his way and must have wandered all night (May 7th); he found my dug out and fell exhausted into my arms. I guided him to the Colonel and got him some stimulant. He was wonderful, he gave his message, received his reply, and went back. He stood in the doorway saluting his Colonel with a smile on his face. He knew he was going back to worse than hell and yet he smiled. I shall never see him again, but I often see that brave boy's face smiling, and hold it as my highest example.[71]

Although rifle fire was a constant and ubiquitous peril, a further difficulty facing the entrenched infantry battalions was establishing effective coordination with their own

---

[69] Sergeant Davies and the other soldier survived the war due in very large part to Charles' gallant and unselfish actions.
[70] Clutterbuck, L.A., *The Bond of Sacrifice, Volume 2, January to June 1915*, Naval and Military Press, 2002, page SOR 436.
[71] Ibid.

artillery support. Donald Kenworthy (Leconfield, 1906) was in the trenches north east of Ypres opposite Steenstraat, when he was killed by shell fire on 17th May in a morning bombardment while in command of B Company, 1st Somerset Light Infantry. The fifth and youngest son of John and Mary Kenworthy, Donald had left College for a career in the army. Commissioned as a second lieutenant in the Somerset Light Infantry, Donald joined the 2nd Battalion in Malta, later serving in Tientsin during the Chinese Rebellion, and then in Quetta.[72] Having seen action throughout the major battles of 1914, he was defending the line with the 1st Battalion near Wieltje during the Second Battle of Ypres and was under fire from artillery shells from both sides. The unit war diary records that the British artillery shells were falling short, as the entry for 15th May states:

> Cool, cloudy day. Our chief trouble today was caused by our own guns bursting high explosive and shrapnel in our own trenches. Could not find out which battery was doing this.[73]

Quite often, the reason behind this desperate state of affairs was that artillery barrels were being worn out by constant use, causing the effective reach of the guns to diminish despite having the correct range settings selected. One solution to this problem was the deployment of Forward Observation Officers to infantry battalions. Officers from the nearby batteries were sent to the front lines to record and report and adjust the fall of the shells and identify new targets of opportunity and priority. In May 1915, Fergus Reid (Boyne House, 1899) was a captain with the 57th Siege Battery, Royal Garrison Artillery supporting the infantry during the attack at Festubert. Having been a scholar at College, winning the Silver Medal for mathematics, he had gone on to the Royal Military Academy at Woolwich to become an artillery officer. He was killed on 16th May by a shell bursting on his position in the front line as he was observing the British bombardment. The loss of such an experienced officer had a significant impact on the battery, his commanding officer noting that:

> He was a man one felt instinctively that one could trust, and one knew that what he was asked to do would not only be done, but well done, and it was so that he was killed. I had instructed his Major to send forward an officer with the infantry, keeping in touch at the same time with him by telephone, so that I should be able to know at once if the infantry require assistance. It was a difficult and responsible task, and his Major at once selected him to do it; this duty he had been performing all day in a most efficient manner in spite of being under fire the whole time, until, alas! he was killed. He died nobly doing his duty, and knowing that he was doing it at a risk which gave him little chance of escape, and yet doing it with all zeal and willingness.[74]

[72] *The London Gazette*, dated 18 September 1908, page 6762.
[73] The National Archives, WO 95/2016, War Diary of 1st Somerset Light Infantry, 1915.
[74] IWM Records, HU 124822.

Fergus was posthumously mentioned in despatches by Sir John French, BEF Commander-in-Chief, on 30th November.

Shortly after Cyril Hillier had been evacuated to England, his replacement officer arrived; he was, by sheer coincidence, a member of the College teaching staff, Second Lieutenant Henry Reed (Common Room, 1914). Some three months junior in rank to Cyril, Henry had taught classics to Cyril at College and was also a house tutor in Cheltondale. Educated at Durham School where he was in the rugby XV in 1900 and 1901, Henry went up to Durham University and then on to Trinity College, Cambridge where he read classics, graduating in 1909. As a good rugby player and Leander rower in the Trinity VIII, he was a very welcomed and talented addition to the College Common Room when he joined in September 1909. Henry was also a cadet corporal in the College Officer Training Corps. Having decided to enlist to serve alongside his young protégés, he was commissioned, and joined the 2nd Monmouths in trenches at St Julien, to the east of Ypres.

Henry was killed on 2nd May during the Second Battle of Ypres. After a heavy gas attack the battalion was withdrawn to the Divisional Reserve where it was heavily shelled. He was 30 years old.[75]

Throughout 1915, poison gas was increasingly used by the Germans, and was a constant and deadly threat confronting troops occupying trenches and dug outs. Being denser than air, the fumes quickly descended into shell holes, pits and tunnels where men were trying to shelter from the shell fire. After the initial introduction of gas to the battlefield at Ypres on 22nd April, the Germans made four more similar attacks there in May. John Vaughan (Southwood, 1914) had not been a subaltern in the 3rd Battalion Royal Fusiliers for long. Having been a corporal in the OTC he left College and applied for entry to the Royal Military College, Sandhurst on 28th March, whilst still only 17 years of age. By May 1915, he was defending the Ypres Salient during the Second Battle of Ypres. His battalion was in a defensive position between the Bellewaarde Lake and the railway line, near Ypres, when the Germans attacked on 24th May with the aid of a particularly dense layer of gas. The unit war diary records the events:

Henry Reed, College Classics Master

> At 2.30am a German maxim started firing followed by the sound of rifle fire. Major Johnson and myself (Major Baker) went out and observed a thick mist rising in front of the German lines, W of the Road. Immediately afterwards we felt the effects of gas and at once put our respirators on.[76]

---

[75] At the time of the Second Battle of Ypres, there was no effective gas mask or respirator available. For further reading see G H Cassar, *Trial by Gas: The British Army at the Second Battle of Ypres*, Potomac Books, Nebraska (2014).

[76] The National Archives, WO 95/2279, Unit War Diary for 3rd Royal Fusiliers, May 1915.

Some in the battalion were not so quick, nor was John so lucky. He was initially reported by telegram as 'missing' but soon after this was amended stating that he had 'died of wounds'. This suggests that John may have been found later in the day and then died from the asphyxiating, drowning effects of the chlorine which attacked the lungs filling them with fluid. The war diary acknowledges that John's death was most likely due to the gas attack endured.

Trying to locate troublesome enemy artillery batteries, as well as gaining a better understanding of German defensive positions, became a preoccupation of the headquarters staff in an effort to reduce casualties, especially those of the attacking infantry. Since the start of the year, aerial reconnaissance by the Royal Flying Corps (RFC) had become the best method of mapping and photographing enemy dispositions, both at the front line and also behind the lines where weapon stockpiles and storage areas could be detected. Such intelligence was invaluable, and reconnaissance aircraft were becoming a most valuable asset to commanders. In preparation for the attack at Neuve Chapelle, for example, some 3,000 detailed maps of enemy trenches and redoubts were issued to attacking troops, produced with the support of aerial photography. For RFC aircrew, flying on low level observation operations was an extremely hazardous duty, with casualty rates approaching 50%, an accepted consequence of the offensive and aggressive approach to British aerial strategy.[77] Eight days after Henry Reed had been killed Isaac Woodiwiss (Boyne House, 1914), a former student of his, became the first Old Cheltonian airman to be killed. In his last year at College, Isaac was a sergeant in the Officer's Training Corps and applied for a commission at the end of his last term in July 1914.

Having spent only three months at the Royal Military College, Sandhurst, he was commissioned as a second lieutenant in the 1st Lincolnshire Regiment.[78] In the spring of 1915, the BEF needed observers in the Royal Flying Corps to carry out essential reconnaissance tasks, and, having volunteered, Isaac was attached to No 3 Squadron, RFC, flying as an observer in a Morane Parasol aircraft. On 10th May, Isaac and his pilot, Lieutenant Denys Corbett-Wilson, were reported missing.

After a fortnight with no news, parental concern was becoming stratospheric, so Isaac Woodiwiss (senior), his father, wrote to the War Office seeking some news of his only son. Two weeks later, after investigation by the authorities, he received the following letter in reply dated 15th June 1915:

Isaac N Woodiwiss

The Military Secretary presents his compliments to Mr IN Woodiwiss, and begs to inform that the following report has just been received from the Base:

---

[77] J. Buckley, *Air Power in the Age of Total War*, UCL Press Ltd, London, (1999), page 43.
[78] *The London Gazette*, dated 10th November 1914, page 9141.

Morane Parasol Aeroplane and crew

"Lieut D Corbett-Wilson and Lieut IN Woodiwiss of the RFC started on a tactical reconnaissance on 10th May, and did not return. The next day a message was received from a German aeroplane to the effect that an English parasol type aeroplane was hit by German artillery, and two officers, who were killed, were buried in a churchyard just east of Furnes. It is considered that this message refers to Lieut Corbett-Wilson and Lieut Woodiwiss as, at the time given in the message, there was only one aeroplane of the parasol type flying in the area."

The Military Secretary is desired by Lord Kitchener to convey his sympathy to Mr Woodiwiss on his loss, and would be glad to know if he accepts the fact of Lieut Woodiwiss' death on this evidence with a view to its publication in the Press.[79]

    His father replied by return of post stating that the family reluctantly felt that they must accept the evidence given. Isaac Newton Woodiwiss, named after both his father and their illustrious family forbear, was only 18 years of age when he was killed.

    Ten days later, Herbert Macdonnell (Boyne House, 1902), one of the earliest of Old Cheltonian aviators, was shot down and mortally wounded. Herbert joined the army and was commissioned in the Royal Irish Rifles in November 1903. By March 1910, he was promoted to captain and decided to learn to fly, gaining his Aviator's Certificate (No 309) in October 1912 from the Bristol Flying School at Brooklands having flown the Bristol Biplane. Although he rejoined his regiment, he stayed on the reserve of the RFC and on the outbreak of war, Herbert was ordered to rejoin the RFC serving with it in France during

[79] The National Archives, WO 339/1071, Personal Record of Captain IN Woodiwiss.

the very first weeks of the war. He flew daily on operational sorties for the next eight months with No 5 Squadron, in one of the very few aircraft specially fitted with a radio transmitter, developing the important use of radio telegraphy in cooperation with heavy artillery to help direct fire and report the fall of shot. Promoted to be a flight commander on 18th May, Herbert was shot down two days later, and died from his injuries on 24th May at Hazebrouck. He was the only son of Colonel Alfred Creagh Macdonnell (Price, 1872), also an Old Cheltonian, who was serving then as the Chief Royal Engineer with 34th Division, one of the New Army divisions training in England.

These latter two incidents, quite common for the time, reflect the ad hoc nature of combat flying in the early years of the war. With only some 90 front-line aircraft available in March 1915, the potential impact of the RFC in support of the BEF's offensive operations was limited in comparison to that of the German and French air forces. In an effort to make aerial bombing more accurate, RFC crews were encouraged to fly low.[80] Air combat, especially the use of the fixed machine guns firing forward through the propeller with the aid of deflector plates or interrupter gearing, was still in its infancy.[81] Therefore, it is unclear whether Isaac and Herbert were brought down by dedicated anti-aircraft artillery (or, as the RFC crews referred to it, 'Archie'). While British 'Archie' was almost non-existent until mid-1916, the Germans had invested in its development in the pre-war period, possessing a distinct capability with some 270 dedicated anti-aircraft guns at the front. Even by the summer of 1915, rarely did RFC aircraft return from operational sorties without being molested by 'Archie'.[82] That said, in an era before the advent of effective airspace coordination between the army and the RFC squadrons, coupled to the performance limitations to aircraft altitude and the requirement to take accurate reconnaissance photographs below the lowest cloud formations, it is quite likely that they may both have been unintended victims: killed by flying into either enemy or friendly artillery bombardments of ground targets.

Over the period from July to mid-September, over 150 battalions of Kitchener's New Army had completed their training and been deployed to France, and were ready for the next 'Big Push'. The new assembly trenches near Loos in preparation for the attack became obvious to German observation. With the spoils of fresh chalk almost glowing, even at night, it was clear that an attack was imminent. In support of Marshal Joffre's wider campaign in Artois, the British offensive at Loos represented the first large scale planned attack by the BEF on the Western Front, and one in which the first elements of Kitchener's New Army, the 21st and 24th Divisions, were introduced. At 6.30am on 25th September 1915, the British attacked at Loos. They did so with the use of some 5,000 cylinders of chlorine gas, the first employment of such a weapon by Britain, released 40 minutes before the whistles were blown and the troops went 'over the top'. The gas was used to offset the lack

---

[80] See JH Morrow, *The Great War in the Air*, Smithsonian Institution Press, Washington, (1993), page 113.
[81] Air to air combat did not start in earnest until mid-July 1915 with the arrival of the Fokker Eindecker in which Oswald Boelke and Max Immelmann became great proponents. Morrow, (1993), page 105.
[82] See Jones, H. *War in the Air, Volume 2*, Oxford, Clarendon Press, (1928), pages 168-171.

of heavy artillery needed to support the infantry assault, a logistical constraint still plaguing the BEF. However, the gas would never clear the defensive wire in front of the German lines. Furthermore, it was released in less than ideal wind conditions as some of the gas cloud drifted back into the British lines impeding the advance. Four Old Cheltonians died in this initial attack, and over the next 18 days of bitter fighting at Loos, a further 20 Old Cheltonians were killed.

Two of the youngest were Edward Adams (Cheltondale, 1913) and Ernest Rimington (Christowe, 1912). Edward was a private in the OTC, until December 1913 when he left and became an under-writer at Lloyds. Following the declaration of war, he applied for a commission in the Territorial Force on 23rd October and was commissioned within two weeks as a second lieutenant on 5th November. He even had his seniority in rank back-dated to 25th September, presumably due to his OTC experience. He was killed exactly a year later on the first day of the battle.

The son of a serving major general, Ernest was a member of the College Boat in 1912. He gained a place at Sandhurst and was commissioned as a second lieutenant in the Cheshire Regiment on 17th March 1915.[83] Ernest joined the 2nd Battalion on 3rd July at Dickebusch near Ypres as a platoon commander in No 1 Company. By the end of September, the battalion had joined the fighting at Loos and had just taken over from the Royal Fusiliers in the front line. On 1st October, it was occupying trenches on the western side of the Hohenzollern Redoubt, a dominating, and therefore hotly contested feature on the battlefield. Ernest was killed in action at 7am that morning.[84] The battalion war diary records events: 'Heavy fire from trench mortars and aerial torpedoes. 2 Lieuts Rimington and Hardy No 1 Coy killed.'[85] The news of his death must have been a bitter blow to his family, particularly to his father who was serving as the Engineer-in-Chief in Mesopotamia. Both Edward and Ernest were just 19 years of age.

The oldest Old Cheltonian to die at Loos was Frederick Fairtlough (Leconfield, 1875); he was aged 54. Educated at College for just the winter term of 1875, he was an experienced soldier and Boer War veteran, commanding the 3rd Battalion, Royal West Surrey Regiment, being mentioned in despatches twice. He was also made a companion of the Most Distinguished Order of St Michael and St George and awarded the Queen's Medal with two clasps. Frederick retired from the Army in 1905 and settled down with his wife Maud and his young family. When war was declared he was recalled as the army expanded and needed experienced commanding officers for its new battalions. Frederick was appointed the first officer to command the 8th (Service) Battalion of his regiment on 1st October 1914, a command he held until he was killed on 26th September 1915 near Vermelles. His body was never recovered, and he is commemorated on the Loos Memorial. Sadly, Frederick's son Gerard, serving in the Royal Engineers, was killed in 1918; for Maud the Great War was thus a double tragedy.

---

[83] *The London Gazette*, 16th March 1915, page 2632.
[84] This rectifies his date of death, which was previously recorded in the College Register as being 2nd October 1915.
[85] The National Archives, WO 95/2276, the Unit War Diary of 2nd Cheshire Regiment, 1915.

Lieutenant Maurice Shaw (Teighmore 1885), was severely wounded at Loos on 26th September fighting with the 12th Battalion, Highland Light Infantry and evacuated to hospital at Le Treport where he succumbed to his injuries three days later. The son of Major General George Salis Schwabe, he was educated at the College's Junior School for five terms with his younger brother Walter, leaving together in July 1885 to continue their education at Marlborough College. Yet Maurice was not recorded in the College's Roll of Honour under either surname, Schwabe or Shaw. In 1892, three years after leaving Marlborough, Maurice was embroiled in a homosexual affair with Oscar Wilde. In accordance with the law of the time, criminal prosecutions for gross indecency and immorality were brought, and, given Oscar's celebrity and notoriety, a very public and widely reported court case ensued in Paris. Maurice's father was not only a successful senior military officer, he had also been a liberal unionist politician, and, at the time of Maurice's trial, was a senior partner in the family firm of Salis Schwabe & Co, Calico Printers, of Rhodes and Manchester. The affair brought shame on the family who banished Maurice to Australia for a time. In Australia during 1911 he changed his name from Schwabe to Shaw. However, after war was declared Maurice returned to England, enlisted and was granted a commission under his newly-assumed surname as a temporary lieutenant on 7th July 1915. [86]

Maurice Shaw (Schwabe)

Maurice embarked for France three days later, being nominally attached to the 12th Highland Light Infantry and appointed as the battalion Transport Officer. Unfortunately, the battalion war diary holds very little detail on any of his associated activity with the battalion, other than that he is recorded as wounded in its entry of 26th September. It appears however, that he may have been employed as a staff intelligence officer, and being fluent in German, was employed interrogating prisoners, a task for which he was apparently complimented by the senior divisional intelligence officers. Irrespective of these details, Maurice died, having volunteered for duty and served with great distinction and bravery at Loos, a factor that reflected very well both on himself and his family. His death compounded the tragic effect the war had already inflicted on the family, as his younger sister Gladys had drowned with her husband and their six children on 7th May when the RMS *Lusitania* was torpedoed and sunk. His brother Walter, although a barrister and appointed as King's Council in 1913, also served during the war as a captain in the 19th Battalion, City of London Volunteers, and survived the war to become the Chief Justice in the High Court in Madras and knighted. Both brothers' names were omitted from the 1919 Register; why such an omission occurred is puzzling. Certainly, public opinion at the time regarding homosexuality and its criminality tended to adopt the attitude of 'the less said the better'; therefore, it is possible that the family or the College authorities may have been trying to avoid any associated social stigma. One hundred years on, and with

[86] Supplement to *The London Gazette*, 19th July 1915, page 7061.

today's more liberal and open-minded attitudes towards sexuality, it is fitting that Maurice and Walter are now remembered alongside all the other Old Cheltonians that served King and Country during the war.

The attack at Loos failed in large part due to familiar problems that had been encountered six months previously at Neuve Chapelle; the inability to clear the wire in front of the German second line which was beyond the range of the artillery; the failure to move the artillery forward to support any infantry progress; and the shortage of artillery munitions and hand grenades. In addition, the Germans were repeatedly evolving and strengthening their defences and tactics between the Allied offensives. When the Loos assault was called off on 13th October, activity on the Western Front descended into the debilitating routine and trauma of trench existence as the second winter's freezing conditions set in. While under the continual threat from enemy shelling and mortar fire, Ernest Taylor, alongside his fellow troopers of the 1st Battalion, Canadian Mounted Rifles, was keeping his head down in the front line, and getting used to the menacing and sometimes deadly monotony. Despite the considerable difficulties, Ernest found time to write to his sister in December:

My dearest Nance,

I think when I last wrote I was stationed with 7 others at a bomb store behind the front line. Well, we had a fairly peaceful time there. They shelled us one afternoon, but it was mostly shrapnel and we felt pretty snug inside the dugout. After four days there we packed up, and at dusk fell in behind our squadron as it went by on the way to the front line. These marches into the trenches by night are something never to be forgotten. You go stumbling along in the dark, single file, just like "follow the leader" and "obstacle race" combined. Sometimes scrambling down into a trench when nothing but the quantity of soft mud at the bottom prevents you from damaging yourself. On you go knee deep in mud, and after a while you scramble out again with a supreme effort. Then perhaps there is open ground to cross in full view of the enemy trenches. Each time the star lights go up illuminating everything like a flash of lightning, the procession stands motionless until the light fades away, then onward once more. On reaching the front line we exchanged our boots for rubber waders. The man that had mine must have fallen down or been in very deep for there was a lot of water inside them, and I used up 4 pairs of socks before they dried out. Life in the trenches is not pleasant in winter time. You are practically wallowing in mud all the time, but still it was a very interesting experience. Looking through the periscope one could see the German trench very plainly about 130 yards away with a lot of ruined buildings behind full of snipers. We had a fairly quiet night, but the next day Wednesday was memorable for poor old C. Squadron. I think the British had arranged to bombard another part of the line, and the Germans, instead of retaliating there, concentrated their fire where they considered it would have most effect. This happened to be a front of about a quarter of a mile, the greater part of which was held by us. Anyhow at noon they started up quite suddenly, and for two hours we experienced one of the worst bombardments that have been for some time. There was nothing to do but sit still and smoke, smoke, smoke, and keep as cheerful as possible. The noise was terrific because the British shells went screeching over only a few feet above our heads. You will understand how warm things were when I tell you that during the two hours we lost nearly a quarter of our men. The Major had his leg broken at the start, and before the Captain, who is also a doctor, could come up he (the captain) was killed. We had nine killed including the sergeant major, a sergeant and corporal and about twelve wounded, and there were others who suffered severely from shock though they were not actually wounded. The front of the trench was blown in in two or three places, and several dug-outs blown to pieces with all the equipment inside them. Bill was knocked by a shell as he was digging a man out from under the debris, but he is not hurt except for being stiff. No Vermilion men were killed, though three that enlisted with us at Vegreville were. None of us grenade men got hurt. The next day we waited in anticipation of a similar ordeal. I made a hearty lunch of cheese and hard tack so as to be well fortified. Soon after, our guns started up on the German trenches. They sent back a few shots, but apparently were loath to take up the challenge, and things soon quieted down. While I was waiting for the shells to come, I received your letter. It had been blown out of the Major's dug-out with the rest of the mail and was wet through and almost out of the envelope, but it was readable and I was very grateful for getting it. We grenade men came out of the trenches yesterday afternoon and are now on the slope of a wooded hill in comparative safety. We had just got settled down, and I had just cooked my supper when I had orders to go at once to a farm about four miles away for rations. I missed the place and spent the evening wandering about, getting back about 9 p.m. I think we may go back for a rest tomorrow, but I don't know whether it will be to our old billets or not. One longs for a high and dry spot where you can get away from the everlasting mud and get cleaned up a bit. One gets caked in mud from head to foot, your food gets coated with it, and one lies down in it. In fact, I should say the most noticeable feature of a winter campaign is mud. The last parcel has not come yet. I have a very good scarf that Amy sent me, but the socks would be useful. Go easy on sending canned stuffs and tabloids. I found I was carrying more round than I needed as tea and sugar and condensed milk were issued in the trenches. The best things to send are cake, chocolate, anything of the sweetmeat variety, raisins or figs, a pot of fish paste occasionally.

Well, old girl, I had better close.
Heaps of love to you all
Your affectionate brother,

Ernest[87]

---

[87] Extracts from the Canadian Letters and Images Project, The Taylor Bury Collection of Letters (online), Dept. of History, Vancouver Island University.

This incredibly descriptive letter, though lengthy, shows through its entirety a clearer picture of the depth of the relationship between the soldier at the front and his loved ones at home. Furthermore, it clearly depicts the importance that soldiers attached to sending letters home, which was as vital as receiving family news. Such letters maintained the essential family link and brought close everyday realities.

If the fighting on the Western Front was brutally costly in terms of Old Cheltonians killed and wounded, so too was the Gallipoli campaign which began on 25th April, just as the BEF in France was learning to deal with gas attacks, and ground on for the remainder of the year.

The Dardanelles

Before Sir John French had finished planning the attack at Neuve Chapelle, trying to bring some movement to the muddy stalemate now established on the Western Front, British strategists had surmised that better, or at least some, progress might be made further afield. Although fully committed on the Western Front, not least to bolstering the ranks of the BEF that had been so depleted by the fierce fighting to date, the British war cabinet was not deaf to the plight of their Russian ally who urged for a diversionary attack against the Turks. An attack on Turkey would relieve pressure on the Russian troops fighting the Ottoman forces at Sarikamish. British focus, particularly sharpened by Churchill's wishful thinking, increasingly converged on the eastern Mediterranean, and specifically the Dardanelles. The Dardanelles operation started out with much hope and expectation, but it swiftly became an unmitigated military disaster and a significant dent to Britain's imperial prestige. Much has been written about Gallipoli, but what is perhaps less well known or indeed unrecorded are the considerable contributions, sacrifice and bravery made by Old Cheltonians throughout this improvident campaign, in which 41 of them died.

For College, the Dardanelles death toll started on Sunday, 25th April. It had been a very quiet night, with hardly a ripple on the Aegean waters as the landing force silently assembled off Cape Helles. As the moon slipped down at 3.00am, the first of the landing force began disembarking quietly into the small pinnaces, cutters and strings of open life boats towed by trawlers that were to get the troops ashore at the four British beach heads. The SS *River Clyde*, a collier requisitioned by the Royal Navy and converted into a landing ship, was to be beached on the shore at V beach, and akin to the renowned Trojan Horse, was to disgorge some 2,000 troops onto the shore from the 'sally-ports' that had been cut in the side of her hull. Just after 6.00am, the ship ran smoothly into the sand and came to a stop in a few feet of water but still some 80 yards from the beach. Oddly, there was almost no reaction from the shore defences. The troops started to disembark from the *River Clyde* into small open boats for the last few yards to the beach.

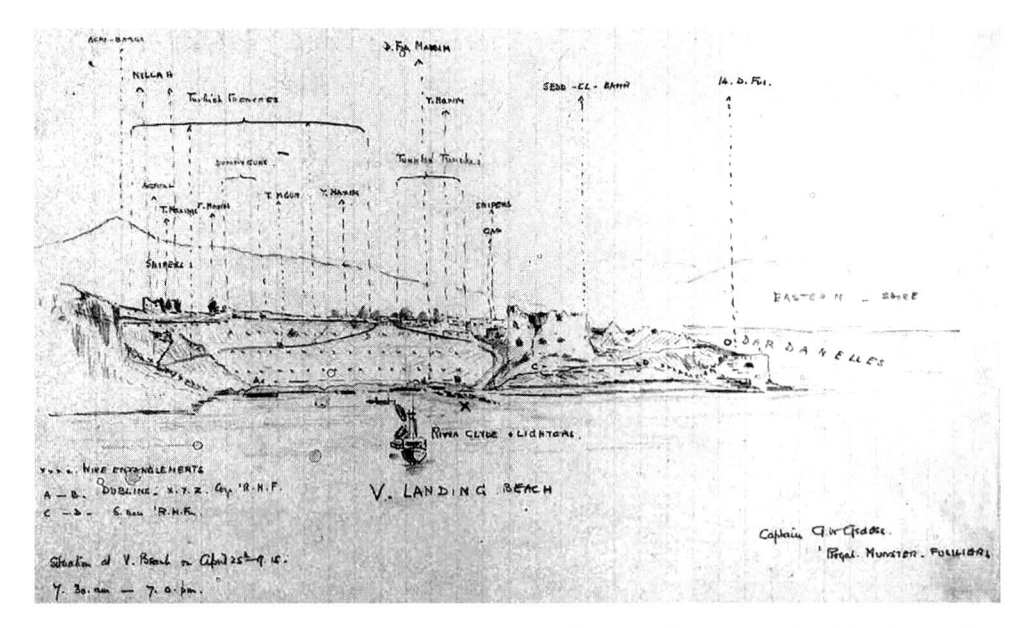

The V Beach Landing, sketch by Guy Geddes

By 7.30am most were on their way under the powerful umbrella of the naval barrage. Amongst the first of these troops were the 1st Battalion, Royal Dublin Fusiliers, including three Old Cheltonian officers. Henry Floyd (Southwood, 1907) had initially been educated at Harrow from 1903 to 1904 and came to College for his last two years, which he shared with George Dunlop (Christowe, 1907). On leaving, they both went on to Sandhurst (albeit Henry a cadet intake behind) and were commissioned into the Regiment in 1909. By contrast, Thomas Frankland (Teighmore, 1890) had left College aged 11 with his elder brother Robert and both had gone on to Charterhouse. While serving as a young officer during the South Africa War, Thomas was taken prisoner and held in a camp in Pretoria, not only with Winston Churchill but also Aylmer Haldane.[88] Thomas later trained as one of the early airmen, being awarded his aviator's certificate (No 679) as a pilot flying the Vickers Biplane at the Vickers School at Brooklands. Later, and now a general, Haldane asked for Thomas by name to serve on the general's brigade staff. When a brigadier, Haldane clearly thought highly of Thomas, recalling that:

> He was an officer who displayed great coolness under fire, and possessed accomplishments much above the average, and from the time I first knew him in South Africa I felt that he would go far in his career.[89]

---

[88] General Sir James Aylmer Lowthorpe Haldane, GCMG, KCB, DSO, who was instrumental in the army's reformation, after the Boer War, and implemented in 1907.
[89] IWM, Catalogue 14069, Private Papers of General Sir Aylmer Haldane.

1915 – THE YEAR OF FALSE HOPE

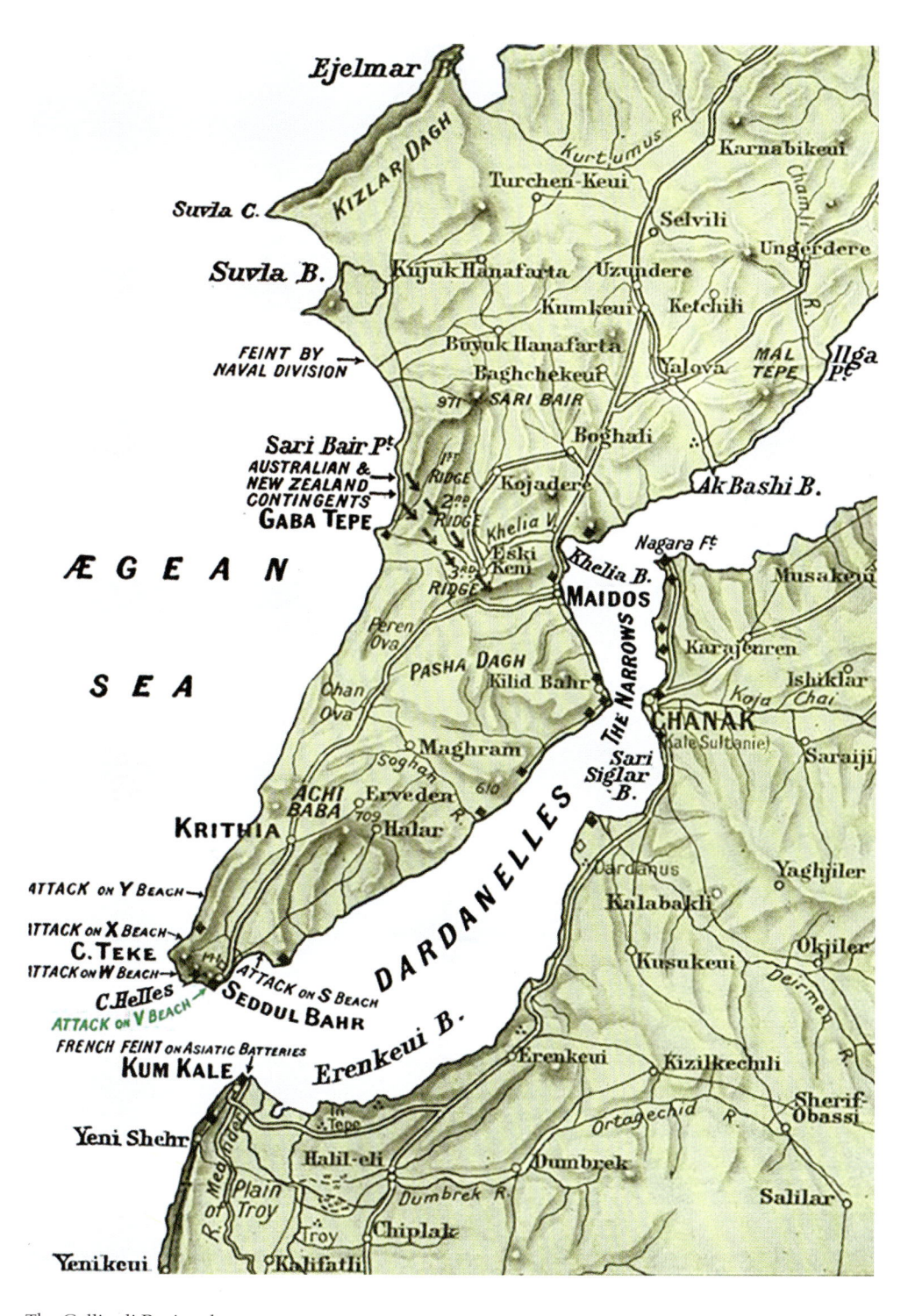

The Gallipoli Peninsula

Just as the lead boats were yards from the shoreline, an eruption of defensive fire burst onto the landing force. A personal letter from May 1915, recently published in the *Irish Times*, vividly describes the carnage that followed:

Dear Mother

This is the first opportunity I have had of writing to you since we left the boat. You will have seen in the papers by now that we have forced a landing, but ourselves and the Dublins got most awfully mauled in doing so. We left Lemnos for Tenedos one day, and from there we got into a collier called the River Clyde, which had been fitted for the purpose of landing. We anchored at midnight, about two miles from the mouth of the Dardanelles, and at dawn the whole fleet began a bombardment of the end of the peninsula, where we were going to land.

At 7.30am the Dublins set off in open boats; their landing place was the same as ours. As each boat got near the shore snipers shot down the oarsmen. The boats then began to drift, and machine-gun fire was turned on to them. You could see the men dropping everywhere, and of the first boatload of 40 men only three reached the shore, all wounded. At the same time we ran our old collier on to the shore, but the water was shallower than thought, and she stuck about 80 yards out.

Some lighters were put to connect with the shore, and we began running along them to get down to the beach. I can't tell you how many were killed or drowned, but the place was a regular death trap. I ran down to the lighters but was sent back by Jarrett, as there was no room on them. Then the wounded began crawling back, the Turks sniping at them the whole time. The men who had managed to reach the shore were all crouching under a bank about 10 feet high, among them Jarrett.

At 2pm the colonel told me to go down on to the barge, collect as many men as I could and join the force on the shore. We jumped into the sea and got ashore somehow with a rain of bullets around us. I found Jarrett and a lot of men but very few not hit. We waited till dusk and then crept up into a sort of position a few yards up. We took up an outpost line, and I had just put out my sentry groups, and Jarrett came up to take a look, when he was shot through the throat by my side. We had an awful night, soaked to the skin, bitterly cold and wet and sniped at.[90]

In just 15 minutes the attacking force was almost destroyed by enemy rifle and machine gun fire: the Dubliners lost 21 officers and 560 men, including George Dunlop. Thomas managed to get ashore but was killed later that day while advancing from V Beach in an

---

[90] Personal Letter from Lieutenant Guy Nightingale to his mother, published in *The Irish Times* on 25th April 2015.

attempt to link up with the forces on W Beach and organise and coordinate the survivors. Henry also survived the landing only to be killed in action less than a week later in the fighting at Gully Ravine.[91]

Also coming ashore at V Beach that morning and witnessing the bloodshed was George Pownall (Southwood, 1898). He left College aged 15 to join the Royal Navy as a cadet on the training ship HMS *Britannia*, having been at school with two friends destined for service in submarines. George was in the same house as Frederick Coplestone (who was killed in action in 1914 as previously described) and at school with Edward Boyle (Day, 1897): all three trained together on *Britannia* and gave distinguished service in the Royal Navy. From their times at College, their subsequent training in HMS *Britannia* and afterwards in the small community of the embryonic submarine service, they would have known each other very well. On 15th September 1899, George passed out first in his batch as a midshipman, and, being assessed as 'most promising', was given six months' seniority in rank.[92] He continued to progress well and on promotion to lieutenant on 1903, George was specially selected for the submarine duties in which he served until 1909, becoming one of the early submarine captains in the newest branch addition to the Fleet.[93] Over the next two years, further happiness and success followed. He married Vera Chichester on 17th December 1910, and undertook a short gunnery appointment on the battleship, HMS *Lord Nelson*, where he was commended for 'having especially contributed towards [good] shooting and efficiency in gunnery in Lord Nelson'.[94] Returning to the submarine service in 1911, George commanded HMS *Onyx*, a torpedo depot ship based in Plymouth. He was promoted to lieutenant commander in 1913 when posted to Malta as First Lieutenant of HMS *Egmont*, a harbour service ship from which command of the Mediterranean Submarine Flotilla was executed. With the landings at Cape Helles imminent, George volunteered to act as the Assistant Beach Master during the disembarkation of the assaulting troops on V Beach. This was an extremely dangerous task. George had to remain on the beach, under the murderous fire from the Turkish defenders in the fort above him and direct the landing forces up the beach to some degree of safety. He also had to order and orchestrate the empty landing craft back for further troop loads so that the

George Pownall

---

[91] The National Archives, WO 95/4310. Brigade War Diary records at 2010 hrs that 'R Dublin Fusiliers quite unable to advance up RAVINE so erected a barricade across RAVINE about 80* North East of junction of H12 with Ravine' and later at 0038 hrs, 'Message dispatched by OC R Dublin Fusiliers reporting that while swinging his left forward and digging in on his right, they had been heavily attacked, and their left flank in danger of being turned.' (The battalion war diaries for this action and the landing disaster of 25th April are missing from the National Archives.)
[92] The National Archives, ADM 196/48/128, personal record Lieutenant Commander GH Pownall RN.
[93] The Royal Navy Submarine Service was formed in September 1902 with the establishment of the 1st Submarine Flotilla, consisting of RN submarine *Holland 1* and its tender HMS *Hazard*, based at Portsmouth. The air arm of the Royal Navy, the Royal Naval Air Service, was formally established on 1st July 1914.
[94] The National Archives, ADM 196/48/128, personal record Lieutenant Commander GH Pownall RN.

landing area remained uncongested. George was killed in action on the beach on the morning of 25th April, aged 31.[95]

Edward Boyle, however, was in command of HM Submarine *E14*, just off the coast of the Dardanelles. This was Edward's fifth submarine command, making him one of the Royal Navy's most experienced submariners. On 27th April, he took the *E14* through the Straits, passed the Narrows, and into the Sea of Marmara causing great alarm amongst Turkish shipping. Several previous attempts to penetrate the Narrows had been made, which entailed diving beneath minefields and avoiding detection in the most confined sea room; almost all had been unsuccessful. For his actions Edward was awarded the Victoria Cross, being gazetted four weeks later:

Edward Boyle VC

The KING has been graciously pleased to approve of the grant of the Victoria Cross to Lieutenant-Commander Edward Courtney Boyle, Royal Navy, for the conspicuous act of bravery specified below:

"For most conspicuous bravery, in command of Submarine E. 14, when he dived his vessel under the enemy minefields and entered the Sea of Marmora on the 27th April, 1915. In spite of great navigational difficulties from strong currents, of the continual neighbourhood of hostile patrols, and of the hourly danger of attack from the enemy, he continued to operate in the narrow waters of the Straits and succeeded in sinking two Turkish gunboats and one large military transport."[96]

Edward's two brother officers on board the submarine were awarded the Distinguished Service Cross, and all 28 seamen in her crew were awarded the Distinguished Service Medal. His Victoria Cross was the second of three such awards to submariners in operations in the Dardanelles. He survived the war and retired in 1932 with the rank of rear admiral.

James Grogan (Boyne House, 1908) applied for entry to the Royal Military College, Sandhurst on 6th March 1908 while still in his penultimate term at College. Commissioned as a second lieutenant into the 1st Battalion, King's Own Scottish Borderers, he was serving at Lucknow in India when war was declared.[97] The battalion was ordered home, returning on 28th December 1914 to join the 87th Infantry Brigade, 29th Division that was earmarked for the Dardanelles campaign. On 18th March 1915, James left England from Avonmouth with the battalion, and, after transit via Alexandria and Mudros, landed at Y Beach just west of Cape Helles on 25th April. Within the first 24 hours, the battalion had lost 296 of their strength, including their commanding officer. On 4th June 1915, James was wounded

[95] See IWM HU128014.
[96] *The London Gazette*, 21st May 1915, page 4894.
[97] *The London Gazette*, 17th September 1909, page 6962.

and reported missing in a daylight attack on the Turkish trenches. In an effort to respond to his mother's queries concerning his fate, the authorities requested information from his comrades. One informant, Private (No 9450) McLachlan, stated on 2nd August 1915 that he was 'killed June 4th by hand grenade along with Comp Sgt Major Pierce'.[98] A machine-gun officer described the assault as follows:

> Mr. Grogan led one of the first two companies to the assault on June 4th. They charged into an absolute hell of rifle, machine-gun, and shrapnel fire, and very few came back. He died a gallant and noble death.[99]

His commanding officer wrote to James's brother:

> Your brother commanded one of the two companies which were in the first line sent forward to rush the Turkish trenches after the bombardment. He and his Company Sergeant-Major were the only two in that company who got right up to the trenches. He was last seen standing on the parapet firing his revolver before he was killed. How he got over the ground swept by such a fire as there was is hard to understand. For this particular attack our brigade was broken up and we were attached to another and, as a regiment, were given the most difficult portion of the line to advance against. Our casualties alone showed what we had up against us. Your brother's death is a great loss to the regiment. I had never met him till I returned to the battalion on the 17th of May. I could quite plainly see how much he was liked by everybody.[100]

James's body was eventually recovered, and he was buried in the cemetery at Twelve Tree Copse.

Also leaving College with James were Frank Ayrton (Boyne House, 1908) and Frederick Gudgeon (Leconfield, 1908); both were talented sportsmen. Frank had been in the College Gym VIII for two years (1905-06) and was the College racquets champion when he left in 1908. Frederick, by contrast, was a good tennis player and rowed at bow in the College IV boat during his last summer term; he was also a sergeant in the Officers Training Corps. They both went their separate ways. Frank went on to the Royal Military Academy at Woolwich and was commissioned into the Royal Garrison Artillery as a second lieutenant, but resigned his commission in 1912.[101] Frederick went on to London University where he matriculated on 23rd April 1914 and went out to Brazil to join his family. When war broke out Frederick returned to England and was reunited with Frank by sheer coincidence, when they both joined the 16th Royal Fusiliers as officers.[102] Both were then attached to the 2nd Battalion before it left for the Dardanelles from Avonmouth in March

---

[98] The National Archives, WO 339/7387, personal record of Lieutenant JC Grogan.
[99] Ibid.
[100] Ibid.
[101] *The London Gazette*, 14th January 1910, page 340.
[102] Supplement to *The London Gazette*, 26th November 1914, page 9976.

1915. Before sailing, Frederick wrote respectfully to his father on 3rd January 1915, closing his letter by saying:

> Well my dear old father there is nothing else except to say thank you for all your numerous proofs of kindness shown to me, for the splendid education and start in life you gave me, and I hope I was never a disappointment to you. I always tried to do the right thing by you.
>
> Fondest love to you, Mother, Katie, Pat and Dondinha, from your affectionate son, FG Gudgeon.[103]

Frank and Frederick both landed at X Beach on 25th April, and although there was little opposition to start with, resistance stiffened as they pressed forward. They were both killed in the fighting near Gully Ravine, both as captains leading their respective companies. In a response to Frederick's mother's request for details of his death, the battalion's commanding officer reported that:

> All evidence goes to prove that he was killed about 20 yards outside the Trench called J12. Officers went with periscopes to try and locate body but failed owing to the number of dead lying near. Body not recovered.[104]

Frank and Frederick are commemorated on the Helles Memorial in Gallipoli, their names beside each other. Frederick's two elder brothers, both Old Cheltonians, survived the war. George served in the Hertfordshire Regiment winning the Military Cross and being mentioned in despatches, before he was badly wounded and invalided out of the army. Stanley, a civilian who was in Germany at the start of the war, was interned in 1914 and held in Ruhleben Camp until his release in November 1918; he went into His Majesty's Consular Service and served back home in Brazil.

Edward Boyle's VC was followed six weeks later by the fourth such prestigious award to an Old Cheltonian during the First World War. George Raymond Dallas Moor (Boyne House, 1914), referred to by his family as Dallas, endured his baptism of fire on V Beach as he too landed on 25th April. He had left College in July 1914, and following the outbreak of war, enlisted at Barnstaple with some friends in the Public School's Battalion of the Royal Fusiliers (becoming Rifleman No 4156) on 18th September 1914 just before his 18th birthday. However, a month later he was appointed to a commission from the Special Reserve of Officers as a second lieutenant in the 2nd Battalion, Hampshire Regiment. Having landed from the SS *River Clyde*, just behind the heavily depleted ranks of the Dublin Fusiliers, the Hampshires ground their way forward for the next six weeks over the half mile towards Gully Ravine.

---

[103] The National Archives, WO 339/2395, personal file of captain FG Gugeon.
[104] Ibid.

But any meaningful advance was thwarted by tenacious Turkish defence and counter-attacks during the bitter fighting that was to be termed as the Third Battle of Krithia. Dallas was awarded the VC for his conduct in one such action:

> For most conspicuous bravery and resource on the 5th June 1915 during operations South of Krithia, Dardanelles. When a detachment of a battalion on his left, which had lost all its officers, was rapidly retiring before a heavy Turkish attack, Second Lieutenant Moor, immediately grasping the danger to the remainder of the line, dashed back some 200 yards, stemmed the retirement, led back the men and recaptured the lost trench.
>
> This young officer, who only joined the army in October 1914, by his personal bravery and presence of mind, saved a dangerous situation.[105]

Dallas Moor VC

As the years have gone by, and modern attitudes to war and the conduct of war have changed, Dallas's VC award has come under some scrutiny and caused a degree of controversy. In the course of this action, his 'stemming the retirement' apparently involved shooting four of the leading retirees, an act which the divisional commander General de Lisle suggested brought other soldiers who were falling back to their senses. Whether the four soldiers shot were wounded or killed remains unclear. But the fact remains that a rout was avoided by Dallas's action, which potentially saved many more lives – his award was fully justified by the higher authorities. Dallas survived the crucible of Gallipoli and would be applauded and again decorated for his bravery later in the war.

Montague Proctor-Beauchamp (Day Boy, 1906) was the eldest son of the Reverend Sir Montagu Harry (7th Baronet) and Lady Florence Proctor-Beauchamp living at Ebley Court in Stroud, Gloucestershire. He was educated at the Junior School for seven terms before leaving aged 12. Montague's death at Gallipoli has been shrouded by a well-known yet unresolved mystery. His uncle, Sir Horace George, was not only the 6th Baronet of the family's hereditary title, but also the Lieutenant Colonel commanding the 1/5th Battalion, Norfolk Regiment. Sir Horace had retired from the army in 1904 but when war broke out, was recommissioned despite being 65 years of age. He raised a territorial battalion from volunteers largely from the Norfolk villages including E Company, which consisted of

Montague Proctor-Beauchamp

---

[105] *The London Gazette*, 24th July 1915, page 7279.

The 5th Norfolk Officers

soldiers recruited from the Royal Estate at Sandringham.[106] Needing officers he knew and trusted, Sir Horace enlisted the help of his young nephew, Montague, who was commissioned as a second lieutenant and attached to the 'Sandringham' Company.

The battalion set sail from Liverpool on 30th July 1915, aboard the luxury liner RMS *Aquitania*. Landing at Suvla Bay on 10th August, in the thick of heavy fighting, it was immediately ordered inland. Montague was killed in action alongside his uncle and the rest of the Sandringham Company in an abortive advance on 12th August. What was mysterious was that after the company had advanced through the smoke of battle, nothing was seen or heard of them. There were no survivors and none of their bodies were found. Conscious of potential royal scrutiny, a despatch was sent from General Sir Ian Hamilton, the commander-in-chief, reporting:

> There happened a very mysterious thing, the Norfolks had drawn somewhat ahead of the rest of the British line; the ground became more wooded and broken, but the Colonel, with sixteen officers and 250 men, still kept pushing on, driving the enemy before them. Among these ardent souls was part of a fine company enlisted from the King's Sandringham estates. Nothing more was ever seen or heard of any of them. They charged into the forest and were lost to sight or sound. Not one of them ever came back.[107]

---

[106] To fill the ranks of Kitchener's New Armies, and the new territorial battalions being raised, many retired officers were recommissioned and irreverently though humorously referred to as 'dug-outs', as they had been 'dug out' of their retirement to command battalions from the dug-outs in the trenches.

[107] See Holroyd. J, and Longford. W; *The Great War Illustrated; 1915*, Pen and Sword, Barnsley, (2015), page 132.

1915 – THE YEAR OF FALSE HOPE

The mystery of their disappearance remained until some evidence of their fate was literally 'unearthed' in 1919. Some 36,000 Commonwealth soldiers were killed during the Gallipoli campaign, of which 13,000 could not be unidentified and were 'known unto God'. Another 14,000 men remained missing and were never found. The War Office, perhaps after some informal royal persuasion from Queen Alexandria (who took an interest in the families serving at Sandringham), commissioned the Reverend Charles Edwards to go to Gallipoli to find the missing Norfolks. Edwards, himself a veteran service chaplain with a Military Cross to his name, found 180 bodies buried beyond the old Turkish front line near an old ruined farm and identified them as Norfolks by the metal shoulder flashes. It transpired that most, if not all, of the bodies had a single gunshot wound to the head. Whether the Norfolks, isolated during the attack, were overwhelmed, surrendered, and then summarily executed by the Turks remains a sensitive and contentious issue.[108]

The reputation and contribution of the Australian and New Zealand Army Corps, the ANZACs, to the Gallipoli campaign is widely respected and well documented. Perhaps less well known is the contribution of the Old Cheltonians to the ANZAC forces. The day after Montague had disappeared with the Sandringham Company, Cornwallis Maude (Boyne House, 1891) was killed at Walkers Ridge near ANZAC Cove on 13th August, fighting with his platoon from the 9th Australian Light Horse. The son of Lieutenant General Cornwallis Oswald Maude, he had left College in April 1891, aged 14 and a half, eventually settling in South Africa. When he was 19, he joined the Cape Mounted Rifles as a trooper in King Williams Town in the Eastern Cape on 23rd May 1896. Three years later Cornwallis was fighting with the Rifles, an irregular cavalry unit, during the South African War. He appears to have been well regarded in the upper echelons of colonial society as he was commissioned on the personal nomination of the Governor of Cape Colony, becoming a second lieutenant on 21st November 1900 in the 3rd Worcestershire Regiment.[109] After the war in 1902 however, rather than returning to England with the regiment and an army career, he resigned his commission and went to live in Australia with his elder brother, Maurice, living in Bourke Street, Goulburn, New South Wales. There, Cornwallis worked as an electrician fitting electric lights to houses and streets in the area. But after war with Germany was declared, he enlisted as a trooper in the 9th Australian Light Horse on 29th October 1914, at Morphettville, South Australia, and embarked for Egypt, leaving Melbourne on 11th February 1915 on the HMAT *Karroo*.[110] His previous military experience was quickly noticed and he was soon promoted to sergeant. On 7th August 1915 he was recommissioned as a second lieutenant in the Australian Imperial Forces.[111] His commission was short-lived as he was killed in action six days later by a gunshot wound to the head and buried in the cemetery on Walker's Ridge. The epitaph on his headstone was chosen by his brother, Maurice, and reads 'Not in vain'.

---

[108] The facilities to accommodate and hold prisoners of war in Gallipoli were exceptionally limited for both sides which made the fighting even more brutal. It should also be noted that the Ottoman authorities' approach to captives and minority groups was ruthless, particularly regarding the Armenians whose persecution by the Ottomans is thought to have begun on 24th April 1915.
[109] *The London Gazette*, 20th November 1900, page 7138.
[110] His Majesty's Australian Transport.
[111] Supplement to *The London Gazette*, 23rd October 1915, page 10483, a posthumous notification.

Born in Cheltenham, Kenneth Bird (Hazelwell, 1904) left College and studied engineering at King's College London. While he was there, he also took art classes at the Regent Street Polytechnic, a skill which he developed, later making a most significant national impact in his later years. Commissioned into the City of Edinburgh (Fortress) Royal Engineers on 11th September 1914, Kenneth deployed to Gallipoli with the 52nd (Lowland) Division in July the following year. He was very seriously wounded by a shell exploding nearby, which broke his spine. Despite the fears of many of the medics who thought his chances of survival were slim, Kenneth was immediately evacuated back to England where he spent almost three years slowly convalescing. But his injuries proved so serious that he was invalided out of the army in 1916. Kenneth turned to art, especially cartoons where he published as early as 1916 for Punch Magazine under the pen name of 'Fougasse', later becoming the magazine's editor. He survived the war and made a tremendous impact during the Second World War with his series of popular propagandist cartoons which emphasised that 'careless talk costs lives'.

While Kenneth was being evacuated to England, Charles Thomas (Leconfield, 1880) was tending to the wounded amongst the flies and filth on the peninsula. He had left College aged 16 and, moving to New Zealand, eventually studied medicine, becoming a doctor in Timaru New Zealand; he also played cricket for South Canterbury. During the South African War he had served as a chief medical officer and surgeon before returning to New Zealand. Life there became settled with the family and besides his doctoring he was also elected president of the South Canterbury Cricket Association from 1904 to 1908, a role he combined with the presidency of the New Zealand Cricket Council in 1906. Being a respected doctor with battlefield experience, he was re-commissioned as a lieutenant colonel when war was declared and given command of the New Zealand Medical Corps (Mounted Brigade Field Ambulance). On 3rd December 1914, he said goodbye to his wife Mildred and his 11-year-old son and embarked for the Mediterranean from Auckland, en route to Suez, Egypt on the HMNZT *Star of India*. He arrived in Gallipoli on 25th April, landing at ANZAC Cove and set up his field ambulance unit. By August, the ANZACs were fighting hard to take Hill 60. But instead of remaining in the relative safety of the dressing station, Charles went with stretcher bearers on 28th August to help the wounded men in the trenches. While sheltering in a trench he was killed instantly when a shell exploded directly above him; he was 51 years of age. Charles' personal letters held by the South Canterbury Museum provide a remarkable insight into his last months in the Gallipoli campaign, opening with his views from Alexandria in March, before his later entries from Gallipoli:

> 1 March 1915: It seems to be an endless, hopeless mess we are in now.
>
> May 8, 1915: Received orders at about 10am to go further up the coast where Australians and New Zealanders landed. Have just arrived and lowered anchor. The place where they landed almost like the side of a steep cliff, covered with scrub going straight down to the beach which is hardly perceptible. Their landing and driving the

1915 – THE YEAR OF FALSE HOPE

Turks up the cliff under some very hot shell and rifle fire was a most creditable performance. It seems an almost impossible task. They had to jump into the water up to their shoulders to do it and of course suffered heavy casualties. Some of the boats scarcely landed a single man.

May 29th, 1915. H.M. Transport "Iverine". Had an easy time on Lemnos Island for five days. Beautiful sea bathing. Played cricket for my unit against the Australians. The Australians won easily. I made 27, second highest score on our side.
July 24, 1915: The safest place on land is in the fire trenches. Some are still killed and wounded before even they put a foot on shore … There is a great deal of sickness on account of the damp dugouts and the flies, which are even worse than here on account of the unburied and partially buried. I have 30 men employed all day and every day digging graves for New Zealanders.[112]

Writing home, Sergeant Bill Tait recalls Charles' last moments:

The death of Lieut.-Col. Thomas will, no doubt, have come as a great shock to Timaru. I can assure you that it gave me a great shock. I was sitting talking to him in the trenches when he was killed. We were up in the New Zealand Mounted trenches while they were attacking three Turkish trenches, and the shells were falling thick and fast all around us, till at last one burst above us. Col. Thomas was killed outright, and died without speaking. I was badly hit, and rolled over towards him, while three or four stretcher-bearers were also more or less badly hit. I thought I was finished, and could do nothing for the Colonel, but after some time they managed to plug me and get me away. The trip back to the dressing station was almost as lively as in the trenches, as shells and stray bullets were dropping all round us. We had some narrow escapes, but managed to get back safety. Our little company was broken-hearted on hearing of the death of our dear Colonel. I could talk for months about him, but you know what he was, and what he has done for me, and for our company. I am proud to have been with him when he died. He was absolutely fearless, and would go anywhere in the face of danger.[113]

Four days earlier, another two school friends were killed. With their birthdays only three days apart, Richard Leslie and Archie Roberts (both Day Boys, 1885) had been together in their house at College for three years. Both went into the army to become officers, albeit through two different avenues. Richard was granted a militia commission as a second lieutenant in the 3rd Battalion, West Yorkshire Regiment on 25th February 1888.[114] However,

---

[112] Personal Letters of Lieutenant Colonel CE Thomas held by the South Canterbury Museum, published in *The Timaru Herald,* dated 20th July 2015.
[113] Personal Letters of Sergeant Bill Tait held by the South Canterbury Museum, published in *The Timaru Herald,* dated 20th July 2015.
[114] *The London Gazette*, 24th February 1888, page 1226.

he transferred to the Dorsetshire Regiment some two years later, and was promoted to captain in 1897.[115] Richard saw active service in the South African War being mentioned in despatches twice for gallantry and receiving the King's and Queen's Medals with a total of seven clasps. Although he resigned his commission in 1905, he retained a reserve commitment to the regiment as a captain under the conditions of the 1900 Royal Warrant.[116] On the outbreak of war he was automatically mobilised, and joined the 5th Battalion, which, after six months work up and training, was ready for deployment.

Archie on the other hand had followed the familiar route into the army from school direct to the Royal Military College, being commissioned from Sandhurst into the Middlesex Regiment as a second lieutenant on 3rd October 1888. Transferring to the Indian Army, he served for the next 12 years and saw active service on the North West Frontier, before resigning from the army in March 1911 as a major. However, with the outbreak of war he volunteered for active service, and had his rank and seniority reinstated, being made the second in command of the 6th (Service) Battalion, Yorkshire Regiment, one of Kitchener's New Army battalion. After training and operational work up, the battalion sailed to the Dardanelles from Liverpool on 3rd July 1915.

Richard landed at Suvla Bay on 11th July 1915 with the 5th Dorsets. Over the next six months, although they lost relatively few in fighting, they suffered heavily from the sickness that was the scourge of soldiers during the campaign. He took over command of the battalion as a major when the commanding officer was invalided back to Egypt on 18th August with sickness. Four days later Richard was killed attacking Turkish positions and trenches.

Archie arrived at Suvla Bay at dawn on 6th August 1915. Almost immediately the battalion went into action, being ordered to take the heights at Lala Baba at the point of the bayonet, one of the first attacks by a New Army battalion. The advance was met with strong Turkish resistance, and although the hill was captured, nearly all the officers were either killed or wounded. He was severely wounded and evacuated to Malta where he died on 22nd August 1915. Richard and Archie, born within three days of each other and schooled together, died on the same day. The Gallipoli campaign is remembered for its brutal fighting in a climate where flies, disease and sickness thrived. It was not the only theatre where Old Cheltonians had to endure such similarly unpleasant conditions.

Mesopotamia

The campaign in Mesopotamia had started on 6th November 1914. Mindful of the need for operational expedience without removing essential military manpower resources from either the Western Front or those needed for the Dardanelles campaign, the British Indian Expeditionary Force, specifically the 6th (Poona) Division, was dispatched to Mesopotamia.

---

[115] *The London Gazette*, 20th December 1889, page 7356.
[116] *The London Gazette*, 24th March 1905, page 2277.

The Division landed on 6th November and quickly took the fort at Fao at the mouth of the Shatt-al-Arab waterway.[117] The inclusion of British Muslim troops from India in the Expeditionary Force also diluted any impression of invasion of historical Muslim homelands in the region by European Christian forces (an important consideration not lost to the minds of today's diplomats, politicians and military commanders). The primary intent of the campaign was to secure Britain's route to India by dislodging the Ottoman Turk forces that threatened British interests, specifically the oilfields of the Anglo-Persian Oil Company.

This would be achieved by occupying the province of Basra up to Kut al-Amara, a town strategically placed on a bend of the river Tigris at its convergence with the Shatt al-Hai waterway. Basra was captured by 21st November 1914, and Qurna, a strategically important town at the confluence of the Tigris and the Euphrates, a month later. After these initial early successes, strategic ambitions of advancing to Baghdad started to cloud operational prudence and judgement as the realities of an over-extended logistical chain and inadequate supporting medical services began to bite.[118]

By March 1915, the British force was established in the region around Basra and one column of some one thousand troops moved north towards the oilfield at Ahwaz to secure the pipeline running down the Karun river valley to the coast and the refineries on Abadan Island. On 3rd March, the first two Old Cheltonians to die in the Mesopotamian campaign were killed at Ahwaz, serving together in the 7th Rajputs; Frederick MacKenzie (Christowe, 1903) and Douglas Bourgoyne-Wallace (Boyne House, 1911). Both had followed the now familiar route to Sandhurst and a commission, and then entry into the Indian Army. On being promoted to captain on 18th January 1914, Frederick was appointed adjutant of the battalion just after Douglas had arrived to become a platoon commander. Both were killed during a confused, hand-to-hand engagement against some 10,000 local tribesmen supplemented with 2,000 regular Turkish soldiers. The unit war diary records that while the British cavalry attempted a flanking manoeuvre, enemy artillery opened fire:

> The 33rd Cavalry galloped around the rear of the ridge, a frontal bayonet attack was made, led by Captain Ogg and the men of the Dorsets. The Arabs gave way and rapidly dispersed. At this point in the battle the Turks opened fire with three artillery guns for the first time, causing British casualties. One of those killed by this enemy artillery fire was Captain Frederick Obre MacKenzie, the Adjutant of the 7th Rajputs.[119]

---

[117] The 6th (Poona) Division was comprised of three infantry brigades: the 16th 17th, and 18th Brigades. Each of the brigades had a regular British battalion as its lead battalion: 2nd Dorsets, 1st Oxfordshire and Buckinghamshire Light Infantry, and the 2nd Norfolks respectively. Each brigade had a further three Indian battalions commanded by British officers. Therefore, the influence of Sandhurst educated and trained officers permeated right the way through the Indian Army.
[118] The similarities to the British contributions to the allied operations in Iraq in 2003 are both clear and uncanny.
[119] The National Archives, WO 95/5124/3, Unit War Diary of 18th Indian Infantry Brigade: 7th Battalion Rajputs.

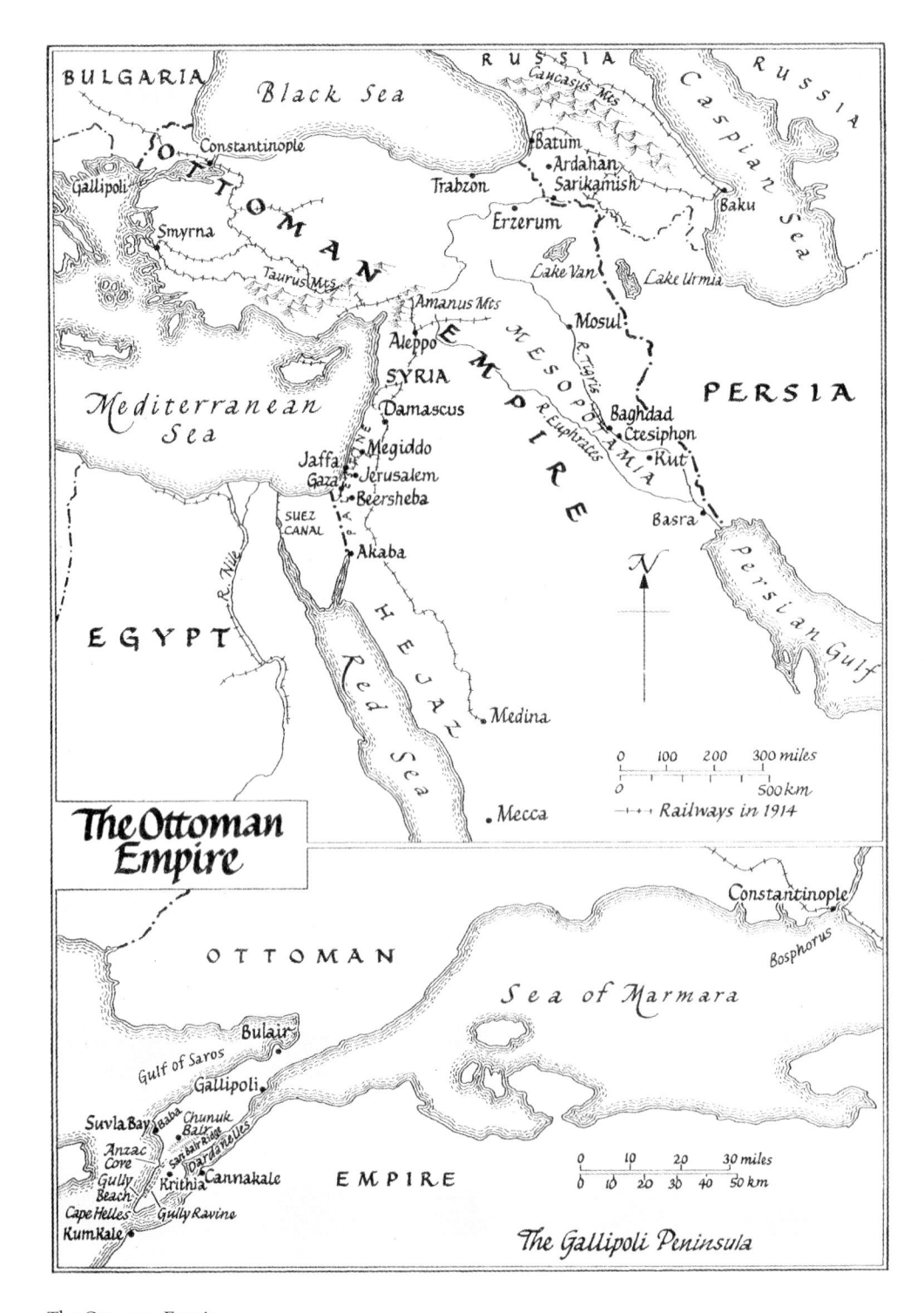

The Ottoman Empire

However, a later account from the Battalion's record amplifies these details, and highlights the fog of battle:

> Groups of swift-moving Arab irregular cavalry rode to get behind the British position. The 1,000 British soldiers were now facing around 12,000 enemy troops, about 2,000 of them Turks. The Right Flank Guard was composed of two companies of the 7th Rajputs commanded by Captain A C Ogg but it became so heavily involved with the enemy that it was reinforced by the third 7th Rajput company and the mountain guns. Around 0715 hours the Brigadier, realizing that his force was in trouble and could be surrounded, ordered a withdrawal but now the lack of pre-planning for this tactic caused serious problems. Lieutenant Colonel H O Parr, commanding the 7th Rajputs, ordered a retirement starting with his left-flank troops and this was executed steadily. Then an order to retire from an unknown source reached his right-flank troops and they also fell back. This isolated Parr's centre and the Colonel was severely wounded in an arm but he fought on with his revolver until he was wounded again in the stomach and hip. Several of the Brigade's supply and ammunition carts had been loaned by the Anglo-Persian Oil Company and, when ponies pulling the carts began to be hit, most of the civilian drivers abandoned their carts, creating confusion on the battlefield. The enemy quickly over-ran and looted the carts. The 4th Rajputs were the Left Flank Guard and poor staff work initiated by the Brigadier caused them to withdraw prematurely and so fail to hold vital ground. The 7th Rajputs rapidly took casualties as the enemy swarmed in and around the hastily withdrawing troops. Three officers of the 7th Rajputs, Captain W A Gover and Lieutenants Douglas Burgoyne-Wallace and Wickham Leathes Harvey were all killed.[120]

Frederick's body was recovered and buried at the war cemetery in Basra. His wife Doris, whom he had married on 25th February 1911 at Christ Church, Kotagiri, in Madras, was waiting in India for his return. With the devastating news of his death, she decided to return to England, eventually settling at 4, Evelyn Court, Cheltenham, close to College where Frederick had excelled in the school's Gymnastics VIII. Sadly, however, Douglas's body was never found, and he is commemorated on the wall of the British War Memorial in Tehran.

A further four Old Cheltonians were killed in Mesopotamia later in the year. Frederick Chadwick (Christowe, 1900) was killed during the fighting at Shaiba on 13th April when the Turks attempted to retake Basra. One of seven children and the eldest son of Colonel Edward Chadwick, Frederick had followed his father into the army. He graduated from the Royal Military College and was commissioned on 19th August 1903. Ten years later, he was a captain in the 104th Wellesley's Rifles and in charge of the battalion's machine gun section. Mentioned in despatches twice for gallantry, Frederick was mortally wounded while leading his gun teams in repulsing the Turkish attacks on British positions and died

---

[120] Ibid.

the same day. Further family tragedy was soon to follow, however, as a month later his youngest brother, Richard, died from wounds received in France.[121] The day after Frederick was killed at Shaiba, Arthur Hind (Boyne House, 1903) was killed at Ahwaz. He too had been mentioned in despatches for gallantry and was serving as a captain in the 110th Mahratta Light Infantry. Having been at College together, their bodies were recovered and today lie buried just yards from each other in the Basra War Cemetery.

Over the next six months, the Indian Expeditionary Force pushed remorselessly northwards along the Tigris valley. By November the Force had reached Kut al-Amarah and was threatening Baghdad, itself defended by a force of 18,000 Ottoman troops in a defensive line at Ctesiphon some 15 miles to the south east of the capital. Here, Owen Mortimore (Leconfield, 1895) was killed on the opening day of the battle at Ctesiphon on 22nd November, aged 37. Though still young, Owen had had an interesting life. Having been in the Engineer Corps of the College OTC, he decided on a military career and was commissioned as a second lieutenant in the 4th Battalion, Devonshire Regiment, a militia unit, on 17th March 1897.[122] Transferring into the regular 2nd Battalion in 1899, he saw active service in the South African War, for which he received the Queen's Medal with five clasps. Although he was promoted to lieutenant in 1901, he resigned his commission some two years later in January 1903. His letter of resignation stated that this was due to the recent death of his father, which incurred some associated financial constraints on the family; 'monetary matters being so unsatisfactory that I cannot afford to remain in the Service'.[123] However, there may well have been other contributing factors that influenced his decision to resign. A week later, on 14th January 1903 at St John's Church, Deptford, he married Constance Eleanor (neé Archer), and they had two children, a son Foster born in October 1903 and named after his father, and then a daughter Ursula some six years later in 1909. The family went to live and farm in South Africa living at Darling Farm, Standerton in the Transvaal. Nevertheless, on the outbreak of war the family returned to England, living at 9 Marine Parade in Dawlish, Devon. Despite being an older recruit with a young family, Owen applied for a commission in the Special Reserve of Officers, rejoining his old regiment. Promoted to captain in the 3rd Battalion, Devonshire Regiment, he was one of 50 men attached to the 2nd Dorsets in Mesopotamia. He was killed in action fighting at Ctesiphon and is commemorated on the Basra Memorial. Lastly, George Townsend (Newick, 1907) was killed at Kut al-Amarah, serving in the Indian Army with the 66th Punjabis as part of the 12th Indian Division. He had fought near Frederick Chadwick at Shaiba and later at Ctesiphon with Owen. Unable to make any progress, the British/Indian column retired to Kut al-Amara, where it was besieged by the Turks. He was killed defending the garrison and was buried in the war cemetery at Kut.

[121] Educated not at College but at Wellington, Richard had gone on to the Royal Military Academy at Woolwich and was a second lieutenant serving with the 11th Siege Battery, Royal Garrison Artillery. He was mortally wounded near Bethune on 13th May 1915 in the front line while observing and reporting the fall of shot of his battery.
[122] *The London Gazette*, 16th March 1897, page 1533.
[123] The National Archives, WO 374/49157, personal file, and his letter of resignation to the Deputy Adjutant General dated 6th January 1903.

West Africa

In the Cameroons, skirmishes between the colonial forces of Germany and the British West African Frontier Force continued. Kenneth Markham-Rose (Hazelwell, 1907) was a scholar at College. He also played for the football XV in his final term, at the start of which on 4th September 1907 he applied for entry to the Royal Military College to embark on a career in the regular army.

Having spent his schooldays in Hazelwell opposite the Lousada twins in Cheltondale, the three young Cheltonians all joined the same intake at Sandhurst. After graduating they all went their separate ways, and Kenneth was commissioned as a second lieutenant in the Essex Regiment on 6th February 1909.[124] He was promoted to lieutenant just eight months later and served in the garrison at home. He must have proved himself and performed his duties well as he was seconded to the Royal West African Frontier Force in South Nigeria on 26th February 1913, a duty that required sound leadership and diplomatic skills for training and leading the locally enlisted Nigerian soldiers. On 19th August 1914, just after war had been declared, he was

Kenneth Markham-Rose

detached for duty with the Gambia Company in the Cameroons to counter the threat from a German force that was advancing along the Mbila river. He was killed in action on 3rd May. But the manner of his death reflects well on his personal integrity and regard for the irregular native soldiers under his command. It also underscores his own sense of duty and selfless service with which he had been inculcated, no doubt through the influence of his indefatigable housemaster at Hazelwell, Reverend Percy Hattersley-Smith. After stemming the German force's advance, Kenneth led a counter-attack and was killed at the height of the action, going to the aid of the company's wounded sergeant major. The action cost the Gambia Company 22 casualties, including Kenneth and three other Europeans who were wounded. The company sergeant major, Ebrima Jalu, was later awarded the Distinguished Conduct Medal. His citation for the award read:

> At the action at Mbila River, Jaunde Road, on 3rd May 1915, CSM Ebrima Jalu was in command of one of the hottest parts of the firing line after Lieutenant Markham-Rose was killed. Although deprived of the moral support of any European for several hours, he displayed the greatest coolness and showed a fine example by the way in which he controlled his men and directed their fire throughout the day.[125]

This fitting tribute to the bravery of Ebrima Jalu is perhaps equally reflective of the example and leadership of Kenneth, the officer who trained and led the Gambia Company.

---

[124] *The London Gazette*, dated 5th February 1909, page 948.
[125] For a full description see Chapter 6 of Costello R., *Black Tommies: British Soldiers of African Descent in the First World War*, University Press, Liverpool (2015).

The Home Front

Each name on the rising casualty lists of 1915, published in the daily papers, represented an individual and personal tragedy, an event that was devastating more and more communities up and down the country and across the empire. While individuals scrutinised the press columns for news of friends and colleagues, families and next of kin waited nervously at home for news of their dear ones serving at the front, dreading the arrival of the telegram stamped 'OHMS' – On His Majesty's Service.[126] When such hammer-blow news arrived, collective and shared sorrow of the entire community was gently and sympathetically offered in support of the grieving families as they stoically attempted to cope with their individual loss. Few examples epitomise this better than the College community's support for the long-serving and dedicated member of staff and Hazelwell housemaster, Percy Hattersley-Smith.

The College Common Room, circa 1895

For 44 years, Percy was an assistant master at College, and therefore would have taught a large number of the Old Cheltonians contained within and beyond these pages. For more than half that time, he and his wife Mary held ownership of Hazelwell, with their large family of six daughters and two sons, Geoffrey and elder brother James. Relinquishing his role as a housemaster, Percy eventually sold Hazelwell to College in 1901 and moved with the family to Pitville Circus Road in the town.

Of his two boys, Geoffrey was educated at the College's junior school for five terms before winning a naval cadet scholarship to HMS *Britannia*. James, on the other hand, was sent to Winchester College, where he was a College Prefect and a member of the

---

[126] Telegrams marked 'OHMS' were sent to the nominated next of kin as soon as a serviceman was reported 'Wounded', 'Missing in Action', Killed in Action', or Died of Wounds'.

rugby XV, before going up to Lincoln College, Oxford on a scholarship to read classics. When war was declared, and aged 38, James immediately enlisted as a private in the 9th Battalion, Norfolk Regiment, declining to accept a commission which might have delayed his arrival at the front. He was severely wounded in the first day's action at Loos, leading his section's attack on the German line, and died in hospital in Boulogne on 7th October. His company officer wrote the following letter to his father, which was immediately published in *The Cheltonian* magazine in honour of Percy's elder son:

> May I say at the outset how deeply the officers, NCOs and men of the company sympathise with you on the loss of your son. I would add that I hope it may be of some comfort to know that when he fell he was doing his duty gallantly leading the men around him in a charge across the open, and he reached a point nearer the enemy than that of anyone else. As regards his life in the regiment, from my own knowledge and what I have gathered from the men I have asked, he was always keen and enthusiastic about his work, always cheerful and imbuing others with his cheerfulness, never holding himself aloof from his fellows. On and off duty he gained the confidence, respect and esteem of all who came into contact with him. Latterly, as a Lance Corporal, he proved himself an efficient leader, and it seems a pity he did not wish for a commission. Finally, when he was lying out in the open, with his thigh severely shattered, he told the two men who went to take him back to leave him and look after the others.[127]

At the outbreak of war, brother Geoffrey was already a lieutenant in the Royal Navy serving on HMS *Pegasus*. He had done well as his personal service record reflected. As early as 1905, while a midshipman on HMS *Implacable* he was assessed as having an 'exceptionally good physique, and should make a good officer'. The following year after joining HMS *Swiftsure*, his report described him as being 'zealous and useful.'[128] Geoffrey had been awarded the Royal Humane Society Bronze Medal for life saving on 16th February 1914. While on *Pegasus*, he dived into the water of Lamu harbour (British East Africa and now Kenya) to save fellow crewman Petty Officer A F Hodge, who had been knocked overboard. Some six months later and now at war, *Pegasus* was disabled and sunk on 20th September 1914 at Zanzibar after action with the German cruiser *Konigsberg*; all the surviving ship's officers were ordered home. However, Geoffrey was too unwell to travel owing to a severe bout of dysentery, and a month later the Senior Naval Officer in Zanzibar reported that 'Lieut Hattersley-Smith in European Hospital with ulcerations of intestines with haemorrhage'.[129] After a further three weeks, his condition was sufficiently improved that he was allowed to travel home to England to recuperate. By 2nd January 1915, Geoffrey was declared fit and appointed to HMS *Lark*, a Laforey Class destroyer based at Harwich with the 9th Destroyer Flotilla. However, on 18th

---

[127] *The Cheltonian*, November 1915.
[128] The National Archives, ADM 196/52/72 and ADM 196/144/422 Lieutenant Hattersley-Smith personal records.
[129] The National Archives, ADM 196/52/72 and ADM 196/144/422 Lieutenant Hattersley-Smith personal records.

September 1915, symptoms of his dysentery returned and he was admitted to Plymouth Naval Hospital with disease of the intestines. Geoffrey died of the illness six weeks later on 1st November; a sad end to a most promising career.

Equally poignant, the telegram reporting Geoffrey's passing arrived at his father's house just 24 days after the one reporting the death of James. Percy must have been devastated by the news, made more difficult to bear as his wife Mary had died five years previously in July 1910. The cumulative effect and desolation of these three family bereavements must have been hard enough to endure, but nonetheless he continued to teach at College to help cover absences and service duties of at least 10 members of the Common Room staff, including Henry Reed, who had left for the war.[130] He would have undoubtedly found strong support and consolation from the College community: from the other members of the Common Room, the boys at College, and at home with his six unmarried daughters. Percy died on 19th January 1918, aged 71.

For soldiers yet to go to France, the programme of training at camps back home intensified; an activity not without its dangers. As the training officer of the 3rd (Reserve) Battalion, Connaught Rangers, Frederic Lewin was doing what he could to improve the bombing capabilities of his men, many of them undertaking this type of exercise for the first time. Therefore, the risk of accidents was relatively high despite Frederic's professional reputation and athletic prowess. While at College, Frederic was quite an athlete, playing in the rugby XV in 1895, as well as being a member of the gymnastics VIII in his last two years. He left school in December 1895 and went up to Merton College, Oxford, eventually becoming a barrister in Ireland; he also served in the East Surrey Militia for a while. On the day war was declared, he applied for a commission in the Special Reserve of Officers and was gazetted on as a lieutenant in the Connaught Rangers, his local regiment in Ireland, which was immediately mobilised.[131] On 10th November 1915 he was supervising a course of grenade instruction with his men on the Preghane Rifle Range at Kinsale, County Cork. Frederic was exploring the viability of using trench catapults to extend the effective range of grenades beyond that of the standard arm's throw. With the British arms manufacturers desperately trying to catch up with the acute operational requirement for rifle grenades, any method that extended the range of grenades beyond that of one's opponent offered a critical advantage, particularly in trench warfare.[132] Sadly, one of the bombs exploded prematurely by Frederic's right hand side, and he suffered very serious injuries to his skull and neck and died shortly afterwards. His death, though accidental and miles away from the front line, was the result of his military service and conduct of his war service duties, and so he takes his place quite appropriately alongside the other Old Cheltonians killed in the war.

---

[130] At least 10 members of the Common Room, the teaching staff, served in the war: Gabriel Grey, Arthur Bishop, Evelyne Byrde, Leonard Butler (killed), Geoffrey Crump, Henry Reed (killed), Arthur Lloyd-Barker, John Reid (killed), Arthur Pilkington, Arthur Catty, and Charles Reynolds. (Sadly, no records exist of the non-teaching staff who served during the war.)
[131] *The London Gazette*, dated 4th August 1914, page 7002.
[132] The BEF entered the war without any rifle grenades, and temporary solutions were improvised. Rifle grenades were hurriedly developed, and throughout 1915 the Hales No 3 Rifle Grenade was increasingly introduced to battalions which increased the range of grenades to some 150 yards.

The Mediterranean

The last four Old Cheltonian fatalities of what was a horrific year for the school's alumni all occurred on the penultimate day of 1915. In London, Malcolm Blest (Newick House, 1909), who had seen action as a captain in the 8th Battalion, Middlesex Regiment at Ypres and Loos, succumbed in London to illnesses the medics attributed to his time in the trenches. Near Armentières, Charles Lee (Boyne House, 1914) was killed in action whilst serving as a young Royal Engineer subaltern with the 126th Field Company. Further afield, 71 miles south east of Cape Martello on the south coast of Crete, the SS *Persia*, a 5,000 ton P&O passenger liner with 519 souls on board, was steaming steadily on her way to India towards Port Said in Egypt and the mouth of the Suez Canal. Amongst her passengers were Earnest Swiney (Day, 1882) and John Lodwick (Day and Southwood, 1899). Both were serving officers in the Indian Army, Earnest a colonel and commanding officer of the 39th Gharwal Rifles and John a captain and company commander in the 3rd Ghurkas. They had both sat down to lunch when, at 1.10pm, a violent explosion ripped apart the ship's port side and within ten minutes the ship had capsized and sunk. Only four lifeboats managed to get away before the ship capsized, resulting in many casualties. Both Earnest and John were among the 343 souls lost. The ship had been torpedoed by the German submarine *U-38*, captained by Kapitänleutnant Max Valentiner, without warning and, controversially, in breach of international law regarding the stop and search of merchant vessels sailing under a neutral flag.

Yet, after 17 months of increasingly global warfare, in which command of the Mediterranean had already become pivotal to Britain's fortunes and an essential, almost umbilical, resupply route, ships were still allowed to sail alone, without any protection of escort vessels or convoy system, adhering to published sailing timetables that were available to all seafarers, including German submarine crews. It was another pitiable example of the naivety of the directing commands and authorities, all too slow to shake off peacetime routine and operation, and indicative of their struggle to keep pace with and counter the latest technological advances being employed by a very astute and inventive enemy.

Year's End

Back in the trenches, the second Christmas of the war had come and gone, with no sign of the fraternisation experienced in 1914. Stalemate in the trench systems, both on the Western Front and in Gallipoli, intensified with a tacit but creeping acquiescence between opposing front-line troops of an attitude of 'live and let live'. All sides took the opportunity to consolidate positions and keep the troops tolerably occupied. On the day the SS *Persia* slipped beneath the waves to its watery grave in the Mediterranean, Ernest Taylor was behind the lines in France and 'in reserve'. As part of a bombing team not immediately required for an attack or trench raid, he found time away from the constant threat of trench mortar and shellfire of the front line to pencil his last letter of the year to his sister at home:

My dearest Doll,

Thank you so much for your letter which I received a few days ago. It is very interesting hearing about yours and Madge's lives at the hospital and the good work you are doing. I am so glad you like it. According to Ronald, if we got a "blighty" we could get into your hospital through virtue of having relations connected with the F.M.S. Wouldn't it be jolly! When a fellow gets wounded the first question one asks is whether it is a "blighty" and if the reply is in the affirmative everyone says "lucky beggar," but of course this must be taken with a grain of salt. However I don't think there is much need to worry about us getting wounded yet awhile. The process of reorganization seems very slow, in fact up to the present there is no visible sign of it, and I think we shall be marooned here for weeks. The regiment held some successful sports on the 28th. There was a football match in the morning when "C" squadron won the regimental championship. We were allowed off for the afternoon so got there in time for the sports. Jack Rowe and I entered for the wheelbarrow race, he being the wheel, but we did not get a place. In the evening there was a smoking concert which went with the usual swing. Cheese, biscuits, fruit, cigars and French beer were supplied free. The Colonel distributed the prizes and remarked when presenting C Squadron with theirs that "C Squadron could evidently play football as well as they could fight." It is very nice having an occasional reunion like that, as in the Grenade Section which is a Brigade affair, you feel a bit cut off from your old regiment. On the evening of New Year's Day 2nd troop are getting up a bit of shine I believe which we must try and get over for. My parcel from the Barwicks arrived last night – a pair of socks from Mrs., tobacco from George and Sid, and a cake of soap from Gladys. Very good of them, wasn't it? I had already written in answer to the letter, so if Ray gets them on the phone when he sees this letter and says how pleased I was with the things it will save me writing again so soon. I went on dental parade today, not that I had been bothered with toothache but I had one that needed filling, and it might have made trouble for me in the trenches when there is no chance of getting anything done for it. There were a lot of aeroplanes out yesterday. At one time I counted as many as sixteen all close together and they looked just like a flock of birds circling round. I wonder what the next development will be in the war. At present there seems to be a deadlock all round. I often have a look at the snapshots Grace sent me of Raymond and the baby and the cattle with my shack and the well-house in the background. It is astonishing how free from colds one keeps in this country in spite of continually having damp feet through splashing through mud all day. I put it down to not having any artificial heat. There are no fires or stoves to sit over, and the barns though frequently cold and draughty keep pretty much at the same temperature. I should think your patients would not miss the picture shows so much through having been over here. The towns and villages here are deadly dull in the evenings. If people were enterprising enough to start a good picture show they would make piles. A Canadian soldier did have a miniature one going here for a few nights. I went one night. The screen was not much larger than a good-sized pocket handkerchief, but the pictures were quite clear, and the room was packed with soldiers.

Good-bye with much love to you and Madge
Ever your affectionate brother
Ernest[133]

From a national perspective, the year had started with hope and expectation, but results on the battlefield yielded few returns as commanders failed to optimise the forces available to them. Time and again the campaign planners and battle managers pitted an increasingly plentiful human resource against an industrialised defensive armoury primarily composed of the machine gun, field artillery, and ever deepening belts of barbed wire. The same costly experiences were repeated, as the dogma from the tactics of past wars prevailed; a case of 19th century tactics being used against 20th century technology wielded by a clever enemy who was also learning to improve his lethal defensive tactics. To be fair to the most senior commanders, they were, for the first time ever, commanding, supplying, managing and transporting armies of millions of men – an experience for which British military leaders had no precedent. For them no blue print or doctrine existed, nor had a suitable training manual for these circumstances ever been conceived, let alone published. It was on-the-job training: their apprenticeship was as painful as any. For the Commander-in-Chief, the increasingly high casualty rates were unacceptable and cost Sir John French his job and his reputation. But, until some game-changing technological solution to break the deadlock could be found, developed, instilled and exploited, the casualty lists would continue to lengthen and the learning curve at both the tactical and operational levels would continue to be long and steep. True, there were some successes. The integration of the fledgling flying corps was of increasing value with the roles of air power extending from reconnaissance and observation to bombing and air superiority. The nation's industrial base was at last starting to turn the corner and provide the necessary resources and munitions in sufficient quality and quantity to supply the burgeoning appetite of the front line. The War was fast developing into a test of which side could endure the most and persist the longest. A war of attrition for 1916, both in men and materiel, was starting to be envisaged and planned by all sides.

[133] Extracts from the Canadian Letters and Images Project, The Taylor Bury Collection of Letters (online), Dept. of History, Vancouver Island University.

From the College's perspective, news of serving Old Cheltonians trickled back to school through various channels: via the Cheltonian 'grapevine'; through letters from families to housemasters; and, unhappily, through scouring the casualty lists and obituaries published in the newspapers. By the year's end, 301 Old Cheltonians had died as a result of the war. What remained undiminished, however, was the sense of duty and service to school, king and country that the current cohort of Cheltonians displayed. Of the rugby XV that finished playing for College that winter term in December 1915, all would serve during the war, all would be commissioned as officers, but three of the side would, alas, be killed.

LIST OF FALLEN OLD CHELTONIANS 1915

On the following pages (96 to 107) are the names and service details of Old Cheltonians who died in the second year of the war.

1915 – LIST OF FALLEN OLD CHELTONIANS

	Died (1915)	Name	Rank
96	6 January	Chads HC	Lieutenant
97	9 January	Orlebar RE	2nd Lieutenant
98	14 January	Conybeare MHC	Lieutenant
99	23 January	Flint RB	2nd Lieutenant
100	25 January	Buist K	Lieutenant
101	3 February	Bannerman OWE	Captain
102	6 February	Warren-Swettenham IREW	Major
103	15 February	Fort L	Captain
104	15 February	Thursby AD	Captain
105	16 February	Grieve WP	2nd Lieutenant
106	16 February	Lloyd GA	Captain
107	17 February	Wood-Martin FW	Captain
108	18 February	Mather JK	Lieutenant
109	21 February	Cutfield H	Trooper
110	25 February	Allen T	2nd Lieutenant
111	25 February	Osborne MG	Captain
112	27 February	Hillier CAH	2nd Lieutenant
113	2 March	Bird FC	2nd Lieutenant
114	3 March	Burgoyne-Wallace DB	Lieutenant
115	3 March	Mackenzie FO	Captain
116	3 March	Turner HG	Captain
117	3 March	Willoughby JG	Captain
118	10 March	Coates GWT	2nd Lieutenant
119	10 March	Sparrow BC	Captain
120	10 March	Saunders AH	Lieutenant
121	12 March	Biscoe AJ	Captain
122	12 March	Griffith RV de B	Lieutenant
123	12 March	Hewett GE	Captain
124	12 March	Sanders AA	Major
125	12 March	Wilson CW	Lieutenant
126	12 March	Wood-Martin JI	Captain
127	13 March	Sackville-Cresswell AE	Captain
128	13 March	Tate WL	Lieutenant
129	14 March	Campbell WUM	2nd Lieutenant
130	15 March	O'Callaghan D McK M	2nd Lieutenant
131	18 March	Eardley-Wilmott FL	Lieutenant
132	23 March	Saward HD	Captain
133	25 March	Odling ERM	Lieutenant
134	2 April	Molson EE	Lieutenant

1915 – LIST OF FALLEN OLD CHELTONIANS

Unit	Age	Place
1st North Staffordshire Regiment	20	Armentières, France
2nd Middlesex Regiment	33	Neuve Chapelle, France
7th Yorkshire Regiment	24	Teignmouth, UK
59th Field Coy, Royal Engineers	23	Lissenhoek, Belgium
B Coy, 1st Black Watch	20	Cuinchy, France
15th Lancers, IA	38	Boulogne, France
2nd East Yorkshire Regiment	48	Ypres, Belgium
2nd East Kent (Buffs) Regiment	33	Ypres, Belgium
3rd King's Royal Rifle Corps	27	Ypres, Belgium
3rd Middlesex Regiment	29	Ypres, Belgium
1st Welch Regiment	26	Ypres, Belgium
1st Suffolk Regiment	34	Ypres, Belgium
1st York & Lancaster Regiment	25	Ypres, Belgium
16th Lancers	19	Ypres, Belgium
1st Irish Guards	27	Cuinchy, France
3rd Rifle Brigade	24	Bailleul, France
2nd Monmouthshire Regiment	17	Farnborough, UK
2nd King's Shropshire Light Infantry	20	Ypres, Belgium
7th Rajputs, IA	21	Mesopotamia
7th Rajputs, IA	28	Mesopotamia
2nd Cheshire Regiment	36	Ypres, Belgium
33rd Light Cavalry, IA	31	Mesopotamia
33rd Battery, Royal Field Artillery	19	Neuve Chapelle, France
39th Garhwal Rifles, IA	33	Neuve Chapelle, France
2nd Royal Berkshire Regiment	22	Neuve Chapelle, France
1st Royal Irish Rifles	34	Boulogne, France
3rd Royal Fusiliers	22	Kemmel, Belgium
3rd Worcestershire Regiment	42	Ypres, Belgium
2nd East Lancashire Regiment	44	Neuve Chapelle, France
2nd Border Regiment	20	Neuve Chapelle, France
2nd Northamptonshire Regiment	40	Neuve Chapelle, France
2nd East Kent (Buffs) Regiment	36	Ypres, Belgium
5th Royal Fusiliers	24	Kemmel, Belgium
1st Highland Light Infantry	29	Neuve Chapelle, France
2nd Duke of Cornwall's Light Infantry	23	Ypres, Belgium
Princess Patricia's Canadian Light Infantry	20	Ypres Belgium
2nd Royal Scots	30	Ypres, Belgium
Royal Engineers	21	Festubert, France
2nd Royal Scots	21	Ypres, Belgium

1915 – LIST OF FALLEN OLD CHELTONIANS

	Died (1915)	**Name**	**Rank**
135	5 April	Lanyon WM	Captain
136	6 April	Gilliatt RHC	Captain
137	6 April	Ferris SBC	2nd Lieutenant
138	11 April	Atlay HW	Major
139	13 April	Chadwick FJ	Captain
140	14 April	Hind ACS	Captain
141	19 April	Clayton WJ	Sergeant
142	23 April	Aikenhead R	Private
143	23 April	Howe GFT	Private
144	24 April	Peel CM	2nd Lieutenant
145	25 April	Dunlop GM	Captain
146	25 April	Frankland THC	Major
147	25 April	Jollie FOH	Captain
148	25 April	Payne JO	Lieutenant
149	25 April	Pownall GH	Lt Commander
150	25 April	Macleod AR	Lieutenant
151	26 April	Banks P d'A	Captain
152	28 April	Geddes AD	Colonel
153	28 April	Shubrick RB	Captain
154	28 April	Wythes CA	Captain
155	30 April	Allen RAS	Captain
156	1 May	Webb EM	Lieutenant
157	2 May	Smith EP	Colonel
158	2 May	Reed HWT	2nd Lieutenant
159	3 May	Markham-Rose K	Lieutenant
160	3 May	Dickinson GB	Lieutenant
161	6 May	MacFadyen ND	2nd Lieutenant
162	7 May	Gard'ner BGC	2nd Lieutenant
163	7 May	Hart AC	Captain
164	7 May	Sim BV	Captain
165	7 May	Waterhouse R	Captain
166	8 May	Cochrane DJ	Captain
167	8 May	Hodson HB	Private
168	8 May	Isherwood FEB	Lt Colonel
169	8 May	Rawlinson LH	Lieutenant
170	8 May	Sorby CMC	2nd Lieutenant
171	9 May	Campbell IP	2nd Lieutenant
172	9 May	Dick JC	Captain
173	9 May	Finke RF	Captain

1915 – LIST OF FALLEN OLD CHELTONIANS

Unit	Age	Place
5th Royal Irish Rifles	34	Flerbaix, France
1st Connaught Rangers	30	Neuve Chapelle, France
1st (Reserve) Cavalry Regiment	26	Tidworth, UK
CO 54th Battery, RFA	42	Ypres, Belgium
104th Wellesley Rifles IA	31	Mesopotamia
110th Mahratta Light Infantry IA	30	Mesopotamia
9th London Regiment	30	Ypres, Belgium
48th Canadian Highlanders	23	Ypres, Belgium
16th (Manitoba) Canadian Scots	29	Ypres, Belgium
2nd Royal Dublin Fusiliers	26	Ypres, Belgium
1st Royal Dublin Fusiliers	26	Gallipoli
1st Royal Dublin Fusiliers	35	Gallipoli
2nd East Surrey Regiment	25	Ypres, Belgium
1st Royal Warwickshire Regiment	31	Ypres, Belgium
HMS *Egmont*, Assistant Beach Master	31	Gallipoli
Y Battery, RHA	23	Gallipoli
57th Wilde's Rifles, IA	29	Ypres, Belgium
CO 2nd East Kent (Buffs) Regiment	48	Ypres, Belgium
1st Royal Inniskilling Fusiliers	24	Gallipoli
4th Worcestershire Regiment	29	Gallipoli
5th (Saskatchewan) Canadian Infantry	35	Boulogne, France
2nd King's Own Yorkshire Light Infantry	36	Boulogne, France
CO 17th Brigade, Royal Field Artillery	51	Gallipoli
2nd Monmouthshire Regiment	30	Ypres, Belgium
att West African Frontier Force	25	Cameroons, Africa
1st East Lancashire Regiment	29	Ypres, Belgium
2nd Cameron Highlanders	20	Ypres, Belgium
att 171st Tunneling Company RE	31	Le Treport, France
2nd Northumberland Fusiliers	33	Ypres, Belgium
4th Middlesex Regiment	26	Ypres, Belgium
1/7th Lancashire Fusiliers	25	Gallipoli
65th Battery, Royal Field Artillery	27	Ypres, Belgium
Princess Patricia's Canadian Light Infantry	23	Ypres, Belgium
CO, 1st York & Lancaster Regiment	45	Ypres, Belgium
2nd Royal Lancaster Regiment	26	Ypres, Belgium
1/3rd Monmouthshire Regiment	20	Ypres, Belgium
1st Cameron Highlanders	18	Festubert, France
2nd Royal Munster Fusiliers	37	Festubert, France
2nd Royal Sussex Regiment	37	Festubert, France

1915 – LIST OF FALLEN OLD CHELTONIANS

	Died (1915)	**Name**	**Rank**
174	9 May	Littledale AC	Major
175	9 May	Lousada BC	Lieutenant
176	9 May	Pottinger ROB	2nd Lieutenant
177	10 May	Attree FWWT	Captain
178	10 May	Riordan H de B	Captain
179	10 May	Woodiwiss IN	Captain
180	12 May	Forbes NE	2nd Lieutenant
181	13 May	Bond FHB	2nd Lieutenant
182	13 May	Brooks TE	2nd Lieutenant
183	13 May	Browne CNF	2nd Lieutenant
184	16 May	Cohen GH	Lieutenant
185	16 May	Dashwood LA	Lieutenant
186	16 May	Humphreys DF	2nd Lieutenant
187	16 May	McCormick JG	2nd Lieutenant
188	16 May	Reid FH	Captain
189	16 May	Robinson DGM	Lieutenant
190	17 May	Hamilton JW	Sapper
191	17 May	Kenworthy D	Captain
192	18 May	Bottomley HR	Lt Colonel
193	18 May	Kuhn AE	Lieutenant
194	19 May	Biscoe F	Captain
195	24 May	Bradley S	Lieutenant
196	24 May	Gresson JE	2nd Lieutenant
197	24 May	MacDonnell HC	Captain
198	25 May	Sykes GW	2nd Lieutenant
199	25 May	Vaughn JM	2nd Lieutenant
200	26 May	Marsden E	Captain
201	27 May	Crawford E	2nd Lieutenant
202	28 May	Floyd HM	Captain
203	28 May	Lowndes EW	Corporal
204	28 May	Raymond EWH	Lieutenant
205	2 June	Creed CO	2nd Lieutenant
206	2 June	Forbes-Semphill RA	Lieutenant
207	4 June	Grogan JC	Lieutenant
208	4 June	Lowry WAH	2nd Lieutenant
209	4 June	Lowther TB	Lieutenant
210	4 June	Brooke-Taylor AC	Lieutenant
211	5 June	Fairbairn AH	2nd Lieutenant
212	9 June	Blomfield CGM	Major

1915 – LIST OF FALLEN OLD CHELTONIANS

Unit	Age	Place
19th Battery, Royal Field Artillery	35	Neuve Chapelle, France
1st York & Lancaster Regiment	26	Ypres, Belgium
2nd Royal Munster Fusiliers	19	Festubert, France
1st Suffolk Regiment	26	Ypres, Belgium
2nd East Surrey Regiment	27	Ypres, Belgium
No 3 Sqn RFC	18	Ypres, Belgium
20th Field Battery, RFA	20	Ypres, Belgium
122nd Battery, RFA	21	Ypres, Belgium
9th Leicestershire Yeomanry	29	Ypres, Belgium
1st Royal Dragoon Guards	20	Ypres, Belgium
5th Kings Liverpool Regiment	37	Festubert, France
2nd Oxford & Bucks Light Infantry	27	Festubert, France
2nd Royal West Surrey Regiment	24	Festubert, France
2nd Worcestershire Regiment	21	Festubert, France
57th Siege Battery, RGA	32	Festubert, France
att 1st South Staffordshire Regiment	20	Festibert, France
38th Field Company, RE	26	Netley, UK
att 1st Somerset Light Infantry	27	Ypres, Belgium
CO, 2nd Royal West Surrey Regiment	44	Festubert, France
2nd Bedfordshire Regiment	20	Festubert, France
2nd Worcestershire Regiment	20	Festubert, France
2nd Suffolk Regiment	23	Ypres, Belgium
att 2nd Cheshire Regiment	34	Ypres, Belgium
att No 5 Squadron, RFC	31	Hazebrouck, France
1/7th West Yorkshire Regiment	18	Flerbaix, France
3rd Royal Fusiliers	18	Ypres, Belgium
64th Pioneers, IA	34	Burma
att 2nd Royal Irish Regiment	34	Wimereux, France
1st Royal Dublin Fusiliers	25	Gallipoli
3rd Australian Light Horse	30	Gallipoli
1st Royal Inniskilling Fusiliers	24	London (Gallipoli)
2nd Grenadier Guards	35	Rouen, France
1/5th Gordon Highlanders	45	Festubert, France
1st King's Own Scottish Borderers	25	Gallipoli
att 14th Sikhs, IA	25	Gallipoli
1st Lancashire Fusiliers	25	Gallipoli
6th Manchester Regiment	27	Gallipoli
2nd Royal Irish Regiment	21	Ostnieukirche, Germany
1st Royal Warwickshire Regiment	36	Ypres, Belgium

1915 – LIST OF FALLEN OLD CHELTONIANS

	Died (1915)	**Name**	**Rank**
213	9 June	Silk NG	Lieutenant
214	15 June	Walker-Coren E	2nd Lieutenant
215	15 June	Woodham CB	Captain
216	16 June	Thomas-O'Donel G O'DF	Captain
217	26 June	Gore ACE StG	Captain
218	28 June	Ayrton FJ	Captain
219	28 June	Gudgeon FG	Captain
220	28 June	Grantham HF	2nd Lieutenant
221	28 June	Bramwell CG	Captain
222	28 June	Clerk RV	Captain
223	28 June	Findlay JT	Lieutenant
224	2 July	Armstrong GP	Lieutenant
225	9 July	Monkton MH	2nd Lieutenant
226	12 July	Maxwell J	2nd Lieutenant
227	17 July	Jowitt TL	Major
228	19 July	Persse CdeBG	2nd Lieutenant
229	23 July	Wallis DB	2nd Lieutenant
230	24 July	Fisher CEH	2nd Lieutenant
231	28 July	Oldham LWS	Major
232	28 July	Onslow BW	Lieutenant
233	7 August	Frankland RCC	Captain
234	7 August	Taylor HM	Major
235	8 August	Willoughby EC	Captain
236	10 August	Beadon BHE	Captain
237	10 August	Carnegy RL	Major
238	10 August	Cunningham CA	Captain
239	11 August	Walter WF	Major
240	12 August	Blagrove RC	Lieutenant
241	12 August	Buckley EM	2nd Lieutenant
242	12 August	Proctor-Beauchamp MBG	2nd Lieutenant
243	13 August	Marten HM	2nd Lieutenant
244	13 August	Maude CCW	2nd Lieutenant
245	15 August	Vanrenen AS	Lt Colonel
246	17 August	Welstead HM	Lt Colonel
247	21 August	Coxwell-Rogers RH	Lieutenant
248	21 August	Cummins HJ	Lieutenant
249	22 August	Leslie RFWF	Major
250	22 August	Roberts A	Major
251	26 August	Goodeve L	Major

1915 – LIST OF FALLEN OLD CHELTONIANS

Unit	Age	Place
2nd South Wales Borderers	20	Gallipoli
38th Brigade, Royal Field Artillery	22	Ypres, Belgium
1st Duke of Cornwall's Light Infantry	40	Ypres, Belgium
Adjutant, 4th Royal Fusiliers	30	Ypres, Belgium
att 1/9th Gurkha Rifles	29	Festubert, France
att 2nd Royal Fusiliers	26	Gallipoli
att 2nd Royal Fusiliers	24	Gallipoli
1st Essex Regiment	20	Gallipoli
Adjutant, 1/8th Cameronians	35	Gallipoli
att 1/7th Cameronians	31	Gallipoli
1/8th Cameronians	24	Gallipoli
34th Sikhs Engineers	24	Estaires, France
att No 8 Squadron, RFC	24	Ypres, Belgium
2nd Royal Scots Fusiliers	26	Gallipoli
5th Highland Light Infantry	46	Gallipoli
att 1st Irish Guards	40	Netley, UK
att 2nd Royal Munster Fusiliers	24	Chocques, France
15th Field Company, RE	19	Sailly-sur-Lys, France
63rd Field Company, RE	45	Bethune, France
11th Lancers, IA	22	Gallipoli
att 1/8th Lancashire Fusiliers	38	Gallipoli
6th Royal Irish Fusiliers	45	Gallipoli
7th Gloucestershire Regiment	34	Gallipoli
1/7th Royal Welch Fusiliers	27	Gallipoli
6th Royal Lancaster Regiment	48	Ypres, Belgium
6th Border Regiment	25	Gallipoli
General Staff	52	Gallipoli
Adjutant, Duke of Cornwall's Light Infantry	24	Ypres, Belgium
1/7th Royal Welch Fusiliers	28	Gallipoli
1/5th Norfolk Regiment	22	Gallipoli
att 2nd Manchester Regiment	20	Mericourt, France
9th Australian Light Horse	39	Gallipoli
CO, 5th Royal Inniskilling Fusiliers	52	Gallipoli
CO, 9th Lancashire Fusiliers	55	Gallipoli
Royal Gloucestershire Hussars	31	Gallipoli
5th Gurkha Rifles, IA	26	Gallipoli
CO, 5th Dorsetshire Regiment	46	Gallipoli
6th Yorkshire Regiment	46	(Malta) Gallipoli
att 6th Royal Scots Fusiliers	33	Vermelles, France

1915 – LIST OF FALLEN OLD CHELTONIANS

	Died (1915)	**Name**	**Rank**
252	28 August	Thomas CE	Lt Colonel
253	31 August	Drysdale HD	Lieutenant
254	17 September	Cooper SG	2nd Lieutenant
255	25 September	Adams EC	2nd Lieutenant
256	25 September	Caruth JG	2nd Lieutenant
257	25 September	Forbes FR	Major
258	25 September	Macrae FL	2nd Lieutenant
259	25 September	Moss EH	Captain
260	25 September	Sweet-Escott LW	Lieutenant
261	25 September	Tindall RF	2nd Lieutenant
262	25 September	Blood B	Captain
263	26 September	Cardew EB	Captain
264	26 September	Daubeney GHJ	Lieutenant
265	26 September	Fairtlough FH	Colonel
266	26 September	Meire WHG	2nd Lieutenant
267	27 September	Waddell JD	Captain
268	27 September	Harvey KW	Lieutenant
269	27 September	Noyes RE	Major
270	27 September	Smith PL	2nd Lieutenant
271	28 September	Gransmore R	Captain
272	30 September	Shaw (Schwabe) MS	Lieutenant
273	2 October	Dickinson RS	Captain
274	2 October	Rimington ECW	2nd Lieutenant
275	3 October	Grant H de B	Captain
276	8 October	Lloyd FCA	Lieutenant
277	13 October	Cobbold CA	Captain
278	13 October	Fleming JH	Captain
279	13 October	Morgan WD	2nd Lieutenant
280	13 October	Thompson RWHEDF	2nd Lieutenant
281	13 October	Wood GD	Lieutenant
282	14 October	Widowfield G	2nd Lieutenant
283	14 October	Woodhouse GS	2nd Lieutenant
284	15 October	Rolph CC	Captain
285	19 October	Stotherd SB	Major
286	21 October	Lockley REH	Major
287	21 October	Shewell PG	Major
288	1 November	Hattersley-Smith GA	Lieutenant
289	15 November	Bligh FA	Major
290	22 November	Mortimore OJ	Captain

1915 – LIST OF FALLEN OLD CHELTONIANS

Unit	Age	Place
CO, NZ Mounted Ambulance Corps	51	Gallipoli
26th Punjabis IA, att Royal Scots	27	La Bassée, France
1st Royal Warwickshire Regiment	32	Acheux, France
1/20th London Regiment	19	Loos, France
att 7th Royal Irish Rifles	18	Ypres, Belgium
95th Field Company, RE	25	Loos, France
8th Seaforth Highlanders	34	Loos, France
10th Gloucestershire Regiment	37	Loos, France
5th Oxford and Bucks Light Infantry	21	Ypres, Belgium
att 2nd Lincolnshire Regiment	25	Armentières, France
att Home Defence Squadron	33	Hounslow, UK
7th Field Company, RE	32	Loos, France
att 2nd Worcestershire Regiment	28	Vermelles, France
CO, 8th Royal West Surrey Regiment	54	Loos, France
1/9th Norfolk Regiment	25	Loos, France
12th Royal Fusiliers	43	Loos, France
19th Anti-Aircraft Section, RFA	24	Ypres, Belgium
10th Yorkshire Regiment	41	Loos, France
10th York and Lancaster Regiment	20	Loos, France
3rd Middlesex Regiment	25	Loos, France
12th Highland Light Infantry	43	Loos, France
1/16th London Regiment	24	Ypres, Belgium
2nd Cheshire Regiment	19	Loos, France
'A' Battery, 65th Brigade, RFA	30	Loos, France
att 12th Highland Light Infantry	31	Le Touquet, France
7th Suffolk Regiment	44	Loos, France
1/5th North Staffordshire Regiment	37	Loos, france
95th Field Company, RE	23	Loos, France
10th Gordon Highlanders	26	Loos, France
7th Suffolk Regiment	24	Loos, France
1st Monmouthshire Regiment	38	Lillers, France
'D' Battery, 64th Brigade, RFA	27	Loos, France
2nd Leicestershire Regiment	27	Loos, France
7th Suffolk Regiment	53	Bethune, France
att West African Frontier Force	37	Crowthorne, UK
Military Secretary to India Office	51	Barnes, UK
HMS *Pegasus*	26	Devonport, UK
'B' Battery, 154th Brigade RA	54	Oakhampton, UK
att 2nd Dorsetshire Regiment	37	(Kut) Mesopotamia

1915 – LIST OF FALLEN OLD CHELTONIANS

	Died (1915)	**Name**	**Rank**
291	26 November	Townsend GJ	Lieutenant
292	26 November	Balders AW	Captain
293	28 November	Shaw RP	Captain
294	7 December	Turner HS	Captain
295	8 December	Lewin FH	Captain
296	13 December	Edwards C o'R	Captain
297	25 December	Birch-Reynardson EV	2nd Lieutenant
298	30 December	Blest M	Captain
299	30 December	Lee CS	2nd Lieutenant
300	30 December	Lodwick JT	Captain
301	30 December	Swiney ERR	Colonel

1915 – LIST OF FALLEN OLD CHELTONIANS

Unit	Age	Place
66th Punjabis, IA	26	(Kut) Mesopotamia
att 1st Nigeria Regiment (WAFF)	30	Cameroon, Africa
att 2nd Royal Fusiliers	28	Gallipoli
46th Punjabis, IA	30	Rawalpindi, India
3rd Connaught Rangers	38	Kinsale, Ireland
57th Field Company, RE	33	Ypres, Belgium
att 1st East Surrey Regiment	21	Mericourt, France
8th Middlesex Regiment	24	Esher, UK
126th Field Company, RE	19	Armentières, France
2/3rd Gurkha Rifles	33	SS Persia, Crete
CO, 39th Garhwal Rifles	52	SS Persia, Crete

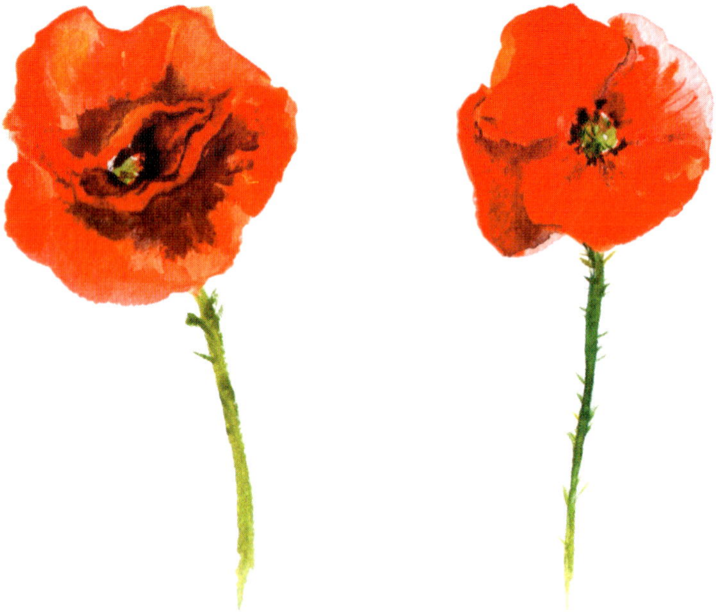

ACTS THREE

1916 – THE YEAR OF ENDLESS SHADOW

Despite the unrelenting and irresistible pressure from the French High Command on its military partners, expressly Britain, to expel the invader from French and Belgian territory, the failures of 1915 pitiably emphasised the vulnerabilities of a doctrine transfixed on the need for offensive action. Quite simply, the attacker had to advance across the detritus-strewn devastation of No Man's Land, exposed to a firestorm from well dug-in machine guns and cleverly concealed field artillery batteries. The advantage favoured the entrenched defenders over their advancing and vulnerable attackers by a ratio of nearly 2:1. During the previous autumn fighting in Artois, for example, the British and French armies lost over 98,000 killed and wounded attempting a breakthrough, compared to 56,000 German casualties defending their lines.[134] Even during those fleetingly rare occasions when advance through the German line was glimpsed, such as at the start of the Neuve Chapelle action, the ability to exploit success simply evaporated. With little change in approach, it was then hardly surprising that the casualty lists from the Western Front were ever-increasing; the same applied to the nugatory effort in Gallipoli. Lessons, even if identified, were just not being learned, and any sign of progress stalled as German defences became deeper and more strongly integrated. A different approach was needed. When Sir Douglas Haig replaced Sir John French as commander-in-chief on 19th December 1915, the Allied commanders agreed that the way to defeat Germany was to attack in concert, with simultaneous assaults on all fronts during 1916. The priority was quite crudely to pin down German reserves and kill Germans in sufficient numbers to make their defences untenable in any subsequent wave of attacks. Once this critical mass had been overcome, a breakthrough could then be achieved. The disastrous consequence of this rationale resulted in a degeneration in the fighting which slowly transformed the war to one of attrition where supremacy in the numbers of soldiers, the output of the munitions industries, the morale of the civil population and workforce, and the strength of the economy held sway and would become the defining factors. Such a war of attrition on all sides, but especially for the BEF on the Western Front, would mark 1916 indelibly in the British psyche with an endless shadow perpetually encapsulated in a single tragic epithet – 'The Somme'.

Evidence of the training focused on clearing enemy trenches and killing their occupants is reflected in the letters sent home by Ernest Taylor, fighting with the 3rd Canadian Mounted Rifles:

---

[134] Official German figures from the *Reichsarchiv: The Operations of 1915: The Events in the West in the Spring and Summer, in the East in the Spring up to the End of the Year,* Mittler, Berlin, 2012 [1932], pages 93-96.

1916 – THE YEAR OF ENDLESS SHADOW

My dearest Mother,

I have an interesting letter from Olive to thank for which arrived three or four days ago. Congratulations to her on passing her two exams. I should like to see her in uniform. I was glad to see the enclosures from Madge and Mrs. Barwick. It is a pity Doll and Madge have to work so hard for no remuneration, the labourer is worthy of his hire, and they deserve it just as the soldier who is fighting for his country. We finished the trenches we have been working on a few days ago. They are complete with barbed wire entanglements, listening posts, dug-outs and everything. In consequence our work has been a bit more varied and rational lately. This morning a general and his staff came along to see us bomb the trench out in approved style. Of course, only a small amount of explosive is used in the bombs on these occasions so as not to damage the trench. Two bomb squads of eleven each, comprising bayonet men, snipers, throwers and carriers go up the trench in single file, followed by a work party carrying sand bags, spades, barbed wire and spare bombs. As each section of the trench is thoroughly bombed out the word is passed along to advance, and when the next danger point is reached you all halt until that is cleaned up of Germans. Every dug-out and side trench has to be bombed, in case the enemy should hide there and attack the party in the rear. When it is considered we have gone far enough in advance of our attacking force, the word is passed back for the work party to come up at the double, and the trench is blocked up with sand bags, wire entanglements put up and machine gun and store bombs put ready at the barricade to stop a counter attack. Of course, the big bugs were above ground watching our progress up the trench, and all went well. This afternoon we threw live stuff, about 50 pounds worth of it. I threw eight myself, and they are worth about five bob each; the time went quite quickly. The weekly parcel came last night and gave the accustomed pleasure. The cake was a picture, quite an echo of Christmas, and it tasted as good as it looked. Tell Olive the peppermint creams were very good. I had supper with Bill in town on Sunday and gave him your letter which he was very pleased with. I walked in again tonight with Jack. We went to the picture show after supper, and it was quite good. One of the films was "She stoops to conquer" played by a good company. The room was packed with soldiers representing dozens of different regiments, English, Scotch, and Canadians, and to hear them laugh at the antics of Charlie Chaplin you wouldn't think they worried much about meeting the Germans or going in the trenches. Well, dearest Mother, I am expecting lights out to go any minute, so I had better stop.

Fondest love to all
Your loving son
Ernest[135]

---

[135] Cheltenham College Archives. Personal letters of Ernest Taylor, letter, dated 23rd January 1916 from France.

To bring the concerted attacks into effect required the BEF to replace the casualties of the preceding 12 months and to prepare for these coming offences. However, as numbers of volunteers had significantly reduced, the British government passed the Military Service Act in January 1916, with conscription coming into force in March. Men aged between 18 and 41 became liable for military duty in the army and for service at the Front.[136]

However, making adjustments on the Western Front was not the sole preserve of the Allies. As 1916 dawned, General Erich von Falkenhayn, the Chief of the German General Staff, was finalising his plans to 'bleed France white' in terms of both manpower and materiel in the killing fields around Verdun; an approach which the German later termed *Materialschlacht*.[137] This major offensive started at dawn on 21st February with a ferocious nine-hour bombardment that lashed eight miles of the French front line. The French immediately began to supply reinforcements into the area to avoid losing this 'sacred' city – suffering the very attrition the Germans hoped for in the process. The fighting at Verdun would last until December and the associated attrition to both sides would account for some 714,000 men. The French needed help, and quickly: Verdun would have an associated and devastating impact on Britain, on the BEF and also on the Old Cheltonians that would gather on the Somme in increasing numbers with the New Army battalions. The events of 1916 would cast an enduring shadow over Britain and the Commonwealth nations and deliver a lasting legacy that would be indelibly etched into their national histories.

Heartaches

One essential pillar of Britain's wartime strategy was the grey-steeled grip of the Royal Navy's blockade of the German North Sea and Baltic ports. Twelve months had passed since Edward Disney narrowly missed the hapless demise of HMS *Formidable* with his timely posting to the light cruiser HMS *Arethusa*. Having been promoted to lieutenant commander on 2nd July 1915, he was now a senior and respected member of the wardroom.[138] Without exception, he was highly thought of, Captain Allenby his previous commander described him as 'a most promising officer in all ways, zealous, and should make a very efficient officer'.[139]

On the evening of 4th January *Arethusa* was battling storm force weather in the North Sea that made conditions on deck

Edward Disney

---

[136] The First Military Service Act in January 1916 did not apply to married men, widowers with children, men in reserved occupation, clergymen, or those serving in the Royal Navy. A second Act was passed in May 1916 removing the protection from service for married men. A third Act was passed in 1918 extending the upper age limit to 51 years.
[137] For details about German operational intent at Verdun, see G Sheffield, *The Somme*, Cassell, London (2003), pages 13-15.
[138] *The London Gazette*, 2nd July 1915, page 6439.
[139] The National Archives, ADM 196/50/250 and ADM 196/143/807, Personal Records of Lieutenant Commander EO Disney RN.

exceptionally perilous. Edward was lost overboard and, given the dark and turbulent seas, was never found; the ensuing Court of Enquiry confirmed that his death was accidental.[140] He was the first of 127 Old Cheltonians to be killed in 1916. George and Cora Disney were still grieving for their only son a year later when they posted the following message in the Times on the anniversary of his death:

> In Memoriam. Disney – In loving memory of Lieutenant Commander Edward Ogle Disney R.N. H.M.S. Arethusa, lost overboard at sea on active service, 4th January 1916.[141]

Sadly, this was not the end to the family anguish. Exactly a year later, on the very date of Edward's death, his father George died after a short illness.

> Deaths: Disney. On the 4th January at 23 Nottingham Place W1 after a short illness, George William Disney, formerly of Behar and Orissa. Funeral at Highgate Cemetery on Monday at 1.30 p.m.[142]

Cora would now have to face the future without the two men in her family.

There were other similar and equally heart-rending episodes. James Landale (Day Boy, 1899) was the elder son of Deputy Surgeon General James, a retired army doctor, and Harriette Rosa Landale, whose family home was at 'Dunholm', The Park, Cheltenham. Deciding to emulate his father's army career, James entered the Royal Military College immediately after leaving school, gaining a commission as a second lieutenant with the Royal Scots Fusiliers in March 1901. Having served in the South African War, receiving the Queen's Medal and five clasps, he transferred to the Indian Army on 30th September 1905. By 1915, he was a major in the 2nd Rajput Light Infantry fighting with the Indian Expeditionary Force in Mesopotamia. He was mortally wounded during the attack on the Dujailah Redoubt at El Singh, near Kut, on 8th March 1916.[143] However, the previous evening, his 79-year-old father had dined out in Cheltenham and was walking home in the dark when he stumbled over an obstruction on the pavement and fell. Being assisted home, he appeared not to have been seriously injured, but he passed away in his sleep that night, almost at the minute as young James died from his wounds.[144]

Rupert Meyricke (Day Boy, 1894) was brother to elder twins Edward and Robert; all entering College together in September 1887 (although Rupert was starting at the College's

---

[140] A month later, HMS Arethusa struck a mine off Felixstowe on 11th February 1916, and drifted onto a shoal while under tow and broke her back.
[141] *The Times*, January 4th 1917.
[142] *The Times*, January 5th 1918.
[143] James had been in command of the regiment since its arrival in Mesopotamia and the manner with which it fought was largely attributed by his brigade commander to James' leadership and fine example. Apparently, he had been wounded in the thigh but took no notice, going on until mortally wounded some time later.
[144] See *The British Medical Journal*, Obituaries (Medico-legal), 25th March 1916, page 470.

junior school). All three were day boys, making their way to school each day from the family home at Nubie House on Lansdown Road.[145]

From College the three boys gained entry to the Royal Military Academy at Woolwich directly from College, the twins becoming officers in the Royal Engineers and Rupert being commissioned as a second lieutenant in the Royal Field Artillery on 1st September 1897.[146] While Edward was attached to the Egyptian Army Robert and Rupert saw active service during the campaign in South Africa. Rupert received the Queen's Medal with three clasps, but unfortunately Robert contracted enteric fever and died in Pietermaritzberg in 1900. Edward died at Aldershot some three years later from injuries sustained when thrown from his horse during a steeplechase race. The loss of the twins left Rupert as the sole surviving son alongside his two sisters, Evelyn and Mabel, to whom he arranged to leave his estate in the event of his death. After serving in India, where Rupert contracted malaria with an associated epileptic episode, he returned to England. After war was declared, he was attached to the Mediterranean Expeditionary Force and embarked for Gallipoli, sailing from Devonport on 1st July 1915. He landed on the Peninsula at Suvla Bay on 9th August 1915 to serve with the 58th Field Artillery. By mid-November Rupert was quite unwell, suffering not only from jaundice but also from a leg ulcer which disabled walking. During his evacuation to Malta, the medical officers on board the Hospital Ship *Kildonan Castle* also noticed that he was showing 'slight undefined nervous symptoms and uncontrollable muscular spasms'.[147] Rupert died on 25th January 1916 at the Bighi Royal Naval Hospital in Malta and was buried on the island, his family being informed that his death was due to illness. Accordingly, on the wall of the Memorial Chapel in St Stephen's Church in Cheltenham, his family recorded his death: 'Major Rupert J Meyricke R H A, who died of blood poisoning in Malta in 1916'. However, this was not the cause of his death, and, given the prevailing criminality in law concerning suicide, one might consider such misrepresentation of the facts as a deliberate attempt to preserve the good reputation of both Rupert and his family. His death in Malta was in fact due to a self-inflicted revolver bullet wound to the head, and, according to the Board of Enquiry findings, caused 'whilst in a state of temporary insanity'. He had shot himself whilst sitting on a garden seat overlooking the Grand Harbour between 9.30 and 10.10am on the morning that he was due to be invalided back to England aboard the Hospital Ship *Soudan*, a ship at anchor and being readied for sailing and one which he could clearly see from the hospital. Despite his orders to embark for England, he preferred to stay in Malta to recover and then return to duty with his battery rather than be repatriated simply because of a troublesome ulcer which, as he might have viewed it, could be treated locally. It appears that he was not aware of his weakening health and delicate mental state. Almost certainly, Rupert was suffering from acute psychological trauma, intensified perhaps

Rupert Meyricke

---

[145] Nubie House and Elm Lodge were both later demolished to make room for Regents Court.
[146] *The London Gazette*, 31st August 1897, page 4876.
[147] National Archives, WO 374/47518, Personal and Medical Records of Major RJC Meyricke.

Last Will and Testament

by a strong sense of loyalty and devotion to his comrades and a sense of guilt that he was going back to 'Blighty' while his fellow comrades faced further danger at the Front. He was to return home without even any obvious war wound to qualify his medical evacuation. Neither he, nor the medical or governmental authorities considered 'shell-shock' a war wound, a condition we now regard very seriously as a silent, invisible mental injury that, if left untreated, can be deadly. The criminality associated with suicide has long since been removed. Thankfully, over the last century attitudes, both to suicide and combat stress, have significantly changed.[148] Given the loss of Rupert's twin brothers a decade before, the family must have

---

[148] The study of psychological trauma associated with combat operations has been the subject of considerable modern research following the campaigns in the Falklands, Iraq, and most recently, Afghanistan. Post-Traumatic Stress Disorder (PTSD) is a subject that is better understood and more sympathetically considered than was the case a century ago. Dr JHA Summerfield, a consultant psychiatrist, offers this useful though brief insight to provide context to the narrative: 'PTSD is a mental illness occurring after very stressful, frightening or distressing events. It can occur after any trauma but typically after an event where the individual feels their life is threatened or witnesses other people dying or injured. The disorder can develop immediately after the experience or later, even starting after some years have passed. It is surprisingly common (affecting about 1 in every 3 people who have a traumatic experience) but it is unclear exactly why some people develop the condition while others in the same scenario do not. Someone suffering from PTSD may experience flashbacks and nightmares (re-living the event), anxiety, avoidance, emotional numbing, hypervigilance (being jumpy and on edge), as well as irritability, insomnia, isolation, and feelings of depression.

The link between exposure to military combat and mental illness gained more public recognition during the 20th century. In the First World War, "shell shock" was often considered a form of weakness, lack of moral fibre or even cowardice. Although some did receive treatment (such as Siegfried Sassoon and Wilfred Owen at Craiglockhart Hospital in Edinburgh), others were tried and even executed when displaying these symptoms. It was not until the 1970s after the Vietnam War, when many U.S. military veterans returned with symptoms of PTSD, that the condition was formerly recognised as a psychiatric diagnosis in the standard international classifications of mental disorders.

There are now well-established, evidence-based, psychological and physical treatments for PTSD. These include forms of psychotherapy (talking therapies) such as Cognitive Behavioural Therapy (CBT) and EMDR (Eye Movement Desensitisation & Reprocessing) and medications, particularly antidepressants. In the UK these treatments can be accessed through the National Health Service (NHS) as well as through military veterans' organisations and charities such as Combat Stress.
Some regions have specialist Traumatic Stress Clinics provided by the NHS including services specifically for military veterans such as the Veterans Mental Health Transition, Intervention and Liaison (TIL) Service in London.'

been devastated by the news of his death, a terrible event made all the worse as his personal effects were lost in transit and could not therefore be sent to his family. His two sisters inherited his estate amounting to £2,098.

The death of Rupert was indeed a tragic case, but he had served his country bravely and faithfully and is respected and not forgotten.

There was heartache too on the Western Front. Douglas Reynolds had been at College briefly with Rupert before they both became artillery officers. As previously recorded, Douglas had gallantly won the Victoria Cross at Le Cateau in 1914. While recovering in England from wounds he had subsequently received he married Doris Petersen, and a year later at the end of January 1916, their only child, Douglas William Sinclair Petersen (called 'Peter' to differentiate from his father) was born.[149] The month before his son's birth, Douglas was back at the Front and was concussed by a gas shell. However, as he appeared to be recovering quickly from its effects, he decided to stay with his battery. Invidiously, the first symptoms of septicaemia began to appear and he was immediately evacuated to No 1 Red Cross Hospital (Duchess of Westminster's Hospital) at Le Touquet, where he died on 23rd February 1916. He never got to meet his son Peter. By sad coincidence, Peter was killed in action 24 years later on 23rd May 1940 serving with the Irish Guards near Boulogne and was buried just 18 miles from his own father's grave at Etaples.

In the opening months of the year, two Old Cheltonians were killed while commanding their battalions. Jasper Radcliffe (Leconfield, 1884) was a regular army officer in the Devonshire Regiment enjoying a rewarding military career. In 1893, Jasper had married Emily Maude Chatterton-Orpen and together resided at 69 Park Mansions, Knightsbridge, London when service commitments allowed. The following year they had their only child, a son, Dering John Jasper Radcliffe, who later attended Wellington College, conveniently placed between the family's home in London and the army's establishments at Aldershot and Sandhurst. Dering subsequently followed his father into the army, firstly in his father's regiment, before transferring into the Grenadier Guards. Meanwhile, Jasper's army career progressed, seeing action during the South African War and being awarded the Distinguished Service Order for conspicuous service.[150] An experienced major by 1914, Jasper impressed during the opening months of the war and was given command of the 1st Battalion, Dorsetshire Regiment from 30th June to 17th August 1915 as a temporary lieutenant colonel. His promotion became substantive on 23rd November that year, when he took over command of the 10th Battalion, Essex Regiment. On the night of 31st January 1916, during a German attack with strong artillery support on his battalion's stretch of line near Arras, he went into the telephonist's dugout to pass a situation report to his brigade commander when it received a direct hit causing a heavy beam to collapse onto

---

[149] Doris was the daughter of Danish ship owner, William (later Sir William) Petersen of Heron's Ghyll, East Sussex. She married Douglas on 29th March 1915 at Epsom, Surrey.
[150] *The London Gazette*, dated 27th September 1901, and reads: 'Jasper Fitzgerald Radcliffe, Capt., Devonshire Regt. In recognition of services during the operations in South Africa.' The award was presented to him by the King Edward VII on 29th October 1901.

Jasper's head and killing him instantly. His son Dering was killed on 31st October 1917 in a fatal accident during grenade training; he was aged 22. In little over 18 months Emily was yet another to lose all the men in her life to the war.

Claude Campbell (PBH, 1894) only attended College for a term, leaving to become a Royal Navy cadet. However, while undergoing training, he opted for service in the army and following Sandhurst, was commissioned into the Cameron Highlanders in 1899. Like Jasper, he too was awarded the Distinguished Service Order, albeit more recently for 'services in the field' during 1915.[151] Given Claude's operational prowess and reputation for strong leadership, he was given command of the 12th West Yorkshire Regiment from 3rd November 1915 to 12th February 1916. After a short spell of leave, he returned to the Front and was appointed to assume command of his own regiment, the 1st Battalion, Cameron Highlanders, with effect from 11th March. Such an appointment, to command the senior battalion of the regiment into which one is first commissioned, is many a professional soldier's dream. Sadly, for Claude this enduring ambition was snatched from him at the 11th hour as events and priorities elsewhere overtook him. The 1/4th Battalion Seaforth Highlanders, a territorial unit, had landed in France in November 1914, but suffered successive maulings during the fighting of 1915, especially at Aubers Ridge and Loos. Consequently, the battalion had been without any formal senior leadership throughout the winter, with one of the company captains assuming temporary command. For much of February 1916, the battalion spent time in reserve, conducting training, doing fatigues and playing football. Claude took over the battalion on 29th February and, after 10 days of route marching, redeployed from billets in the Amiens area to the front line at Louez, to the north west of Arras. On 10th March, he organised the battalion to take over their allotted portion of the front line, the Lewis gunners and signallers going in first to establish defensive firing points and communications, followed by the four companies – two to the front line and two in support. Except for some sporadic shelling and sniper fire, the front was relatively quiet. On 14th March, after the companies had switched positions the previous night, Claude made his first inspection of the line; the war diary records that:

> Beautiful day and very quiet. Lt Colonel Campbell our new CO was killed this morning by a sniper while observing. He had only been with the Battalion 14 days. He was a grand type of soldier and his fine personality will be missed by all ranks.[152]

The battalion was relieved the following day and went into Brigade Reserve. Claude had certainly made in impact on his men in the fortnight he had been with the Seaforths, and he was buried by them in the Louez military cemetery, just behind the lines.

Every life lost in the Great War was a tragedy and heartbreak to the respective family. While these individual cases hold their own particular poignancy, they by no means

---

[151] *The London Gazette*, dated 29th June 1915.
[152] The National Archives, WO 95/2888/1, War Diary of the 1/4th Battalion, Seaforth Highlanders.

diminish or underestimate the grief and anguish suffered elsewhere on campaign fronts in the other corners of the world as the war ground remorselessly on. The silence between letters from soldiers at the 'Front' would have been stressful enough for their families: when the letters stopped for any extended period the wait and the uncertainty would have been unbearable.

Missing in Action

When soldiers went 'missing in action', their absences were most immediately felt by their comrades. Invariably, considerable efforts were made to establish their safety, or the circumstances of their fate. The disappearance of Noel Blakeway (Leconfield, 1914) was not an unusual case. Noel was educated initially at the Crypt School in Gloucester before coming to College in September 1909. During his final term preparing for matriculation for London University, he applied for a commission in the Special Reserve of Officers on 5th December 1914. With a strong recommendation from Captain APS Newman, commanding the College OTC contingent at the time, Noel was commissioned as a second lieutenant (on probation) just 11 days later.[153] By March 1916, he was a platoon commander in C Company of the 1st Dorsets, and on the 26th undertook a night raid on part of the German line held by 109th Infantry Regiment (part of the 14th Reserve German Army Corps) with the aim of intelligence gathering by bringing back prisoners for interrogation. However, the German trench was largely unoccupied and also filled with barbed wire entanglements to ensnare any attackers, who would then be killed during counter-attacks. The battalion war diary graphically describes the night's events:

> At 12.27am a mine was exploded opposite La Boiselle. This was a pre-arranged signal for a raid to be made on Y sap and the enemy's trenches to the right of it for the purpose of taking prisoners. The raiding party (86 men) led by Lieut Mansel-Playdell, 2Lieut Blakeway and 2Lieut Clarke, all under the direction of Capt Algeo, then went forward in two parties. One party went to the left to enter the front trench of Y sap and the other to the right to enter the front German trench on the right of the Bapaume Road. Both parties managed to get through the gaps already cut for them in the German wire although a considerable amount of loose wire had been put out, and the majority of the men got into the German trenches. Immediately, they came under heavy fire from grenades, bombs, 'oil-cans', artillery, machine guns. The Y sap appears to have been empty, and only one or two Germans were seen running away. One was shot. The bombing was so heavy that when the signal to retire was given at 12.35am as arranged the left party had not got as far as had been anticipated. Our casualties were 2 killed, 14 wounded, and 2 Lieut Blakeway wounded and missing. The latter was seen lying on the German parapet and

[153] *The London Gazette*, 15th December 1914, page 10700, confirmed in rank on 8th June 1915 (page 5519).

though every possible effort was made to remove him, this was found impossible. Parties were at work assisting to get in the wounded until dawn, a task that was rendered extremely difficult and dangerous by German machine-gun fire.[154]

Although Noel was reported as missing believed wounded by his comrades as soon as they had regained the safety of their own trenches, when it was light enough efforts to establish his whereabouts and condition were made. A report from the 14th Brigade records that:

A notice was put up in front of our trenches asking for news of 2/Lieut Blakeway who was missing and known to be wounded. An answering notice was put up by the enemy stating that 2/Lieut Blakeway had died of his wounds.[155]

On the strength of these pieces of information which were reported up the chain of command, telegrams were sent to Noel's parents, George and Florence at home at Tuffley in Gloucestershire. The first announced that Noel was 'missing believed wounded'; a later amendment stated that he was 'missing believed killed'. One can barely imagine the consternation this would have caused to his family. Was he alive or not? Had he by any chance been taken prisoner? Without any concrete evidence, this uncertainty caused the family to endure a lengthy period of suspended torment, as without any firm evidence of his loss a death certificate could not be issued, and they could not seek closure. By 5th December 1916 Noel's fate was still unresolved, so after an exchange of letters between the family and the War Office, witness statements were sought from his comrades that had been with him on that raid. Despite the interval of some eight months, 53 informant reports (all from C Company) were accumulated and described the action. One statement from Sergeant (7015) Webb reported that:

A raiding party of some 90 men were gathered under Lt Blakeway being [in command] C Coy. We had black cap covers and charcoaled our faces and necks. After a good supper, we moved down to Keats Redan at 11.30pm, waiting for the REs to blow a mine which went off but was short, doing no damage, and only caused the enemy artillery to open up a violent fire on us. At this time we were crawling towards their trenches with Mr Blakeway leading. By the light of a star shell we saw him wave to us and call on C Coy to follow him, then saw him disappear into the trench and we never saw him again. We followed but could do nothing for the enemy deluged the trench with his fire, his own troops being withdrawn to the 3rd line. A Coy joined us later on when the fire slackened, but none of us saw this officer. He was a dare devil, always up to some deal with the enemy – taking their iron plates, etc, on the Kaiser's birthday, the enemy put up a

[154] The National Archives, WO 95/2393/1, War Diary 1st Dorset Regiment, March 1916.
[155] The National Archives, WO 339/30750, Personal Record of Second Lieutenant NC Blakeway.

paper in front of their trench – Mr Blakeway went and took it. A fine officer, much respected.[156]

Sometimes, such testaments only added to the uncertainty. While Sergeant Webb's account was close to the war diary record, some of the other witness statements were quite contradictory, which made any circumstantial assessment of Noel's death quite complicated. Other avenues of enquiry were then followed. The War Office would pass the details of each individual case to the diplomatic staff in the Foreign Office, or in the Colonial Office if the individual was fighting with the various imperial contingents, who would then contact their embassies, consulates and legations in the neutral countries seeking support of the investigation.[157] But with the grindingly slow turn of the machineries of the various officialdoms, this process could take many months or even years to complete, often without result.

Unsurprisingly, some anxious families resorted to other more desperate, yet sometimes more expeditious and fruitful means. Mrs Emily Campbell, for example, was living across College Field at No 4 College Lawn when her son Ian Campbell (Boyne House, 1914) was reported missing by telegram on 9th May 1915. Ian had enjoyed a full education at College, being the Racquets Champion (1913-14), and winning the Ladies' Prize in his final year; he was also a corporal in the OTC. After graduating from Sandhurst, he was a platoon commander with the 1st Cameron Highlanders when he went missing in action near Festubert in 1915. After months of no news, Emily placed an advertisement in the Morning Post asking for any news of her missing son. Several weeks later, she received a reply by letter from Lieutenant Erule James Corse-Scott, of the 2nd Battalion, Gurkha Rifles:

> I am sorry to say a party from my regiment buried your son's body the other night. He evidently fell amongst his men, close to the German trenches where we were burying. Two cheque books were all there was to identify it as being your son. Your son is buried with his men where they fell.
>
> With sincerest sympathies.[158]

Though terrible news to receive, at least the uncertainty was finally removed, and Ian was no longer missing. He is commemorated in the Guards Cemetery, at Windy Corner near Cuinchy; he was 18 years of age.

---

[156] The National Archives, WO 339/30750, Personal Record of Lieutenant NC Blakeway.
[157] The neutral countries included Switzerland, The Netherlands, Denmark, Sweden and Norway. Acting as intermediaries, these countries would then engage with their German colleagues, as well as non-governmental organisations such as the Swiss Red Cross, who would scan the lists of prisoner of war intakes and medical records at German Field Hospitals in an effort to shed light on each episode. It was not until 1998 and the release to public scrutiny of the confidential military records held in the National Archives that many of the associated ambiguities were finally resolved.
[158] The National Archives, WO 339/13981, Personal Record of Second Lieutenant IP Campbell.

Personal Effects

Whenever battlefield conditions allowed, the gloomy task that followed every fatality was the collection, package and return of all the individual's personal effects to his family, accompanied by letters of condolence from comrades. For soldiers, this task quite often consisted simply of a box containing the few letters, photographs, and small personal memorabilia that he would have carried in his knapsack. For officers, particularly those in the regular army, it would consist of his officer's valise containing all his possessions that he may have had with him at the front, including his sword (in the opening years of the war), service revolver, binoculars, and other items specific to officers such as a Burberry trench coat. These personal possessions would be carefully packed, often by the officer's manservant or batman and sent home to his next of kin. Charles Cobbold (Cheltondale, 1889), for example, had married Theodora on 12th October 1896 in Toronto, Canada. Though he was killed at Loos in October 1915, she waited patiently at 46, Devonshire Street, Portland Place, London for his personal effects to be returned. At the beginning of January 1916, the package was finally delivered, containing a letter case, a pair of silver sleeve links, a silver match box, a silver cigarette lighter, and a packet of her letters in a waterproof bag. Cases of lost personal effects occurred throughout the war, even in its last months. For example, George Woolstenholme (Southwood, 1914), who left College aged 16 to become a cotton apprentice, gained a commission in the Special Reserve of Officers in 1916. He was killed in action fighting with the 9th Yorkshire Regiment at Beaurevoir in France in the last month of the war. His personal effects included an 18-carat gold signet ring, a pair of cuff links, six regimental buttons and badges, a broken wristwatch, a cigarette case, and four silk handkerchiefs. These two examples are typical of the personal effects of the middle-class officer at war.

Unfortunately, as many of an officer's personal items were valuable and attractive, several cases of petty pilfering were recorded on the personal files of fallen Old Cheltonians; contents, such as family signet rings, being absent from the respective inventory. Even more reprehensible was the theft of items from the mortally wounded at dressing stations and hospitals. Francis West (Day Boy, 1901) had gone up to St John's College, Oxford where he gained a BA (Hons) in 1905. Having then trained as a barrister at law, he also held a Territorial Army commission in the Royal Field Artillery. Established comfortably in civilian life in Bilton near Rugby, his life was complete when he married Agatha Mary on 2nd June 1909 in the Rugby School Chapel, and they started a family, having four daughters, the last two being twins. On 5th August 1914, he was mobilised and by the summer of 1916 he was a temporary lieutenant colonel commanding the 243rd Brigade, Royal Field Artillery. On the 28th September, he was seriously wounded and taken to the Canadian Dressing Station, situated some 500 yards west of Pozières on the road to La Boisselle. He died of his wounds at the dressing station and had his watch and pocket book stolen.

1916 – THE YEAR OF ENDLESS SHADOW

That said, there were also remarkable acts of great generosity and altruism at moments of extreme suffering. Edward MacBryan (Teighmore, 1903) was mortally wounded on the Somme on 2nd July 1916. Sergeant Harry Hunt, a member of his company, had seen a family request for news of Edward in the papers the following week, and wrote to his father nine days later:

Dear Sir,

Please accept my sincere sympathy in your sad loss. I saw your son before he died and made him as comfortable as possible. I am glad to tell you he suffered but little and was real plucky. When I took off his equipment I asked him what I should do with his revolver and he requested me to give it to the Adj of his battalion (as a gift). This Officer was killed. I therefore could not carry out your son's wishes but I saw the present OC and the Adj of 1st SLI and gave them the revolver, holster, and belt and requested them to forward same home and I trust same will reach you. I have in my possession two silk handkerchiefs which I used to bathe his forehead and etc. I will forward these to you at the first opportunity. At present it is impossible. I feel greatly for you, for your son faced the music like a man. I happened to see the Daily Mail of the 8th inst, and that is why I have written you, yours faithfully...[159]

Edward's commanding officer also wrote to the family:

He was a splendid soldier and his company were simply devoted to him: his death has been a terrible blow to it.[160]

For officers in the Indian Army, however, their personal effects tended to be far more extensive, and mirrored their privileged lifestyle back at their home garrisons in India. A fair example is that of Lynton White (Leconfield, 1905). He had died of wounds in September 1914 from the action at Nery during which his school mate Claude Champion de Cressigny (Christowe, 1905) was also killed, both fighting with 2nd Dragoon Guards. Unsurprisingly for a cavalry officer, his personal effects reflected his status and interests. The property belonging to his estate in India included two polo ponies, a bay water mare called 'Game Girl' and a grey Arabian thoroughbred called 'Ali Baba'. It also included, in a very full inventory on his file: a puppy, a piano, a dining room table and a sideboard. Much of this was sent to auction under the aegis of a military adjusting committee sitting in India.[161]

For the soldiers in the front line on the Western Front, where the post and parcel service were regular and reasonably timely, their personal effects consisted of largely

---
[159] The National Archives, WO 339/17275, Personal Record of Lieutenant C MacBryan.
[160] Ibid.
[161] The National Archives, WO 339/7112, Personal Record of Lieutenant LW White.

what was sent over by their families or what they could 'scrounge' locally. Ernest Taylor received frequent updates from his family, and replied downplaying the risk to himself and his comrades, describing in February 1916 harrowing events and daily perils on the front line as matters of minor irritation:

My dearest Madge,

If the Germans will allow me I will try and get a few lines off to you. This is about the time when a daily strafing begins, and if it does so we have to vacate our dug-outs. At present however it is fairly quiet except for a few of our shells going over. We left our last billets last Monday at 9 a.m. A steady four hours march brought us to some tents a couple of miles behind the firing line, where we stayed the night. I got in with a pretty nice crowd five of them being B.C. men from another battalion. They were the public school type with the swank knocked out of them, and it was a pleasure to hear their well modulated English voices discussing interesting topics after the harsh Canadian voices of so many of our men. I always think the hour or two before lights out when under canvas is rather fascinating. Pleasantly tired after our march we lay in our blankets watching a brazier of red hot coke near the door of the tent, and gradually the sound of voices singing drifted over from various tents. Soon it was taken up by ours and to the accompaniment of a mouth organ most of the old and new songs were gone through before we fell asleep. The next morning we took it easy and at 3 p.m. set out for the trenches. Our first objective was some "dug-outs" a couple of hundred yards or so behind the front line. One squad of eleven went on to the trenches, and the other two, one of which I was in, stayed there. We were there three days and it was not too bad. The dug-outs were roomy and two of the nights were undisturbed. The first night I was on sentry, but the time went fairly quickly. This country must have been well settled judging by the ruined farms one sees on every hand. During the daytime one could move round a little with care as there was a hedge between us and the enemy. This devastated country behind the trenches has the same fascination for me that old ruins at home always have. I crept over to the ruined farm close by and poked about. It was little more than a pile of brick dust, but in one room I found the remains of a nearly new cream separator. On going to a field close by for water I found the remains of a threshing engine and separator all set in line ready for work. The unfortunate people must have been at it when they had to leave and I could picture the busy scene and then someone rushing it to say the Germans were coming. The greatest excitement at this place was going for rations after dusk. There was no communication trench so we could only move after dark. There were numerous plank bridges to be crossed in the dark over yawning trenches. Sometimes a flare would go up when one was in the middle of one of these lighting everything up distinctly only to make the darkness blacker than ever when it died out. The return trip with a bag of food or a box of bombs was even more precarious and I was always glad to get back without a fall. One night just as we were getting back crossing an open field in view of the German trenches, a flare went up. We all froze into statues, but the white sacks must have shown up. A machine gun went pat-pat-pat. You could feel them playing it up and down the line and hear the bullets hiss in the long grass, but no one was hit. After three days in this place my squad took its turn in the front line. The trench here is drier than the last one I was in, but we don't get much rest even in the daytime. We stand-to most of the night and I am thankful this is the last one as I can barely keep my eyes open. We get relieved tomorrow night. Then we spend six days back in the tents and then come back for another six days. Then six more days in the tents after which the brigade moves back for a rest. I got -----

8:30 a.m. Monday. I was brought to a sudden stop yesterday by a couple of shells coming over. We hastily scrambled out and squeezed up close to a parapet. They sent them over pretty steadily for an hour and a half. Nothing like as bad as we had it before, but it was by no means pleasant. Several burst on either side of the trench a few yards from us and you are all the time expecting one to drop beside you. Four men were killed, all old Squadron men. One of them was from Vermilion. He used to fix up the telephones for a time, and once he told me he thought he had been at Newhaven, because he called one afternoon at a house near Alton's and two English girls were having afternoon tea and gave him a cup. Thank goodness we have done our last night, two hours on and two hours off seems to be one continual waking up just as you have gone to sleep. Then having to keep out of the dug-outs in the daytime does not give one much chance to sleep. We got the first mail since leaving our old billets yesterday and the parcel made a most opportune arrival. Our wood supply was damp and an officer made me put my fire out because it was smoking too much before the water was boiling or the bacon cooked. One can't live on raw bacon or steak, so I was dependant on bread and jam, and the cake and lobster paste were much relished. Many thanks to you all for everything. Please thank Ol for her letter and interesting enclosures. I had a very interesting one from Ray too. What a busy life you and Doll are leading, it must be very tiring and trying too at times. I am afraid this letter is very grubby, but I am horribly so myself and I have not shaved since we came in the trenches. The place we bombers are patrolling at night is rather exposed. There are several isolated buttresses of sand bags about eighty feet apart in front of the trench. We each occupy one but have to keep moving through the open part between to keep in touch with each other. The German snipers have established themselves about a hundred yards away and keep potting at us all night long. I don't mind it as it rather breaks the monotony. This morning they evidently thought we had gone to breakfast and started their fires up. We saw smoke and fired several rounds at it. I expect they were pretty well dug in and would not get hit, but it was satisfactory to see how quickly they put their fires out and to know that we had at least spoilt their breakfast. I expect we shall get relieved about eight o'clock tonight and have about three miles to march to the tents where we shall be in reserve for six days. I expect it will be getting pretty near the end of the month before we go back for a rest. Then I hope they will get a wiggle on with the leave. At present only about two are going per week from the battalion. Well I am going to try and get a little sleep in case the guns start up later on.

Good-bye old girl. Love to all
Ernest[162]

This again is another telling, lengthy testament of the stoic nature of soldiers at the front line. Such personal accounts, deliberately downplayed the realities and horrors of the war so as not to alarm families at home, and was not just confined to the Western Front, but was a common feature of all those serving in the various expeditionary forces deployed across the other areas of campaign.

Forgotten Fronts – Mesopotamia and Salonika

As the strategists in the War Office were shuffling the troops withdrawn from the Dardanelles at the start of the year and redeploying them to the other operational theatres, their attention and focus was snapped back to the Western Front when the first shells crashed on to the French troops defending Verdun at dawn on 21st February. The concentration of 1,220 German guns rained a torrent of high explosive on just eight miles of the French front line, and from that moment on operations in France became the centre of Allied attention and the strongest magnet for attracting resources, both men and materiel.

Thus, for the Indian Expeditionary Force, attempting to force progress towards the capture of Baghdad, conditions were to become increasingly desperate. The advance had been checked by the Turks at Ctesiphon and, having fallen back to the garrison at Kut-al-Amarah, the Force had been besieged. Several attempts to break out from the Ottoman encirclement followed, in which twelve Old Cheltonians were killed in action or died of their wounds. Arthur and Hunter Forbes-Robertson (Day Boys, 1898 and 1905 respectively) followed their father's footsteps, first to College and then into the army.[163] Both had been mentioned in despatches for gallant conduct and were serving in battalions trying to break the Turkish encirclement at Kut. Hunter was killed in

---
[162] Cheltenham College Archives, Personal Letters of Ernest Taylor.
[163] Colonel George Forbes-Robertson left College in 1854 and served with the 95th Highlanders and the Argyll and Sutherland Highlanders, seeing active service with the Indian Army including the Indian Mutiny of 1857.

action on 6th April serving with 51st Sikhs, the following diary entry recording the sorry events:

> April 6th. The 7th Division, parading at 1.30 a.m., made a night march on to the Sannaiyat position, to be assaulted at 4.55 a.m. The Provisional Battalion was on the right of the 28th Brigade – the right of the firing line.
>
> The force arrived late at the position of deployment, and, owing to lack of reconnaissance, had to advance over the open in daylight. About 5 a.m. heavy fire (artillery, machine-gun, and rifle) opened from the Turkish trenches. The Battalion advanced and did splendidly but was wiped out. Practically every officer was killed or wounded, and only 17 men were left at the end of the day. I was knocked out comparatively early. Poor Foljambe was shot through the head almost at once; Hammick was hit twice, through the chest and arm; and Tatton through both hands and one leg. Altogether it was a very hot corner, and we got most of the enemy's attention, until the Composite Battalion of Black Watch and Seaforths came up on our left.[164]

Just 11 days later, Arthur was killed in action serving with the 128th Pioneers alongside another Old Cheltonian, Harold Birch (Hazelwell, 1903). After leaving College, Harold became apprenticed to an engineering firm for seven years before emigrating to Assam in 1910 to become a tea planter. While working in Assam, Harold also held a commission in the Reserve of Officers in the 32nd Sikh Pioneers of the Indian Army. In 1914, he was called forward for duty, promoted to lieutenant and attached to the 128th Pioneers. Harold too was mentioned in despatches for distinguished service but died of wounds four days after the regiment's action at Beit Aiessa in which Arthur had been killed.

Such coincidences where former school chums were reunited during service or killed fighting together in the actions around Kut were not uncommon. Anthony Davis and Arthur Saunders (Boyne House, 1901 and 1903 respectively), were in the same house together at College, then went their separate ways, before finding themselves together fighting and attacking adjacent objectives. Anthony came from a large family and was the eighth of 10 children to Lawrence and Margaret Davis who ran the family milling business in Twyford. Anthony's father had died when he was at College, and on leaving, returned home to train as a miller and to assist his mother in the business. When war was declared he was the manager of several flour mills, yet he enlisted in the 16th (Public Schools) Battalion, Middlesex Regiment as a private on 22nd September 1914. While in training, he applied for a temporary commission in the regular army on 16th January 1915, joining the 3rd Battalion, Oxfordshire and Buckinghamshire Light Infantry. His training completed, Anthony embarked for Mesopotamia at Devonport on 20th January 1916 on board HMT *Alaunia*, arriving at Basrah a month later to join the regiment's 1st Battalion. He was killed on 6th April attacking the Turkish positions at Sannaiyat, not far from Harold Forbes-

---

[164] The National Archives, WO 95/5140/5, War Diary of the 51st Sikhs, 1916-1917.

Robertson. Arthur Saunders was killed some four weeks earlier leading the last assault on the nearby Dujailah Redoubt, alongside two other Old Cheltonians, Alister Arbuthnot (Day Boy, 1898), a Royal Engineer officer, and James Landale (Day Boy, 1899). All three had been at College together and all three were killed in the same attack. However, not all fatalities were due to enemy action. As conditions in the Kut garrison degenerated, and with provisions and medical resources running low, infections were increasingly difficult to limit and disease and illness swiftly took hold. For example, Francis Lambert (Christowe, 1879), an experienced doctor and a major in the Royal Army Medical Corps, sadly contracted typhoid and died on 29th March.

Similarly, in Salonika illness and disease was endemic. The British Salonika Force had begun landing at the Greek port of Salonika (now Thessaloniki) from Gallipoli and France in October 1915. By mid-1916, a strong coalition of forces from Britain, France, Italy, and Russia, as well as from their respective colonies faced the Bulgarian Army, an ally of the Central Powers. The British contribution to the Salonika front numbered some 220,000 troops in a two-year campaign that was largely 'out of sight and out of mind' to British public perception. As on the Western Front, both sets of combatants established extensive trench systems, in which the greatest threat to occupants was from disease.

Alfred Llewellyn (Leconfield, 1909) was the first Old Cheltonian to die in Salonika. Having gained a classics exhibition to College he enjoyed a successful education, playing rugby in the XV of 1908; he left College and continued his rugby with Clifton RFC. When war was declared, Alfred was employed as a clerk by Downing and Hancock, a solicitor's firm in Cardiff. Yet he enlisted on 2nd September in the city, joining the 2nd Battalion, Welsh Regiment as a private. He clearly impressed while undergoing training, as he was promoted to lance corporal on 5th November. Alfred was discharged a month later on being granted a commission as a temporary second lieutenant on 7th December in the 8th Battalion, South Wales Borderers.[165] His battalion sailed for Salonika as part of the Mediterranean Expeditionary Force from Folkestone on 5th September 1915 and onwards from Marseille on 30th October. By June 1916, Alfred and the battalion were in the trenches conducting routine training. The battalion war diary records that he was killed accidentally on 14th June:

> Revolver practice by Officers. All specialists carried out training from 1600 to 1800hrs. A regrettable accident occurred to a party of bttn bombers when undergoing training Lieut Harold Alfred Llewellyn and No 8/16422 Pte John Sullivan being killed through a faulty fuse, the bomb coming back almost immediately after leaving the last-named man's hand.[166]

Although seven other men were wounded in this particular event, the greatest risk to troops serving in Salonika was that of disease. Arthur Montgomery (Christowe, 1892) had

---

[165] *The London Gazette*, dated 8th December 1914, page 10452.
[166] The National Archives, WO 95/4857, Unit War Diary of 8th Battalion, South Wales Borderers.

left College and spent some time working in Australia, at Glanalmond College Perth, before returning home in County Tipperary to undertake a BA degree at Trinity College Dublin. When war was declared he became the superintendent of the Remount Department in Clonmel. Seeking a more active role in the war, Arthur applied for a commission on 18th January 1915 and was commissioned as a second lieutenant a month later with the 5th Battalion, Royal Inniskilling Fusiliers.[167] The battalion landed at Suvla Bay, Gallipoli on the 7th August where it immediately joined the assault on Chocolate Hill. Owing to its casualties, the battalion was withdrawn from Gallipoli to Salonika seven weeks later. Serving as a subaltern with the 31st Infantry Brigade over the subsequent Balkan winter, Arthur contracted dysentery and died at No 5 Canadian General Hospital on 21st June 1916. Two further Old Cheltonians would die on the Salonika Front during the year. John Reid (Cheltondale, 1909) was killed in action on 8th September at Horseshoe Hill near Lake Doiran, and Herbert Evans (Southwood, 1912) lost his life on 4th October at Jenikoj, Macedonia. While both the Salonika Front, or 'Muckydonia' as the troops irreverently but aptly called it, and the campaign in Mesopotamia may have appeared to have been overlooked in the layman's broader perception of the First World War, neither are forgotten. Each Old Cheltonian who courageously fought and died there continues to be rightfully commemorated.

Endless Shadow – The Somme

By May 1916, the titanic struggle at Verdun increasingly preoccupied the minds of the French General Staff and the initial strategic plan of a combined Franco-British offensive against the Germans on a 60-mile frontage astride the Somme had to be adjusted radically.[168]

Furthermore, the pressure from General Joffre on Sir Douglas Haig for the BEF to execute a large-scale offensive on the Somme to divert some attention away from the hard-pressed French Army was becoming overwhelming. After all, this was a coalition war, and Britain hitherto had remained the junior partner. The original concept of a combined, equal effort by the two nations was completely overturned by events at Verdun. In January, France had contemplated allocating 40 divisions to the offensive on the Somme, but by May this figure had been reduced to 25.[169] The BEF was required to play the leading role in the offensive, particularly once the continued and immense strain on the French Army reduced their participation further to only 11 infantry

---

[167] *The London Gazette*, dated 16th February 1915, page 1561.
[168] Following the Second Inter-Allied Military Conference on 6-8th December 1915, General Joffre had garnered political support from the Allies for simultaneous large-scale attacks to wear down the German Army on several fronts. Although April 1916 was initially considered for a start, Haig was concerned that the battalions of the New Armies would not be sufficiently trained and logistically ready and therefore the start of the offensive was planned for the end of June or the beginning of July. The Somme Offensive was planned with little secrecy and therefore the Germans knew where and approximately when the blow would fall.
[169] See M. Gilbert, *The Somme*, Henry Holt and Company, LLC, New York (2006), page 25.

divisions.[170] The fighting on the Somme would become an affair almost entirely for Britain and her Dominion contingents. The battle would test the mettle of Kitchener's New Armies with their scores of thousands of volunteer soldiers, many in the recently established 'Pals' battalions, being put to the test alongside the troops sent from Canada, Newfoundland, Australia, New Zealand, and South Africa.

Training in the military camps up and down Britain entered a final phase of activity as brigades reached their full establishments and prepared for embarkation. On 27th May, Neil Mackinnon (Southwood, 1901) was conducting grenade instruction at Blackdown Camp (now Deepcut Barracks) near Camberley as a lieutenant in the 14th Battalion, Highland Light Infantry. One of his soldiers under instruction failed to clear the parapet with his bomb, which rolled down into the mud at the bottom of the training trench. Neil immediately leaped forward to seize the bomb but was impeded by the soldier who, having realised the immediate peril was endeavouring to get clear. Neil managed to find the bomb, after groping for it in the mud, and just managed to hurl it clear of the trench before it exploded. There were two other soldiers in the trench at the time besides Neil and his unfortunate bomber and a very serious accident was averted by Neil's quick thinking and courage.[171]

The Albert Medal, for gallantry

For his actions Neil was awarded the Albert Medal, an award almost as rare and prestigious as the Victoria Cross; he also survived the war. Two weeks later, his battalion was in France and making its way to the Front.

As the first of some 400,000 additional troops began to assemble in Northern France, not to mention the 100,000 additional horses to support the offensive, the new arrivals began training and conditioning, by conducting practice attacks behind the lines in preparation for the 'Big Push'. Yet the daily routine and danger continued for those manning the British trenches that now stretched from the Somme to Ypres. Trooper Ernest Taylor was still holding the line at Hooge, south of Ypres, with the 3rd Canadian Mounted Rifles, with whom he had fought for the last five months. An ardent letter-writer, as we have seen, reporting back regularly to the family at home, Ernest wrote to his sister in May 1916:

My dearest May,

Thank you very much for the tempting parcel you sent me. I have enjoyed the cakes so much & the [cake tin] has just come in handy for the trenches. I expect we shall

---

[170] The French XX Corps supported the attack on the north bank of the Somme with the 11th, 39th, 72nd and 153rd infantry divisions. South of the river, the French 1st Colonial Corps (2nd, 3rd, 16th and 99th (Territorial) Divisions) and XXXV Corps (51st, 61st and 121st Divisions) were integrated into the attack.
[171] See *The Glasgow Herald*, 30th August 1916.

be off there again tomorrow night. I got an interesting letter from Olive two nights ago, & one from Amy yesterday, for which I send them my hearty thanks. I am afraid Alfred must have had a pretty hot time in Ireland, how anxious you would all be. I saw the appalling number of casualties among the officers of the S.F. in the paper, but never thought of it being his battalion. When I wrote my last letter I spoke too soon about us being too near the firing line for inspections etc. I should have touched wood when I said that for the next day we had an inspection by the O.C. We were all clean & shaven, but had not cleaned our boots. That is a thing we have never done since coming to France, & no stuff had been issued for the purpose. Indeed it is little use cleaning boots when as soon as you step out of your hut you step into inches of mud or dust according to the weather. For this crime we were made the subject of some very insulting remarks, such as being a disgrace to the battalion and the badges we wore etc. The fact that when in the trenches the bombers are put in the most dangerous & unpleasant spots, & that during three months of leave only two men have been allowed away, does not weigh much against the crime of dirty boots. There is too much fuss made about the outside of the platter in the British Army. The O.C. called another inspection for the following day & dubbin was issued in the meantime. The next morning we rubbed our boots over every five minutes & even then there was quite a sprinkling of dust on them at the inspection. However we were told the improvement was very marked. Curiously enough, in the morning paper there was an account written by an officer in the trenches, which rather bears on the same subject. I have no doubt the staff officer in question told the sentry he was a disgrace to the uniform he wore & such insulting remarks. I am sorry to hear about Hubert cutting his hand so badly. I hope it won't be a long business getting better. How clever Marjorie seems to be at the Bank. It seems to me there ought to be some equivalent of the D.C.M. she ought to get for discovering so many forgeries. What a long time the hot weather is lasting. I expect the rain is waiting till we get in the trenches. One of the men returning from leave told me that all men taking commissions had now to train for four months in the O.T.C. first of all, so Ronald will have some hard work ahead of him. That kind of thing would not appeal to me at all. Sixteen days out of the trenches is almost too long. Things gradually get more regimental, & then off you go to the trenches & begin to think & act more like a man & less like a puppet. The Germans have been putting some shells over this way this morning. One of them killed four men & wounded two or three. They were out drilling. I must stop now as I have about three more letters to write. Dearest love to you all.

Ever your affectionate brother
Ernest
I wonder who sent me the waterproof socks.[172]

[172] Cheltenham College Archives, Private Letters of Ernest Taylor.

It was to be his last letter home. He was killed later that day and his friend Wilfrid, who had been with Ernest in the battalion's ranks, quickly reported the sad news and sent his condolences to Ernest's mother back home in Derbyshire:

My dear Mrs. Taylor

It is hard for me to write to you. I have just heard that Ernest was killed this morning, and I cannot realize it at all. He is in a different post to me, but I will try and learn the particulars before posting this. I am most awfully sorry for you all. It is a tremendous blow to me too for he has always proved a real true friend. Somehow, I was quite sure he would come through all right and get safely home. I have seen quite a lot of him lately for we were in the same camp and I said Goodbye to him, as we always did before going into the trenches, yesterday afternoon. I am afraid nothing can quite fill the void for you and us, but we should try to comfort ourselves with the remembrance that all of us have to die when our time comes, and a man could not wish for a finer end than Ernest's. This will be a frightful blow to you all, but you have the consolation of the above thought, which you wouldn't have had if he had died in peace time. All the boys mourn a splendid comrade and send you their most sincere sympathy.

I saw a quotation in a story the other day which I think Ernest would whisper to you if he could "Dulce et decorum est pro patria mori."

Goodbye dear Mrs. Taylor, I am so sorry.

Yours very sincerely
Wilfrid Bury

Monday I have not been able to get first hand information, but I believe he was hit on sentry-go and killed instantly without any suffering. [173]

Ernest was buried in the military cemetery on the Menin Road; he was 30 years of age. In the assembly areas behind the lines west of the town of Albert stockpiles of equipment needed for the attack were building apace. On 8th June the first of seven daily trains arrived with ammunition for the guns. Once unloaded at the railheads, munitions were transported onwards to the batteries, often by pack mule and horse. While all these preparations were going on, normal 'service' in the front line had to be maintained. Two days later, while the long ammunition trains continued their relentless 'clickety-clack' to and from the army service corps sidings, Walter North (Hazelwell, 1901), a corporal in the 22nd Battalion, Royal Fusiliers, was holding the line with his battalion in the trenches

---

[173] Cheltenham College Archives, Personal Letters of Ernest Taylor.

near Vimy.[174] Having gained an exhibition to Caius College, Cambridge the year before he left College, Walter graduated in 1904 and became a master at Llandaff Cathedral School. But when war was declared, he enlisted in September 1914 and began a year's training with the battalion.

Once operationally ready, and being suitably manned and equipped, the battalion deployed to France from Folkestone, landing at Boulogne near midnight of 16th November 1915. After two days of final acclimatisation and briefings, the battalion entrained for the Front with 30 officers and 991 other ranks. Walter was initiated into trench warfare on 29th November and

Walter North

obviously impressed as he was soon promoted to corporal. Six months later, on 10th June 1916, the battalion was battle-hardened and used to the daily routines and troop rotations associated with the BEF's operations in Flanders, Artois and Picardy. In the process of relieving the 1st Battalion, King's Liverpool Regiment in the front line that morning and while preparations for the offensive were being made, Walter was killed in the trenches, a '"routine" casualty of the attritional nature of daily trench warfare from trench mortar, machine gun fire, or sniping'.[175] Walter and Ernest Taylor, both well-educated and articulate, had been at College at the same time, and yet both had chosen to serve in the ranks rather than take a commission as officers. Walter now lies with his comrades in the British cemetery at Cabaret Rouge.

On Friday 24th June, the preliminary barrage erupted, and the harbinger of terror and destruction descended on the German lines. Over the next seven days, some 1,500 artillery pieces of varying calibre beat a non-stop 'drumfire' of over 1.7 million shells. The effect of this relentless barrage on the German defenders was considerable, driving many hysterical as they cowered in their deep, reinforced, chalky dug-outs while choking any attempts to resupply them with provisions and water from their support lines. However, material damage to the enemy's positions, especially their barbed wire entanglements, was much less impressive. Many of the shells were duds and failed to explode. Although the bombardment had a thrilling effect on the morale of the British troops starting to gather in the assembly trenches, the inability of the British artillery to adequately clear the obstacles in No Man's Land, suppress German machine gun positions, and neutralise the enemy's artillery batteries behind their lines would have unexpected and devastating repercussions.

At 7.30am on 1st July, the whistles blew, and across some 19 miles of front troops scaled the trench ladders, formed into their assault waves on the parapet, and set forward at a walk towards the German lines. The attack on the Somme had started. A further 66 Old Cheltonians were killed over the next three and a half months of the Somme offensive, six

---

[174] 22nd (Service) Battalion, Royal Fusiliers, known as the Kensington Battalion from where it was raised on 11th September 1914 at White City by the Mayor of Kensington.
[175] The unit war diary, WO 95/1372, records that the battalion was located in the line near Carency and that no assault was made, or attack from the Germans received.

on the infamous opening day – 1st July 1916. The respective battalion war diaries record the catastrophic events. George Cope (Cheltondale, 1914), promoted from the ranks and now a captain in the 20th Battalion, Northumberland Fusiliers (Tyneside Scottish), led his company across No Man's Land towards the village of Ovillers:

> The Battalion attacked up MASH VALLEY in four waves, 100 yards between waves. A special bombing party was sent into LA BOISELLE. Prior to the attack the bombardment which had been continuous for the last seven days became intense, and LA BOISELLE was subjected to a concentrated bombardment for the last twelve minutes. The mines were also exploded at -2 (7.28am) one on each side of LA BOISELLE. When the advance began at 7.36am the Battalion came under a heavy enfilading machine gun fire from OVILLERS-LA BOISELLE partly due to the fact that the 2nd Division had not been able to advance from their trenches. It is difficult to discover what happened, but though a few reached the German line, the remaining survivors fell back to our front line under cover of darkness. Not a single officer who went forward escaped becoming a casualty. Officer casualties: killed 10 including Capt Cope, wounded 10, missing 7. Other ranks were 62, 305, and 267 respectively. A casualty rate of some 90%.[176]

George was just 20 years of age. His body was never found, and he is commemorated on the Thiepval Memorial. Edward Matthey (Christowe, 1911) was a captain commanding 'A' Company 2nd Lancashire Fusiliers attacking at Beaumont Hamel and the Hawthorn Redoubt, two of the most heavily defended positions on the Somme.

> The battn (sic) was badly cut up by enemy's MG/rifle fire, suffering 508 casualties and 21 officer casualties. At dusk we returned to our trenches but held and consolidated Sunken Road. The battalion fought nobly but had no chance of success against enemy's MG fire.[177]

Just to the north, Hugh Adams (Hazelwell, 1900) led his company alongside the rest of the 1st Battalion, Hampshire Regiment over the top towards Beaumont Hamel at the start of the attack:

> As soon as we left the trenches, heavy MG fire was brought to bear on them from all directions and it was impossible to reach the German front line. Officer casualties were 100%, most lay in shell holes all that day.[178]

John (known as 'Jack') Macpherson (Leconfield, 1909), a scholar at College, was a qualified architect working in his father's practice in Tennant Street, Derby. After war was declared he

---

[176] The National Archives, WO 95/2462/4, War Diary of the 20th Northumberland Fusiliers, 1916.
[177] The National Archives, WO 95/2300, War Diary of the 2nd Lancashire Fusiliers, 1916.
[178] The National Archives, WO 95/1495/3, War Diary of the 1st Hampshire Regiment, 1916.

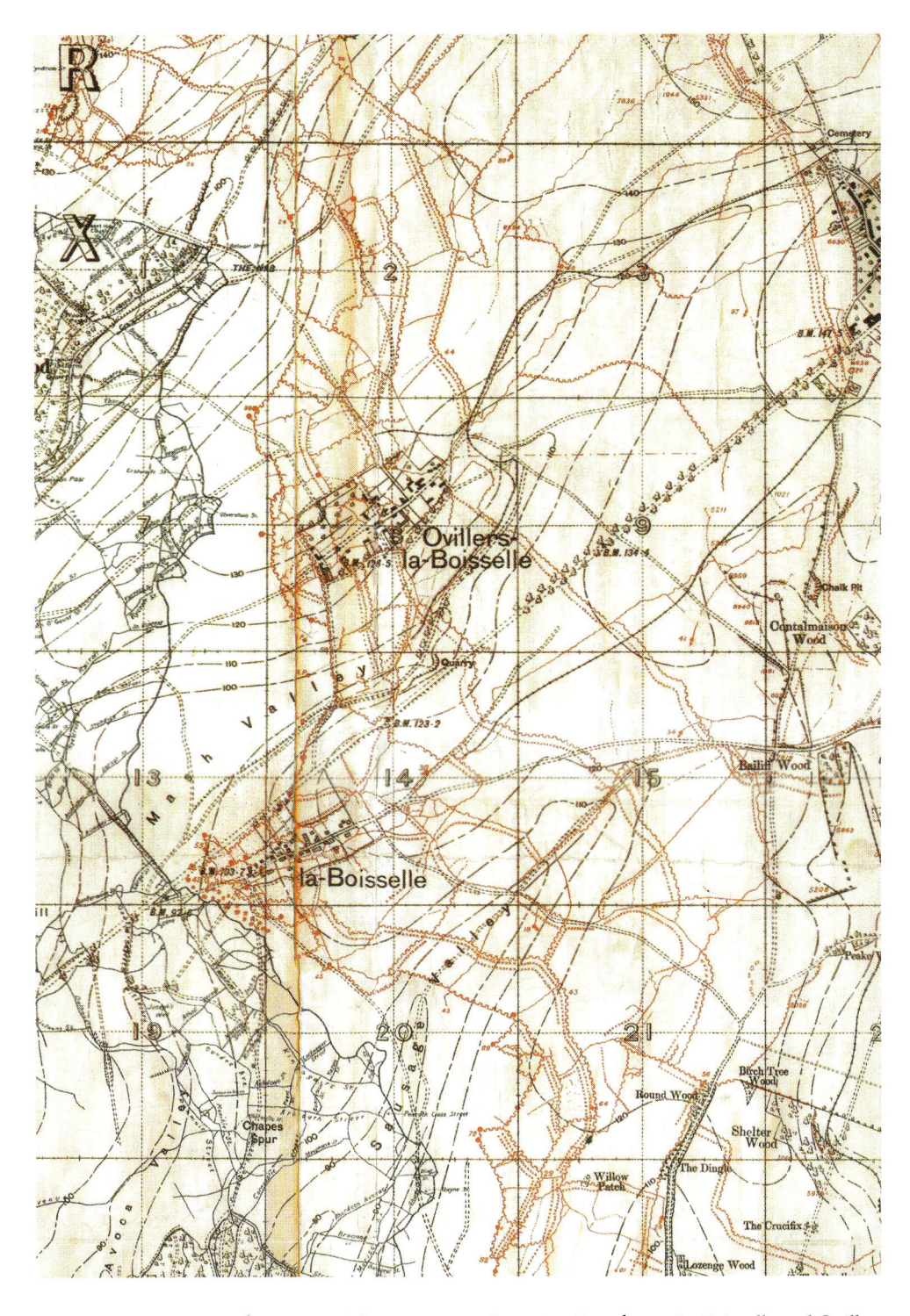

The Somme Offensive 1916 – Opposing Trenches at La Boisselle and Ovillers

enlisted and attested on 31st August 1914 in Nottingham as a private in the 6th Battalion, Royal Fusiliers, but quickly submitted an application for a commission on 5th October 1914. Once commissioned in the 1/7th Battalion, Nottinghamshire and Derbyshire Regiment (Sherwood Foresters), he was later promoted captain commanding 'B' Company. Jack reached the German first line under withering machine gun and rifle fire but with so few survivors of the assault could not hold the position. He was one of many killed that morning, his battalion suffering a 77% casualty rate – one of the highest rates of the assaulting battalions that morning.

At the opposite end of the assault sector at Carnoy, Gerald Neame (Hazelwell, 1903) commanded a company of the 7th Battalion, East Kent Regiment (The Buffs) attacking the Montauban Ridge that morning. His battalion suffered heavy losses early in the initial assault and Gerald's company, which had been held in reserve, was required at midday to go forward and take the final objectives. It was during this engagement in the early afternoon, that Gerald was also killed in action; aged 31.

Opposite Fricourt, Cecil Hirst (Boyne House, 1911) was killed advancing with the 9th Battalion, Devonshire Regiment. From College, he had won a history scholarship to Keble College, Oxford and as president of the Essay Club, had much in common with the young poet Noel Hodgson with whom he now served. They were of similar age and at Oxford together developing their respective literary interests and style, and now they were serving as young subalterns together. One of the battalion's company commanders, Captain Martin, had noticed the position of a German machine gun post built into the foundations of a shrine, just south of Mametz village, which covered their proposed line of advance. Realising the deadly danger that the gun posed, Captain Martin produced a plasticine model of the gun's position and took it to the artillery battery, who would be supporting their attack, to include the machine gun as a high priority in its target list. The artillery bombarded the position. Cecil and Noel were both killed attacking the village of Mametz early that morning. So too was Captain Martin. The artillery barrage on the machine gun had been ineffective and the gun claimed all three officers. A few days prior, Noel had written these prophetic lines in his famous poem *Before Action*, which was published in the *New Witness* on 29th June just two days before the fateful attack:

> By all the glories of the day
> And the cool evening's benison
> By that last sunset touch that lay
> Upon the hills when day was done,
> By beauty lavishly outpoured
> And blessings carelessly received,
> By all the days that I have lived
> Make me a soldier, Lord.
>
> By all of all man's hopes and fears
> And all the wonders poets sing,

> The laughter of unclouded years,
> And every sad and lovely thing;
> By the romantic ages stored
> With high endeavour that was his,
> By all his mad catastrophes
> Make me a man, O Lord.
>
> I, that on my familiar hill
> Saw with uncomprehending eyes
> A hundred of thy sunsets spill
> Their fresh and sanguine sacrifice,
> Ere the sun swings his noonday sword
> Must say good-bye to all of this; -
> By all delights that I shall miss,
> Help me to die, O Lord.

Cecil was buried in Danzig Alley Cemetery, while Noel and Captain Martin, killed earlier in the day, were buried in Devonshire Cemetery, dug from the very trench from which the Devons launched their attack that morning.[179]

Not every Old Cheltonian attacking that morning was among the casualties. Charles Pigg (Southwood, 1906) had enjoyed a most successful education at College, being a scholar, a College prefect, playing both rugby and cricket for the school, and being a cadet captain in the OTC. He had won a scholarship to Jesus College, Cambridge, and was a regular member of the Cambridgeshire County Cricket XI and the Blackheath rugby XV.

Having enlisted in 1914 for war service, Charles was now a captain and attached to the 2nd Battalion, Worcestershire Regiment, when he led his company over the top on 1st July. His diary entries record the fighting of the first two days:

Charles Pigg, College Master

> Our guns were timed to put down a barrage on the enemy reserve line, and eight Stokes mortars were to fire thirty rounds a minute as a box barrage on each flank of the attack. Our orders were to occupy the German front and second lines, to remain there for an hour, to complete their destruction, and to bring back a few prisoners for identification. We left in our dug-outs our spare kit and anything by which we might ourselves be identified. We had worked out every movement and position to the last detail, and shortly before midnight, July 1st and 2nd, we crept quietly out and lay down in front of our wire in two lines of platoons extended to a couple of paces.

---

[179] The inscription at what is known as Devonshire Trench reads: 'The Devonshires held this trench, the Devonshires hold it still.'

1916 – THE YEAR OF ENDLESS SHADOW

The night was quiet and dark save for an occasional star shell or bullet. I waited with Baxter at the head of a sap between the four platoons; with me were my runner, the signallers with the telephone, and four sappers carrying portable mines for the destruction of dug-outs. The preliminary bombardment had been timed for from twelve fifteen to twelve eighteen, and at twelve eighteen a small mine to be sprung on our right front was to give the signal to advance. I was hoping that it would not be sprung beneath us.

The bombardment when it came was terrific, and after a minute a sixty-pounder shell dropped short and just in front of our noses. For a few seconds when it exploded the men thought the mine had gone up for the advance; but we checked them, and then at last, after what seemed ages, up went the mine with a great shake of earth, and we were into the remains of the enemy wire and through it in a moment. Each officer and man knew his task to an inch and went straight to his post. The German trench, as I stood above it, seemed very deep and much more soundly constructed than ours. Jumping down, I found Private Raven with his bayonet at the throat of a German soldier. Raven was a young, dark, devil-may-care, up to anything when out of the line, though in the line he was a first-rate soldier; the German was a good-looking boy, in appearance about sixteen, wearing a neat and new field grey uniform and cap. He looked like one of our own young cadets, and faced his death fearlessly with his hands at his side. But I told Raven to spare him and take him back safely as a prisoner.

We soon fixed company headquarters at the point previously determined, and immediately I was speaking to Leman two or three hundred yards away; the noise was deafening and only by shouting could we use the telephone at all. Our organisation worked perfectly, and at one fifteen, after an hour which had passed very rapidly, I gave the signal to withdraw. Our own firing ceased and the trenches were rapidly cleared. Presently the runner and I were left alone and we walked along the new empty lines to ensure that no one had been left behind. It was a curious experience in the comparative silence; and the climb out of the deserted trench and the walk back across the open was uncanny. Direction might have been easily lost, but to guide us we had German guns which were now slowly shelling no man's land. The shells rushed past us in the darkness and burst in front of us along our parapet. and we were relieved to pass our wire and drop in to our own lines.

I found in my dug-out three prisoners whom Baxter had kept for me to see; he had sent on others to headquarters. One of them was badly shaken and frightened; but I tried to talk to another, Karl Jager, of Zittau, of the two hundred and forty-second Reserve Regiment. He was short, elderly and unsoldierly in appearance. Then all three were marched back to the Colonel.

Our Company roll call disclosed that we had two men missing, believed killed in the explosion of one of our own mines, and a dozen or so wounded, mostly very lightly. Our total casualties were two killed and fifteen severely wounded. Later we learnt the full result of the efforts of the two companies. We had entirely wrecked a considerable sector of the German front and second lines, blown in their mineshafts and dug-outs, killed a large number, and brought in eleven prisoners and some machine guns. Our opponents were the two hundred and forty-second and two hundred and forty-fourth Reserve Regiments, the latter of which had been one of the regiments routed by the battalion at Gheluvelt in 1914. We were delighted with our success and did not sleep that morning, but, having recovered our possessions from Old Boots trench, again took over the front line. Very early a runner brought me the best reward of all in a note from the Colonel, and throughout the day congratulations poured in upon us. I spent some time in drafting a report and recommendations. Wilmot, who had had the responsible task of guarding our right flank, had done his work most efficiently; he had established a block in the trench at the correct spot and held it throughout. He told me that as he was doing this a German officer coming up had run into him round the traverse and that he had fired point blank and killed him. But his work was typical of all, and I could not find that anything had gone wrong with our arrangements.[180]

His colonel expressed his admiration in a personal note to Charles the following day:

Dear Pigg,

My heartiest congratulations to you and all your gallant fellows. They did splendidly and I hope to have soon an opportunity of seeing them. Right well have you upheld the traditions of the dear old Battalion.

Yours ever,
L. M. STEVENS.[181]

Charles survived the war having won the Military Cross. He then resumed his interests within academia, first as the principal of the Lancaster ex-Service Men's Training College, before returning to College where he became an assistant master and then housemaster of Cheltondale in 1922.[182]

Many of the Old Cheltonians fighting on the Somme were veterans from earlier in the war. Calverly Bewicke (Day Boy, 1910) had already been wounded: on 7th September

---

[180] Extracts from the Diary of Captain CH Pigg OBE MC, held in the Regimental Archives, Norton Barracks, Worcester.
[181] Ibid.
[182] His younger brother, Bernard William Pigg, was educated at Tonbridge School where he was Head of School. He was killed in action at La Boiselle on the Somme on 3rd July 1916 while serving in the 10th Worcesters, and by unhappy coincidence at the same time as these diary entries were being written.

1915 he was hit by a rifle bullet to his scalp while in action at Kemmel with the Welsh Regiment and evacuated to England from Boulogne to Dover the same day. Having recovered, he returned to the Front and became embroiled in the bitter struggle during the battle to capture the village of Pozières:

> 26 July-16 – At 3.00pm another attack is organised at MUNSTER ALLEY. It is carried out by "B" Company under Captain C. P. CLAYTON. Good progress is made until 5.00pm when the objective is reached. By this time all the Battalion bombers have been called up and all are in a very exhausted condition. The enemy then counter-attacks in large numbers and eventually we are pushed back to our original position. Another attack is then organised and with the assistance of 17th AUSTRALIAN Battalion 150 yards of MUNSTER ALLEY is re-won and consolidated. About 9.00pm the relief of the Battalion is commenced by 10th NORTHUMBERLAND FUSILIERS. Casualties for 25th-26th, Lieutenant C.G. BEWICKE and 2nd Lieutenant E. C. McGROARTY killed. 131 other ranks killed wounded and missing.[183]

However, a fuller picture of the action, and Calverly's significant contribution to it, is found in the diaries of Captain Clayton, commanding 'B' Company during the attack who wrote a few days afterwards:

> But a few minutes later comes the nastiest experience, I think, which can come to a soldier. All of a sudden, as we are busy with our bomb supply, there is a strange wild shout and men begin to rush back upon us out of the battle trench. I am almost bowled off my feet with the rush. At the same time more men come running over the open from the front and jumping down upon us. They all come running as if the devil is at their heels. Their faces show abject terror and some in their haste fall headlong into the trench and fight madly to regain their feet. They have cracked. They begin to line the side of the trench but only, at first, to start a wild burst of wild firing at nothing. But this is better than unreasoning terror. They are recovering. Sliding down into the trench I try to get them to come and start bombing up the trench again but I can get none to stir. Young Bewicke is at a bend in the trench a few yards away and most of the men are between him and me. It is a great relief to me to hear his Lewis gun open out. He is letting off sharp bursts. His gun has done more to steady the men than anything else. Without his dashing work with his Lewis gun I doubt whether the men would have recovered from their panic sufficiently to make good the lost ground as they have done. He died at his gun, after he had done his bit.[184]

---

[183] The National Archives, WO 95/1281/3, War Diaries, 3rd Infantry Brigade, 2nd Battalion Welsh Regiment, 1916
[184] Edited diaries of Captain CP Clayton, MC, reproduced on-line by Leicestershire County Council, War Memorials Project, at www.leicestershirewarmemorials.co.uk/war/casualty/view/17107.

1916 – THE YEAR OF ENDLESS SHADOW

The Battle of the Somme continued for over three months. On 27th August, the 1/5th Battalion, Gloucestershire Regiment made a successful attack against a particularly obstinate part of the German Line near Mouquet Farm, one of the strong points in the Ovillers-la-Boiselle sector of the Front.[185] While reaching their objective near Pole Trench, and taking 50 prisoners in the process, they sustained casualties amounting to six officers and 98 other ranks. Two of the officers killed were Old Cheltonians, Arthur Apperly (Boyne House, 1896) and Cyril Winterbotham (Day Boy, 1906). Also fighting with them in the battalion was Cyril's elder brother James (Day Boy, 1902). All three were lieutenants in the battalion, and each, in their different ways, had enjoyed distinguished backgrounds before their experience of soldiering with the 1/5th Glosters in the First World War.

Arthur Apperly

Arthur had made the most of his time at College. In his final year, he was appointed as a college prefect and was a member of both the school's rugby first XV and the gymnastics VIII. He also excelled at shooting, being in the College VIII for four years and winning the Spencer Cup at Bisley in 1894.[186] But perhaps the one area of endeavour that would influence his life the most was the time he spent in the Officers Training Corps. In his last year, he was a cadet captain in the Engineering Corps, after which he was commissioned as a lieutenant in the 1st Gloucestershire Royal Engineer Company, a volunteer unit within the county's militia structure.

At the same time, Arthur trained as a chartered accountant to support the family's woollen textile business, as well as being a stalwart of the Stroud Rugby Club. Although he resigned his militia commission in 1902, taking up a bursar's appointment at St Andrew's College in Grahamstown, South Africa, he returned to support the family business becoming a director. After war was declared, Arthur secured a commission with the Glosters' territorial battalion. Having agreed to serve overseas, he was commissioned on 15th November 1915 into the 1/5th Battalion.[187]

Cyril Winterbotham left College some 10 years after Arthur, going up to Lincoln College, Oxford where he gained a Law degree and became a member of the Inner Temple. Cyril was a practising barrister when war was declared; his application for a commission was granted on 26th September 1914, becoming a second lieutenant in the same battalion as Arthur.[188]

Cyril Winterbotham

---

[185] Mouquet Farm was known to the Tommy as 'mucky farm' or 'moo-cow farm' and was a very distinctive and strongly held position.
[186] The Spencer Cup, presented in 1861 by Earl Spencer, was an individual trophy competed for by one representative of each school competing at Bisley that year and awarded to the best overall shot.
[187] Supplement to *The London Gazette*, dated 22nd November 1915, page 11585.
[188] *The London Gazette*, 25th September 1914, page 7604, and appointed to the 1/5th Gloucestershire Regiment.

Having deployed to France on 30th March 1915, the battalion was sent to the Artois sector of the line where Cyril recorded his surroundings:

> It is a strange sight, this firing line. Imagine two untidy lines of sandbags, looking more like rubbish heaps in the distance and between them straggling lines of wire on rough poles at all sorts of angles with a dead cow here and there and odd articles scattered about. Then dotted about are ruined houses with tileless roofs and broken walls standing in the remains of their gardens. Over all, absolutely no sign of life or movement.
>
> I sat and looked round on Sunday morning. An aeroplane was being shelled up above and the sky was dotted with little white puffs of smoke. I couldn't help trying to reconstruct the scene in peace and imagine all the roofs on and all the mess cleaned up... Waller and I remarked simultaneously that the whole thing is preposterous nonsense and that men ought to leave each other in peace to enjoy the weather and, I added, go fishing. After which we went off to try and spot a sniper and if possible put a bullet in him. [189]

In April 1915, in an effort to keep up morale, the battalion's commanding officer, encouraged the production of the *'Fifth Glo'ster Gazette'* a trench magazine containing poems, jokes, notices, and serious and humorous articles about the battalion's experiences and their lives in the trenches. This was an early publication replicating the type of content found in a parish newspaper.[190]

'Bong Jour Alf! Have you changed your socks today? If not, why not?'

Cartoon in the *Fifth Glo'ster Gazette*, circa 1916

---

[189] Van Emden, R, *The Soldier's War: The Great War through Veterans' Eyes,* Bloomsbury, London, (2010).
[190] A more celebrated example of a trench magazine was *The Wipers Times*, begun in February 1916 and even now a topic of both television and West End productions by Ian Hislop and Nick Newman.

1916 – THE YEAR OF ENDLESS SHADOW

The Gazette provides a powerful testimony for combining its seemingly matter-of-fact events and routine with the backdrop of extreme danger and extraordinary circumstances. Cyril was a constant contributor of poems, two of which were first published (sadly, posthumously) in London in November 1917 in *The Muse in Arms*, including his poignant and prophetic poem, *The Wooden Cross*:

> God be with you and us who go our way
> And leave you dead upon the ground you won.
> For you at last the long fatigue is done,
> The hard march ended; you have rest to-day.
>
> You were our friends; with you we watched the dawn
> Gleam through the rain of the long winter night,
> With you we laboured till the morning light
> Broke on the village, shell-destroyed and torn.
>
> Not now for you the glorious return
> To steep Stroud valleys, to the Severn leas
> By Tewkesbury and Gloucester, or the trees
> Of Cheltenham under high Cotswold stern.
>
> For you no medals such as others wear –
> A cross of bronze for those approved brave –
> To you is given, above a shallow grave,
> The Wooden Cross that marks you resting there.
>
> Rest you content; more honourable far
> Than all the Orders is the Cross of Wood,
> The symbol of self-sacrifice that stood
> Bearing the God whose brethren you are.[191]

Cyril became the editor of the *Gazette*, and, with the help and prolific contribution of another war poet, Will Harvey, supervised its publications until both Arthur and Cyril were killed in action in the attack on 27th August.[192] The battalion war diary describes their final action:

---

[191] See E.B Osborn, *The Muse in Arms: A Collection of War Poems, for the Most Part Written in the Field of Action, by Seamen, Soldiers, and Flying Men Who Are Serving, or Have Served, in the Great War*, Frederick A Stokes Company, New York (1917).

[192] The 25 editions of the *Fifth Glo'ster Gazette* were published, and full copies are held at both the Imperial War Museum and the Soldiers of Gloucestershire Museum. Lieutenant Frederick William Harvey, DCM, known as the 'Laureate of Gloucestershire', was captured during a reconnaissance patrol on 16th April 1916 and spent the rest of the war as a POW. Thus, he was not present during the fateful attack on 'Mucky Farm' with the Winterbotham brothers.

C Company attacked on the right and B company on left both in two lines across the open. A Company 2 platoons advanced up a communication trench. Intense barrage for 3 minutes. Right company entered trench in their own barrage and left company at the moment of lift with few casualties. The bombing platoons met with considerable opposition in the communication trench and a large party of Germans held out, but were ultimately forced to retire across the open when our Lewis guns accounted for all but 3. Several dugouts were bombed and trench was consolidated and held. About 50 prisoners were taken and the enemy's other losses were estimated at about 200 killed and wounded. One machine gun was captured.

Our casualties

Killed: Lt L W Moore Lt C W Winterbotham 2nd Lt AL Apperly, Missing: 2n Lt Brien, Wounded: 2nd Lt NH Graves-Smith 2nd Lt WF Bigger.[193]

James Winterbotham had enjoyed a full and illustrious career at school. Having been appointed a College prefect he played in the rugby XV in his last year. But it was on the cricket field where he really excelled, being in the XI for three years and as captain in his last term in 1902. Going up to Oriel College, Oxford, he gained his 'Blue' the following year and played briefly for Gloucestershire, mainly as a steady left arm orthodox bowler. After graduating in 1905, he joined his father and two brothers, John and Cyril, in the well-established family solicitors practice in Cheltenham, all four being Old Cheltonians. Here his life developed into a comfortable middle-class idyll where his growing professional reputation was enhanced by his continued sporting prowess. On midsummer's day the following year he married Jean at St Giles's Cathedral in Edinburgh, subsequently settling down in their family home. Two years later, on 12th September 1906, their first daughter, Beatrice, was born, followed by a second daughter, Hilda in August 1911. However, when war was declared, this peaceful milieu was quickly upended.

James enlisted in the ranks of the Public School's Battalion on 4th September 1914 and after initial training was quickly commissioned on 6th February 1915, joining younger brother Cyril, ironically some four months senior to James in rank, in the same battalion of the Glosters.[194] James survived both the attack on the Somme,

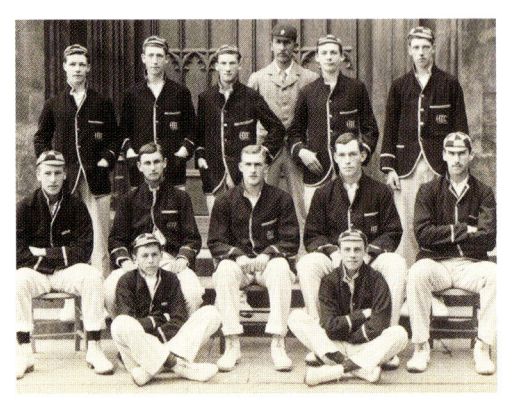

James Winterbotham, College XI, sitting far right

[193] The National Archives, WO 95/2763/1, War Diary of the 1/5th Battalion, Gloucestershire Regiment, March 1915-November 1917.
[194] Supplement to *The London Gazette*, dated 13th February 1915, page 1530.

which saw his brother Cyril and Arthur Apperly killed, and also the war, serving with great distinction and gallantry: he was mentioned in despatches and awarded the Military Cross. He also became the adjutant of the battalion before being badly wounded in the right leg by shell fragments on 6th August 1917 while holding the line near Ypres. [195]

The bodies of Arthur and Cyril were never recovered from the Somme battlefield. They are commemorated on the Thiepval Memorial, the evening summer shadows of which almost fall on the very spot near 'Mucky Farm' where they both fell; two of the 73,000 British soldiers who died on the Somme whose remains were never found. James never fully recovered from his wartime experiences and passed away in Cheltenham on 2nd December 1925 after a short illness. Aged just 42 his relatively premature death, if not a direct consequence of his wartime service, was no doubt exacerbated by the wounds, privations and stress that four years of trench combat would have imposed on his medical strength and constitution, and thus perhaps making him all the more vulnerable to sickness and infection.

Vivian Newton (Leconfield, 1911) was just 19 years of age when he embarked for the Front on 24th May 1916, being posted as a replacement officer to the 1st Battalion, Welch Fusiliers. He was the most junior and inexperienced officer in the battalion when he joined on 1st June. A month later, he was fighting during the battalion's attack to the south of Fricourt, serving alongside the Great War poet Siegfried Sassoon. They had struck up a friendship when they were holding a bombing post near Wood Trench just after the battalion had captured the Quadrangle near Mametz on 4th July. Vivian was a popular and respected young subaltern who later featured in Sassoon's 1930 novel *'Memoirs of an Infantry Officer'*, as the young officer 'Fernby'. Vivian received a serious shrapnel wound to the head during the attack at Ginchy on 3rd September, was evacuated to No 8 General Hospital at Rouen, where he died at 9.00am on 15th September. His commanding officer, Lieutenant Colonel Stockwell, wrote to his parents describing Vivian as:

> A charming boy – always keen and full of pluck; so much so that I especially selected him to go to the grenadier company, the picked company of the battalion... His loss will be felt by all of us who were his brother officers as he was universally liked because of his straightness and keenness.[196]

At the other end of the teaching process at College was assistant master Leonard Butler (Common Room, 1914). He had been to Rugby School, being a member of the OTC before going up as a scholar to New College, Oxford. After graduating, he embarked on a teaching career and was appointed as a master at College; he was also made a fellow of St John's College, Oxford. When war was declared, he applied for a temporary commission on 7th October 1914 along with several other colleagues from the Common Room. He received

---

[195] Supplement to *The London Gazette*, dated 1st January 1918, page 50.
[196] See McPhail. H., and Guest. P., *Sassoon and Graves: On the Trail of the Poets of the Great War*, Pen and Sword, Barnsley, 2001, page 112.

his commission as a second lieutenant in the Rifle Brigade some two weeks later.[197] Though initially posted to the depot and training unit, he was transferred to the 3rd Battalion and fought with them from mid-1915 on the Western Front. On 21st August 1916, and now promoted to captain, Leonard and the battalion were involved in an attack on the German line north of Guillemont, where the fighting through Trônes and Delville Woods was particularly difficult. Following the attack, he was reported as 'missing believed wounded' in the telegram to his mother three days later. Lieutenant Colonel Pigot, his commanding officer, wrote to Leonard's brother on 25th August:

> He is put down as missing but I fear there is no hope. He was last seen by a Rifleman whom I have carefully questioned, badly wounded, paralysed and dying fast. It seems an awful sort of death for anyone but if anyone ever died a hero's death it was your brother. On the 18th our first attack, he had greatly distinguished himself in command of his Coy when his Captain had been hit and for the way in which he then acted. I would have recommended him for a reward. In the 2nd attack on the 21st he was first of all hit by a bullet close to the German trench which we were trying to enter. He was soon after hit by a bomb and later by another bomb, all the time he was encouraging the men round him to hold on, saying 'I know you are all good boys, and will hang on'. Some men then tried to get him away, but he would not let them touch him. It was certain death to anyone that tried to carry him away. Again, when the remnants of his Coy were ordered to withdraw, they tried to get him away but he would not let them. He had destroyed all his papers and maps and was practically dead when last seen. I sent out at night to try and find him but it was impossible. There was heavy shelling at the time and I am afraid that he may have been blown to pieces by a shell. I think his death is the finest I have ever heard of. The whole of his Coy that are left speak so highly of the way he acted and put up such a fine fight.[198]

It is clear from this letter that Leonard was an inspirational character, and just the sort of individual to motivate young students at College as well as, later, the soldiers under his command. His body was never found and Leonard is also commemorated on the Thiepval Memorial to the missing. He was just 26 years of age.

Amphibians

Enduring the frightful suffering and adversities throughout the Somme offensive was not just the preserve of the army's battalions. The Royal Navy's participation in the land fighting had already made a significant contribution through the employment of the 63rd Royal Naval Division. Drawn up from a surplus of some 25,000 Royal Navy and Royal

---

[197] *The London Gazette*, 23rd October 1914, page 8520.
[198] The National Archives, WO 339/21676, Personal Record of Captain LG Butler.

Marine reservists who were not required for sea duty, parts of the Division had already fought with distinction at Antwerp in 1914 and then at Gallipoli the following year. On 29th April 1916 operational authority for the Division was passed from the Admiralty to the War Office, and it moved to the Western Front in May 1916 where it served for the remainder of the war. By November 1916, two Old Cheltonians were fighting with the Royal Marines on the Somme, holding a line of trenches near Beaumont Hamel. Murdoch Browne (Cheltondale, 1904) was a company commander with the 1st Battalion, Royal Marine Light Infantry. He had already served in Gallipoli, having landed at Y Beach on 25th April 1915. Wounded on 12th May with a gunshot wound to his right shoulder and evacuated to the Royal Navy Hospital in Malta, he had recovered and returned to his battalion in Gallipoli in June. He was subsequently awarded the Distinguished Service Cross in recognition of his service during operations on the Gallipoli Peninsula, especially for his exploits during the night on 12th July.[199] Murdoch had been sent out with is company during the abortive attack along the Achi Baba nullah and found himself cut off. With his men, he took an advanced trench and held it throughout the following day without food or water until the front line was re-established and stabilised. He was commended for his personal courage and example which maintained the morale and fighting spirit of his men. His personal file on record shows that he was:

> A very good officer, hardworking and always cheerful. A good example to his men, great ability and a good leader.[200]

With him on the Somme near Beaumont Hamel was Edward Abelson (Day Boy, 1915). A College prefect and a member of the OTC at school Edward had won an open history scholarship to Emmanuel College, Oxford. Rather than pursue his studies, he enlisted in the Royal Marine Light Infantry, graduating from Dartmouth on 15th January 1916; his progress being recorded as 'average, but zealous – will make a good officer in time'. Edward then undertook his Royal Marine professional training, on completion of which he was promoted to lieutenant and sent to the machine gun school at Belton Park near Grantham for a course of instruction. Suitably qualified as a machine gun officer, Edward was attached to the Machine Gun Corps, but appointed to the 190th Company to give direct support to 1st Royal Marine Light Infantry. He embarked on the SS *Huntscraft* at Southampton on 3rd September 1916 to join Murdoch and the other Royal Marines in the brigade on the Somme.

Just before first light, on the very misty morning of 13th November, both Murdoch and Edward took part in the final push to capture Beaumont Hamel, one of the most stubbornly held objectives of the opening day of the battle at the beginning of July, and yet still in German hands. Their final objective was the village of Beaucourt a little further up the Ancre valley. The battalion war diary records the events:

---

[199] 5th Supplement to *The London Gazette*, dated 5th November 1915, page 11029, published 8th November 1915.
[200] The National Archives, ADM 195/64/165.

> The attack commenced on the opening of our barrage at 5.45am when Bttn (sic) advanced in 4 waves – one platoon of each company in a wave. There was a very thick mist. Every Company Commander was killed before crossing German Front line. Enemy trenches were practically obliterated by our artillery. No Man's Land and ground between various German lines, as far as slope down to STATION ROAD was pitted with shell holes, deep & very muddy. Ground crossed by this Battn was particularly muddy which made advance difficult. Within a minute of our barrage starting, enemy replied with artillery barrage on support lines and No Man's land, where they also opened a heavy Machine Gun fire. It is estimated that at least 50% of casualties occurred between No Man's Land & German front line. Between 2nd & 3rd line, ground was swept with MG fire. Here also were heavy casualties. Isolated parties of this Battn followed the barrage as far as YELLOW LINE & got in touch with HAC on right. They were not however sufficiently strong to close gap between HAC and Battn on left. Remnants of this Battn held dotted BLUE LINE during night in partially constructed trenches W of STATION ROAD. Touch was maintained during night with 4th Gordon Highlanders on left.[201]

The battalion advanced nearly 500 strong, yet only 138 Royal Marines could answer the muster when it was later taken; 47 men were killed, 210 wounded and 85 were missing in action. Of the 22 officers who took part in the battalion's attack, only two returned unscathed; six, including Murdoch, were killed, 11 were wounded, and three were missing. Dangerously wounded, with a gunshot wound to his right shoulder and thigh and a fractured spine, Edward was quickly recovered and taken to the Casualty Clearing Station and then to No 8 General Hospital at Le Havre. Sadly, his wounds proved so serious that his condition slowly deteriorated and he died at 5am on 1st December. In his post-action report Edward's brigade commander recorded that:

> The MG Coy had little scope. They advanced with the object of rendering what aid they could but became involved in the mist and confusion, and while the German guns trained to sweep areas of ground in defence were effective even in the fog, our machine guns found it difficult to locate the target.[202]

The commanding officer of the 190th Machine Gun Company recorded in a letter to his parents:

> Your son was a most efficient, in fact, the ideal MGC officer. He was much liked by his brother officers, respected by his men, extraordinarily reliable, and had special abilities which fitted him for this work. In my dispatch to the Brigadier after the action, and in reporting your son being wounded, I described him as a most capable and efficient officer.[203]

---

[201] The National Archives, WO 95/3110/1, Battalion War Diary of 1st Royal Marines Light Infantry, 1916.
[202] The National Archives, WO 95/3119, Brigade War Diary, 190 Infantry Brigade, Royal Naval Division.
[203] The National Archives, ADM/137/3069.

The offensive on the Somme was brought to a halt on 18th November when the most significant change to the rate of bloodshed on both sides was decided by the weather, which, with the arrival of the heavy autumn rains, had churned the battlefield up into a muddy, bloody morass, and where any substantive movement became impossible.[204] Both sides were exhausted, badly depleted and increasingly disillusioned by the dreadful casualty rates, and the worsening weather only served to lower morale further. Arguably, the battle might be considered as a German defensive victory based on the greater number of casualties to the Anglo-French aggressors, over 620,000 on the allied side compared to nearly 500,000 Germans. But, despite the horrendous cost, the primary objective had been fulfilled. The German assault against the French at Verdun had been halted and then pushed back at the cost of approximately 400,000 casualties on each side. By the year's end, the pressure on the German Army was sufficiently acute as to make a tactical withdrawal the following year the most prudent operational option. Specifically, a newly structured, straightened and strengthened front line would improve the German defensive system, requiring fewer troops to hold the trenches as they slowly overcame exhaustion and battle fatigue with the arrival of fresh replacements. However, at the strategic and political level, the German withdrawal gave the Allied High Command the incentive to perpetuate their offensive intent.

Somme Aviators

An essential element during the fighting on the Somme was the employment of aircraft of the RFC to cooperate with both the artillery and infantry. Although still in its early stages of development, air power by 1916 had already proved its worth on the battlefield, especially in the role of reconnaissance and artillery observation. In simple terms, the army that could most accurately monitor the unfolding circumstances of combat operations on the ground, and then most speedily reorientate and execute the necessary tactical adjustments to the battle plan, maintained the tactical and operational edge. The efficacy of air power on the Somme, particularly in the reconnaissance and intelligence gathering phase of operations was proven. The need for aviators, both pilots and observers, to undertake these crucial roles remained a high priority. To satisfy the increasing demand for military aviators, many Old Cheltonians volunteered for duty in the RFC in this new combat environment.

Kenneth Brooke-Murray, for example, was serving with the Army Service Corps (ASC) from the outset of the war, being, as previously noted, the first member of the BEF to step ashore in France in August 1914. The ASC units, responsible for providing all the food, equipment, transport and ammunition to the fighting troops, were critical to the war effort, yet were often regarded by the fighting soldiers as rear echelon elements and disparagingly

[204] Author's note: Given the dreadful winter conditions, it could be argued that the term 'amphibian' was equally applicable to the entire British Expeditionary Force on the Western Front rather than simply to the Royal Marines and the Royal Naval Division fighting on land as infantry.

referred to as *Alley Sloper's Cavalry*.[205] However, seeking, perhaps, to avoid this unwarranted epithet and make a more direct impact on combat operations, he volunteered for service in the RFC. On 9th June 1916, he was transferred as an observer (on probation), and, having proven his worth, was appointed to flying duties on 27th August 1916 with No 15 Squadron RFC. As aerial observation for the artillery made the effect of their fire on enemy positions more accurate and deadly, reconnaissance aircraft and observation balloons remained high priority targets for fighter aircraft and anti-aircraft units. Flying over the Somme battlefield on 16th September from his base at Marieux, his BE 2c aircraft was involved in aerial combat with three enemy aircraft. Kenneth was mortally wounded, receiving several gunshot wounds and a compound fracture to his leg which necessitated immediate amputation of his left leg above the knee. He was evacuated to No 7 Stationary Hospital, Boulogne where he died at 11pm on 23rd September. His mother, after being informed by telegram of his injuries, was granted permission to travel to Boulogne to see him in hospital. Sadly, due to delays in telegraphic traffic, she arrived just minutes too late to see him on the day he died. His gravestone carries the crest of the RFC as opposed to the ASC and the patriotic epitaph selected by his mother:

Went the day well? We never knew. But ill or well, England, we died for you.

Geoffrey Allen (Day Boy, 1905) left College at the age of 15 and went to Blundell's to complete his education. When war was declared he enlisted at Clapham Park on 28th August 1914 and was appointed to the 'C' Squadron, Surrey Yeomanry in September acting as a despatch rider. Geoffrey served in Egypt from 19th March 1915, attaining the rank of lance corporal, but just a fortnight later on 1st April 1915 applied for and was granted a commission, being gazetted on 13th July. Geoffrey became a second lieutenant (on the General List) in the RFC and was posted to No 11 Squadron as an observer flying in the FE 2b biplane. Flying from his base at Izel le Hameau on 2nd September, he was killed in action near Thiepval and buried in the military cemetery extension at Mesnil.

George Bidie (Christowe, 1910) was commissioned on 3rd September 1913 as a second lieutenant in the 1st Battalion, Royal Scots, joining them on garrison duty in India. When war was declared, the battalion was soon recalled to the UK, and quickly re-equipped for active service on the Western Front. By Christmas 1914, it was in Flanders getting accustomed to the dangerous routine of trench warfare and the constant rotation between holding the line and being relieved to rest and provide working parties; all conducted in dreadfully wet and freezing conditions while facing the threat from enteric fever and violent demise. The experience was a complete contrast from their more placid garrison duties in India. George was wounded in action twice. Just four weeks after their arrival in Flanders, he sustained a bullet wound in the leg and was evacuated to St Thomas' Hospital, London on 25th January 1915. Once recovered, he returned to the Front only to

---

[205] Ally Sloper was an early comic strip character of the day made infamous for his scheming to make money on the side of his duties, for avoiding hard work, and for drinking whenever the opportunity arose.

be wounded again 12 weeks later, this time from a gunshot to the face during the Second Battle of Ypres. He returned to the UK and to St Thomas's for treatment on 12th May. After convalescing, and although still slightly lame from his first wounding, he felt sufficiently recovered to apply for RFC service, obtaining his pilot's certificate in May 1916. During this period in the UK he married his wife, Maria Bradbury. Posted to the recently inaugurated No 43 Squadron, he was tasked to fly a BE2d (serial number 5793) from Farnborough to Folkestone to join the squadron assembling in France and readying themselves for the Somme offensive.

George Bidie

Joining him as a passenger on the trip to Folkestone was Air Mechanic (2nd Class) William Charles Manning. While flying along the coastline near Whitstable their engine began to misfire; this required George to land the aircraft immediately, which he began to prepare for. However, on his final approach to what appeared to be a suitable field he saw a wire across his intended flight path. He quickly pulled the nose of the aircraft up and side-slipped in a low turn. Losing all his airspeed in the process, the aircraft stalled and began to spin into the ground. Without any altitude to effect a recovery, the aircraft crashed nose first into the turf from a height of some 25 feet. William Manning was killed instantly and George was very badly injured. A local GP from Whitstable, Doctor Witney, who had witnessed the crash, quickly attended the scene and took George to hospital where he died from his injuries just three minutes after their arrival. His body was taken back to his wife's home near Helensburgh where he was buried; today his resting place is commemorated by an impressive memorial cross. He was regarded highly by his former commanding officer, Colonel Callender of the 1st Royal Scots, who acknowledged George for his zeal and gallant conduct.

FE 2B aeroplane and crew

Chaplains

Francis Tuke (Day Boy, 1886) was one of three brothers who all went to College, coming from the large family of Henry and Jane Tuke who lived in Lansdowne Crescent in the town. Of the three, Francis was a particularly talented athlete, being in the Gym VIII in his last two years at College, after which he went up to Trinity College, Cambridge with a view to taking Holy Orders. Ordained in 1890, Francis spent 15 years as a village priest, first at Ripley in Surrey and afterwards at Hope-under-Dinmore in Herefordshire where he also played cricket for the county. When war was declared, he was more aware than most of the pressures that would face the volunteers rushing to the colours. His elder brother Martin had retired from the Royal Engineers having fought in Egypt and the Soudan and his younger brother Arthur was a military doctor who had joined the Indian Medical Service in 1911. Eager to 'do his bit' in the war for the fighting soldiers, he enlisted as a Chaplain 4th Class on 19th July 1915.

Almost exactly a year to the day later, he was killed during the Battle of the Somme on 20th July 1916, while bravely carrying water to troops of the 6th Royal Berkshires who were in action near Bernafay Wood; he was 49 years old.

Francis was one of 21 Old Cheltonians who served as chaplains in His Majesty's Forces during the First World War, both in the field and on board the Royal Navy's warships. In an era when the concept of 'muscular Christianity', based on a sense of patriotic duty, manliness, athletic pursuit, teamwork, discipline, and self-sacrifice, prevailed and permeated throughout private school education in the late 19th Century, it is hardly surprising that so many Old Cheltonians became service chaplains during the Great War. The fact that all of the College's principals since the school's foundation in 1841 had been ordained clergymen was also, perhaps, no coincidence.

Francis Tuke

Arthur Finnimore (Leconfield, 1875) was ordained in 1885 and felt driven to conduct missionary work in Asia, first in India, then in Mauritius where his only son David was born, and finally in Ceylon. David was educated in England, initially at Ascham Preparatory School in Eastbourne and then, like his father, at College (Leconfield, 1913). David then went into the army via the Military Academy at Woolwich becoming an officer in the Royal Engineers almost at the outbreak of the war. David served in France, being mentioned in despatches for his distinguished service erecting pontoon bridges for the infantry. Arthur, however, wishing to be closer to his son, finished his missionary work and volunteered to serve as an army chaplain on the Western Front while his wife Mary and the rest of the family remained at their home in Painswick Road, Cheltenham. Sadly, after two years of active service in the fields of Flanders and Artois, David contracted pneumonia and was invalided back to England to the Cambridge Hospital in Aldershot where he died from septicaemia aggravated by diabetes on 10th May 1917 aged twenty. David was buried at Aldershot Military Cemetery.

James Fitzgerald (Hazelwell, 1884) had played rugby for the College XV in 1883, and the following Easter he went up to Exeter College, Oxford. After being ordained in 1888, he gained his first Master's degree in 1892, and then a second MA from Durham University in 1895. From 1900 until the outbreak of war he administered to the priesthood in Yorkshire but volunteered for service as a forces chaplain soon after war was declared. He was appointed as a Chaplain 4th Class on 5th December 1914, and subsequently served throughout the war, in the challenging conditions on the Western Front in France, then in Salonika and finally in Palestine.[206] He was mentioned in despatches on four occasions for his distinguished service and appointed as an officer of the Most Excellent Order of the British Empire.

However, one Cheltonian family in particular epitomised the highest ideals of 'muscular Christianity'. In 1892, Reverend Thomas Hodson became the vicar of St Mary's Church in Charlton Kings, and he and his wife, Catherine, lived in the vicarage with their nine children – seven sons and two daughters. All of the seven boys went to the College and all contributed significantly in their various subsequent careers. Gerald (Day Boy, 1898), the eldest, entered the Royal Navy at the age of 14 and fought in the First World War winning the Distinguished Service Order before retiring as a Commander in 1923. Thomas (Day Boy, 1901) went on to Wadham College, Oxford and later joined the civil service in Ceylon. During the war he served as a second lieutenant in the Royal Army Service Corps in Flanders. Cyril (Day Boy, 1904), the third son, was a scholar at College and a fine shot winning the Ashburton Shield at Bisley in 1903 with the school shooting VIII. He too went on to Wadham College, gaining his MA in 1911 and becoming the first of three brothers to be ordained; he then served as an army chaplain during the war. The twins Harold and Reginald (Day Boys, 1906) also went to Wadham College after College, a route now becoming a well trodden family footpath to adulthood. Both undertook their theological education at Wells in 1910 and both then served as service chaplains in the war, Harold winning the Military Cross with the army, and Reginald on duty in the Royal Navy. Hubert (Day Boy, 1908) emigrated to Canada to farm, but when war was declared he enlisted at Valcartier, Quebec on 24th September 1914 into the 6th Battalion, Canadian Infantry (East Ontario). However, he transferred into the Princess Patricia's Canadian Light Infantry in the field on 11th April 1915, though barely four weeks later he was killed in action at Bellewaarde during the Battle of Second Ypres. Having no known grave, Herbert is commemorated on the Menin Gate memorial. Francis (Day Boy, 1914), the youngest son, served in the 7th Battalion, Gloucestershire Regiment, fighting in Gallipoli, Mesopotamia and Italy. He was wounded four times during his exploits with the battalion, winning the Military Cross and retiring as a captain. This remarkable family history is not only testament to the principles of 'muscular Christianity' as practised within their family and school environment, it also demonstrates the strength of moral fibre of each of the boys and, perhaps, of their wider generation. The strength of character, self sacrifice,

---

[206] *The London Gazette*, 19th March 1915, page 2740.

duty and loyalty displayed by every chaplain that served the armed forces during the conflict, no less than that of our 21 Old Cheltonian Great War chaplains, is impressive. To seek to go into the foulest of conditions of filth and injury, to venture into harm's way undefended and highly vulnerable, and administer to the sick, wounded and dying was quite an extraordinary and most humbling undertaking. Their awards for bravery and distinguished service, along with our deepest respect, are fully justified.

DINNER TIME

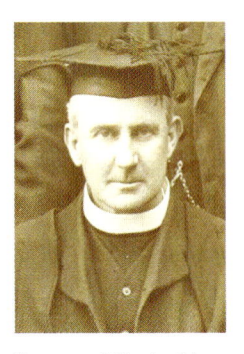

Reverend Reginald Waterfield, College Principal

On Wednesday, 20th December, 53 Old Cheltonians assembled at the Second Army Headquarters at Cassel and sat down to dinner. Presiding over the dinner was Major-General Arlington Chichester (Teighmore and Baxter, 1882), the Second Army's quartermaster general, who had been in recent letter contact with Reverend Reginald Waterfield, the principal of College at the time.

Reginald was intrigued to think that Old Cheltonians, so gripped in the process of attritional warfare, wished to hold a reunion dinner just 13 miles behind the infamous and active front line at Ypres. Furthermore, Reginald was also mindful of the dreadful number of Old Cheltonian casualties sustained during the year, the vast majority a consequence of the Somme offensive that had petered out only five weeks before. He wrote a letter, which was read out to the guests as part of the after-dinner speech:

> We think of you all a good deal. The boys are sending the College and House ribbons to decorate your table. Best wishes to your gathering, which I see you are holding on my birthday. We have beaten Rugby and Clifton at football this term.[207]

With a more sombre note, he also added that:

> There are no fewer than 3,161 Old Cheltonians who, in some form or another, are helping to mould the destinies of our great empire. Out of that number about a third, nearly a third, I am sorry to say are casualties in one form or another. On the other hand there are about one-fifth who have been decorated in some form. Out of these there are 4 V.Cs, 2 G.C.B., 1 K.C.B., 1 C.V.O., 20 C.B., 27 C.M.G., 1 C.S.I., 75 D.S.O., 124 M.C., 2 D.S.C., 574 mentions, besides a number of foreign decorations.[208]

---

[207] *The Cheltonian*, 1917, January/February, page 30.
[208] Ibid.

His letter and news from College was met with great applause and cheering from the assembled diners, one of whom was Major-General Charles Harington (Leconfield, 1890). Before embarking on his illustrious military career, Charles had played cricket for the College XI going on to play for the MCC, the Free Foresters, and the I. Zingari cricket teams.[209] He had also played racquets for the army. Now as the Second Army's chief of staff, he was a highly regarded and popular officer, and was asked to say a few words. He chose as his theme the notion of 'esprit de corps':

> Where did we first learn that spirit? We learned it first when, as quite little fellows, we lined the touch line and by the force of example of others learned to shout 'College'. That was the dawn of the right spirit in us, the foundation of 'Esprit de Corps'. We learned it on the touch line and it is our mainstay of the field of life and on the field of battle. We are glad, therefore, to pay tribute to those to whom the credit is due for infusing this spirit into us Cheltonians. It is due to the Cheltenham masters. Before any of us were born they were striving day in and day out to gain this end. They were striving in our day. They are doing it today and will do it tomorrow. They have only one object, viz, to make men of the material that passes through their hands and to send forth that material into the world to uphold the honour and name of Cheltenham College. All honour is due to them. We owe them a deep debt of gratitude.[210]

It was during the informal conversations at this dinner regarding the numbers of Old Cheltonian casualties that the first seeds for some kind of formal memorial were sown. After toasting the health of the king, the principal, and the College masters, the diners returned to their various duties in the front line. Of the 53 Old Cheltonians that attended dinner that evening, four would be killed later in the war.[211] Behind each of the Old Cheltonians killed during the Battle of the Somme lies a personal story, unique in itself, all of which have been researched and are now recorded in the College archives. Through each one runs the common thread of inspiration for their individual and collective feats of bravery, duty, loyalty and leadership.

The end of the year marked another subtle change in the attitudes of the British soldier fighting the war. The first two and half years of total and industrialised warfare had seen the demise of Britain's small regular army. The Territorial Army had been raised, trained, sent abroad, and then badly battered at Loos and on the Somme. So too were the ranks of Kitchener's New Armies and the Pals' battalions, now lying in the surfeit of cemeteries between Montauban and Serre. Many of those eager volunteers, who had rushed to the

---

[209] These amateur cricket clubs were often nomadic by nature, their members playing fixtures around the world often considered to be of first class cricket standard.
[210] *The Cheltonian*, 1917, January/February, pages 32-33.
[211] Authors note: Interestingly, these sentiments, despite being articulated in a slightly old-fashioned manner (hardly surprising given the passing of a century), are replicated to some extent in the attitudes of today's cohort of Cheltonians, a dynamic witnessed when again College beat Rugby and Clifton on the rugby field in the 2017 season.

colours in the autumn of 1914, were gone, replaced by others who were now beginning to be conscripted. Equally brave though the conscripts were, (and though they had to be), the fact of their forced enlistment was a new and challenging dynamic for the military leadership. War 'weariness' was setting in – on the Home Front as well as the fighting fronts. A conflict that was envisioned to have been concluded by its first Christmas was now facing its third. There was an underlying reluctance to prosecute the war with quite the same offensive vigour and 'esprit de corps' that Charles Harington had alluded to at the Old Cheltonians' dinner. This was not only due to the era of conscription, a deeply unpopular yet essential contingency, it was also embodied in a change of political attitudes. With Lloyd George succeeding Herbert Asquith as Prime Minister on 7th December, Haig inherited a sceptical, if not critical, political master to whom the casualty rate, with its associated and growing public concern, exhorted consideration of alternative strategies. The commander-in-chief, despite having the tacit support of the king, would now be required to seek endorsement from politicians to confirm his campaign to align it with a national co-ordinated response of men and materiel as well as support from the Dominions. The burgeoning military effort and its increasing demands, not just in Europe but across the seas between the four other major campaigns, had to be harmonised with a holistic approach to industrial, agricultural and economic output.[212] Furthermore, while patriotic fervour was eroded bit by bit with every newspaper publication of the latest casualty lists, it was essential to maintain the focus of public opinion on final victory, so as not to betray the countless sacrifices already made. If 1916 had been challenging, the following year was likely to be doubly difficult.

---

[212] Four significant campaigns were being fought simultaneously in Salonika, Palestine, Mesopotamia, and Africa (both East and West). It should also be noted that increasing numbers of troops were required for garrisons in Ireland following the April uprising.

LIST OF FALLEN OLD CHELTONIANS 1916

On the following pages (156 to 163) are the names and service details of Old Cheltonians who died in the third year of the war.

1916 – LIST OF FALLEN OLD CHELTONIANS

	Died (1916)	**Name**	**Rank**
302	4 January	Disney EO	Lt Commander
303	21 January	Jenkins RA	Captain
304	25 January	Meyricke RJC	Major
305	31 January	Prendergast CR	Captain
306	31 January	Radcliffe JF	Lt Colonel
307	11 February	Bingen CM	Lieutenant
308	12 February	Ievers OG	Lt Colonel
309	14 February	Hore CO	Colonel
310	20 February	Gatacre, EG	Captain
311	20 February	Wiseman-Clarke CFR	Lieutenant
312	23 February	Reynolds D (VC)	Major
313	26 February	Reeves VCM	Major
314	28 February	Jamieson GA	Major
315	2 March	Mason AEK	Captain
316	8 March	Arbuthnot ADS	Captain
317	8 March	Landale JR	Major
318	8 March	Saunders AHR	Captain
319	14 March	Campbell CH	Lt Colonel
320	27 March	Blakeway NC	Lieutenant
321	29 March	Lambert FC	Major
322	5 April	Conybeare EB	Captain
323	6 April	Davis AH	2nd Lieutenant
324	6 April	Forbes- Robertson H	Captain
325	17 April	Forbes-Robertson A	Brevet Major
326	21 April	Birch H	2nd Lieutenant
327	21 April	Stewart B	Lieutenant
328	22 April	Armstrong MRL	2nd Lieutenant
329	26 April	Steinman BP	Captain
330	7 May	Mansfield CJ	Sgn General
331	7 May	Taylor EM	Trooper
332	15 May	Aldin DC	2nd Lieutenant
333	19 May	Soames WN	Lieutenant
334	20 May	Deakin CG	2nd Lieutenant
335	25 May	Clarke HC	Captain
336	25 May	Purdey MS	Major
337	31 May	Robinson HA	Major
338	1 June	Maxwell J McC	Lieutenant
339	10 June	North WBG	Corporal
340	13 June	Whitehead H	2nd Lieutenant

1916 – LIST OF FALLEN OLD CHELTONIANS

Unit	Age	Place
HMS *Arethusa*	29	North Sea
97th Deccan Infantry, IA	29	Mesopotamia
58th Brigade, Royal Field Artillery	38	(Malta) Gallipoli
28th Punjabis	28	Mesopotamia
CO, 10th Essex Regiment	48	Arras, France
5th Royal Sussex Regiment	20	Somme, France
GSO2, late Royal Sussex Regiment	52	Ireland
CO, Royal Garrison Regiment	55	London
2nd West Riding Regiment	31	Somme, France
108th Heavy Battery, RGA	19	Ypres, Belgium
37th Battery, Royal Field Artillery	34	Le Touquet, France
1/1st Dorsetshire Yeomanry	29	Agagia, Egypt
9th Bhopal Infantry	39	(Mesop), India
att 6th Royal Fusiliers	22	Loos, France
20th Coy, 3rd Sappers/Miners, RE	34	Mesopotamia
2nd Rajput Light Infantry, IA	25	Mesopotamia
1/2nd Gurkha Rifles	30	Mesopotamia
CO, 1/4th Seaforth Highlanders	37	Arras, France
att 1st Dorsetshire Regiment	20	Somme, France
Royal Army Medical Corps	37	Mesopotamia
9th Worcestershire Regiment	23	Mesopotamia
1st Oxford and Bucks Light Infantry	31	Mesopotamia
51st Sikhs, IA	29	Mesopotamia
128th Pioneers, IA	35	Mesopotamia
128th Pioneers, IA	30	Mesopotamia
1st Seaforth Highlanders	22	Mesopotamia
150th Field Company, RE	26	Somme, France
att 1st East Kent (Buffs) Regiment	41	Rouen, France
CO, RN Hospital, Haslar	54	Haslar, UK
3rd Canadian Mounted Rifles	30	Hooge, Belgium
105th Field Company, RE	19	Vimy, France
1/1st Cheshire Yeomanry	27	Egypt
14th Hussars	22	Mesopotamia
33rd Division Train, ASC	35	Bethune, France
Army Remount Service	38	Sussex
2nd Loyal North Lancashire Regiment	45	German East Africa
459th Battery, 118th Brigade, RGA	21	Ypres, Belgium
22nd Royal Fusiliers	34	Vimy, France
Trench Mortar Battery, 4th Div, RFA	18	Somme, France

1916 – LIST OF FALLEN OLD CHELTONIANS

	Died (1916)	Name	Rank
341	14 June	Llewellyn HA	Lieutenant
342	21 June	Montgomery AS	Lieutenant
343	29 June	Allaway TR	Captain
344	30 June	Turner GP	2nd Lieutenant
345	1 July	Adams HI	Lieutenant
346	1 July	Cope GE	Captain
347	1 July	Hirst CP	2nd Lieutenant
348	1 July	MacPherson J	Captain
349	1 July	Matthey EG	Captain
350	1 July	Neame GT	Captain
351	2 July	Damiano WH	2nd Lieutenant
352	2 July	MacBryan EC	Lieutenant
353	3 July	Crooke EH	Captain
354	8 July	Bidie GMV	Lieutenant
355	8 July	Chard RAF	Captain
356	10 July	Boothby EB	2nd Lieutenant
357	10 July	Braithwaite HL	2nd Lieutenant
358	10 July	Lucas CM	2nd Lieutenant
359	11 July	Mather E	Private
360	11 July	Davidson GL	Lieutenant
361	12 July	Williams FT	Lt Colonel
362	14 July	Woollatt PR	2nd Lieutenant
363	16 July	Barnes GG	2nd Lieutenant
364	16 July	Elliot WCA	Lieutenant
365	18 July	Patrick DB	Lieutenant
366	20 July	Tuke FH	Chaplain
367	20 July	Vaughan GC	Captain
368	21 July	Trimmer WC	2nd Lieutenant
369	21 July	Shurey C	Captain
370	22 July	Loch AAF	Captain
371	22 July	Thornton LN	2nd Lieutenant
372	23 July	Boothby JH	2nd Lieutenant
373	26 July	Bewicke CG	Lieutenant
374	27 July	Turner CRS	2nd Lieutenant
375	29 July	Ramsbottom R	2nd Lieutenant
376	30 July	Harries-Jones LA	2nd Lieutenant
377	31 July	Rainey EF	Lt Colonel
378	1 August	Footner HE	Captain
379	2 August	Owen RM	Major

1916 – LIST OF FALLEN OLD CHELTONIANS

Unit	Age	Place
8th South Wales Borderers	25	Salonika
5th Royal Inniskilling Fusiliers	39	Salonika
att 2nd Welsh Regiment	24	Egypt
att 116th Trench Mortar Battery	34	Loos, France
1st Hampshire Regiment	34	Somme, France
20th Northumberland Fusiliers	20	Somme, France
9th Devonshire Regiment	24	Somme, France
1/7th Notts and Derby Regiment	25	Somme, France
2nd Lancashire Fusiliers	23	Somme, France
7th East Kent (Buffs) Regiment	31	Somme, France
2nd Royal Dublin Fusiliers	19	Somme, France
att 1st Somerset Light Infantry	22	Somme, France
8th Gloucestershire Regiment	25	Somme, France
1st Royal Scots att No 43 Sqn, RFC	22	Whitstable, England
8th Royal Fusiliers	29	Somme, France
13th Rifle Brigade	35	Somme, France
171st Tunneling Company, RE	31	Ypres, Belgium
att 15th Welsh Regiment	30	Somme, France
17th King's (Liverpool) Regiment	25	Somme, France
6th Dorsetshire Regiment	30	Somme, France
2nd Northamptonshire, Regiment	38	Rouen, France
7th Queen's (Royal West Surrey)	21	Somme, France
6th Worcestershire Regiment	23	Somme, France
1st Royal Marines Light Infantry	25	Vimy, France
att 28th Machine Gun Corps	31	Somme, France
Army Chaplain's Department	49	Somme, France
1st Devonshire Regiment	26	Somme, France
1/4th Oxford and Bucks Light Infantry	19	Somme, France
att 10th Royal Fusiliers	25	Somme, France
1st South Wales Borderers	20	Somme, France
att 10th Gloucestershire Regiment	21	Somme, France
U Battery, 1st (Indian) Brigade, RHA	23	Somme, France
att 2nd Welch Regiment	19	Somme. France
att 1st King's Royal Rifle Corps	19	Somme, France
att 17th Royal Fusiliers	32	Somme, France
att 24th Manchester Regiment	24	Somme, France
72nd Punjabis	51	Srinagar, India
35th Heavy Battery, RGA	39	Somme, France
2nd Oxford and Bucks Light Infantry	25	Somme, France

1916 – LIST OF FALLEN OLD CHELTONIANS

	Died (1916)	**Name**	**Rank**
380	10 August	Hunt JCM	Lieutenant
381	11 August	St Hill FH	Private
382	12 August	Tosswill WR	Captain
383	13 August	Sharp FL	Lt Colonel
384	16 August	MacNeece JDG	Captain
385	18 August	Baghot de la Bere CJ	2nd Lieutenant
386	18 August	Layng GRS	2nd Lieutenant
387	21 August	Butler LG	Captain
388	21 August	Kellett RHV	2nd Lieutenant
389	21 August	Woollatt CH	Captain
390	27 August	Apperly AL	Lieutenant
391	27 August	Winterbotham CW	Lieutenant
392	31 August	Crawford JC	2nd Lieutenant
393	1 September	Philpot G	Captain
394	2 September	Allen GM	2nd Lieutenant
395	3 September	Du Boulay HLH	2nd Lieutenant
396	3 September	Vyall LE	Corporal
397	5 September	Walker R	Major
398	6 September	Bertram RG de la V	Lieutenant
399	8 September	Reid JG	Captain
400	8 September	Worsey TA	Lieutenant
401	9 September	Bren HAH	Lieutenant
402	9 September	Purdon TO	Captain
403	13 September	Dawe RH O'N	2nd Lieutenant
404	13 September	Wilson GD	Lieutenant
405	15 September	Cully GMG	Captain
406	15 September	Herbert JG	Rifleman
407	15 September	Newton VF	2nd Lieutenant
408	16 September	Walter B	Major
409	19 September	Williams RB	Captain
410	22 September	Louis AG	Private
411	23 September	Brooke-Murray K	Captain
412	25 September	Gosset RF	Captain
413	28 September	West FCB	Lt Colonel
414	4 October	Evans HTP	2nd Lieutenant
415	9 October	Wood RP	Lt Colonel
416	15 October	James EG	Captain
417	21 October	Mackinnon RF	Lieutenant
418	25 October	Scott D	2nd Lieutenant

1916 – LIST OF FALLEN OLD CHELTONIANS

Unit	Age	Place
B Battery, 47th Brigade, RFA	21	Somme, France
NZAC Training Unit, Trentham	25	New Zealand
1st East Lancashire Regiment	22	Ypres, Belgium
CO 39th Brigade, Royal Field Artillery	49	Somme, France
CO 51st Battery, Royal Field Artillery	25	Somme, France
10th Gloucestershire Regiment	20	Somme, France
10th Gloucestershire Regiment	20	Somme, France
att 3rd Rifle Brigade	26	Somme, France
B Battery, 74th Brigade, RFA	20	Somme, France
8th Queen's (Royal West Surreys)	29	Somme, France
1/5th Gloucestershire Regiment	39	Somme, France
1/5th Gloucestershire Regiment	29	Somme, France
F battery, 14th Brigade, RHA	18	Somme, France
15th Siege Battery, RGA	25	Somme, France
No 11 Squadron, RFC	22	Somme, France
att 1st Wiltshire Regiment	19	Somme, France
2nd Canadian Division (Signals)	27	St Omer, France
105th Field Company, RE	39	Somme, France
8th Canadian (Manitoba) Infantry	25	London, England
11th Worcestershire Regiment	26	Doiran, Salonika
7th Canadian Infantry	34	Somme, France
att 7th Leinster Regiment	24	Somme, France
7th Leinster Regiment	28	Somme, France
1st Devonshire Regiment	18	Somme, France
2nd (London) Brigade, RFA	45	Rouen, France
11th Royal West Kent Regiment	33	Somme, France
7th Rifle Brigade	31	Somme, France
1st Royal Welch Regiment	19	Somme, France
43rd Battery, Royal Field Artillery	34	Somme, France
176th Tunneling Company, RE	29	Vimy, France
Royal Army Medical Corps	42	Prestbury, England
ASC, att No 15 Squadron, RFC	24	Boulogne, France
1st East Yorkshire Regiment	21	Somme, France
CO, 243rd Brigade, Royal Field Artillery	32	Somme, France
98th Brigade, Royal Field Artillery	22	Jenikoj, Salonika
CO, 2nd York and Lancasters	26	Somme, France
1st Shropshire Light Infantry	23	Rouen, France
11th Lancashire Fusiliers	27	Somme, France
54th Battery, 39th Brigade, RFA	19	Somme, France

1916 – LIST OF FALLEN OLD CHELTONIANS

	Died (1916)	Name	Rank
419	28 October	Terry WG	Captain
420	13 November	Browne MC	Captain
421	15 November	Stock JMT	Captain
422	18 November	Torrie TGJ	Lt Colonel
423	19 November	Hall AH	Captain
424	1 December	Abelson EG	Lieutenant
425	7 December	Richardson G St J	Lieutenant
426	10 December	Crooke HN	2nd Lieutenant
427	16 December	Cheetham AH	Lieutenant
428	23 December	Murray GR	Lieutenant
429	28 December	Barnes J	2nd Lieutenant

1916 – LIST OF FALLEN OLD CHELTONIANS

Unit	Age	Place
Royal Artillery	55	Plymouth, England
Royal Marines Light Infantry	24	Somme, France
8th East Lancashire Regiment	26	Somme, France
CO, 7th East Lancashire Regiment	36	Somme, France
att 8th Somerset Light Infantry	25	Somme, France
Royal Marines Light Infantry	18	Le Havre, France
7th (Duke of Connaught's) Rajputs	27	Mesopotamia
67th Field Company, RE	19	Somme, France
2nd West Riding Regiment	20	Somme, France
13th (Duke of Connaught's) Lancers	36	Mesopotamia
1/7th Sherwood Foresters	25	Somme, France

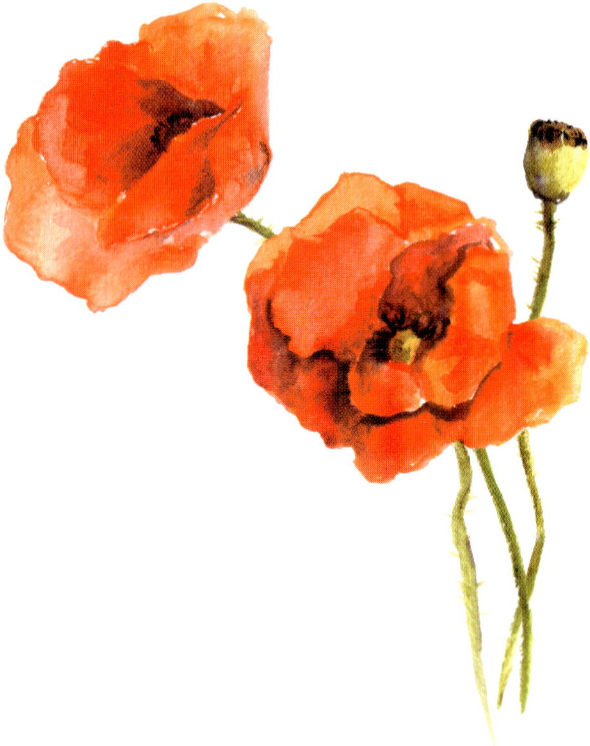

ACTS FOUR

1917 – THE YEAR OF STOIC RESOLVE

After two and half years of mounting casualties without very much measurable progress, jingoistic fervour had started to wane within the British psyche. The turn of the new year showed little change to the sense of duty and service to nation felt by the College community. The adventurism and enthusiasm displayed in 1914 had been overtaken by an enduring patriotism and stoicism firmly focussed with steely purpose on a final victory. For example, of the College cricket XI from the season before, all served during the war; George Shelmerdine (Newick, 1918) being one of five Old Cheltonians from the family who saw active service.

All of these cricketers, and the five Shelmerdine brothers, survived the conflict. Similarly, of the 1916 rugby XV, whose victories over Clifton and Rugby had been lauded by General Charles Harington to the assembled Old Cheltonian officers dining together in Flanders the previous December, all volunteered for service in the army with one exception. Theodore Walsh (Boyne House, 1918) was simply too young, being just sixteen when he first played for the College XV that season. He went on to play in the next two seasons, captaining the team throughout his last term in the autumn of 1918.[213] The remaining members of the XV, however, were all commissioned into the army. The personal stories behind three particular young team mates (Lionel Maby, Noel Russell and Patrick Henderson) exemplify the close and integral lives that the College community shared. Having started as a day boy, Lionel Maby (Cheltondale, 1916) became a boarder at College, even though his family lived locally at Marie Hill House, Cheltenham.[214] Besides being a member of the rugby XV in his final term, he was also appointed the school's senior prefect and was a cadet second lieutenant in the school's Officers Training Corps. Whilst still at school Lionel applied for entry to the Military Academy at Woolwich with a view to becoming a Royal Artillery officer. Perhaps realising that this would entail an extended period of training and eager to play his part, he also applied for a commission in the infantry, subsequently gaining a place at Sandhurst from which he was commissioned as a second lieutenant into the 2nd Battalion, Scots Guards, with which he fought during the last several months of the war. Noel Russell (Day Boy, 1917) took over from Lionel as the senior prefect at College, leaving at the end of the

---

[213] Theodore Edwin Walsh also played in the 1st XI cricket for two years and was a College prefect. He went up to King's College, Cambridge playing rugby for the University and gaining his BA in 1921, before going on to qualify as a doctor in 1925. He emigrated to America and became a professor at the University of Chicago and one of the world's leading experts in the field of otolaryngology. He died in St Louis, Missouri, on 29th April 1971.
[214] His father, Joseph, was a railway contractor and sent Lionel and his two younger brothers, Joseph and Alfred to College; both were day boys.

WOOF. W.H.JESSOP. I.J.KILGOUR. L.W.HASLETT. G.N.RODMAN. P.T.HARRISON. F.C.CHISNELL. BURROWS.
G.O.SHELMERDINE. P.B.SANGER. J.A.S.JACKSON. O.L.ROBERTS. C.P.GUISE.
L.F.HANCOCK (ABSENT.)

College XI 1916, all served and survived

following summer term. Having enlisted and attested at Cheltenham on 18th December 1916 Noel was placed on the Army Reserve while completing his schooling. On 30th July 1917 he was posted to No 1 Royal Field Artillery Officer Cadet School at St John's Wood and would receive his commission as a second lieutenant on 12th January 1918.[215] Patrick Henderson (Newick, 1917) was a scholar, a College prefect and like Lionel, a cadet lieutenant in the Corps. Again like Lionel, Patrick also applied early for a temporary commission in the autumn term on 12th November 1916 and during his last term at College the following summer, was attested into the army at Horfield Barracks, Bristol on 5th June. He was immediately posted to No 5 Officer Cadet Battalion at Trinity College, Cambridge. Patrick was commissioned three months later as a second lieutenant in the West Riding Regiment on 26th September, and after further professional training with the reserve battalion was sent to the Front as a replacement officer.[216]

Across the nation, patriotic enthusiasm for war service was on the decline as the effects of conscription and war weariness began to bite. In addition, growing industrial unrest, food shortages and the continued issue regarding Irish nationalism clouded the national focus, conspiring to undermine national cohesion for fighting the war to a successful conclusion. These domestic and political pressures at home had a sapping effect on the morale of troops engaged at the Front. However, from the College's perspective, the

---

[215] Supplement to *The London Gazette*, dated 21st January 1918, page 1068.
[216] Supplement to *The London Gazette*, dated 13th October 1917, page 10560.

beginning of 1917 showed no sign of any slackening in the resolve of the boys to volunteer and serve the nation's cause. Of the other 11 members of the 1916 rugby XV, seven gained commissions after passing through the Royal Military Academy at Woolwich with several on the same cadet intake, two were commissioned after their course at the Royal Military College, Sandhurst, and two were commissioned from the ranks. Furthermore, 10 of the XV were appointed as College prefects, with wider responsibilities in College and their respective Houses. Given the dreadfully depressing casualty figures being published, the vast majority resulting from the recent fighting on the Somme, what maintained such a strong motivation within the student population to go to war? Clearly, the evidence suggests an overwhelming consensus within the senior elements of the College's student population to serve their country, all of them going into the army and all becoming junior officers. As several of these boys began their individual application process before they left school, it is highly likely that volunteering for military service was not only a commonly felt duty, it was also a hot topic for discussion and collusion between the boys. Furthermore, as their applications for commissions would have needed supporting testimonials, chiefly from the Principal, Reverend Reginald Waterfield, but also from the various housemasters and even the officers in the College's Officers Training Corps and with tacit support from parents, the recruiting process was embraced by the whole College community. In addition, although the idea of heroic adventure, so common in the opening stages of the war, may have faded to some degree there was still a shared and firmly held belief in the righteousness of the cause. If the cause was right then the war had to be won, not least to ensure that the fallen had not died in vain. Consequently, there remained manifest within the College's society abiding patriotism and stoicism in the face of unparalleled hardship and sacrifice, epitomised through the release in late 1916 of the official war film *The Battle of the Somme*.[217] Alongside this there remained an enduring sense of duty and determination to embrace and uphold the school's history, ethos and reputation.

There were also other less lofty but equally valid motivations. Playing in his first season of rugby in the XV, John MacNeece (Hazelwell, 1918) was the youngest of three brothers, all educated at College, who fought in the war. The boys had grown up in a military environment, as their father Thomas had been a colonel and an army doctor. Eldest brother William had left College in 1907, and after being commissioned from Sandhurst, began his career in the army. Before the war he trained as a pilot, and was awarded his Royal Aero Club aviator's certificate (number 671) on 31st October 1913. As the fledgling potential of air power became increasingly appreciated by the upper echelons of the army, William was amongst the early numbers whose flying expertise was transferred to the reserve of the Royal Flying Corps (RFC) on 28th April 1914. When war broke out some three months later, he was quickly seconded to the RFC. By 1917, after flying many reconnaissance sorties with No 3 Squadron, he was commanding a wing with the rank of lieutenant colonel and

---

[217] The official war film was released on 21st August 1916, edited by C Urban and G H Malins and was booked by over 2,000 cinemas by October 1916; a large proportion of the British population viewed the film that autumn.

had just been awarded the Distinguished Service Order in the 1917 New Year's Honours list.[218] So as young John applied for his own military service during 1917, undoubtedly buoyed by pride in his eldest brother's recent award and achievements, he already had much to admire and emulate. Sadly, however, the middle brother James was less fortunate. James had been both the senior prefect and captain of the rugby XV at College, leaving in 1909 to go to Woolwich to become an artillery officer. After war had broken out, he fought in the early bitter actions at Ypres, Neuve Chapelle, and Loos. By 1916, he commanded the 51st Battery, Royal Field Artillery moving to the Somme in the early summer of 1916. During a short period of leave before the major assault commenced in July, James married Mary Heath, daughter of Major General Sir Gerard Heath, on 1st June 1916. As both families were well-connected, it was no doubt quite a social event and well attended family occasion, despite the privations and apprehension of serving in France. As it transpired, such trepidation was well founded. James was killed in action on 16th August by enemy rifle fire in No Man's Land near Delville Wood, while looking for a forward position from which to observe the fire of his battery's guns. James' body was never found. In Mary's anxiety to locate the whereabouts of his body, an informant, Gunner Young, stated later that:

> Capt Macneece (*sic*) was in my battery- very popular and a fine soldier. We were in action on Montauban Ridge in Aug. Signaller Buckley (51st Batt) was out observing with him. I saw them both start and I saw Buckley come back alone. He told me that he had seen Capt Macneece killed by machine gun fire, 15 yds from the German trenches. We tried to recover his body but it was too close to the German lines.[219]

Perhaps with the emotion of losing his brother James, and seeing sister-in-law Mary so quickly widowed, John had added incentive to join the ranks and fight for victory.

BRIEF INTERLUDE

By January 1917, College had lost 429 Old Cheltonians during the preceding 29 months of warfare, a depressing monthly average of nearly 15 deaths a month. So, the 13 Old Cheltonians killed during the first two months of 1917 represented somewhat of a brief improvement over the carnage of the preceding six months and that which was soon to follow. Of course, it gave little solace to the ever-lengthening list of grieving families. Of these 13, only three were killed in action on the Western Front. Raymond Doherty-Holwell (Hazelwell, 1899), a maths scholar at College and later a lieutenant colonel in the Royal Engineers with a Distinguished Service Order to his name, was killed near Ypres supervising improvements to the communications systems between the front-line trenches

---

[218] He would become Air Vice Marshal William Foster MacNeece Foster, CB, CBE, DSO, DFC.
[219] The National Archives, WO 339/7952, Personal Record of Captain JDG MacNeece.

and brigade and divisional headquarters. William Pym (Cheltondale, 1906) was involved in an abortive attack on 17th February on the German line near Miraumont on the Somme. He had left College when he was 17 to become a rubber planter in the Federated Malay States, but on the outbreak of war, he returned to England and enlisted in the Royal Fusiliers in November 1914. The battalion war diary records the action that day:

> By 5.30am all the [Companies] were reported as ready however, from 4.30 onwards the enemy had spotted the attack and kept a 'steady bombardment' upon the newly forming lines. The [Companies] stayed in good form and the enemy's attacks slackened and therefore, they eventually managed to progress and move forward at 5.45. However, the enemy quickly launched an intense machine gun fire causing severe casualties to many officers.[220]

Those severe officer casualties included two killed, one who died of wounds and 11 wounded, leaving the attacking troops with weakened leadership. The diary goes on:

> To progress further at 'GRANDCOURT TRENCH' there was wire that needed cutting and this delay also resulted in more casualties. By this time the Battalion units had all merged and were considerably diminished in numbers. The battalion finally reached 'S. MIRAUMOUNT' in the north of France in the Somme area. The wire at this location was 'inadvisable' to cut through. Therefore, the troops were forced to occupy shell holes. They remained in this situation for around 30 minutes until the enemy in the centre launched an attack. Troops retired from the left and right as it was 'advisable to withdraw'. The Battalion failed to reach its final objective. However, the diary states that after the disaster regarding the loss and wounding of the officers of the 11th Battalion, the remaining troops 'displayed the greatest gallantry and devotion to duty' and fought valiantly in the circumstances.[221]

The Battalion lost 42 other ranks killed and 162 wounded, during the attack, and a further 69 were reported as 'missing'. Fusilier William Pym was one of these missing soldiers: his body was never found, and he is commemorated on Thiepval Memorial to the Missing.

Younger than William, but in the same House was Frank Simpson (Cheltondale, 1909). An energetic member of the Officers Training Corps, Frank was a member of the School's shooting VIII in his penultimate term and had gained his Certificate A, the set of competency tests for army cadets believed to prepare them for a territorial commission. At the end of the following term, he applied for entry to the Royal Military Academy at Woolwich to join the Royal Field Artillery (RFA), having gained a supplementary certificate in mathematics from the University of Birmingham to bolster his application. Frank and

[220] The National Archives, WO 95/2045, War Diary of the 11th Battalion, Royal Fusiliers, 1917.
[221] Ibid.

his father, had their eyes set on the 'dash and gallop' associated with the ethos of the RFA as this element of the Royal Artillery tended to be where the young artillery 'thrusters' were appointed and won their spurs. The example of Douglas Reynolds's VC action in saving the RFA's guns at Le Cateau in the first month of the war, would no doubt have provided a source of pride and inspiration in the minds of the College's OTC cadets. However, on completion of his artillery course, Frank was commissioned in 1911 into the Royal Garrison Artillery (RGA).[222] Naturally disappointed not to have achieved his aspiration of an RFA commission, his father wrote to the Academy for an explanation, to which the reply explained that as Frank 'did not pass high enough in Riding and Field Artillery drills to secure a vacancy in the Royal Field Artillery', he was considered more suitable for service with the heavier siege gun batteries of the RGA.[223] When war was declared, he served on the Western Front initially with the RGA but, perhaps still seeking the élan and thrill of a more nimble 'mount', transferred to the Royal Flying Corps and trained as a pilot. Successfully gaining his wings, Frank was posted to No 53 Squadron where he quickly made a name for himself for developing air to ground communications for coordination with the infantry battalions; he was promoted to Captain in July 1916. Earlier that summer Frank had married Eleanor Coleman and they were expecting their first child at the end February 1917, who, tragically he did not live to meet. Late on the morning of 16th February, the squadron put up several aircraft on an escorted artillery observation mission, to support the effort against 28 designated targets that day. The squadron's sorties, however, met with mixed results. Second Lieutenants David Kerr and Frederick Elstob shot down a German Halberstadt aircraft which crashed south of Ypres near Wytschaete shortly after midday.[224] Frank however, was killed during the mission flying with Sergeant Charles Edlington as his air gunner when their BE2c (No 6313) broke up in a vertical nose dive after descending out of control from 9,000 feet and crashing behind the British line near the battle torn village of Nieppe, north west of Armentières. Both bodies were recovered to No 77 Field Ambulance where they were buried beside each other in the Pont de Nieppe communal cemetery.

During these early months, three Old Cheltonians died in hospital, one from wounds and two from illness, reflecting the poor sanitary conditions and inability of soldiers to resist infection in a time before antibiotics from their service in the appalling conditions of the various front lines. William Denne (Hazelwell, 1895), a good cricketer at College playing in the XI for two years, served on the Western Front from 1914, temporarily commanding the 2nd Battalion, Bedfordshire Regiment from November 1914 until January 1915. William was severely wounded at Neuve Chapelle, an action for which he was subsequently awarded the Distinguished Service Order. The war diary records that the battalion was holding front line trenches amongst the remains of the small and broken village of Piètre, two miles east of Neuve Chapelle, when;

---

[222] *The London Gazette*, dated 22nd August 1911.
[223] The National Archives, WO 339/7955, Personal Record of Captain FWH Simpson, (letter of explanation dated 30th August 1911 from the Academy to his father).
[224] See C. Bowyer, Royal Flying Corps Communiqués, 1917-1918, (Grub Street, London), page 20, Communiqué No 75.

> The salient was rushed by the Germans early in the morning of 12 March [1915] until about noon. (At 7am) Major W H DENNE prepared to make a counter attack on the captured trench with part of A Coy. Maj DENNE was severely wounded.[225]

William was quickly evacuated to England and sent to the Queen Alexandra's Hospital in Highgate. Sadly, his wounds were so severe that they finally took his life almost two years later, on 21st February 1917. He bravely endured constant pain during his entire, unbroken stay at the hospital.

Reginald Loye (Cheltondale, 1903) also died in hospital, but from illness. In finance before the war, he was conscripted in March 1916 as a private in the 12th Battalion, Royal Fusiliers (the 'Bankers' Battalion). Embarking for France that August as part of a reinforcement draft, Reginald was engaged in special duties and patrols into No Man's Land during various actions on the Somme. After extreme risk and danger from action between the front lines, he died of pneumonia at a casualty clearing station (CCS) near Bethune. The illness had been contracted earlier in the winter while under canvas at a base camp, undergoing a course of machine gun instruction. In another example Robert Carew (Christowe, 1876) died in a military hospital in Bournemouth from carcinoma which was thought to have been contracted during his service in Salonika during August 1916. Disease during the summer months specifically enteric fever and malaria was the source of significant casualties owing to the climate and poor sanitary arrangements.[226] He was medically evacuated from Egypt in October but died in the military hospital in Bournemouth some four months later and was buried back in Ireland at the Waterford Protestant Cemetery.

The other seven Old Cheltonians that died during this short period were all killed fighting in Mesopotamia, where at last some progress was becoming apparent. After the debacle of General Townshend's surrender at Kut the previous year, the British army in Mesopotamia had been reorganised and reinforced.[227] Its new commander, General Maude, initiated an offensive up the River Tigris on 13th December 1916, gaining ground from the Turks and recapturing the city of Kut, after two days of heavy fighting, on 24th February. Two Old Cheltonians, Henry Crichton (Cheltondale, 1912) and Aubrey Reilly (Newick, 1911), were both killed in the initial assault on Kut of 22nd February. Having attended College at the same time, Henry and Aubrey represented the school's gymnastic and shooting VIIIs respectively. They both went on to the Royal Military College at Sandhurst and were commissioned into the Indian Army. Henry was leading his platoon from the 51st Sikhs and Aubrey a company of the 69th Punjabis against strong Turkish defences by the River Tigris when they were both killed. Forward momentum was maintained however, Baghdad falling to the British some two weeks later on 11th March. Both these significant successes served to restore, to a large

---

[225] The National Archives, WO 95/1658, War Diary of the 2nd Bedfordshire Regiment, 1915.
[226] The National Archives, WO 153/1344 Salonika – Charts and Graphs: British strengths, casualties etc., 1915-1918. For most months recorded in Salonika, the number of casualties listed as 'died of disease' exceeded the number 'killed' and often even the number 'wounded'.
[227] In April 1916 the British garrison at Kut, consisting of 13,000 British and Indian troops, surrendered to the Turks after a 147-day siege. This was the worst surrender in the history of the British Army to that point.

degree, the tarnished British military reputation in Mesopotamia, a process in which Old Cheltonians played their full part.

While distinct success was beginning to materialise in Mesopotamia, fighting in the German colonies of East Africa had continued from 1914 in a campaign smaller in scale and subsequently less renowned than those being waged in Europe and the Middle East. However, East African engagements were equally as brutal. In his despatch to the War Office, Lieutenant General Hoskins, the commander-in-chief of the East African Expeditionary Force, describes the circumstances affecting the campaign in February 1917:

> The approximate total strength of the efficient troops of the enemy in the field was computed at 1,100 whites and 7,300 Askaris, with four guns of 4in. or 4.1in. calibre, sixteen smaller ones and seventy-three machine guns.
>
> It was clearly necessary to push the enemy off the Rufiji River and as far south as possible so as to be able to use the Rufiji River for transport purposes; and the operations of the Kilwa and Rufiji Columns had been conceived with this object. From native reports and such statistics as were available three more weeks of fine weather could be expected. But the supply and transport situation was not at all satisfactory. There was no reserve in the advanced depots; the number of porters was insufficient; the animals in transport units were dying and the drivers of the mechanical transport were falling sick so rapidly that the numbers of troops in the front line could not be maintained there.[228]

By February the rainy season had begun in earnest, heralding one of the wettest seasons in the region for some time. This made movement of troops and supplies through the thick bush countryside difficult, as rivers flooded, tracks became impassable and some patrols had to be carried out by canoe. Frederick Booth (Hazelwell, 1905), joined the British South African Police in 1912, but was seconded to the Rhodesian Native Infantry as a sergeant during the campaign in East Africa. On 12th February, he was one of the few white officers operating with native soldiers near Songea as part of a force under Colonel Byron charged with harassing the German irregular companies. General Hoskins' despatch records that the German force:

> Appeared on the Wiedhafen-Songea road, attacked two of our posts without success, and moved south on the 11th, hotly pursued by Colonel Hawthorn, whose column had been moved most opportunely. Kraut's men were reported to be in a discontented state, probably from lack of supplies; his retirement was therefore rapid, and though his rearguards were frequently roughly handled by our pursuing column, he managed to make good his retreat with six companies and three guns to the Portuguese border due south of Songea.[229]

---

[228] *The London Gazette*, dated 27th December 1917, page 30447.
[229] Ibid.

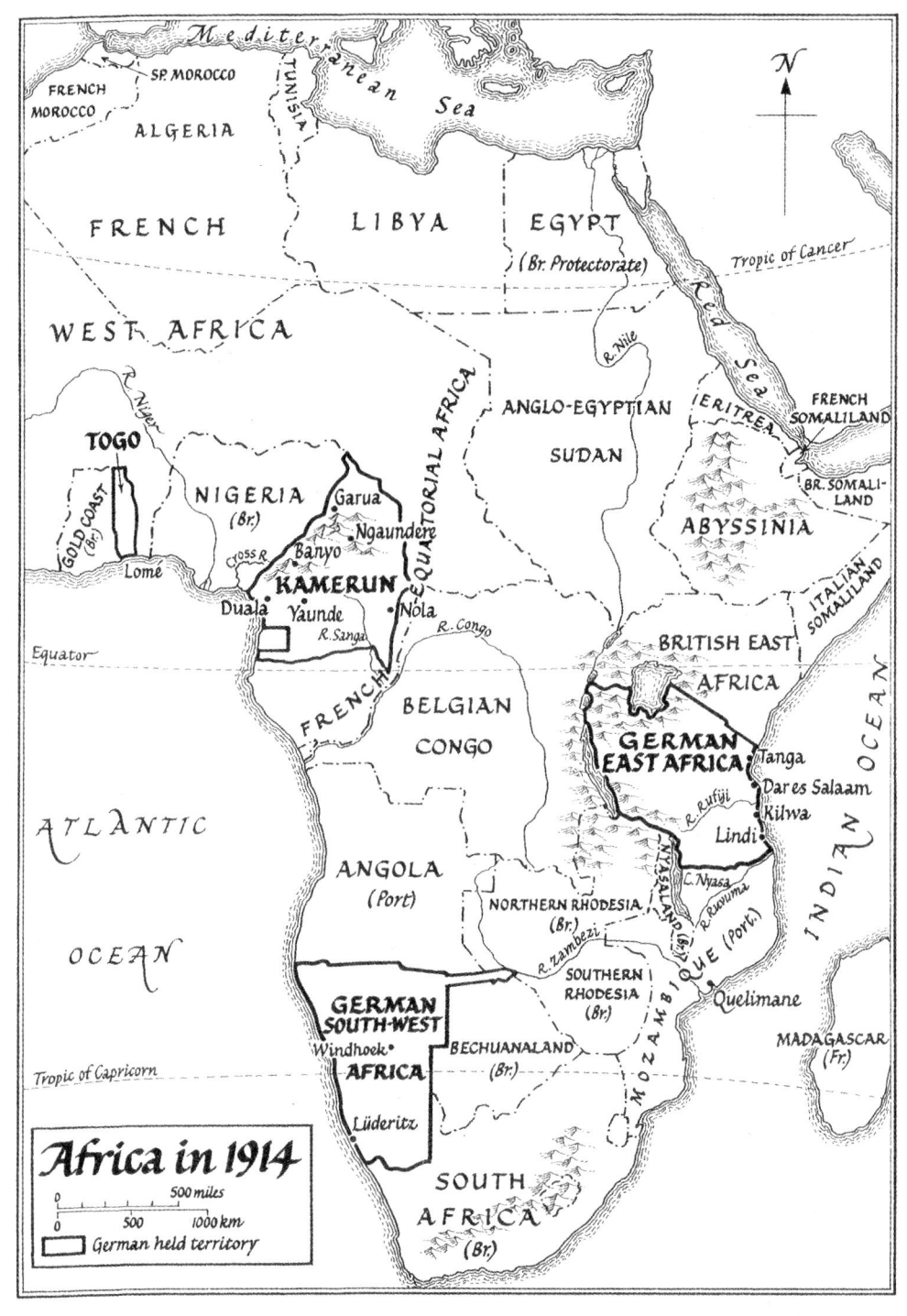

Africa in 1914

Frederick was awarded the Victoria Cross for his actions that day by the Rovuma River at Johannesbruck, near the town of Songea, as his citation records:

> For most conspicuous bravery during an attack in thick bush on the enemy position. Under very heavy rifle fire, Sergeant Booth went forward alone and brought in a man who was dangerously wounded. Later he rallied native troops who were badly disorganised and brought them to the firing line. This NCO has on many previous occasions displayed the greatest bravery, coolness and resource in action, and has set a splendid example of pluck, endurance and determination.[230]

Frederick was further decorated with the Distinguished Conduct Medal just three months later on 15th May:

> For conspicuous gallantry on many occasions. Booth showed a splendid example of courage and good leadership, inspiring confidence in his men. He twice carried despatches through enemy lines.[231]

Frederick Booth VC

Frederick was wounded in action shortly thereafter and eventually invalided back to England. He was invested with his Victoria Cross by King George V at Buckingham Palace on 16th January 1918 becoming the fifth Old Cheltonian VC recipient of the Great War. A month later he was appointed to a permanent commission in the Middlesex Regiment as a captain. Spared the harrowing experiences of the Western Front, he survived the war.

The relatively quiet period in France and Flanders during the opening two months can be partly explained by three distinct though mutually linked factors. Firstly, the three key belligerent armies on the Front, through the long, sapping pugilism of Verdun and the Somme, had fought their opponents 'toe to toe' almost to a standstill in terms of expended manpower, munitions and materiel, without any side delivering a decisive 'knock out' blow. The German, French and British armies were simply exhausted, and for a short period the cost of any further offensive action was unaffordable. Secondly, the deteriorating weather and freezing temperatures of bleak mid-winter perpetuated a 'live and let live' attitude, with all sides slipping into a survival mode of existence as the foul and flooded conditions in the trenches became the common primary foe. However, this suited the German High Command, who realised that, with regard to the third factor of the Allied naval blockade strangling subsistence resources for the population at home and their industrial capacity for war, they were slowly losing the '*Materialschlacht*' – the battle of equipment. Therefore, on 9th February, the German divisions, under the careful guidance

[230] *The London Gazette*, dated 8th June 1917
[231] *The London Gazette*, 26th May 1917.

and planning of Crown Prince Rupprecht, withdrew from their lines on the Somme to the newly constructed defences of the Hindenburg line. This tactical withdrawal shortened their front line by some 25 miles and in the process reduced the defensive manpower requirement by 14 infantry divisions. This generated a healthier troop reserve for the Germans to resist further Allied pressure on the Western Front.

However, there were several developments which allowed Britain's optimists to sound a more confident note. Besides the recent progress and regained momentum in Mesopotamia, industry and new technologies were being harnessed for war fighting on a scale never seen before in Britain. Many of the armament vulnerabilities, so evident over the previous two years, were being addressed. During early 1917, the introduction in numbers of the No 106 Fuse, which detonated instantaneously on the slightest contact, greatly reduced the number of 'duds' that had been fired hitherto and facilitated a much-improved capability for clearing barbed wire entanglements. More controversially, the use of artillery to deliver chemical shells became a routine procedure of the BEF. Again, to locate and neutralise the enemy's artillery batteries, the principal nemesis for attacking infantry and invariably positioned well behind the lines, flash spotting (observing and triangulating night-time muzzle flash) and sound ranging by listening posts and ground stations was introduced. This integrated effort was used very effectively during the successful Canadian assault of Vimy Ridge. With such technical innovations and ever-increasing effectiveness between artillery and aircraft coordination and communication, counter battery fire was developed to a high degree. On the opening day of the British attack at Arras on 9th April, for example, German heavy artillery capability was reduced to as little as 20%.[232]

In addition, two further developments underpinned renewed British optimism. A recent rejuvenation of tactics had gripped the BEF from top to bottom with the introduction of a series of new training manuals. Lessons from the Somme offensive, particularly its profligate use of waves of infantry walking towards the enemy, had been learned, new tactics were evolved and widely adopted and new guidance and training programmes issued and put into effect. Even at the lowest command layer, the sections and platoons, specialist teams of bombers, bayonet men, snipers and 'moppers up' trained together, and worked with other teams which would 'leap-frog' forward to gain new ground and objectives as tactically directed and coordinated between battalion and brigade headquarters. Additionally, increasing use of the creeping barrage, where these infantry teams followed very closely behind a slowly advancing barrage, ensured that by the time the barrage lifted from the enemy's front line, the attacking groups were already infiltrating German trench systems, giving defenders little or no time to bring their machine guns into action.

Secondly, in the BEF's sector in and around Arras over the previous several months, the tunnelling companies of the Royal Engineers had been very busy. By the beginning of April, an enormous labyrinth of passages and galleries from the subterranean chalk quarries

---

[232] G. Sheffield, *Forgotten Victory: The First World War – Myths and Realities*, Headline, London, (2002), page 194.

extended beneath the German Lines. So extensive was this electrified and plumbed underground system, containing command and control centres, latrines, cooking facilities, a narrow-gauge railway and a hospital for some 700 patients, that some 24,000 fully equipped troops could be accommodated in relative safety away from the relentless enemy gunfire and the unseasonably bitter weather.

The scene was set for the Allied spring offensive, which was to be launched as a three-pronged attack; the Canadians at Vimy, the British east of Arras, and the French further south on the Chemin des Dames.[233] Allied plans and objectives for this combined Anglo-French spring offensive had to be adjusted to take account of the new German positions on the Hindenburg Line, especially on the BEF's area of operational focus, a frontage of some 15 miles stretching from Vimy Ridge to the north of Arras to the east of Bapaume.

BLOODY APRIL

For all these detailed preparations and tactical innovations, however, there was to be little change of fortune with regard to casualty figures. To the minds of most military historians, 'Bloody April' refers to the losses suffered by the Royal Flying Corps at the hands of the dominant German fighter squadrons, the *Jagdstaffeln*, immortalised by Manfred von Richtofen; a topic that will shortly be developed.[234] Yet the Battle of Arras would become Britain's most costly encounter of the war in terms of the daily casualty rate.[235] For Old Cheltonians, the term 'Bloody April' could be attributed just as appropriately to the land battles. Over the ensuing five weeks of fighting, 22 Old Cheltonians were killed during the Arras offensive. On 9th April, the opening day of the attack, as the snow and sleet covered the ground, the five-day preliminary but intensive barrage reached a terrifying and shuddering crescendo during its final hour. At 5.30am, the BEF forces rose from their troglodyte domains to attack, making significant progress over the next six hours. That morning, Sydney Trevenen (Day Boy, 1911), a lieutenant in the RFA had been in the thick of the action on the south side of the River Scarpe to the east of Arras.

The son of an established local solicitor, at their comfortable family home 'Welton' in Christchurch Road, Cheltenham, Sydney had already been awarded the Military Cross. His citation read as follows:

---

[233] The French assault in the Champagne area would become known as the Nivelle Offensive, after the French Commander in Chief General Robert Nivelle, which having publicly and loudly promised success, ultimately failed, with very high casualties. In the week commencing 16th April, over 130,000 French casualties were sustained. This led to Nivelle's dismissal and a malaise in the French army that resulted in mutiny in several French divisions. (See P Hart, *The Great War 1914-1918* Profile Limited, London (2014), pages 338-345).

[234] The losses to the RFC in April 1917 amounted to 275 aircraft and some 400 aircrew casualties (of which over 200 were killed), compared to the loss of 66 German aircraft. See P. Hart, *Bloody April: Slaughter in the Skies over Arras, 1917*. Weidenfeld & Nicolson, London, (2005).

[235] The Battle of Arras (9th April – 13th May 1917) lasted for 34 days, and cost the BEF 158,000 casualties, a rate of 4647 casualties per day, compared with the Somme – 2978 casualties per day, and Passchendaele – 2696 casualties per day. (These figures remain disputed by historians and are approximate.)

For conspicuous gallantry. He crawled out some 1,000 yards in front of our forward trench, and brought back useful information. He twice acted as liaison officer and showed marked resource and coolness.[236]

Sydney and his guns of the 49th Battery (40th Brigade), had been in continual action for the previous week. Just after midday he had a short time to make a hurried note in his diary describing events and the effects of the artillery's barrage:

Sydney Trevenen MC

By 1pm, the Huns were seen retiring from this line in great disorder long before our troops were near them. I had a great time at Bde HQ passing on all information from the firing line direct to my Brigade. But the most interesting thing of all was seeing prisoners being interrogated. Although muddy, they were nearly all shaved. One of them said the Cambrai Road was mined N of Tilloy, but although he was sent back to indicate the spot no entrance could be located. During the preliminary bombardment they suffered heavy casualties and had been unable to bring up any rations for two days and nights. Needless to say their moral (sic) was bad in the extreme, whilst on the other hand there was no holding our men back. I was ordered to rejoin the battery in action East of the Girls School at about 3pm. In the evening the WL moved up to a grass field just outside Arras.[237]

As Sydney made his way back to his battery that afternoon, Basil Thomas (Leconfield, 1913) became the first Old Cheltonian fatality of the battle. Two years behind Sydney at school, Basil had rowed in the College boat in 1913. After war was declared, he applied for a temporary commission on 19th September 1914 and his commission as a second lieutenant in the 15th Battalion, Royal Welch Fusiliers was gazetted three months later.[238] In 1916 he was transferred to the Machine Gun Corps and after specialist training at Belton Park near Grantham, joined the 27th Company on 26th October and appointed as second in command three days later. On 9th April, Basil's company was supporting the 9th Scottish Division's advance eastwards from Arras towards Gavrelle on the north bank of the Scarpe. The previous day Basil's company of machine gunners had been kept busy supporting the effects of the barrage, by preventing the German defenders from repairing their damaged barbed wire:

large number of gaps which have been cut in the enemy's wire are now being kept open by MG fire[239]

[236] *The London Gazette*, 20th October 1916.
[237] Cheltenham College Archives, The Trevenen Diaries. WL refers to Wagon Lines supporting the batteries with ammunition.
[238] Supplement to *The London Gazette*, dated 12th December 1914, page 10664.
[239] The National Archives, WO 95/1773/3, War Diary of the 27th Company, Machine Gun Corps, April 1917.

The following day, as the artillery barrage lifted and moved forward, Basil went forward with his machine gun teams. The war diary records that:

> At 5.30am the attack commenced. Weather wet and cold. ..... Pack mules with ammunition moved forward to PONT DE JOUR during the afternoon. Lieut Thomas, 2nd in command of the Coy, was killed near the third objective (PONT DE JOUR).[240]

Within the 27th Company, Basil was the only officer to be killed that day, alongside nine of his men. He was buried at Roclincourt later in the day. Snow fell heavily that evening.

The following morning, on the opposite side of the river, Sydney Trevenan was trying to keep up with the infantry's initial progress.

> After an undisturbed night, due to the fact that the Hun was out of range, I rode down to the new WL. The only cover for the entire battery was three wagon tarpaulins and another large one which we found. Luckily we managed to raise four tents. A strong North wind and frequent snow storms did not make camping out in the open any more pleasant, but as we have got the Hun on the run small discomforts such as these do not worry us. In the afternoon, my Brigade advanced another 5000 (yards) in support of the Infantry to a position about a mile east of Tilloy.[241]

Richard Wilkinson

Two days later, Richard Wilkinson (Salter, 1892) was killed with the 13th Battalion, Royal Fusiliers during their attack on the fortified village of Monchy-le-Preux. Over the next few weeks, eight Old Cheltonians were killed in attacks against this stubbornly defended redoubt bristling with machine guns and trench mortars, and though each individual case is, of course, a personal and family tragedy, Richard's story is especially poignant. The youngest son of a successful corn mill owner in Skipton, Richard left College at the age of 16 to complete his education at Leeds Grammar School and help with the family business. Just before the outbreak of the South African War, he was commissioned as a second lieutenant on 30th April 1898 in the West Yorkshire Regiment, a volunteer militia battalion that would send service companies to fight the Boers.[242] Richard was promoted to lieutenant on 13th February 1900, but it appears that he may not have gone to South Africa as he was not awarded any of the associated campaign medals with which the regiment was associated.[243] Resigning his commission in 1901, he settled back to life in Yorkshire, marrying Violet Walmsley in July 1910, the daughter of a

---

[240] Ibid. The diary records the position as Pont de Jour, although contemporary spelling is Point de Jour which is where the Military Cemetery and the memorial to the 9th (Scottish) Division is located.
[241] Cheltenham College Archives, The Trevenen Diaries.
[242] *The London Gazette*, 10th May 1898, page 2894.
[243] *The London Gazette*, 13th February 1900, page 1003.

local vicar, with whom he had two sons. The family were comfortably settled in Southport when war was declared, but just before Christmas 1914, Richard applied for a temporary commission in his old regiment and was swiftly gazetted as a lieutenant in the 13th (Reserve) Battalion.[244] He was attached to the 9th Battalion, which was readying itself to reinforce the Gallipoli campaign, and with training and farewells complete, Richard sailed for Egypt on 16th May 1915. However, on arrival at Alexandria, Richard came down with an attack of acute bronchitis and was evacuated back to England. He was in hospital in York when the rest of his battalion landed at Suvla Bay on 6th August and immediately went into action. Perhaps this had a distinct bearing on what was to follow. Within a fortnight, Richard was sufficiently recovered to be declared fit by his medical board on 14th August; discharged from hospital he was sent back to the Dardanelles to rejoin the battalion. By the time he arrived at Suvla in October, the battalion, especially his brother officers who were obliged to add the burden of his tasks to their own already full list of duties, had been acclimatised to the prevailing battle conditions over the preceding nine weeks. Richard, on the other hand, was abruptly initiated into a nightmare of constant risk and danger, the thump and shatter of shellfire, the crack and whizz of rifle shot, and the squalid living conditions of the trenches – no doubt a lonely experience as the 'old sweats' carried on with their established routines. Furthermore, being somewhat older than his fellow subalterns at 40 years old, and with his young family far away at home from his new isolation, it is perhaps unsurprising that Richard began suffering with his nerves. In November, an incident occurred which questioned his behaviour under fire, and the circumstances and outcomes were the subject of a confidential report made up the chain of command as recorded in the following extract:

> On the 9th November 1915, this officer was warned by the Acting Adjutant to take charge of a 2nd relief of a working party (Dardanelles), but he did not put in an appearance with his party when the time came and the officer who was to be relieved, Lieut Price, found him taking cover. Lieut Price asked him why he did not proceed in relief and he replied that it was not safe as the Turks were shelling. The shelling had stopped some time, however, and Lieut Price told him so but still he would not go forward whereupon Lieut Price said that if he would not do so he himself would and Lieut Wilkinson could take the relieved party back. He accepted the offer and acted on it even when Lieut Price told him he was placing himself in a serious position by his actions.
>
> Lieut Wilkinson admits the facts and regrets he 'had to take the steps he did' but the fact was that he felt his nerves would not stand the test put on them.
>
> It is shown that on the 30th October he had told the CO that he was suffering from nerves, but the Medical Officer could find nothing wrong with him, and he was put

[244] Supplement to *The London Gazette*, 4th January 1915.

under supervision for a time and seemed then to do his work properly, but he stated he failed when the test came. He was questioned by the CO to whom he said that he could not 'make himself' go on; he was placed under arrest.

The GOC Division said it was not fair on anyone to be placed under command of Lieut Wilkinson; GOC the 9th Corps thought the case not one for disciplinary action as the officer only committed the offence of over caution; and he recommended that he be allowed to resign in order that his career might not be ruined.

GOC-in-C MEF has decided not to try Lieut Wilkinson by Court Martial, but he is quite unfit for military employment and accordingly was being sent home with instructions to report in writing the War Office on arrival.[245]

The ramifications of this report would prove to be deadly serious. Being a 'temporary' officer meant that Richard's commission was on probation and had yet to be made substantive. What was not shown in the official report was the final damning and contradictory comments made by the commander of IX Corps, Lieutenant General Julian Byng, whose growing reputation and rank carried significant weight:

> I do not think this is a case for disciplinary action as this officer only committed the offence of over caution.
>
> I recommend that he be allowed to resign his commission in order that his career may not be ruined.
>
> He is obviously not fit to be in the face of the enemy, nor should he be in command of men.[246]

Clearly, Byng's last sentence could only ruin Richard's career, and with such a judgement the uncanny, unhappy and untimely law of unintended consequence was ignited. Richard reluctantly resigned his commission on 13th January 1916. A fortnight later the Military Service Act (1916), better known as conscription, received Royal Assent thus making single men aged between 18 and 41 years liable for service in the military. In May 1916, owing to an ongoing shortage of manpower, especially for the army, this liability was extended to married men. Richard came within this latter bracket by just ten months, and was duly conscripted into the 13th Battalion, Royal Fusiliers as a private, a rank he retained no doubt due to Byng's pejorative judgement. Richard was killed in action on 11th April in

---

[245] The National Archives, WO 339/13753, Personal Record of Lieutenant RHS Wilkinson. Report written by Colonel HW Lawrence, AG3, dated 30th December 1915.
[246] The National Archives, WO 339/13753, Personal Record of Lieutenant RHS Wilkinson. Hand written recommendation by Lieutenant General Byng.

a prolonged attack that had started two days earlier. He was one of the 296 casualties the battalion suffered over four days of continuous fighting and one of the many thousands more to fall in the crucible of Monchy-le-Preux during the Battle of Arras. The battalion war diary and the narrative from the battalion's commanding officer, Lieutenant Colonel Layton, describe Richard's last hours:

> April 10th. In accordance with instructions we retired to BROKEN HILL and bivouacked in FEUCHY from 6am until about noon when we received instructions to move forward for the attack on MONCHY. During the morning of the 10th the prize of the BROWN LINE which had held us up on the 9th had been captured. We advanced over the northern end of ORANGE HILL and then swung half left towards the outlying works west of MONCHY. The 10th RF were in touch on our right. The whole continued to go forward under a heavy barrage which caused many casualties.[247]

The following day at 5am, the attack on Monchy-le-Preux was resumed:

> To time and on this occasion tanks cooperated and proved invaluable in silencing MG emplacements which had hitherto defied our efforts. The attack was delivered with such vigour that the enemy was driven out of the town and park and retired to the slope of the opposite ridge where he rallied and reformed in a remarkably short time. This battalion became mixed up with the battalion in front of it and isolated groups fought their way forward independently. Much good work was done by the battalion in this final attack and great initiative was displayed by all ranks at a time when NCOs and men had to act for themselves to fulfil the common objective.[248]

Given Richard's commissioned background, it is quite possible that the men in these confused moments would have looked to him for leadership during the attack. Irrespective of the part he played, the report undermines the hasty conclusion drawn by General Byng that Richard should not be allowed in the face of the enemy. In reading Richard's personal file and the personal letters it contains, it is clear that he was a gentle, sensitive, and honourable man. He had married Violet when she was already pregnant with their first son Richard, and he had left for Gallipoli with her expecting their second son, John. It is hardly surprising, therefore, that he was nervous under fire, no doubt with the constant worry and potential of leaving the family fatherless. In today's army, such cases as Richard's Gallipoli experience, undoubtedly another episode of psychological trauma, would be quickly diagnosed and dealt with in a far more sympathetic manner, and therefore viewed less harshly. When finally conscripted and sent to the Western Front, with John aged just one, Richard had grounds to resist this second enlistment. Yet he did

---

[247] The National Archives, WO 95/2532, War Diary of the 13th (Service) Battalion, Royal Fusiliers.
[248] Ibid. (Report of Lieutenant Colonel AB Layton, CO 13th Royal Fusiliers, dated 15th April 1917.)

not, finally serving as an elderly private in the infantry. Whatever else one feels about his specific circumstances and earlier conduct, one cannot deny that in the final analysis Richard was a brave man.

By the second week of May, it became clear that no break-through was achievable and, with the exception of the Canadians' spectacular assault and occupation of Vimy Ridge and the initial success of the first three days, few further gains had been made. Fighting in the sector reverted to a familiar state of trench warfare and stalemate. At his battery positions, east of Arras, Sydney Trevenen caught the mood of war weariness and melancholy, writing on 9th and 10th May:

> May 9th. During the morning the batteries of my brigade were heavily shelled, the 6th Bty having one gun knocked out and the 23rd two. We fortunately escaped, though we knew this would happen sooner or later if we persisted on firing 800 every 24 hours from those positions. I took the fat Whizbang out for exercise after lunch.
>
> May 10th. I rode into Arras in the afternoon and had tea at the 130th Bty mess. The trees are all green now, and some blossom on them making one wish for England, Home and Beauty.[249]

When the offensive was finally called off seven days later, Sydney wittingly recorded the disappointing lack of progress made over the last several brutal weeks of the battle. Observing the enemy he noted that it was:

> Very misty all day. In the afternoon I tried to register (the guns) but the light was too bad. The Huns amused themselves occupying our late position and blowing up the ammunition.[250]

April 1917 had been a costly month: the following April would yield little change around Arras with more devastation being heaped on old.

Flying Officers

If the term 'Bloody April' applied quite appropriately to the outcome on the fields around Arras, it most certainly related to the skies above. In the build-up to the battle the need for photographic reconnaissance and artillery observation was acute. Equally, so was the German urge to deny the same by establishing air superiority over the battlefield. Such fierce and deadly competition commenced in earnest in early March and continued as often as the weather permitted.

---

[249] Cheltenham College Archives, The Trevenen Diaries.
[250] Ibid.

Douglas Gabell (Day Boy, 1915), for example, was a young pilot with No 5 Squadron flying the BE 2e on artillery observation and reconnaissance missions. He belonged to a long-established Cheltonian family. His grandfather was a well-known solicitor and magistrate in the town, who had begun the family association with College by sending Douglas's father Arthur and his uncle Henry to College in the 1860s as day boys. Arthur was ordained into the clergy and became the Rector of St Lawrence's Church in Bishop's Cleeve near to the town. Thus, the family was brought up in Cheltenham.

Douglas Gabell

Douglas's three elder brothers, Richard (Day Boy, 1904), Ifor (Day Boy, 1905) and Cyril (Day Boy, 1907) had all been educated at College, and all were now serving in the war; Richard, a despatch rider in the RFC, Ifor, a captain in the Machine Gun Corps, and Cyril a captain with the Monmouthshire Regiment. Douglas, on leaving school, went immediately through the Sandhurst course, and though commissioned as a regular officer into the Gloucestershire Regiment in July 1916, was quickly seconded to the RFC. By March 1917, he had already seen considerable service flying on the Western Front and had been twice brought down by enemy fire. Yet on 1st March 1917 whilst flying BE2e (Serial No 5821) with his observer Lieutenant G E Craig, he was in combat with six enemy aircraft and shot down near Achiet le Petit. His personal file records that near La Boiselle,

> Machine was attacked by Enemy Aircraft. His engine hit in combat, forced landing. Machine turned over in shell hole, and pilots wrist broken.[251]

Douglas was one of five airmen wounded that day, and he was repatriated to England for hospitalisation and recuperation. His war was far from over.

As Douglas began his recovery back in England, day by day in the skies above Arras the fighting for air superiority intensified and greater concentrations of German aircraft were being encountered as the RFC struggled to pinpoint the German artillery batteries. With the competition in aircraft performance becoming critical, new and more powerful machines were quickly brought onto strength; sometimes too quickly. The problem was one of airframe integrity, particularly the disparity between the combination of greater engine performance and weight bearing requirement versus the wing loading capacity. In short, the faster the aircraft could fly, the better it could outpace, outclimb and outperform its competitors. But also, with these higher airspeeds came greater potential stresses from gravitational (or G) force, when the weight of the aircraft on the wing, which was producing the necessary lift, increased as turns were tightened. Furthermore, as the need for additional armaments escalated, two or even three machine guns and ammunition drums for the fighters and larger bombs for the ground attack aircraft, the greater the weight or

---

[251] National Archives, WO 339/66959 and AIR 76/174/4, Personal records of Captain DRC Gabell.

wing loading was placed on the aircraft's structure, especially the main spars of the wing.[252] With main spars still made of wood, their structural integrity, or lack of, was an even more critical and vulnerable factor, especially from the aircrews' perspective. Such was the problem with the French Nieuport 17 fighter, which when flown at high speed, notably when in a dive, the lower wing tended to fail, folding catastrophically.

Nieuport 17 Scout Aeroplane

At their base at Filescamp Farm northwest of Arras, No 60 Squadron was in the process of converting to their new fighter aircraft, the Nieuport 17 Scout. Alongside the famous fighter ace, Billy Bishop, one of the squadron pilots familiarising himself with the new machine was Chalenor Caffyn (Southwood, 1908), who at College had risen to sergeant in the OTC.[253] An engineering graduate of Zurich University, Chalenor was a fluent French and German speaker, working as a civil engineer in London when war was declared in 1914. Like so many other Old Cheltonians, he promptly applied for a commission in the Special Reserve of Officers on 22nd August, which was quickly approved by War Office letter just 13 days later.[254]

Chalenor Caffyn

During 1915 he served with the East Surrey Regiment in the trenches on the Western Front, at the same time as his elder brother, Harold, who was killed in action on 22nd March fighting with the 1st Battalion, North Staffordshire Regiment near Ploegsteert. In 1916, Chalenor was attached to the RFC and, having gained his pilot 'wings', was posted to No 60 Squadron. So, on the cold, bleak and blustery morning of Wednesday 28th March 1917, some of the squadron's pilots, including Chalenor, were practising air to ground gunnery on the airfield. This process involved diving down to fire at a fixed target and then pulling sharply away to avoid any ricochets. Sadly, during the exercise two of the Nieuport 17 aircraft broke up in flight:

> Caffyn's and Brakenbury's [aeroplanes] collapsed when practicing firing at ground targets on the aerodrome, and the former was killed.[255]

[252] To the main spar of the wing and attached by screws were the key aerofoil shaping devices, the ribs and the stringers, over which was stretched a doped fabric skin. Additional strength to the wing was provided with braces and wires, which if damaged could prove catastrophic.
[253] Air Marshal William Avery Bishop, VC, CB, DSO & Bar, MC, DFC, was a Canadian pilot and Victoria Cross recipient of the First World War. He was officially credited with 72 victories, the leading Canadian ace of the war. He was awarded his VC while serving with No 60 Squadron.
[254] *The London Gazette*, 8th September 1914, page 7102.
[255] See A.Scott, *Sixty Squadron RAF; A History of the Squadron from its Formation*, Naval and Military Press, Uckfield, (2015), page 46.

Chalenor was buried the following day with full military honours, at the little village cemetery at Avesnes-le Comte near his airfield at Filescamp Farm, by his squadron comrades including Billy Bishop, who just five weeks later was awarded the Victoria Cross for his courageous lone attack on a German airfield.

Two other Old Cheltonian aviators were killed on operations with the RFC over the Arras salient during the offensive. The first to fall was James Stuart (Hazelwell, 1915), a young pilot killed on 13th April. His formative years were spent in Australia, first at the family home in Townsville, Queensland where his father owned and managed large cattle stations, and then for two years at the King's School, Parramatta, Australia's oldest independent school.[256] In April 1912, he arrived at College aged 15, becoming a lance corporal in the OTC. While still at school he applied for entry to the Royal Military College on 19th January 1915 and once accepted left College the following April. Although commissioned into the Royal Inniskilling Fusiliers, he was quickly attached to the RFC as a pilot in September 1915. Awarded his flying 'wings', he went to France with his squadron as a second lieutenant that December and flew on active service on the Western Front until the following September, when he was posted to No 59 Squadron, a new RFC squadron being formed at Narborough airfield in Norfolk and equipped with the recently designed and produced RE 8 aircraft. With training complete, the squadron deployed in groups to France on 13th February 1917 with 21 pilots, 17 observers and 12 aircraft on the unit's strength. James, though still only 20 years of age, was now a senior member of the

No 59 Sqn Record, James Stuart's last flight

[256] Founded in 1831, 10 years before Cheltenham College.

squadron, being both a captain and a flight commander. Within two weeks, the squadron had bedded in to its home airfield of Cagnicourt, an advanced landing ground close to the front lines, and began operations largely consisting of artillery observation and escort sorties. Friday 13th April 1917 began ominously for the squadron's airmen; the weather that day at Cagnicourt being recorded in the Record Book as 'strong winds and snow – bright intervals'. At 8.15am five aircraft took off, one on a photography mission, and another four to act as its escort. James was flying with Lieutenant Maurice Wood as his observer in an RE 8 (Serial No A 3190). None of the aircraft returned.

The formation was engaged by German fighters behind the German lines near Vimy Ridge and he was shot down. Though initially reported as missing, it was not until 10th September that formal notification of his death finally came through from the Geneva Red Cross.

Twelve days later, Charles Darnell (Cheltondale, 1912) was shot down and crashed behind enemy lines in the same area near Willerval east of Vimy, while providing fighter cover for observation aircraft. Having left school, Charles was articled to a chartered accountant when he applied for a commission in the Special Reserve of Officers on 31st August 1914. However, his passage to becoming a fighter pilot was somewhat convoluted, despite the overwhelming need for young officers. During the application process, he sought a recommendation from his past headmaster at College. Reverend Waterfield duly obliged and supported his application, just one of many, with the headmaster's typically meticulous and forensic attention, born out of a thorough knowledge of each of his former students:

> He attained a very fair standard of education before he left, having reached the Lower Fifth form on the Military Side before he was 17. From that form boys sometimes pass into Sandhurst; from the form next above they seldom fail. At that point, however, not being a candidate for the Army, he transferred to the Special Fifth for his last 2 terms here.[257]

Charles initially wished to join the artillery and was appointed as a gentleman cadet in the Antrim RGA, a territorial garrison unit providing shore defence for ports in Ireland. He was gazetted as temporary second lieutenant on 11th September. However, as he had not passed the entrance exam for either the Royal Military Academy or College at Sandhurst, he could not go immediately to either establishment from the Special Reserve, which thereby delayed his participation in actions at the Front. Therefore, over the next year, he revised for the Sandhurst entrance exam and once passed, resigned his commission in the RGA on 19th January 1916.[258] Charles was subsequently commissioned into the 1st Battalion, Connaught Rangers on the 16th August.[259] However, by early 1917, he gained his pilot wings and transferred as a pilot to No 25 Squadron, RFC. On 25th April, after taking photographs of

---

[257] The National Archives, WO 339/71125 and WO 339/37447, Personal Records of Captain C V Darnell.
[258] *The London Gazette*, 28th January 1916, page 1137.
[259] *The London Gazette*, 15th August 1916, page 8029.

German positions and attacking enemy observation balloons, he was involved with other members of the squadron in aerial combat with the Albatross scout aircraft of Manfred von Richthofen's *Jasta 11*.[260] In what developed into a whirling, turning dog fight, while Lothar von Richthofen was attacking the FE2b (A5505) of Second Lieutenant Maurice Arthur Hancock and Lieutenant Vivian Smith, Lothar was himself attacked by Charles and his air gunner George Pawley in another FE2b (A387). With his controls shot away, Lothar was forced to make a crash landing. However, Charles' aerial victory was short lived, as moments later Lothar's wingman, Leutnant Karl Schaeffer shot Charles' aircraft down in flames and both Charles and George were killed. Charles was just 22 years old.

Nine other Old Cheltonian aviators were killed during the remaining months of 1917, their specific circumstances typifying the spectrum of risk associated with flying in those early years of combat aviation. Con Cole-Hamilton (Boyne House, 1912) was in the College rugby XV for two years. Having graduated from Sandhurst into the 2nd Battalion, Royal Scots in January 1914, Con transferred to the RFC and gained his aviator's certificate (No 1952) on 26th October 1915, completing initial flying training on the Maurice Farman biplane at No 5 Training School, Castle Bromwich. Wounded in air combat over the Western Front early in 1916, Con was evacuated to England, and when recovered, he was posted to No 56 (Reserve) Training Squadron based at London Colney. Here he not only had instructional and flight testing duties, but also flew home defence sorties against the Zeppelins and Gotha bombers that were terrorising civilians in Britain. On 13th June 1917, for example, 20 Gotha bombers launched the first daytime air raid on London, dropping over 100 bombs on the capital, killing 162 people (including 16 children in a school in Poplar) and injuring another 432.[261] Con was airborne with his air gunner Cecil Keevil that morning in a Bristol F2b Fighter (A7135) and attacked three Gothas over Ilford. However, they were unsuccessful, and were themselves shot up by the considerable defensive machine gun fire from the Gotha which killed Cecil. Three weeks later, Con was conducting an air test on a Spad S VII (Serial No A8965), an aircraft renowned for its sturdiness with good climbing and diving characteristics. Suddenly, the fabric skin was stripped from the ribs of the wing owing to a small tear which propagated catastrophically through the material during a dive. The aircraft crashed: Con was killed instantly.

Noel Rayner (Day Boy, 1915) was commissioned in the 2nd Battalion, West Yorkshire Regiment. After fighting with the battalion on the Somme in 1916, Noel transferred to the RFC and flew with No 57 Squadron. The squadron, re-equipped in May 1917 with the more modern Airco DH4, changed its role to long-range bombing and reconnaissance sorties. Flying from Boisdinghem on 27th July in support of the offensive at Ypres and Passchendaele, his aircraft crashed and he died from his injuries, including a badly fractured skull, at 6.30pm the same evening. However, one can tell much about Noel's kind and sensitive character from the letter of condolence he wrote in November 1916 to the mother of a close friend and

---

[260] *Jasta 11* is the abbreviated version of Jagdstaffel – or fighter squadron, the squadron commanded by Manfred von Richthofen, the famed Red Baron.
[261] For further information on the air defence of London, see A. G. Lee, *No Parachute*, Grub Street, London [1968] (2013), pages 95-104.

comrade Captain Barcroft Fayle, who was killed in action when they were both serving together with the West Yorkshires:[262]

>Dear Mrs Fayle
>
>Thankyou (sic) very much for your letter. I am afraid I have not had much time to write as I had intended. My aunt will probably have told you that Barry Fayle and I were great friends although he was considerably older than I.
>
>I admired him immensely as he was always so gentle and kind hearted. He was a typical Cliftonian. He and I (as A/Adjutant) always shared the same dug-out or room wherever we were, and consequently became great friends.
>
>Capt Fayle came to us in September and when he heard that I was Mervyn's cousin he asked me not to say that he had transferred as it might have caused you anxiety.
>
>As you probably know, we have lately been in action. I last saw Capt Fayle about an hour before his death. He had been working hard all day attending to the wounded, and towards evening he told me that he was going to visit the Forward Aid Post to help another Bn.
>
>I did not see him again, as he was killed, (I think by an H.E. shell), shortly after leaving the forward aid-post. The trench in which he was killed was completely flattened out. The only person who knew the exact details was Capt Kidner, who was killed shortly afterwards, so we have never exactly discovered. Some people say he was buried, but in my opinion he was buried by the shell when the trench was flattened. I am afraid that I have had to tell you things rather bluntly, but I have told you all the facts to the best of my knowledge. I would like to add that Capt Fayle was simply splendid on every occasion, and I had often to warn him to take care when he was exposing himself to help the wounded.
>
>I feel that I have lost a great friend, but I am sure that he could not have died in a better way. I cannot say any more, but I am sure you will understand how I feel his loss. Hoping that I may be able to render you service in the future, and with deep sympathy for you in your distress,
>
>I am yours very sincerely, Noel R Rayner.[263]

---

[262] Captain Barcroft Joseph Leech Fayle, RAMC, was the Medical Officer of the 2nd West Yorkshire Regiment. Killed in action at Longueval during the Battle of the Somme on 24th October 1916. He was educated at Clifton College, Emmanuel, College Cambridge and the Bristol Medical School.
[263] Letter posted on Clifton RFC website, www.cliftonrfchistory.co.uk/memorial/WW1/fayle.htm, and submitted by Greg Fayle.

No doubt one of Noel's squadron colleagues wrote a similarly moving testament to his family waiting anxiously at home.

John de Lisle Bush (Hazelwell, 1913), though wounded by a gunshot to his right calf on 1st November 1914 while serving with the 1st Battalion, Somerset Light Infantry, recovered and was transferred to the Royal Flying Corps on 28th July 1916, first as an observer, but later undergoing pilot training. Posted eventually to No 41 Squadron, John was heavily involved in the continued air combat over the Arras front in August 1917 during the prolonged spell of unseasonably wet weather which drowned British aspirations in Flanders.

On Saturday 25th August, John started the engine of his DH 5 (Serial No A9212) fighter, taxied over the sodden grass at his aerodrome at Léalvillers, and at 5.26am took off into the grey leaden skies for an offensive patrol. His aircraft was last seen over the German lines at Sorel-le-Grand an hour later heading east. He was subsequently shot down south west of Cambrai, the second of 30 aerial victories attributed to Josef Mai, an up-and-coming fighter pilot flying with *Jasta 5*. Crashing behind enemy lines and badly wounded, he was taken prisoner. Nothing was then heard of him until an official German 'List of Dead' was forwarded to the War Office through the Geneva Red Cross. Another report through the Netherlands Legation stated that he died on 25th August near Walincourt, Selvigny. John is buried at the Honnechy British cemetery, south east of Cambrai. He was 21 years old.

Six days later, schoolmate Arthur Roberts (Boyne House, 1913) was killed. A College prefect and member of the rugby XV in 1912, he was commissioned from the Oxford University OTC on 24th November 1914 and served with the 10 Battalion, Cameronians (Scottish Rifles).[264] He transferred to the RFC and was serving at home with No 10 Training Squadron when he was accidentally killed while flying solo in a Martinsyde G100 'Elephant' (Serial No 7463) which caught fire whilst on a bomb test from Hounslow Heath, Middlesex, crashing at Hanworth. Aged 22, Arthur was buried by his family in their local village churchyard at Byfleet.

At 28 years of age, Alister Stewart (Southwood, 1907) was a little older. After College, he had trained in land agency at Cirencester Agricultural College, and when war was declared he held an important post in the War Land Department, as Britain sought to maximise food production in the face of the relentless U-Boat attrition of the Atlantic re-supply routes. Despite living in relative peace and comfort with his wife Dorothy at Heath Farm House near Petersfield in Hampshire, he decided in 1917 to seek service in the RFC. He began his flying training on 8th April 1917 at the School of Military Aeronautics at Reading and progressed well. Deemed suitable for fighter aircraft, he was posted to the Central Flying School at Upavon in Wiltshire and began his advanced flying training on Sopwith Camels. With its powerful Bentley rotary engine and tremendous manoeuvrability, the Camel could prove difficult to handle:

---

[264] *The London Gazette*, 24th November 1914, page 9695.

> In the hands of a novice it displayed vicious characteristics that could make it a killer; but under the firm touch of a skilled pilot, who knew how to turn its vices to his own advantage, it was one of the most superb fighting machines ever built.[265]

On 13th October, Alister was flying at low altitude in a Sopwith Camel (Serial No B3812) when he stalled the aircraft, which then nosedived towards the ground. With insufficient height to recover, he was killed in the ensuing crash. He never saw active service abroad, yet one can only admire his determination and personal motivation to leave a life of relative ease and embark on one of the most difficult and hazardous military occupations of the war.

Eleven days later, in completely different circumstances, John Hough (Leconfield, 1914) was killed flying with No 1 Squadron, Royal Naval Air Service (RNAS). Just before his 16th birthday and a month before war was declared, he had gone to live in Canada with his family. However, when aged 18, John sought and gained entry to the RNAS on 7th February 1917 and was appointed as a probationary flight officer. He conducted primary flying at Chingford from 19th May to 14th July, before going on to Cranwell, where he graduated with his 'wings' on 29th August 1917. His personal records confirm that he had done well, being assessed as a *'VG pilot indeed. Recommend for scouts. A good officer'*.[266] After a short spell of leave, he was sent down to Manston in Kent on 18th September for some final operational training, and then flew across to Dunkirk on 8th October. On Wednesday 24th October John was reported as missing when he failed to return from a patrol flying in his Sopwith Triplane (Serial No A/17154). His personal record states that he was;

> last seen near Gheluvelt when the patrol dived on to a formation of scouts. Report of a total loss of a Sopwith Triplane behind enemy lines.[267]

Just five months after this talented and brave young pilot had started his flying career he was killed, aged 19.

Frederick Laverton (Day Boy, 1913) spent just a term at College, leaving at the age of 15. His family lived at Innsworth, so when war was declared he successfully applied for a commission with the Gloucestershire Regiment and served for some time with the 1st Battalion in France, including the Somme, until after training as a pilot he was seconded formally to the RFC, as a flying officer, on 8th November 1916. Frederick spent the next year being posted to several flying stations in Scotland and England, before joining No 3 (Auxiliary) School of Aerial Gunnery at New Romney ranges in Kent on 23rd November 1917. Three weeks later, and just seven days before Christmas, he was severely injured when his Sopwith 1½ Strutter (Serial No A1014) was in a ground collision with another aircraft. In the process of taking off, his aircraft developed engine trouble before it left the ground and unavoidably collided with the other aircraft. Frederick was swiftly placed in an ambulance but died from his injuries whilst on his way to Shorncliffe Military Hospital. His

---

[265] R. Jackson, *Britain's Greatest Aircraft*. Pen and Sword, Barnsley (2007), page 2.
[266] The National Archives, ADM 273/13/75 page 75. Personal record of Sub-Lieutenant JEC Hough RN.
[267] Ibid.

observer/gunner, Sergeant Frederic Querry, was uninjured in the crash. Frederic, like John Hough, was only 19 years of age.

Each of these specific cases underlines the precarious nature of combat flying in the First World War. Not only were the aircraft still remarkably flimsy, but the sciences of aerodynamics and the physiological effects on the human body, including extreme cold and hypoxia, were still very much in their infancy. When one adds the requirement to adopt the latest technological advances, such as in radio telephony, aerial gunnery and photography, there was much with which these gallant young men had to contend. Furthermore, the early aviators, many straight out of school, did not have the benefit of parachutes. This was partly due to the fact that parachute design was not yet sufficiently developed to be feasible for use in aeroplanes as they added additional weight and bulk to an already overloaded airframe. More ominously, some senior officers held the opinion that parachutes might prejudice the fighting spirit of the aircrew and cause them to abandon their machines prematurely. However, these views were eventually overtaken by the fact that a qualified and experienced pilot was too valuable an asset to waste needlessly. The simple truth that over time dawned on such dogmatic attitudes was that it took months to train a pilot to operational status, but weeks to produce an aeroplane. Thus by 1918, parachutes, already an essential piece of equipment used by balloon observers in their precarious and exposed airborne eyries, began to be introduced in aircraft.

But by the end of the year, the efficacy of air power and the courage of the aircrews had already permeated the most senior levels of military command, as the success of the artillery and infantry was shown to be increasingly and inextricably linked to the effectiveness of the Royal Flying Corps' photographic, observation and ground attack sorties.[268] The official communiqué of 7th December confirms this close integration:

> December 7: Low clouds prevented much flying during the day.
>
> Artillery Co-operation: With aerial observation, 26 batteries were successfully engaged for destruction, while with balloon observation of the 2nd Brigade four hostile batteries were successfully dealt with and 31 other targets. 5140 rounds were fired at ground targets by aeroplanes at low altitude.[269]

Music Masters

On that particular day Herbert Dyer (Day Boy, 1895) was killed flying over enemy lines near Ypres. Not only does his story complete the year's sad toll of Old Cheltonian aviators, it offers a vivid impression of the College family as a whole, and that of the broader Cheltonian community, before and during the war years. Doctor Arthur Edwin Dyer, an Oxford

---

[268] J. Morrow, *The Great War in the Air*, Smithsonian Institution Press, London, (1993), page 201.
[269] C. Bowyer (ed), *Royal Flying Corps Communiqués, 1917-1918*, Grub Street, London (1998), page 181.

University music graduate, was the College's musical director, organist and choirmaster from 1875 to his death in 1902. Living with his wife, Jessie, in the family home on Bath Road close to the College, they had a large family; four daughters, Kate, Ada, Dorothy and Winifred, and three sons, Leslie (Day Boy, 1893), Francis (Day Boy and Common Room, 1895) and Herbert (Day Boy, 1895). All three boys were educated at College and served during the war. The eldest son, Leslie, opted for a career in the army and on graduating from the Royal Military College at Sandhurst, saw considerable active service as a captain with the 1st Cheshire Regiment in the South African War for which he received both the Queen's and King's Medals with a total of seven operational clasps. A major in 1914, Leslie fought at Mons and was subsequently captured and made a prisoner of war having been awarded the Military Cross. In 1918, the Germans transferred him to a more open detention centre in Holland from where he was eventually repatriated following the Armistice.

Francis left College imbued with his father's love of music and went to Christ's College, Cambridge on an organ scholarship where he not only gained his master's degree, but also became a fellow of the Royal College of Organists. However, with his father's sudden death in 1902, an immediate replacement was needed at College. Francis, stepping most appropriately into the breach, was quickly appointed Cheltenham's musical director and organist, a post he held until the war intervened. In 1915, he was one of several members of the Common Room to enlist, being commissioned into the Royal Navy Volunteer Reserve and ultimately commanding a motor launch (ML 564) and operating in the southern North Sea.[270] Following the Armistice, Francis resumed his duties at College and remained there until 1923. Clearly, teaching was a strong family suit as Kate became a schoolmistress (and later headmistress) at a local secondary school for girls.[271]

Herbert shared his family's love of music and like his father, went to Oxford where he gained his degree. He was appointed the Head of Music at Bromsgrove School, a post he held from 1901 to 1907. During this period, he established a solid reputation as a composer of hymns and lyrics, such as the 1916 versions of '*At rest*' and '*Bromsgrove*', the latter dedicated to the school where he taught. He also composed the '*Encore Pieces*' which were widely used and set for the piano. But with war declared, Herbert enlisted, being attested into the army at Grove Park on 10th December 1914. Aged 36, he was somewhat older than most recruits, and interestingly, on his enlistment papers he gave his occupation as 'Motor Lorry Driver'. Quite why he did this, as opposed to seek a commission, especially for someone with his qualifications and experience, is open to conjecture. But his trade endorsement enabled him to join the motor transport branch of the Army Service Corps and Herbert spent the next two years acting as a signaller and a dispatch rider in France. His potential for further responsibility and a more demanding role was clearly recognised and though still a private, he was attached to the RFC as an observer on probation in November 1916. Within a month, he had clearly impressed the squadron hierarchy with his reliability and aptitude, and was

---

[270] *The London Gazette*, 21st September 1915, page 9320.
[271] Presumably, she was one of the five members of staff at Pate's Grammar School which had become co-educational with the induction of 82 girls in Livorno Lodge in North Place, Cheltenham in 1905.

No 65 Sqn aircrew at Wyton

commissioned as a second lieutenant, effective on 11th December.[272] He then completed seven months of operations over the Western Front acting as an observer, before returning to England to start pilot training at the military school in Ruislip, gaining his pilot's certificate and 'wings' on 29th July 1917. Herbert was posted to No 65 Squadron, recently formed and busy working up to operational status at the airfield at Wyton near Huntingdon on their new aircraft, the Sopwith Camel, before deploying to France the following month.

On the morning of 7th December, as the patrol took off towards the low layer of stratus clouds over the lines, Herbert was trying to resolve a rough running engine on his Sopwith Camel (Serial No B2464) with his mechanic. After some minor adjustments to the carburettor, he took off some eight minutes after the rest of the formation and attempted to catch them up in the briefed patrol area. But by now the flight was 15 miles away, and he was on his own, in poor visibility and without the safety of any of his wingmen. He was never seen again, and when several hours overdue he was reported missing. News of Herbert's death was later confirmed when a German airman dropped a message in the Allied lines, although no amplifying details were given. Later enquiries by his family, led by his sister Ada, generated renewed investigation through the Geneva Red Cross Society to the German authorities. Finally, a reply came on 14th May the following year and contained the short report that Herbert had 'Died 7th December 1917, Buried in Geluvelt.' His grave was never found and he is commemorated on the Arras Flying Services Memorial. His death was felt by the school communities at College and at Bromsgrove, to which the members of the Dyer family had contributed so much.

[272] *The London Gazette,* 12th January 1917, page 498.

Mediterranean Menace

In the afternoon of 15th April 1917, all the troops on board the RMS *Arcadian* were summoned to their stations as part of a boat drill, to man the life boats and don their life jackets in an emergency practice exercise: what fortunate timing this turned out to be. Now employed as a troopship, the 8,929 ton *Arcadian* was a converted cruise liner requisitioned by the Royal Navy in 1915 which had served as General Sir Ian Hamilton's headquarters ship at the start of the Gallipoli campaign.

RMS *Arcadian*

Having disembarked the troops destined to serve in Salonika, the *Arcadian* had left Thessaloniki the day before, with her single destroyer escort from the Imperial Japanese Navy. It was one of the first of such missions which the Japanese would conduct as Britain's ally in the Mediterranean.[273] Bound for Alexandria with reinforcements for the Palestine campaign, the *Arcadian* was 26 miles north east of the Greek island of Milos and with the weather set fair, now was a good opportunity to conduct the necessary safety and evacuation drills. Among the throng of soldiers making their way up to the boat deck that afternoon was Alexander Baines (Christowe, 1898), who was familiarising himself with the emergency procedures and helping to direct men towards their allocated lifeboats. Though in peacetime a managing partner of Messrs. Eden, Baines, and Kennaway, a land and estate

---

[273] At Britain's request, and in accordance with the Anglo-Japanese Alliance, Japan sent her 2nd Special Squadron, consisting of 14 destroyers and the cruiser *Akashi* to operate from Malta to defend allied shipping, especially the troop transports, in the Mediterranean.

agent firm based in Dorset, Alexander had joined the Army Service Corps as a captain in October 1914. Now a major, he was the senior supply officer on board. At 5.30pm, and with the drill satisfactorily completed, the troops began to disperse to their respective mess decks for dinner. Five minutes later the ship convulsed and shuddered as a simultaneous explosion sent a jet of flame and water high into the air above her port side. Within seconds, the *Arcadian* began to list to port, and the order to abandon ship was given. In just six minutes, the *Arcadian* capsized and, bow first, plunged to the depths, taking many of her complement and crew with her. However, as the troops had just conducted the boat drill many were well placed and conversant with the escape procedures and equipment, and because of this, many lives were saved. Of the 1,335 company and crew, 1,058 were rescued, either through their independent efforts in making for shore or saved by the escorting Japanese destroyer. Many more would have been saved had the ship not capsized so quickly. Adding to the immediate danger to survivors was the considerable amount of loose wreckage that came to the surface with such great force from the sinking ship that this debris struck and killed many of the troops struggling in the water. Alexander survived the sinking but was seriously injured. With the other survivors, Alexander was taken back to Thessaloniki and admitted to one of the stationary hospitals established there for the campaign. Sadly, his injuries were so severe that he died 11 days later; he was buried in the Lembet Road cemetery just to the north of the town alongside the 277 others that died in the incident: 19 army officers, 214 other ranks, as well as 10 naval ratings and 34 members of the crew. The *Arcadian* had been sunk without warning by a single torpedo, the fourth of 37 ships to be dispatched by the German submarine *SM UC-74*.

On the morning of 19th August, Charles Garstang (Cheltondale, 1893) stood on the bridge of the SS *Gartness*, a British cargo steamer as she chugged her way through the gentle swell and warmth of a balmy Mediterranean morning tended by her small but busy crew of 13.

Having left College aged 15, he had entered the Mercantile Marine as a cadet sailor and had worked his way up through the ranks. The wash astern of *Gartness* revealed she was steady on her westerly course toward the Straits of Gibraltar, destined ultimately for Middlesbrough with a cargo of manganese ore, lead and arsenic.

Visibility was slightly hazy, so Charles, the ship's master, was keeping a wary eye out on the partial but empty horizon for anything untoward, even though she was some 180 miles south east of Crete and well away from land. The *Gartness* was torpedoed suddenly and without warning by the German submarine *U-40* and sunk: Charles was drowned. There were no survivors.

Charles Garstang

By sheer coincidence, Charles' younger brother, Walter (Cheltondale, 1893) had qualified as a doctor, and was serving in the Royal Army Medical Corps in one of the

SS Gartness (commissioned as the SS *Charles T Jones* in 1890)

hospitals based in Thessaloniki during 1917. Whether he might have treated Alexander Baines is not known, but he would quite possibly have treated some of the other casualties from the *Arcadian* sinking and would certainly have been well aware of the tragedy. Walter may even have treated Kenneth Parsons (Leconfield, 1894), who was at College at the same time as the Garstang brothers. Kenneth, a qualified barrister in the Supreme Court in Shanghai, had returned home in December 1914 and applied for a commission. Gazetted as a second lieutenant two months later, Kenneth served with the Royal Irish Regiment in Gallipoli landing at Suvla Bay on 7th August 1915. Transferred to Salonika at the beginning of October 1915, he was appointed as the deputy assistant adjutant general on the staff of the Salonika Army when he contracted malaria and died from the illness in August 1917.

Whether Walter and Kenneth met is not known, but certainly Old Cheltonian associations were spread far and wide, and chance meetings not uncommon. John Wills, for example, was visiting the dentist in Amiens when such a meeting occurred during March:

> At this time our troops were slowly pressing towards Bapaume and my dentist was full of 'les braves Anglais'. The same room at Le Rhin housed me for the night. In the morning I paid a fourth visit to the dentist and then just before lunch ran into Law who was with me at Cheltenham.[274]

[274] Imperial War Museum, (17538), Private Papers of Lieutenant JP Wills MC.

The Mediterranean remained the main artery through which the lifeblood of troops and munitions for Salonika, Palestine and Mesopotamia had to pass and it had to remain open. Furthermore, essential reinforcements from India, Australia and New Zealand continued to route through the Suez Canal on their way to Marseille and thence on to the Western Front. The Imperial German Navy, and, to a lesser extent, that of Austria-Hungary, was well aware of this significance and invested in submarines accordingly. Operating primarily from Pola and Cattaro in the Adriatic, and despite the partial blockage of the limited Otranto barrage, enemy submarines operated throughout the Mediterranean in increasing numbers and with considerable success. In 1917, for example, their number increased from 25 to 34, equalling the number of U-Boats operating from Flanders. Indeed, over the period of the war 1,409 allied ships fell victim to U-Boat attacks in the Mediterranean, representing almost 45% of the civilian vessels lost to submarine action. Only in the North Sea was more Allied shipping lost to submarines. Therefore, it is hardly surprising that many Old Cheltonians serving in the Mediterranean Expeditionary Force were threatened by this sub-surface menace, with several, unhappily, becoming its victims.

The significance and extent of the submarine war in the Mediterranean remains somewhat under-recorded in the historiography of the Great War, being largely overshadowed by events in the Atlantic and the North Sea. Notwithstanding Germany's opening naval actions close to, and on occasion against, Britain's shoreline communities in 1914 and culminating in the inconclusive yet decisive engagement at Jutland (1916) which sealed the naval blockade on Germany's northern ports, it was the sinking of the Lusitania in 1915 that precipitated the most significant strategic consequence. It lit the long political fuse to America's eventual entry into the war two years later. With Germany's subsequent reversion to unrestricted submarine warfare in February 1917 and the sinking of increasing numbers of American merchant vessels, alongside the revelations and reverberations of German Foreign Minister Arthur Zimmerman's telegram a month later, America's neutrality combusted when President Wilson and Congress declared war on Germany on 6th April 1917.[275] Furthermore, Britain's food crisis that year was largely due to the effectiveness of Germany's submarines which operated very effectively in the Atlantic. Hence, it is unsurprising that in terms of geo-strategic focus, the Mediterranean played 'second fiddle' to events in the Atlantic.

---

[275] The 'Zimmerman Telegram' was a secret diplomatic communication issued by the German Foreign Office in January 1917 proposing a military alliance between Germany and Mexico in the event of the United States declaring war on Germany. It also included Germany's support of Mexico retaking US land in Texas, New Mexico and Arizona. The telegram was intercepted and decoded by British Naval Intelligence and passed on to the American Government. American public opinion was outraged, especially after the German Foreign Secretary, Arthur Zimmermann, publicly admitted in March 1917 that the telegram was genuine.

Summer's Solstice

The apogee of the BEF's fighting during the year began just before dawn on 7th June, as part of the strategic effort to deny Germany the use of the captured Belgian ports which posed an abiding threat of attack to Allied shipping in the North Sea and the Channel. At 3.10am, 19 mines erupted under the German lines along the Messines Ridge south of Ypres; so powerful were the combined explosions that their reverberations were recorded in London. Immediately, nine divisions of General Plumer's Second Army, including the II Anzac Corps swept forwards in the ensuing confusion towards the ridgeline, supported by tanks and aircraft in a carefully planned and well executed combined assault. It represented a stark contrast and improvement to the BEF's offensive performance on the opening day of the Somme offensive; and for once the weather remained fair. Advancing with the Anzacs was Private Leslie Dighton (Day Boy, 1907). He was educated at College from May 1902 to April 1907, after which he was in business in Jamaica, Athens, Austria, and West Australia. When he enlisted as a private in the 2nd Battalion, New Zealand Expeditionary Force (NZEF), Leslie was the manager of the Neuchatel Asphalt Company in New Zealand. The battalion took part in the successful assault of the Messines Ridge. By 4.58am it had captured all its objectives without meeting serious opposition, except from retaliatory shell fire and gas later in the day. Casualties were five officers and 38 other ranks killed, with another 277 wounded. Sadly, Leslie was one of the fatalities, and left a widow, Evelyn Dighton, of 8 Lansdown Terrace, Cheltenham.

Two other Old Cheltonians were killed that morning. Major Duncan Campbell (Day Boy, 1900) was supporting the advance with his battery of 18-pounder guns of the 112th Brigade, RFA. Duncan had already won the Military Cross in 1916:

> For conspicuous gallantry when directing the fire of his battery. After his observation post had been destroyed and the infantry near him had been withdrawn, he remained for four hours exposed to heavy fire, and successfully cut a wide lane in the enemy's wire.[276]

Duncan's elder brother, Colin, was also a major and a battery commander, who was killed with the 296th Brigade at Ypres some three and half months later; both brothers were mentioned in despatches for gallant conduct in the field. Their parents had a memorial marble plaque placed on the wall of their local church of the Holy Trinity at Back Hamlet, Ipswich in their memory. It reads:

> TO THE GLORY OF THE TRIUNE GOD AND IN PROUD AND LOVING MEMORY OF (PAR NOBILE FRATUM) THE ONLY TWO SONS OF LT COLONEL DONALD ARCHIBALD CAMPBELL AND OF CHARLOTTE, HIS WIFE. DUNCAN DONALD CAMPBELL MC. COLIN ARCHIBALD HERON CAMPBELL.

[276] Supplement to *The London Gazette*, 15th March 1916, page 2876.

1917 – THE YEAR OF STOIC RESOLVE

In the village of Clare in Suffolk where the family lived, the church bells were rung half-muffled on the centenary date of their deaths.

Second Lieutenant William Dickson (Boyne House, 1894) was the only person in his battalion to be killed that day. Having been the cox in the College Boat for two years and serving three years in the OTC, he left College and qualified as a solicitor, settling into a county lifestyle at Orwell House in Chippenham. He was therefore well qualified, even at the relatively senior age of 38, to be granted a commission when he enlisted, although he chose to be attested as a private in the 14th Battalion, London Regiment (London Scottish) at Chippenham on 10th December 1915. Although mobilised on 15th March 1916, after four months he applied for a territorial army commission and was subsequently appointed as a second lieutenant in the 4th Battalion, Loyal North Lancashire Regiment on 25th January 1917. He was killed on the first day of the battle advancing on the Messines Ridge, as the battalion war diary describes:

> At 2.45am a green light was seen to go up followed by two red lights near Messines Ridge. There was quite a lull for 20 minutes, and then exactly to the minute there was a dull roar and the ground shook from miles around and simultaneous with this our real attack for the ridge commenced with a magnificent barrage. Casualties: Killed: 1 officer which was Dickson.[277]

His younger brother, Arthur (Boyne House, 1897) was a doctor in the Royal Army Medical Corps, who had been awarded the Military Cross the previous month for his gallantry in German East Africa in 1916. Arthur survived the war.

The employment of tanks in coordination with an infantry attack was still in its infancy, not least because the machines were notoriously prone to mechanical failure, as Ewen Bruce (Cheltondale, 1908) discovered. A lieutenant in the Machine Gun Corps, he was attached to the 'Heavy' section, a pseudonym for the tanks which were still shrouded in secrecy. He was awarded the Military Cross in July:

> For conspicuous gallantry and devotion to duty in salving tanks under heavy shell fire. He repaired and brought in two tanks which had been abandoned in full view of the enemy. By his energy, resource and courage he has salved many other apparently hopeless tanks, to the value of many thousands of pounds, and his personal example under shell fire and under most difficult conditions has raised the standard of salvage to a very high pitch.[278]

A colourful though unconventional character, Ewen had gained his pilot's certificate and his 'wings' on 25th March 1915 at Farnborough but was then appointed to help commission tanks. He later had an arm amputated after it had been shattered by a shell at Passchendaele, but continued to instruct tank crews in France for the rest of war and act as the deputy commander of the Tank Salvage Companies.

---

[277] The National Archives, WO 95/2978, war diary of the 4th Loyal North Lancashire Regiment, June 1917.
[278] *The London Gazette*, 17th September 1917.

Autumn Agony

During the last six months of the year, 66 Old Cheltonians were killed in action or died as a result of their military service. Of these, 37 were killed during the late summer and early autumn in the horror that became the Third Battle of Ypres – known infamously since as 'Passchendaele'. This three-and-a-half month bloody and awful struggle was continued due to a deadly combination of factors. The British High Command, and Douglas Haig in particular, was largely persuaded by over-optimistic and unrealistic intelligence reports about the reduced fighting state and shaky resolve of the German Army, added to which was the significant disarray in the ranks of the French Army. Due to their disastrous casualty figures arising from the Nivelle Offensive the previous spring, which was designed to coincide with the British assault at Arras aiming to maximise the pressure of combined attacks on the German army, many French infantry units were refusing to go on the offensive. With the Americans still mobilising, the BEF would have to fight this battle alone. Furthermore, with the U-Boat war significantly restricting food supplies for the nation, there was a very acceptable political and strategic case to drive towards the German submarine bases on the Belgian coast and expel them. At Ypres in 1917, Britain was no longer the junior partner to France on the Western Front. She was at least an equal partner with, finally, a well-equipped and resourced continental-sized army to match, and week by week the BEF took more of the combat effort.

As brigades were transferred to Ypres for the offensive, amongst them was Sydney Trevenen's battery. The main British assault at Ypres began on 31st July at 3.50am. By early afternoon a steady drizzle turned into a downpour which continued almost continually; it became the wettest August for thirty years and, with almost five inches of rain falling on 1st August, stalled the advance almost from the start. Half way through September, and with no let-up in the dogged determination to carry on, the BEF was preparing for renewed assault on the German defences, as Sydney recalled:

> Sept 19th. About 6pm the main road was packed with infantry going forward for the attack that is to take place tomorrow.

> Sept 20th. We attacked at dawn on an 8 mile front and were fairly successful. I sent up ammunition all day and went up myself to see how things were going at the guns. I and the major walked up to the OP but could not see much. The hostile artillery fire was practically nil except from shells from long range guns, one of which landed about 25 yards from us.

> Sept 21st. I was roused several times during the night by enemy shells passing overhead and bursting. I should say not more than a quarter of a mile away. Poperinghe was also shelled intermittently throughout the night. The last straw

was when an aeroplane bomb fell about 30 yards from my tent at 5.30am and splashed it with earth. No damage was done, however, I rode over to the 55th D.A. in the morning, attended a burial service in the afternoon and stopped the rest of the day at the WL. Lt Warburton came down from the guns. Just before dinner a Hun aeroplane came over and dropped three bombs. It was picked up by searchlights and was hotly engaged by anti-aircraft and machine guns.[279]

It was not just shelling, bombs, or rifle fire that threatened life and limb. During this fighting, two Old Cheltonians were also killed by the ubiquitous use of gas shells. Not simply a common feature of warfare, chemical weapons were now deemed an essential and integral consideration of almost every attack plan. Ralph MacGeough-Bond (Leconfield, 1915) came to College from Monmouth Grammar School in 1912. On 29th April 1915, while still at school, he applied for entry to RMA Woolwich to join the Royal Artillery and thereby follow in his father's footsteps. Commissioned as a second lieutenant a year later, he underwent final tactical gunnery training and, posted to D Battery (46th Brigade), embarked for the Front.[280] Over the next year, Ralph was involved in some of the most brutal fighting of the war, seeing action on the Somme and later at Arras. An enemy gas barrage was an inherent danger to gun crews as gas was a favoured tactic used specifically to suppress hostile artillery units, forcing gun crews into respirators thus reducing their efficiency and rate of fire – as well as causing casualties. On 22nd August south of Ypres, the gas alarms sounded as the Germans began to bombard his battery's position. Unable to don his respirator quickly enough and badly gassed, Ralph was taken to No 42 Field Ambulance nearby where he died from its poisonous effects that evening; a dreadful end to 19 years of life. He was buried by the medical staff that evening at nearby Voormezeele alongside several other victims of the same attack.

A week later, Marshall Featherstone (Day Boy, 1910) died near Frezenberg. He was a student at the South East Agricultural College at Wye near Ashford when war was declared. Marshall enlisted and attested on 17th August 1914 at Ashford into the 5th Battalion, East Kent Regiment (The Buffs). However, as his training got underway, he transferred six months later to the 28th Battalion, London Regiment (Artists' Rifles), a public schools' battalion in which many other public schoolboys were serving as privates; Private Featherstone was thus one of many. Embarking for France on 28th March 1915, the battalion served as an unofficial officers' training unit, and, given the education and experience of many of its soldiers, provided a steady stream of combat-experienced candidates

Marshall Featherstone

---
[279] Cheltenham College Archives, The Trevenen Diaries. (OP refers to observation post, DA to the director of artillery, and WL Wagon Lines supporting the batteries with ammunition.)
[280] *The London Gazette*, 9th May 1916, page 4560.

with the necessary leadership potential for commissioning. Marshall very much met these criteria, and, having applied for a temporary commission in the Royal Engineers on 13th March 1916, began his officer training.[281]

Marshall was appointed to the Special Companies, which were used to employ chemical weapons (predominantly chlorine gas and later phosgene), using the Livens projector as an offensive weapon prior to an attack. On 2nd September 1917, he was supervising the positioning and arming of a battery of these mortars on the Frezenberg Ridge to the east of Ypres in support of the infantry who were about to slog their way forward through the sludge and beyond the match-sticked poplars. In the loading process, he was overcome by gas leaking from one of his own projectiles. Marshall died from the effects, aged 23, and was buried by his comrades later that day.

On 6th November, the pitted piles of bricks and muddy pavé that once comprised the village of Passchendaele fell to the Canadian Corps which had been specifically transferred into the Salient for this final task. Having gained an enviable reputation as assault troops after their gallant assault on Vimy Ridge for skill and élan in attack, the Canadians finished the assault in the Flanders swamp which had cost the BEF some 250,000 casualties. Several Old Cheltonians fought in the ranks of the Canadians; three were sadly killed.

After leaving College, Henry Sulivan (Newick, 1906) went to Canada in 1910 and settled into business in Montreal. When war was declared, however, he immediately enlisted and was given a commission in the Princess Patricia's Canadian Light Infantry, becoming a member of the initial Canadian contingent to land in Britain in October 1914. Crossing to France on 20th December, the 'Patricias' were the first Canadian infantry unit to reach the battlefield. Henry was wounded on 24th February 1915 by a bullet that fractured his right leg: he was evacuated to England. Promoted to captain while convalescing Henry held several administration posts until he returned to France in June 1916. By then an acting major, he was appointed to command a company in the battalion which remained in the Ypres sector. Given the freezing dampness of a Flanders winter, it is unsurprising that he contracted a bout of influenza in March 1917, spending the next four weeks in hospital at Camiers. At the end of October 1917, during the final push to capture Passchendaele, the BEF were consolidating their 'bite and hold' doctrine. Returning to his company Henry was shot in the chest by a sniper after taking command of the battalion's front line. He died of his wounds on 31st October while he was being taken across the cratered, pond-filled battlefield, a torturous lurching and jolting final journey to No 10 Field Ambulance. His commanding officer wrote:

> No more gallant a fellow ever made the great sacrifice. On the evening of the 30th he brought up reinforcements, and while consolidating the position was shot through the shoulder, chest and arm, and died on his way to the dressing station. He had the

---

[281] While undergoing officer training, he became Pioneer Featherstone (No 130887) and was commissioned as a temporary second lieutenant on 2nd October 1916 – see *The London Gazette*, 12th January 1917, page 498.

confidence and the following of the men, and the friendship and admiration of his brother officers. From his long experience in the field, he thoroughly realized the magnitude and danger of the task he was asked to perform, and simply did his duty.[282]

Henry was from an eclectically educated yet military family and was undoubtedly imbued with a sense of service and duty. His father, an Old Harrovian, had seen active service in Afghanistan and South Africa, and continued to serve throughout the war commanding reserve battalions of the East Surrey Regiment. His youngest brother, Philip, an Old Malvernian, was killed in action on his 20th birthday, 27th August 1914, during the retreat from Mons and while fighting a rear-guard action at Etreux. He was buried by the Germans at the cross-roads nearby with eight of his brother officers who fell in the same action. Younger brother Eugene was an Old Wellingtonian and served in his father's regiment, until reported missing presumed killed at Fresnoy on 8th May 1917. To lose one child would have been bad enough, but to lose three sons in a war in which one was also serving is unimaginably heart-breaking.

Richard Garrett (Newick, 1908) a member of the OTC, had been in the same house as Henry Sullivan at College. Similarly, he too left for Canada to seek work. As an only son, his parents, Richard and Florence Garrett, who were living and working in South Africa, would surely have missed him. When war was declared, Richard was an established banker as well as being a commissioned member of the Canadian Militia in the Welland Canal Force. Realising that the militia units were unlikely to be deployed to France, Richard applied for active service abroad and was transferred into the 98th Battalion, Canadian Infantry (Lincoln and Welland) on 23rd November 1915 at Welland, Ontario where he was living. After training Richard sailed for Britain on 16th July 1916, where the battalion provided reinforcements to the Canadian Corps in the field. He joined the 3rd Battalion, Canadian Infantry in France and though wounded on 3rd May 1917, he was a platoon commander in 'A' Company when he was killed on 5th November just before Passchendaele fell to the Canadians. His commanding officer wrote:

> In Dick I lost a sincere friend, as the gallant officer was a great favourite of us all.[283]

Richard was buried behind the lines at Vlamertinghe Military Cemetery.

The youngest of three brothers, Bernhard Montagnon (Day Boy, 1905) left school when he was 16. His parents, Louis and Sarah Montagnon, lived at Marlborough House in the town and had previously sent his two elder brothers, Louis (Day Boy, 1873) and Denis (Day Boy, 1878) to College. As the family were of French Canadian descent, it was somewhat predictable that Bernhard might return to familial roots in Canada. This he did in 1910 with his education complete, becoming a teacher in 1913 at Highfield School in Hamilton, Ontario where he also played cricket. Two years later with the war raging and the Canadian

---

[282] Newman, S.K., *With the Patricia's in Flanders 1914-1918*, Bellewaerde House Publishing, Saanich, BC, 2000, pages 121-136.
[283] Notice in *The Toronto Star* edition, dated 26th November 1917.

contribution to it ever-increasing, he enlisted in the Canadian Infantry in May 1915 and returned to England becoming an instructor at the Machine Gun School at Shorncliffe. He was eventually sent to France in February 1917 with the 16th Machine Gun Company: a most hazardous duty. Constantly in the open and moving forward to support the infantry advancing in their fighting platoons and sections, machine gun sections and positions were quickly identified and allocated to the field artillery as priority targets. At the end of October, Bernhard was seriously wounded by shrapnel at Passchendaele while leading his gun sections most effectively in very difficult conditions. Evacuated to the base hospital in Le Touquet, he succumbed to his injuries on the 14th November. The unit war diary records 'his great gallantry and courage in the face of grave danger', and he was posthumously awarded the Military Cross.[284] The Highfield Review stated that:

> Mr Montagnon came to Canada with all the enthusiasm of a school boy. He had little experience of teaching, but he was full of energy and high spirits. He was a splendid cricketer and devoted to all kinds of sports.[285]

Bernhard was buried in Etaples Military cemetery, just across the river from the town and overlooking the peaceful opal beaches at Le Touquet.

Noel Saw

The care and attention paid to the wounded by the front line members of the Royal Army Medical Corps (RAMC) gave witness to many acts of extreme bravery removing casualties off the battlefield and out of harm's way, and ensured battalion medical officers were well liked and highly respected. No better example of this deep relationship is there between a regiment's officers and their adopted doctor than Noel Saw (Newick, 1909). Noel was a house mate of Richard Garrett, both killed within a month of each other at Passchendaele. After leaving College, Noel went up to Guy's (Teaching) Hospital to qualify as a doctor, becoming first a licentiate of the Royal College of Physicians and, finally in 1915, a member of the Royal College of Surgeons.

That year in February, he applied for a commission in the Special Reserve of Officers and was commissioned as a lieutenant (on probation) from that date in the RAMC.[286] He left for Gallipoli in July 1915 and was attached to the 4th Battalion, Worcestershire Regiment as its Medical Officer, a post he held for the next two years. In that time, he became an integral and significant part of the battalion, getting to know all the officers and men well, providing immediate medical attention in the heat of battle and in

---

[284] A. Renshaw (ed), *Wisden on the Great War: The Lives of Cricket's Fallen 1914-1918*, Bloomsbury London (2014), page 350.
[285] Ibid.
[286] Supplement to *The London Gazette*, 24th February 1915, page 1958.

quieter moments a friendly and sympathetic ear when morale and spirits needed lifting. As he was always included in the battalion's headquarters company, he witnessed first-hand the pressures and priorities of the command group and though outside the formal chain of command, could provide significant input advice to support the battalion's operational tasks. Not only that, over his two-year appointment with 4th Battalion, Worcesters he was present during the battalion's most challenging actions. He took part in both Gallipoli evacuations, first at Suvla Bay and then at Cape Helles. He served the battalion during the hard fighting on the Somme, especially the bitter struggle to take Beaumont Hamel, where, in recognition of his gallantry during the first five days of July, he was awarded the Military Cross:

> For conspicuous gallantry and devotion to duty. He worked incessantly for five days and nights tending the wounded brought in from 'no mans land'. He went out himself to direct operations connected with collecting the wounded quite regardless of the heavy fire from the enemy.[287]

The battalion war diary describes the attack on 1st July and the circumstances Noel faced:

> At 11.30 a.m. came orders for the 4th Worcestershire to advance. Immediately in front of their position the enemy had put down a barrage of heavy shells between the British front and reserve lines, and through that curtain of explosions the Battalion had to pass. The platoons filed forward as best they could, along smashed communication trenches choked with wounded men. Before the front line was reached a hundred (6 officers (Lts. R. C. Wynter and L. T. H. Leyland, 2/Lts. J. S. Wesson, A. E. Allsopp, K. Mossman and J. Scott) and 96 other ranks.) of the Battalion had been killed or wounded.[288]

At the end of July 1916 the battalion was removed to a quieter sector of the line near Ypres to rest, recuperate and re-equip before returning to the Somme in September. Over the next 12 months, Noel had time to reflect on his future and was sufficiently committed to his military doctoring tasks with the battalion that he applied for a permanent commission in the army on 19th September 1917. Three weeks later, he was killed near Ypres by a shell exploding on his Forward Aid Post, killing him instantly while he was tending the wounded. His commanding officer, Lieutenant Colonel Charles Linton, reflected the shock felt by the battalion by Noel's death, and wrote to his parents stating that:

> Your son had been with this battalion for so long, and was so popular with all ranks, that we all feel that we have lost a good friend.[289]

---

[287] *The London Gazette*, 22nd September 1916.
[288] The National Archives, WO 95/2309/2
[289] Guy's Hospital Reports, Vol. LXX, *Hospital Gazette*, 8th March 1919.

Such was the respect and admiration for Noel that one of his brother officers was also moved to write:

> His long connection with the battalion, his sharing of all its vicissitudes and dangers, his even, cheery disposition, and above all his utter unselfishness, endeared him greatly to us all. His friendship and the memory of his life will long be a powerful inspiration to those who knew him. He was buried on the 11th October at the British Military Cemetery at the base.[290]

Noel Saw and the hundreds of other battalion doctors who were so dedicated to the troops they tended, provided an island of humanity in a sea of death and devastation; one remarkable story of many remarkable men.

Despite the grim stagnation that once again enveloped the salient at Ypres, the final 'push' by the BEF during 1917 took place at Cambrai. For the first time, the use of massed formations of tanks with supporting infantry and air cover were to be employed. Preceded by a hurricane bombardment of over 1,000 guns, all of which had been surreptitiously pre-registered on their targets to maintain the element of surprise, 378 tanks rolled forward over a six-mile front at 6.20am on 20th November. With 19 infantry divisions committed to the attack, the initial results were a staggering success. Penetrating the Hindenburg Line in several places to a depth of over four miles, some church bells in England were rung to herald the accomplishments. Sydney Trevenen, whose artillery experiences we have followed through 1917, had been transferred from Ypres to Bullecourt to support the attack at Cambrai and witnessed events; his breathless diary continues:

> Nov 19th Wide gap in the enemy's lines and the cavalry are going through to capture Marcoing and Mesnières and that is to be the first days advance and if it is possible the battery might advance.
>
> Nov 20th Our attack was quite successful at Bullecourt but the one further south was beyond words. The cavalry broke through and the latest message I've received says we are well on our way towards Cambrai. It was fine in the morning luckily but as usual it had to drizzle for the rest of the day.
>
> Nov 21st It drizzled all day thus rendering observation from the air quite impossible. The advance down south continued but I expect it has been greatly hampered by the beastly weather. We fired in response to an SOS call in the early hours of the morning but for the rest of the day nothing happened. Lt I MacGregor has been attached to the battery.

---

[290] Ibid.

> Nov 22nd Registered the guns during the morning and the Huns sent a few crumps near the OP which was rather unpleasant. We are still advancing down south and great things are expected to take place on this part of the front.[291]

Sadly, Sydney's optimism was a little premature. After three days of advance only 98 tanks remained operational and the poor weather limited air observation and ground attack support. Furthermore, the age-old problem of effectively moving the artillery forward to maintain the impetus of the attack returned. By 30th November the German Second Army, with a break in the weather and the support of large numbers of ground attack aircraft had recoiled, stabilised and repelled the advance almost to the starting lines of 10 days before.

Although William Meikle (Boyne House, 1915) had been commissioned directly on leaving College into the King's Own Scottish Borderers (KOSB), his participation in active service had been somewhat delayed.[292] While training with the 3rd (Reserve) Battalion in Edinburgh, a motor cycle accident left him unconscious in the Royal Infirmary for several days, suffering a fractured skull and haemorrhage to his left eye. William took nearly 10 months to recover and, though still blind in his left eye, was declared fit on 14th February 1917. He completed his training and finally embarked for France as a replacement officer on 4th May, joining the 1st Battalion KOSB in the field five days later. His baptism of fire came during the heavy fighting in the Arras offensive around Monchy-le-Preux. By the end of November, he had been promoted to lieutenant and his battalion was hanging on to positions at Marcoing near Cambrai by its fingertips. The battalion war diary for 30th November records that morning's events:

> The enemy had attacked heavily on our Right and broken through part of the line held by the 20th Div and that this Division was at that moment retiring over the hill on our right. The battalion was aroused to take up a position forming a defensive flank on the right of the Division with the left of the battalion resting on the road south of Marcoing Copse. At about 11am these Coys (A and B) attacked the enemy who were working round the right of Marcoing and drove them back some 600 yards enabling the battalion to occupy a line.[293]

William was killed in this rear-guard action. Five days later the BEF's offensive was wound down; both sides had suffered some 40,000 casualties. However, events at Cambrai had shone a light on the way ahead where fixed defence lines could be penetrated by the use of technology, combined arms, surprise, and superiority in materiel. If a way of getting the guns rapidly forward to support the later phases of an attack could be achieved, stalemate could be avoided. The stoic slog through hectares of slime and debris, were, perhaps, starting to be a thing of the past.

---

[291] Cheltenham College Archives, The Trevenen Diaries.
[292] *The London Gazette*, 23rd November 1915, page 11601.
[293] The National Archives, WO 95/2304, Unit diary for the 1st King's Own Scottish Borderers, November 1917.

The final 1917 Old Cheltonian death in action, in what had been a brutal year testing the resolve of British troops to the limit, was that of Frederick Vicat (Boyne House, 1909), the second of two brothers to die in the war. After leaving College, he went to India and Kashmir to travel, and had only just returned when war was declared. Although Frederick applied immediately for a commission in the Royal West Kent Regiment, he developed acute appendicitis, requiring immediate surgery, followed by a considerable time in recovery; consequently, his commission was delayed. Yet, as soon as his doctor deemed him fit enough, he joined the Young Men's Christian Association as an ambulance driver. Frederick was seconded to a Red Cross detachment, which was supporting the French Government, and served on the Western Front, including Verdun, for eight months until May 1916. Returning to England he was appointed to a reserve cavalry unit. However, he sought a commission in the Special Reserve of the Scots Guards, which was granted on 30th May 1917.[294] In August, he was transferred again, this time to the West Riding Regiment, finally returning to the Western Front on 4th November attached to its 2nd Battalion. Just over a month later near Arras, in the late evening of 8th December, he was killed in action by a shell bursting in his trench, a shell splinter killing him instantly. His commanding officer wrote to console his mother:

> We were all very sorry to lose your son. He had not been with us many days but everyone took to him at once and his men had already learned to love him. This is, of course, the greatest test, love of an officer by his men. I can assure you that when I saw his Company the next morning it was striking how unhappy his death had made them. I regarded him as a very promising officer and together with another young officer who was also killed that night, he was noted as likely to command a Company much sooner than his service with is us would otherwise have warranted.[295]

He was buried the following day by the members of his platoon in the military cemetery at Monchy-le-Preux, another case of a second brother being killed during the war and more young promise cut short.

Memorial Plans

In the 1917 June issue of *The Cheltonian* magazine, it was suggested that a memorial should be established in memory of all the fallen Old Cheltonians, inviting comments and suggestions on the form this memorial might take. Throughout the following months, the magazine's editor received a steady stream of suggestions, with many offerings of financial support to whatever undertaking was finally decided. Jack Cohen (Nestor-Schnurmann, 1903) who was serving with the BEF in the 1/5th Battalion, King's Liverpool Regiment at Ypres responded and wrote about a memorial:

---

[294] Supplement to *The London Gazette*, 19th June 1917, page 6121.
[295] M. Bell, *Sevenoaks War Memorial: The Men Remembered*, Amberley Publishing, Stroud, (2014). See Vicat entry.

> May I propose that this should take the form of a Drill Hall? After the War, OTC will be more important than ever, and, when I left Cheltenham in 1903, the only covered-in place belonging to the Corps was a small shed opposite the Armoury.[296]

Jack's suggestion was considered but not pursued. Shortly after writing, Jack, having served with the battalion from the outset of war, was seriously wounded near the Menin Road during the Third Battle at Ypres, losing both legs above the knee. However, Jack's considerable disabilities did not diminish his determination to serve, and he was elected the MP for Liverpool Fairfield in December 1918, a seat he held for the next 13 years, being knighted for his service to politics and the community. Jack's two brothers, George and Stanley (both Nestor-Schnurmann, 1897 and 1896), also served in the same battalion during the war. George was killed in action at Festubert in 1915, and Stanley was wounded and gassed in 1917 during the same action at Ypres in which Jack lost his legs.

Another suggestion for a memorial in the June edition of *The Cheltonian* proposed the building of a memorial concert hall. Astley Terry (Beaufort, 1885) responded quickly, and, in denouncing this proposal with true Cheltonian candour, instead planted the seed of an idea that over the next 18 months would germinate and grow within the Cheltonian community. On 8th July 1917, the day after the successful attack at Messines had gone in, he wrote to the editor:

> Sir – With reference to the proposed War Memorial: it was suggested in the Editorial of the June *Cheltonian* that it should take the form of a Concert Hall. Personally, I can conceive nothing less suitable, and I don't think this suggestion will commend itself to anybody who has lost a relative – say a son – at the front. I hope the Cheltonian Society will favour the building of cloisters between the Quad and Chapel, which are badly wanted and would be a fitting memorial to our dead. I conclude that either there, or in the Chapel, the names of those who have fallen will be inscribed: and I sincerely trust the great error on the South African Memorial will not be repeated; (I mean the omitting of the rank and regiment). I think too that the action and date should be added. 'X.Y.Jones, Diddlesex (sic) Regiment, Messines Ridge, June 7, 1917' gives the *personal* touch which to my mind is so essential, and a 'lesson in stone' to future Cheltonians for all time.
>
> Yours truly, Astley Terry, Colonel

At the time, Astley was a colonel in the Army Service Corps commanding the Woolwich District and responsible for munitions and armament shipments to the Front. His only son, also named Astley (Cheltondale, 1914), was serving in the Royal Engineers

---

[296] *The Cheltonian*, 1917, page 184. (Author's note: The same shed was still being used by the CCF in his day in the early 1970s.)

on the Western Front; this family context no doubt shaped his views and this proposal, which in the months to come would be taken forward. During 1918, Astley's suggestion increasingly garnered support from the College community, so much so that it would, quite literally, be set in stone.

LIST OF FALLEN OLD CHELTONIANS 1917

On the following pages (212 to 217) are the names and service details of Old Cheltonians who died in the fourth year of the war.

1917 – LIST OF FALLEN OLD CHELTONIANS

	Died (1917)	Name	Rank
430	9 January	Doherty-Holwell RV	Lt Colonel
431	11 January	Wiggin NH	Lieutenant
432	26 January	Thompson IFR	Lt Colonel
433	31 January	Loye RP	Private
434	3 February	Baines HPB	2nd Lieutenant
435	3 February	Woollcombe JM	Major
436	7 February	Stokes TF	Captain
437	11 February	Carew RT	Colonel
438	16 February	Simpson FWH	Captain
439	17 February	Pym WP	Private
440	21 February	Denne WH	Major
441	22 February	Crichton HR	Lieutenant
442	22 February	Reilly AST	Captain
443	5 March	Astley AGL	Captain
444	6 March	Tannett-Walker FW	Colonel
445	15 March	Beale RA	2nd Lieutenant
446	19 March	Cockshott FW	Civilian
447	28 March	Caffyn CHM	2nd Lieutenant
448	28 March	Thomson HGA	Major
449	30 March	Dove EH	2nd Lieutenant
450	9 April	Thomas BLB	Lieutenant
451	11 April	Wilkinson RHS	Private
452	11 April	Shaw GH	Lieutenant
453	12 April	Wilson SC	Private
454	13 April	Stuart JM	Captain
455	14 April	Eyre SHR	2nd Lieutenant
456	15 April	Harvey-James AK	Captain
457	15 April	Renny GM	Lieutenant
458	19 April	Joseph WGA	2nd Lieutenant
459	19 April	Macleod GC	Lieutenant
460	20 April	Taylor CM	2nd Lieutenant
461	21 April	Webster JAC	2nd Lieutenant
462	22 April	Bullock TEG	2nd Lieutenant
463	23 April	Knox AR	Major
464	23 April	Solomon LI	2nd Lieutenant
465	24 April	Capel-Davies JR	Gunner
466	24 April	Fawcett BJA	Captain
467	24 April	Grant IAW	2nd Lieutenant
468	25 April	Darnell CV	2nd Lieutenant
469	26 April	Baines AFCT	Major

1917 – LIST OF FALLEN OLD CHELTONIANS

Unit	Age	Place
Royal Engineers	34	Ypres, Belgium
66th Brigade, Royal Field Artillery	26	Kut, Mesopotamia
CO, 26th Punjabis, IA	49	Hai, Mesopotamia
12th Royal Fusiliers	40	Bethune, France
att 7th Gloucestershire Regiment	35	Dahra, Mesopotamia
1st Devonshire Regiment	38	Hai, Mesopotamia
82nd Punjabis, IA	25	Kut, Mesopotamia
att 6th Rifle Brigade	56	Bournemouth, UK
No 55 Squadron, RFC	25	Nieppe, Belgium
11th Royal Fusiliers	27	Miraumont, France
2nd Bedfordshire Regiment	40	Highgate, UK
51st Sikhs, IA	22	Falayiah, Mesopotamia
att 92nd Punjabis, IA	23	Sannayiat, Mesopotamia
14th Hussars	35	Lagg, Mesopotamia
Royal Engineers	57	Leeds, UK
1st Gloucestershire Regiment	19	Somme, France
HM Inspector of Steel	32	Newcastle, UK
No 60 Squadron, RFC	26	Arras, France
Royal Warwickshire Regiment	39	Sailly sur Lys, France
1st Royal Welch Fusiliers	19	Monchy, France
att 27th Coy, Machine Gun Corps	21	Arras, France
13th Royal Fusiliers	41	Monchy, France
att 6th Bedfordshire Regiment	23	Monchy, France
7th Suffolk Regiment	22	Arras, France
No 59 Squadron, RFC	20	Arras, France
1st Essex Regiment	19	Monchy, France
8th Royal East Kent Regiment	41	Loos, France
92nd Brigade, Royal Field Artillery	21	Havrincourt, France
att 1/5th Norfolk Regiment	21	Gaza, Palestine
att 1/5th (KO) Scottish Borderers	26	Gaza, Palestine
27th Brigade, Royal Field Artillery	19	Vimy, France
1st Seaforth Highlanders	19	Istabulat, Mesopotamia
1st Royal East Kent Regiment	19	Loos, France
18th Reserve Battery, Royal Artillery	54	Woolwich, UK
1st Kings Own Scottish Borderers	32	Monchy, France
Royal Field Artillery	30	Arras, France
8th East Lancashire Regiment	24	Arras, France
70th Brigade, Royal Field Artillery	20	Arras, France
No 25 Squadron, RFC	22	Vimy, France
Royal Army Service Corps	36	Salonika, Greece

1917 – LIST OF FALLEN OLD CHELTONIANS

	Died (1917)	Name	Rank
470	28 April	McCammon TVP	Lt Colonel
471	3 May	Hovenden AL	2nd Lieutenant
472	3 May	Nicholson BH	Lieutenant
473	3 May	Stock JLW	2nd Lieutenant
474	6 May	Littleton CF	Captain
475	8 May	Jones VHS	Captain
476	10 May	Finnimore DK	Lieutenant
477	11 May	Bridgeman HHO	Lieutenant
478	11 May	Kershaw SR	2nd Lieutenant
479	11 May	Robinson AT	Lt Colonel
480	12 May	Jeune H StH	Captain
481	15 May	Willis SA	Captain
482	15 May	Wise AVD	Captain
483	24 May	Wilson CR	Lieutenant
484	2 June	Peile JSC	Lieutenant
485	7 June	Campbell DDH	Major
486	7 June	Dickson WH	2nd Lieutenant
487	7 June	Dighton LP	Private
488	16 June	Gulland AF	Captain
489	18 June	Dickson AG	Major
490	20 June	Momber EMF	Major
491	22 June	De Lautour HA	Lt Colonel
492	25 June	Collins PRM	Major
493	25 June	Mills HV	2nd Lieutenant
494	29 June	Durand RHM	Lieutenant
495	1 July	Kerr HG	2nd Lieutenant
496	2 July	Cole-Hamilton CWE	Captain
497	14 July	Crofton EVM	Lieutenant
498	21 July	Boyd TC	Captain
499	23 July	Tanner JA	Brig General
500	26 July	Bowen GES	Major
501	27 July	Rayner NR	Lieutenant
502	31 July	Hope-Johnstone HM	Lt Colonel
503	31 July	Scott AH	Captain
504	11 August	Tate FH	Captain
505	12 August	Willis HD	Captain
506	14 August	Parsons KJT	Captain
507	19 August	Garstang CH	Ship's Master
508	19 August	Smith JB	2nd Lieutenant
509	22 August	MacGeough-Bond RS	2nd Lieutenant

1917 – LIST OF FALLEN OLD CHELTONIANS

Unit	Age	Place
CO, att 2nd Hampshire Regiment	42	Camiers, France
7th East Surrey Regiment	18	Monchy, France
att 4th Royal Fusiliers	23	Monchy, France
att 6th Somerset Light Infantry	29	Arras, France
att 5th Cameron Highlanders	26	Aubigny, France
1st Royal Marines Light Infantry	35	London, UK
Royal Engineers	20	Aldershot, UK
Household Battalion	25	Roeux, France
att 1st London Regiment	32	Arras, France
CO, 7th Ox and Bucks Light Infantry	44	Salonika, Greece
att 12th Gloucestershire Regiment	23	Arras, France
4th Middlesex Regiment	24	Camiers, France
Royal Engineers	23	Marquaix, France
att 88th Coy, Machine Gun Corps	30	Arras, France
190th Brigade, Royal Field Artillery	21	Ypres, Belgium
112th Brigade, Royal Field Artillery	33	Messines, Belgium
4th Loyal (N) Lancashire Regiment	40	Messines, Belgium
2nd Canterbury Regiment, NZEF	28	Messines, Belgium
att 8th Royal East Kent Regiment	26	Messines, Belgium
123rd Brigade, Royal Field Artillery	39	Le Treport, France
CO, 177th Tunnelling Company, RE	29	Hooge, Belgium
Surgeon, NZ Defence Forces	67	Invercargill, NZ
CO, 13th Seige Battery, RGA	26	Dikkebus, Belgium
321st Seige Battery, RGA	35	Ypres, Belgium
38th Central Indian Horse	25	Peronne, France
9th Queens Royal Lancers	20	Lens, France
Pilot, Royal Flying Corps	23	London Colney, UK
61st Field Coy, Royal Engineers	28	Ypres, Belgium
att 7th Cameron Highlanders	20	Wimereux, France
Chief Royal Engineer, 22nd Division	57	Arras, France
83rd Brigade, Royal Field Artillery	29	Ypres, Belgium
No 57 Squadron, RFC	20	Ypres, Belgium
CO, 12th Royal Fusiliers	31	Ypres, Belgium
Royal Engineers, 12th Infantry Brigade	28	Ypres, Belgium
10th King's Royal Rifle Corps	22	Ypres, Belgium
RAMC, att 3rd Worcestershire Regiment	34	Ypres, Belgium
att 5th Royal Irish Regiment	40	Salonika, Greece
SS Garstang (sunk by U40)	40	Crete, Mediterranean
att 14th Royal Warwickshire Regiment	23	Arleux, France
46th Brigade, Royal Field Artillery	19	Ypres, France

1917 – LIST OF FALLEN OLD CHELTONIANS

	Died (1917)	Name	Rank
510	25 August	Bush JS de L	Captain
511	26 August	Osmaston OCH	2nd Lieutenant
512	30 August	Wrigley HN	2nd Lieutenant
513	31 August	Roberts AD	Lieutenant
514	2 September	Featherstone MB	Captain
515	5 September	Woodhouse B	Captain
516	10 September	Gregory HW	Lt Commander
517	13 September	Campbell AB	Captain
518	26 September	Swales GM	Captain
519	28 September	Harington WG	Major
520	1 October	Marker TM	2nd Lieutenant
521	5 October	Cardew JH	Captain
522	9 October	Holme JE	Captain
523	9 October	Moore RCD	2nd Lieutenant
524	9 October	Saw NHW	Captain
525	9 October	Villar RH	Private
526	11 October	Saltren-Willett AJ	Lt Colonel
527	13 October	Stewart AD	Lieutenant
528	20 October	Adams-Mathieson HFR	Lieutenant
529	20 October	Greatwood H	Lieutenant
530	22 October	Bell-Irving K	Captain
531	24 October	Hough JEC	Sub-Lieutenant
532	26 October	Noel FM	2nd Lieutenant
533	28 October	Dickinson WV	Colonel
534	31 October	Roberts RJ	Lieutenant
535	31 October	Sulivan HE	Major
536	5 November	Garrett RD	Lieutenant
537	6 November	Gloster GCE	Lieutenant
538	14 November	Montagnon BC	Lieutenant
539	19 November	Abraham GWP	Captain
540	20 November	Best TAD	Lt Colonel
541	20 November	Wakefield MS	Lieutenant
542	30 November	Meikle WRD	2nd Lieutenant
543	1 December	Cameron DA	Lieutenant
544	4 December	Mayne AB	Major
545	7 December	Dyer HA	2nd Lieutenant
546	7 December	Iohnson EF	Captain
547	8 December	Vicat FH	2nd Lieutenant
548	12 December	Hawkins AE	Major
549	19 December	Laverton FK	Lieutenant

1917 – LIST OF FALLEN OLD CHELTONIANS

Unit	Age	Place
No 41 Squadron, RFC	21	Cambrai, France
12th Field Coy, Royal Engineers	20	Loos, France
Royal Field Artillery, 53rd Division	26	Cairo, Egypt
No 10 (Training) Squadron, RFC	22	Hounslow, UK
No 2 Special (Gas) Company, RE	23	Ypres, Belgium
RAMC, att 10th Royal Welch Regiment	28	Ypres, Belgium
CO, HMS *Hoverfly*	31	Basra, Mesopotamia
att 8th Royal Sussex Regiment	40	Ypres, Belgium
att 1/8th Trench Mortar Battery	20	Ypres, Belgium
5th Gurkha Rifles	32	Ramadi, Mesopotamia
1st Royal Lancaster Regiment	19	Ypres, Belgium
73rd Battery, Royal Field Artillery	35	Ypres, Belgium
16th Royal Warwickshire Regiment	28	Ypres, Belgium
2nd Honourable Artillery Company	20	Ypres, Belgium
RAMC, att 4th Worcestershire Regiment	25	Ypres, Belgium
1/6th Gloucestershire Regiment	35	Ypres, Belgium
CO, 66th Heavy Group, RGA	51	Ypres, Belgium
Central Flying School	28	Upavon, UK
159th Brigade, Royal Field Artillery	20	Ypres, Belgium
36th Brigade, Royal Field Artillery	30	Ypres, Belgium
8th East Surrey Regiment	25	Ypres, Belgium
No 1 Squadron, RNAS	19	Ypres, Belgium
9th Devonshire Regiment	28	Laventie, France
GHQ, Assistant Adjutant General	61	Rouen, France
179th Coy, Machine Gun Corps	38	Beersheba, Palestine
Princess Patricia's Canadian Light Infantry	29	Ypres, Belgium
3rd Infantry (Toronto) Regiment, Canada	25	Ypres, Belgium
1st Devonshire Regiment	20	Ypres, Belgium
16th Coy, Canadian MGC	28	Le Touquet, France
att 24th Welsh Regiment	22	Port Said, Egypt
2/5th Duke of Wellington's Regiment	38	Havrincourt, France
1st Sherwood Foresters	25	Ypres, Belgium
1st King's Own Scottish Borderers	19	Cambrai, France
Corps of Guides, IA	24	Cambrai, France
Royal Field Artillery	57	London, UK
No 65 Squadron, RFC	39	Ypres, Belgium
310th Brigade, Royal Field Artillery	36	Cambrai, France
2nd West Riding Regiment	25	Monchy, France
181st Brigade, Royal Field Artillery	23	Manancourt, France
School of Aerial Gunnery, RFC	19	New Romsey, UK

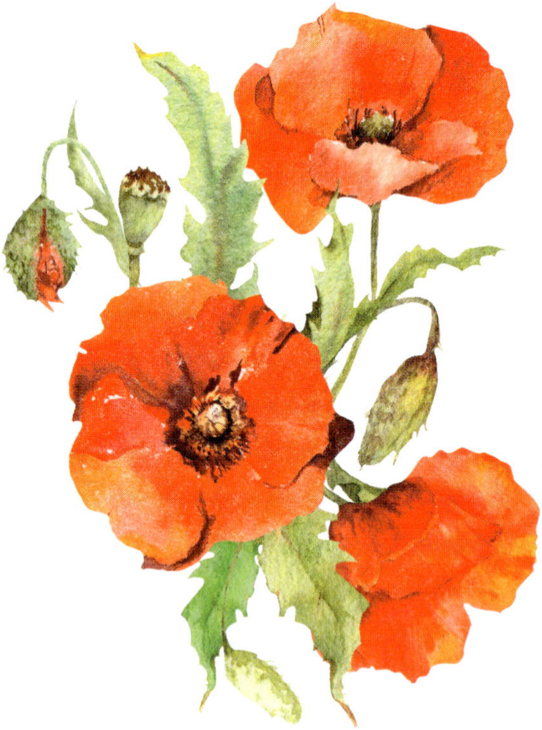

ACTS FIVE
1918 – THE YEAR OF TURNING TIDES

The muted acknowledgements of another wartime New Year's Eve reflected a mood more of grim determination than of exuberant aspiration more usually associated with the occasion. A significant meeting was held in London the following week. At 3.00pm on 9th January, a large and illustrious group of Old Cheltonians, College parents and supporters met at the Criterion Restaurant in Piccadilly and convened under the chairmanship of Sir Arthur Lee, an Old Cheltonian himself and the Director-General of Food Production under Lloyd George. He was also the president of the College council and the sitting Member of Parliament for Fareham.

The purpose of the meeting was to set in motion the necessary funding associated with erecting a permanent memorial at College to honour and commemorate all the Old Cheltonians killed in the war. The meeting was not just noteworthy as far as College was concerned, it also captured the growing popular mood for a suitable and lasting symbol to commemorate and honour the hundreds of thousands of British fallen. After much outpouring of loyal, patriotic and noble sentiment from Sir Arthur, reinforced in kind by others, most notably Reginald Waterfield, the College's principal, the meeting set in train firm plans for the building of the Memorial Cloisters. This project was similar to the proposal by Colonel Astley Terry nearly a year before. Sir Arthur also drew the meeting's attention to another roll of honour, acknowledging with considerable pride that during the war to date Old Cheltonians had won:

Sir Arthur Lee, standing right

> No fewer than 5 Victoria Crosses, 180 D.S.O.'s, 5 bars to the D.S.O., (and everyone knows that that is one of the greatest honours that could be achieved), 255 Military Crosses, 14 Bars to Military Cross, 3 D.S.C.'s, 1,043 mentions in despatches, 145 mentions for valuable service in connection with the War, 39 French, 19 Russian, 10 Italian, 10 Belgian, 2 Rumanian, 13 Serbian, and 10 Egyptian honours.[297]

---

[297] *The Cheltonian* magazine.

Noble of thought and gesture as such a memorial would be, it was not, perhaps, the highest priority in the minds of those still fighting in the various campaigns across the globe, and in particular Brigadier Edward Grogan (Boyne House, 1867) and his family. Edward had five sons, two by his first wife Meta, who had sadly died of typhoid in 1881, and three by his second wife, Ida. Edward and Ida set up their family home in Cheltenham at Huntley Lodge in Montpellier Grove for some domestic stability while the younger three boys attended College and during his absence when away on duty in the army or serving abroad. His eldest son, George, had been educated at Haileybury and was already a career soldier, serving as brigadier in command of the 23rd Infantry Brigade on the Western Front. George would win the Victoria Cross for his gallantry in the intense fighting on the Aisne in May 1918. But, just the day before the Cheltonian meeting in London, Gerald (Day Boy, 1901), the eldest son of his second marriage, was killed; the second of Edward's sons to die during the war.[298]

On leaving College, Gerald went to the University in Edinburgh to study science, intending to be a doctor but did not take to pathology and his interests changed. He went to Camborne College to study Mining Engineering, yet despite his science background, was working by early 1914 as a published author and journalist for the *Throne* and *Pall Mall* magazines in London and living in Sydney Street, Chelsea.[299] Already a member of the Honourable Artillery Company as Private Grogan, he was mobilised at Armoury House, Finsbury the day after war was declared. As the 1st Battalion was quickly reinforced to war strength, Gerald completed some final training, and after the battalion had been inspected by King George V on 12th September, it deployed to France six days later and went into the line near Ypres. On 16th January 1915 while serving at the Front, he applied for a temporary commission, no doubt with some powerful encouragement as his application was approved by the commander of 26th Infantry Brigade, a certain Brigadier General Edward Grogan. Supporting Gerald's application, his father wrote:

> I have the honour to forward herewith Form MT/393, an application from my son No 1395 Private Grogan, GF, No 2 Company, The Honourable Artillery Company Service Battalion, for a Commission in the 6th Service Battalion Leicestershire Regiment. He is now at the front with his Battalion and has been there for some months. He did not apply for a Commission before as he was doubtful how long the war would last. I trust that now his application may be favourably considered, and the fact that myself and all my five sons – one of whom has lately been severely wounded – are serving at the present time may be taken into account as giving extra claim for consideration of this case. I should not have recommended him did I not think he would make a good Officer,
>
> EG Grogan, Brigadier General, Commanding 26th Infantry Brigade.[300]

---

[298] Lieutenant James Grogan (Boyne, 1908) was killed in action in Gallipoli on 4th June 1915, as recorded in Acts 2.
[299] See G Grogan, *A Drop in Infinity*, John Lane, London, (1915), and *William Pollok, and Other Tales*, John Lane, London, (1919).
[300] The National Archives, WO 339/31461, Personal Record of Lieutenant G F Grogan.

Gerald was duly commissioned a month later into the 6th Leicestershire Regiment, one of the New Army battalions being brought up to strength.[301] However, after a short period holding the line near Tilques, he decided to make use of his mining experience and transferred into the Royal Engineers on 8th April 1916 to join one of the early drafts for the new tunnelling companies being raised for mining operations for the Somme offensive. Following a course at the School of Military Engineering at Chatham, Gerald returned to France with 183rd Tunnelling Company and began work on mining operations, specifically preparing the laying of four charges and camouflets under the German trenches at Mametz and a further three near Carnoy. During his time near the trenches at Guillemont, he wrote the poem 'Arrowhead Copse', the opening words of which captured the striking and prophetic atmosphere of his war:

> Bodies of men in the funk-holes
> Who in suffering crept there to die,
> Struck,— Even so may I perish;
> Even so may I lie
> Dead—and a desolate twilight shrouding a dying sky.[302]

The following year the company was employed in the construction of deep dugouts for troop accommodation near Arras, the digging of communication subways and 'Russian Saps' leading out into No Man's Land from the British front line to within yards of the German positions. After two years with the 183rd, Gerald was transferred to one of the other companies working north of Ypres. While working with his team in a forward area on 8th January 1918, he was killed by a high explosive shell which burst right above him, sadly a victim of routine and sporadic shelling that day. He was buried, poignantly, in Bard Cottage Cemetery the same evening.

However, the opening weeks of January seemed to hold a restrained atmosphere and a curtailed tempo to the fighting, both sides apparently content to adopt a tacit agreement to 'live and let live'. Sydney Trevenen, just returned to his battery after some well-earned Christmas leave in England, recorded the somewhat sedentary battle environment permeating around his gun positions near Achiet-le-Grand, northwest of Bapaume. In fact, the only thing battering the front lines appeared to be the weather:

> Jan 16th. There was a howling gale and flying showers all last night and today. After breakfast I struggled up to the WL [wagon lines] and found Lieut Davidson there. We lunched at the Club and in the afternoon improved the hut I now live in.
>
> Jan 17th. As it rained all the morning I finished off fitting up my hut, and it is now very snug and cosy. Except for the horse standings, the WL is a sea of mud 6 inches deep.

---

[301] *The London Gazette,* 12th February 1915, page 1455.
[302] See the privately published book of collective poetry, *Poems*, Whitefriars Press, London, 1925.

> Jan 18th. Went for a ride on Whizbang after breakfast and took Pongo with me. He followed quite well and thoroughly enjoyed the outing. I had dinner at Brigade HQ as tomorrow they go up into action again.[303]

With not a mention of German belligerence in his diary entries, it seemed, rather suspiciously, to be very much a case of 'all quiet on the Western Front'. Was this the calm before a storm, or even the tidal precursor to a tsunami?

During the first 10 weeks of the year, the war claimed only eight Old Cheltonian lives, and four of these were from illness associated with the hardships of wartime military service. Two Old Cheltonians were killed in action holding the line at Ypres, and the other two deaths were caused by flying accidents, one in training in England and the other on an operational sortie in Palestine.[304]

Harald Hewett

Having left College, Harald Hewett (Leconfield, 1911) spent a short period tea planting in Ceylon, before returning to England in 1914 to undergo army officer training at Sandhurst.

Commissioned as a second lieutenant into the Royal Berkshire Regiment in February 1915, he spent barely seven months with his battalion before being seconded to the Royal Flying Corps (RFC) as an observer that October. By 1918 he was a flight commander with No 113 Squadron, an experienced aviator with a Military Cross to his name.[305] On 4th January, Harald was killed during a bombing raid on the airfield at Jenin in Palestine while flying in an RE 8 aircraft piloted by Second Lieutenant Alfred Butt. Their aircraft was involved in a mid-air collision with another RE8 (Serial No B5854) from No 67 Squadron piloted by an Australian crew; Lieutenant Jack Sumner-Potts with Second Lieutenant Vincent Parkinson acting as his wireless operator and observer. On being attacked by an enemy Albatross scout, Alfred took immediate evasive action, a dangerous manoeuvre when in close proximity to other members of the formation, but collided with Jack and Vincent's aircraft. Vincent was the only one of the four to survive the crash, but, badly injured with a fractured skull, was taken prisoner by Germans serving alongside their Turkish allies.

The three airmen were buried with full military honours by Germans who set a broken propeller to the head of the grave: the inscription, written in German on the cross, when translated states 'Here rest in God three fearless English flyers, fallen 4/1/18'. These latter two cases are equally sad, though interesting as both were caused by the inherent dangers

---

[303] Cheltenham College Archives, Diaries of Captain Sydney Trevenen, MC.
[304] During 1918, the Palestine and Sinai campaign front was gaining increasing political significance as General Allenby's Egyptian Expeditionary Force pressed on towards Damascus after the fall of Jerusalem in December 1917. Air operations in the Middle East, particularly the bombing campaign, was an integral part of the allied strategic plan to secure Palestine and Syria, and interrupt, if not sever, Turkish rail links to Mesopotamia.
[305] Supplement to *The London Gazette*, 24th February 1916, page 2080.

The wreckage

associated with flying in formation, a recently developed and increasingly used tactic aimed to maximise the use of defensive armaments against enemy scout aeroplanes as well as to usher a larger number of bombs on to their designated targets. Whether flying in close formation or in a defensive battle formation, both activities require proficiencies that take time and practice to master, but in 1918, the development of the necessary skills and associated training was still in its infancy.

Terence Manly (Hazelwell, 1911) left College at the age of 17 and moved to Canada where he eventually trained to be a school master. A good all-rounder, his sporting interests included rugby, cricket and motor-cycling. At the outbreak of war, he enlisted into the Canadian Expeditionary Force in November, and was promptly made a sergeant instructor at No 106 School of Signalling while also working in the Muster Department of the Canadian Pay Office. However, he applied for a commission on 9th November 1916 in the RFC to be a pilot and having successfully graduated with his pilot wings, was commissioned on the General List (RFC) as a second lieutenant.[306] By March 1918, he had amassed some 460 hours of flying time. Sadly, on 6th March Terence, accompanied by Lieutenant Montgomery of the US Air Service as his passenger, was killed accidentally when his Armstrong Whitworth FK8 aircraft was flying in formation with other aircraft from No 1 Auxiliary School of Aerial Gunnery, Hythe. With the formation's manoeuvres, their machine hit the slipstream of one of the other aircraft and was upset, spilling petrol from the fuel tank over the hot engine. The aircraft quickly caught fire as it dropped from the formation. Terence fell out of the aircraft at 800 feet, and moments later the machine

[306] Supplement to *The London Gazette*, 17th May 1917, page 4785.

crashed inverted with Lieutenant Montgomery still inside. Not until September 1918 was the use of parachutes for aircrew (as opposed to balloon observers) authorised, although parachutes did not reach operational service until after the Armistice, sadly far too late for these intrepid aviators.

Elsewhere, the war ground on remorselessly and at Achiet-le-Grand in France, Sydney, Trevenen was still as domestically orientated as conditions would allow:

> Jan 19th. Rode over to arrange about a Wagon Line Orderly and exercised Whizbang. The Padre blew in for tea and afterwards we dined at the Club.[307]

Percy Hattersley-Smith, College master, 1907

However, back in Cheltenham the very same day one significant death occurred which shook many in the broad Cheltonian community; not just the College family, but also several other associations throughout the town. On that Saturday morning Reverend Percy Hattersley-Smith, the legendary housemaster of Hazelwell, passed away aged seventy. Percy had spent virtually all his post-graduate life at College as an assistant master and a popular member of the Common Room. For 44 years he had taught mathematics to generations of College boys, including most of those who were fighting or who had already fallen in the war.

Percy had tutored many more in a more pastoral role during his 23-year tenure as a housemaster, encouraging and enthusing many budding young cricketers at school. If the deaths of his former students from the war were not sufficient enough sorrow to carry, he had also suffered personal grief with the loss of both his own sons during 1915: James dying of wounds received in action at Loos; Geoffrey of dysentery while serving in the Royal Navy.

Born in Cambridge, Percy had attended Perse Grammar School in the town and went up to the University as a scholar at Emmanuel College. Though a good all-round games player, he excelled at cricket, playing first class cricket for Gloucestershire in the 1870s and also for the MCC, the 'Incogniti' Cricket Club, and Cheltenham's town cricket club. He also helped the foundation of the East Gloucestershire Cricket Club, whose ground in Charlton Kings today provides facilities for tennis, squash and ladies' hockey. In his later years, Percy and his wife Mary lived at the family home at Glenfall Lawn, Pittville Circus in the town. Their daughter Dorothy was also well known, and at the time of his death was the assisting quartermaster of the Red Cross Hospital at Suffolk Hall. Dorothy had taken on the mantle as mistress of the family home when Mary passed away in 1910. Three years later Percy retired from teaching, but willingly returned once the war had

[307] Cheltenham College Archives, Diaries of Captain Sydney Trevenen, MC.

started to help replace those members of the Common Room who had volunteered to serve. With Percy's death, it seemed that an era in the life at College, and an enduring presence around the cloisters, had come to an end. Reverend Reginald Waterfield, most poignantly and eloquently addressed the whole school in Chapel during his evensong sermon the following day:

> Though he had retired from service after forty-four years of as strenuous a service as any master ever gave to a school, he returned to help me in my difficulties, when the claims of our country called so many of the younger men away; and he was working here beyond the age of three score years and ten when the illness took him which, after long months of weariness, proved fatal at last. Mr Hattersley-Smith was admired and respected and loved by many generations of Cheltenham boys. He was a great exponent of games, and a keen enthusiast for all manly and healthy sports. But he was no idol-worshipper of athletics. He insisted upon the prior claims of the intellectual activities of boys and men. A stern moralist and a rigid disciplinarian, he was nevertheless a most generous appraiser of both men and boys. He passed kindly judgement in his conversation about others; he blamed without bitterness, he praised without stint. He loved this school. He loved his House, and to every boy in it he was a friend, but none the less the master. He loved this Chapel and its services. Those of us who have known him longest will him most of all here. And that is as it should be.[308]

One of his old Hazelwell boys was moved to write:

> The advent of Mr Hattersley-Smith effected a magical alteration. Tremendously keen, thorough in everything he undertook, strong of limb, stout of heart, and beloved by every boy young and old in the House, his forcible personality inspired us to emulate his example and imbued us with tremendous enthusiasm and keenness for the House and the College... He was out to 'play the game', and he played it in everything, great and small, that he did in his long life, and he taught us boys to play it too.[309]

This pair of remarkable and revealing testaments, just two of many other similar obituaries published during the course of that spring, offer not only insight into Percy's life and contribution to College, they also highlight the ethos of 'muscular Christianity' which public schools of the period embraced. More pertinently perhaps, and especially in the context of this narrative, the concept espouses many of the qualities demonstrated by the alumni serving during the war. Percy is commemorated in the College Chapel, alongside the fallen Old Cheltonians, many of them his former pupils, of the Great War.

---

[308] *The Cheltonian* magazine, March 1918, page 96.
[309] Ibid.

By the end of February, the shock of Percy's passing had, to some degree, subsided with normal routines and timetables resumed in College. In parallel, on the Western Front the fighting remained relatively light and mostly reactive in nature. The foremost reason for these somewhat dormant conditions was the universal problem of the provision and availability of additional military manpower. From the German perspective, the Russian and Romanian suspension of hostilities in December had released some 33 divisions for westwards transfer to augment and reinforce their weary troops holding the line in Belgium and France. On the other hand, the British were finding themselves short of men. The calamitous and profligate casualty figures from 1917, especially from the fighting at Arras, Passchendaele and Cambrai, on top of the dark shadow still cast by those losses from the Somme the previous year, made an already reluctant and sceptical Lloyd George even more unenthusiastic about meeting Haig's request for yet another 330,000 troops. By mid-March 1918, only half this number was forthcoming. This manpower shortage manifested itself throughout the British divisions and battalions, all of which fell into a state of perpetual reduced strength. With the French army continuing to suffer a malaise in morale, and the American Expeditionary Force still emergent in size, experience and equipment, there would be a short period during the spring when the German Army on the Western Front would hold a numerical advantage of 36 divisions. If Germany was to break the Allies before the American factor became irresistible and overwhelming, she had to strike now, and preferably against the BEF, who, now having grown to the size of a continental army, had been forced to adopt the mantle of senior partner. Accordingly, by March German battle plans for the *'Kaiserschlacht'*, the Kaisers battle, were complete and focussed on the British armies. If, through a sequence of coordinated attacks, the British 'domino' was knocked over, surely the others would quickly fall.

Spring Tide

The Allied High Command was well aware of the comparative manpower mathematics and impending German offensive intentions; aerial reconnaissance provided consistent photographic evidence of increasing troop concentrations and burgeoning supply dumps. The key question was not 'if' but 'when'. On 20th March, Sydney Trevenen was with his battery, supporting 40th Brigade to the south east of Arras, and everything appeared normal. There was the routine church parade on the previous Sunday morning, a VI Corps concert party the following evening, and the next day when the brigade colonel was inspecting his wagon lines he seemed well satisfied with arrangements. Sydney recorded in his diary:

> March 20th. A beastly morning but a nice afternoon of which I took advantage and went for a ride. I hear we go into reserve again about Sunday next for three weeks.[310]

[310] Cheltenham College Archives, Diaries of Captain Sydney Trevenen, MC.

How wrong Sydney would be. During the night of 20th March, over a wide area from Arras to the south of St Quentin, the wind remained slight and, with a clear sky and the damp ground, pockets of fog began to form. By 4.30am the fog had become quite thick and extensive, especially in the British forward zone where the front line was lightly held by observation patrols, snipers and machine gun posts. Most of the Allied troops were concentrated behind the immediate battle zone, out of range of the German field artillery, but ready to go forward if and when required. Fifteen minutes later, the leading crest of the tsunami broke on the Allied lines in the shape of a tremendous wave of bombardment from 6,400 guns and 3,500 trench mortars, drowning the defenders with high explosive, shrapnel and gas shells. Longer-range artillery, pre-registered on their targets, dislocated Allied communications. John Wills was asleep next to his battery when the barrage erupted further south, yet coming dangerously closer minute by minute:

> March 21st. For some time before I awoke I was half conscious of a great rumbling in the distance. Cropper and I rubbed our eyes and realised that the much vaunted 'Michael Day' had dawned at last. There could be no doubt of it for even at the Wagon Lines – six miles or more from the front – the noise was tremendous and the earth shook continuously as from an earthquake. Every minute or so, high velocity guns were firing into Arras or over our heads on to the road to St Pol.[311]

The first wave of skirmishers that poured over the British lines five hours later consisted of 62 German divisions of storm-trooping infantry. Given the bad visibility, which made command and control impossible, the British Third and Fifth Armies could do little initially to resist.

Wilfred Desages (Day Boy, 1898), who had enlisted so readily in 1914 from his job as a clerk at the Caxton Publishing Company, was by now a company commander with the 5th Battalion, East Lancashire Regiment in the trenches near Hargicourt as the grey tide of infantry quickly inundated his position. Wilfred was the middle brother of three serving at the front that morning, all of whom had managed to survive the intervening three and half years of warfare. Elder brother Gordon (Day Boy, 1896) was a private serving in the Artists Rifles and younger brother Owen (Day Boy, 1908) was a captain with the 1st Wiltshire Regiment. The family had grown up in Cheltenham, at their home at Rowanfield House, 20 Imperial Square. Their father Paul, was an established master in the College's Common Room who had taught French there since 1885; he eventually retired in 1924. Wilfred had first arrived in France as a private in the 6th Battalion, King's (Liverpool) Regiment on 24th February 1915 which deployed immediately to Flanders; from then on, his next three years as a soldier would prove eventful. Eight weeks after his introduction to trench warfare, while sheltering from a heavy bombardment in the casemates at Ypres, Wilfred was wounded in the left arm by shell splinters and subsequently evacuated back to England on the HS *St Patrick*. Once recovered, he rejoined his battalion on 12th August. Two months later,

[311] Imperial War Museum, (17538), Private Papers of Lieutenant JP Wills MC.

while the battalion was trying to set up an ambush near Vaux, Wilfred accidentally fired his rifle, ruining any element of surprise. Put on a charge for negligently discharging his weapon he was awarded five days' Field Punishment No 1 by the battalion's commanding officer.[312] Not long afterwards and still with the battalion in the field, Wilfred applied for a territorial commission which was strongly supported by Lieutenant Colonel Harrison, clearly an officer without prejudice as this was the very commanding officer who had awarded Wilfred's Field Punishment only weeks before. Although initially commissioned into the 24th Battalion, London Regiment, Wilfred's connections with his former regiment were maintained quite by coincidence as he had been attached to the East Lancashires again as a company commander when the offensive broke that morning on 21st March.[313] At 6am the battalion was moved up to the battle zone, but after just a few minutes of contact with the enemy, it was forced to withdraw behind a defensive flank and hold position formed by Wilfred's company. Nothing further was heard of him and he was posted missing believed captured, until one of his subalterns, himself a prisoner of war in the 'Offiziergefangenenlager,' at Rastatt (Baden) was contacted by the Swiss Red Cross on 8th April. In a statement, Wilfred's fellow officer confirmed:

> I was captured on 21st March, poor old Desages (my captain) was killed immediately on my right.[314]

Wilfred's body was never recovered, and he is commemorated on the Arras Memorial to the Missing.

But such action was typical of the fighting on that first misty morning of the German attack. From his battery's position, Sydney Trevenen also recorded the events of those first few days as they unravelled:

> March 21st. The long-expected Hun offensive started today. At about 5am he attacked on a wide front from Bullecourt southwards, and we heard he had captured Ecoust which overlooks the battery positions in that neighbourhood. After lunch I reconnoitred a cross country route to the Am L [Ammunition Lines], and got chased by a low flying Bosche aeroplane firing a machine gun. Coming back one solitary HE shell exploded in the track I had just left a few minutes previously. I passed nearly 3 doz Yanks going into positions of readiness.
>
> March 22nd. The day dawned quietly but heavy firing commenced about 11am and continued all day. We did nothing but send up ammunition. I went with the Staff Capt to reconnoitre new W L further back and spent the afternoon lolling in a chair outside

---

[312] Field Punishment No 1 entailed the convicted soldier being fettered or tied to a fixed object, such as a gun wheel or a fence post, for up to two hours each day as a form of public embarrassment and acknowledgement of his crime.
[313] Supplement to *The London Gazette*, 29th November 1916, page 11691.
[314] The National Archives, WO 374/19351, Personal File of Captain W R Desages.

the mess. We have heard nothing officially though the tales one hears are wonderful – one rather significant fact is that the Divisional train has moved back.

March 23rd. At 12 30am I received an order to take the gun limbers up to the position as the 3rd Division was withdrawing to the 3rd Line System in order to conform to the division on its right. This gave the villages of Guemappe, Wancourt, Heninel and Henin to the Bosche. We were out all night and I did not get back till 8.30am. In the afternoon I was summoned to Bde HQ, which is now the old RA HQ to be shown our new positions just outside Boisleux au Mont. I then rode up to the guns with the limbers, came back and spent the rest of the night bringing up the ammunition wagons.[315]

With all the British artillery positions under threat from the rapidly advancing German army, many other units were starting to withdraw. Charles Creagh (Boyne House, 1914) had a long and strong military heritage. His uncle, General Sir O'Moore Creagh, had won the Victoria Cross in Afghanistan in 1879 and had succeeded Lord Kitchener as commander-in-chief of the Indian Army; he retired in 1914. On his mother's side Charles was related to General Sir Thomas Picton who had won fame during the Peninsula War and at Waterloo a century before. Charles was acting as the signals officer to 94th Brigade, and under shell fire yet again. Previously wounded in 1915 from being hit by shell fragments on the left side of his head, he had first-hand knowledge of the very unpleasant experience of being under a German barrage. Charles went missing on 23rd March as his artillery battery pulled back under almost continuous shell fire. For three months the family agitated for news of his whereabouts, and the War Office finally managed to contact members of 'C' Battery who shed light on his fate. One informant, Gunner Thompson, reported that:

Lt O'Moore C Creagh was an officer of my battery and I saw him blown off his horse by a shell, and he was reported killed in the retreat from Moislains, or near there on 23/24th March 1918. We were going away with supply wagons, so I cannot say what became of his body.[316]

Although this information on its own was still rather inclusive, a second eye-witness from Charles' battery, Bombardier D Kane of C Battery, 108th Brigade, RFA independently confirmed the story:

On 23rd Mar, about 1 or 2 in the afternoon, we were forced to retire from the left of Peronne, we had been retiring all the morning. I saw Lt Creagh killed by a shell within 10 yards of me. He fell from his horse which I fetched back. He was one of the finest officers in the Brigade and very well thought of by the men who were very sorry to hear of his death. I am quite sure he was dead.[317]

---

[315] Ibid.
[316] The National Archives, WO 339/43239, Personal Record of Lieutenant OC Creagh.
[317] Ibid.

Charles' body was never found: he too is commemorated on the Arras Memorial to the Missing; he was 21 years of age.

The infantry fared no better, and the experiences of the 2/5th Battalion, Gloucestershire Regiment provide a graphic example of the ferocity of the German assault. John Rickerby (Day Boy, 1914) and Noel Lake (Day Boy, 1912) were at school together in the same House and were now both serving in the 2/5th Glosters. Both came from local families in Cheltenham. John was born in the town and his father, being a local solicitor, established the family home in Shurdington. Noel's father was an admiral in the Royal Navy and retired to Marle Hill in 1905 where the family grew up; sadly, Admiral Lake passed away in 1915. Both John and Noel joined the battalion in its infancy shortly after the declaration of war, being commissioned into it on 26th September 1914. Two years later, for action near Aubers Ridge John was awarded the Military Cross:

> For conspicuous gallantry. He defended his post with the greatest determination against two strong attacks by the enemy, preceded by heavy bombardment. When his signallers had all become casualties, he went himself under fire to the signal dugout to ask for reinforcements. On his return he beat off another attack by machine-gun fire, and then counter-attacked with the bayonet.[318]

Noel, on the other hand, after leaving College in 1912 had sought a career within his father's naval background but was unsuccessful in his application for a commission in the Royal Marines owing to short sightedness. Putting this disappointment aside, he quickly gained an apprenticeship with Messrs. Turner and Company, a shipping agent and merchant business with its head offices in London and Liverpool. When war was declared Noel was working at the company's London Office and enlisted as a private soldier into the 16th (Service) Battalion, the Middlesex Regiment. He applied for a commission on 24th February 1915 while still in training and, although gazetted several months after John in July 1915, the two Old Cheltonians were finally reunited in the battalion in August 1916 when Noel arrived as a replacement officer.[319] From then onwards, they fought alongside each other on the Somme later that year, and again in 1917 against the Hindenburg Line.

In the early morning fog of 21st March, John and Noel's battalion was in support of the front line, near Holnon Wood, west of St Quentin, when the order to 'stand-to' was given at 4.45am. Immediately after the first hostile artillery barrage had fallen on their billets in the wood and Holnon village, the battalion moved forward about 300 yards into the battle zone. The intense bombardment continued for more than four hours but the battalion held its position and began firing at point blank range at the advancing enemy. Brutal fighting continued for the rest of the day, and by the early morning of 22nd the Germans had managed to infiltrate to the rear of the battalion. After another heavy enemy barrage the

---

[318] Supplement to *The London Gazette*, dated 22nd September 1916, Issue 29760.
[319] Supplement to *The London Gazette*, 7th July 1915, page 6677. Clearly, the eye sight criteria and standards for commissioning were relaxed to enable suitable candidates to be commissioned: the well-publicised story of John Kipling, epitomised in the 2007 film *My Boy Jack*, is a case in point.

battalion was ordered to fall back towards Beauvois, arriving there in groups at 5pm. During the withdrawal John was killed by a shell near Holnon Wood. His commanding officer wrote that:

> Capt. Rickerby's death was a disaster for the Battalion. He was of a type to whom clean life and hard living are a part of a deep religion. Possessing a stern sense of duty and full of the joy of living, yet completely regardless of death, he was the ideal Company Commander.[320]

New defensive positions were quickly established, but around midnight the Germans were observed working around the battalion's right flank and therefore the battalion was ordered to pull back again, first towards the Voyennes area and then further westwards to Languevoisin the following day. Now three days without rest, on 24th March the Glosters were ordered to cover the withdrawal of other elements of the BEF which were crossing the Canal du Nord at Buverchy. Already a confused situation appeared to be worsening. No sooner had positions been prepared at Buverchy, than the battalion was ordered to move a mile north to Brueil to defend the canal there. During the night of the 24th and the early morning of the 25th, the tired battalion launched a counter-attack in an attempt to staunch the tide of enemy troops flowing westwards:

> "C" Company crossed the canal and was advancing in open order to take up positions on the right flank, when it was enfiladed by German machine-gunners. Lt Lake, who was gallantly leading the Company was killed.[321]

Noel's body was another never recovered and he is commemorated on the Pozières Memorial to the Missing. He and John were just two of some 6,000 casualties suffered by the 61st Division (2nd South Midland), during the first two weeks of Germany's spring offensive.

Some six miles further north near Villers Carbonnel Auriol Lowry (Southwood 1910) and his younger brother Cyril (Southwood, 1915) were together fighting a determined but precarious rear-guard action with the 2nd Battalion, West Yorkshire Regiment.

The brothers' family had a long connection with the College. Not only had their father and three uncles all attended the school, but so too had their eldest brother William (Southwood, 1908), who had been killed in Gallipoli three years earlier leading the 14th Sikhs in a bayonet charge against the Turkish lines at Krithia. Auriol had chosen to join the army rather than take up his university place at Cambridge, and once commissioned joined the 2nd Battalion, West Yorkshires in Malta immediately before the outbreak of war. He went with the battalion to France in November 1914, becoming its adjutant in March 1915. Auriol had won the Military Cross that year and, after several staff appointments, had rejoined the

---

[320] See A. Barnes, *The Story of the 2/5th Battalion Gloucestershire Regiment, 1914 – 1918,* The Crypt House Press, Gloucester, (1930).
[321] Ibid.

Cyril Lowry

Auriol Lowry MC

William Lowry
(in Gallipoli, 1915)

battalion as its second in command in 1917 before assuming command as an acting lieutenant colonel. Cyril on the other hand was commissioned straight from College into his brother's regiment in 1915. Cyril, like Auriol, had already seen more than his fair share of fighting. He was first wounded in the right arm by a shell splinter near Loos in April 1917 and admitted to No 14 General Hospital in Boulogne, from where he was evacuated to England to recover. Declared fit three months later, he rejoined the 1st Battalion in France but was wounded again; this time on 25th September with a nasty gunshot wound to the face. After three further weeks' medical leave in England he returned to France and was attached to his brother's battalion as one of the company commanders.

By 25th March, Auriol and Cyril were together facing the approaching wave of field grey storm-troopers and trying to stem the German momentum crossing the bridge over the Canal de la Somme at Pont les Brie. It was an important feature as the canal formed the last natural obstacle on the German line of advance, with nothing but gentle rolling farmland running on to Amiens just 20 miles to the west. The battalion was ordered to counter-attack early that morning with two of its companies combined together to make a force of some 300 men. In the action Cyril was mortally wounded. The unit war diary records that at 8am that morning:

> Received news that Eterpigny bridge had been crossed and enemy had to be counter-attacked. C and A Coys under Capt Cropper proceeded to attack (at 9.30am). Came under heavy MG and rifle fire about 500 yds W of Eterpigny on the ridge and the attack was smashed up. All officers C Coy out of action.[322]

The war diary entry, however, is far from complete and hides a most remarkable and moving set of events. Auriol was close to his soldiers making the attack, but under the weight of the German advance the battalion had to withdraw. Cyril too came back, carried on a stretcher to the battalion headquarters mortally wounded and too badly injured to be moved further. As the rest of the battalion retired, Auriol remained and held Cyril in his arms as he lay dying. Auriol was captured a few minutes later by the advancing Germans when his headquarters dug out was overrun and he was taken back

[322] The National Archives, WO 95/1714, War Diary of 2nd West Yorkshire Regiment, 1918.

behind German lines. But, at an unguarded moment that evening after dusk, he picked up a discarded German trench coat and helmet, put them on, and walked back along the trench system and through the German lines. His shadowy figure was fired at by both sides during his daring escape, but he eventually made it back to his battalion and resumed command. When in an area of comparative safety later on, Auriol had to complete the entry above in the battalion's war diary including the circumstances of the death of his own brother, signing off the entry simply as 'Lt Col AE Lowry'. Cyril's body was never recovered, and he is commemorated on the Pozières Memorial to the Missing.

The following day, another school and battalion contemporary of Noel Lake and John Rickerby was killed while attached to another regiment. Minden Badcock (Day Boy, 1914) enjoyed a full life as a schoolboy at College.

A member of the rugby XV in 1913 and a College prefect, Minden was also a cadet second lieutenant in the College Contingent (the Junior Division) of the OTC. His parents, Francis and Adele lived at the end of College Field at 1 College Lawn, where they had retired after working abroad with the Indian Civil Service; so conveniently making Minden's daily commute to College one of the shortest of any of the day boys.[323]

Minden Badcock

1, College Lawn, Cheltonian Home and House

[323] This house has recently been acquired by the College, renovated, and is now used as a girls' boarding house, appropriately named College Lawn.

Although when he left College in July 1914 he was due to go up to Brasenose College, Oxford, the outbreak of war caused him to change his plans and like so many of his College contemporaries, he applied for a commission in the army. Given his military training and experience as a cadet officer, this was swiftly granted, and Minden was appointed to a territorial force commission as a second lieutenant in the Gloucestershire Regiment on 3rd October, joining the 2/5th Battalion just after it was formed. He served with the battalion throughout the war and remained with it, with the exception of normal leave periods and two instances when he was evacuated to England after being wounded in action. By October 1916, he had been promoted to captain and was given command of 'C' Company. Minden clearly moulded this group of some 120 infantry soldiers into a coordinated team as, a year later, they took part in a highly successful trench raid for which he was awarded the Military Cross; his citation in the *London Gazette* recording it was:

> For conspicuous gallantry and devotion to duty in command of a successful raiding party. The party captured four prisoners and a machine gun, killed fifteen of the enemy, and destroyed several dug-outs. Before the night of the raid, he personally took out a patrol over the ground and gained valuable information. When returning, he ran into an enemy post, which he dealt with successfully, bombing them and getting the whole of his party back without casualties. During the raid he shot one of the enemy with his revolver when he attempted to bayonet him. He was the last to leave the enemy's trench and, finding a mobile charge which had not been used, returned up the trench and threw it down a dug-out.

When the German spring offensive began, Minden was absent from the battalion attending a course of instruction at one of the army schools behind the lines. Due to the weight and momentum of the German assault, all the students at the schools of the Third and Fifth Armies were quickly returned to their units or filled immediate vacancies in other battalions. Minden was sent to the 9th Battalion, East Surrey Regiment, stationed in an unfamiliar sector of the Somme. Fighting with a different team of soldiers, with an unknown company commander, and all under the most extreme combat pressure, Minden was killed in action near Rosières. Like Noel, his body was never recovered, and like Noel, he is recorded on the Pozières Memorial to the Missing.

On 27th March, Robert Mather (Day Boy and CCJS, 1912) was killed in action. He was the youngest of three brothers and the last one of the three to die during the war. Robert left College early aged 17 and moved to Liverpool with his elder brother Ellis, working as a clerk with Nicholson and Wrigley, cotton brokers. On 1st September 1914, he enlisted and attested in Liverpool with Ellis, both as privates in the 17th Battalion, King's (Liverpool) Regiment, which had begun forming on 29th August in the old watch factory at Prescot. The battalion has the distinction of being the first of the 'pals' battalions to be formed in Kitchener's New Armies. After training he embarked to France the following year with the battalion, sailing from Folkestone to Boulogne on 7th November 1915 as a member of No 1 Company. However, he found getting used to front line service, with all its additional requirements, somewhat of a challenge. On 30th December while mounting guard near Beaumetz, Sergeant Major Hancock found Robert's water bottle to be empty, an offence for which he was confined to barracks for three days. On 12th March the following year near Maricourt, he was reported by Corporal Howden as having lost his gas helmet for which he was given one day's Field Punishment No 1. Two weeks later, on 28th March, he was found to have a dirty valise at a General's Inspection, for which he received three days of Field Punishment No 1. But despite these setbacks, he was promoted to lance corporal on 12th August and then to acting corporal on 2nd October; a case of poacher turning gamekeeper perhaps. This transformation was completed when he was recommended by his commanding officer the following month for a commission and Robert was sent to No 5 Officer Cadet Battalion at Trinity College Cambridge where he underwent officer training from 25th December 1916 to 29th May 1917. Commissioned as a second lieutenant the following day, he rejoined his old battalion and fought with them throughout the next year.[324] On 27th March 1918, Robert was killed while holding the line in a defensive position west of the village of Folies during a German attack in strength. Robert was the third brother to be killed in action during the war. Eldest brother John had been killed in action near Ypres in February 1915, and Ellis, with whom Robert had enlisted, was killed at Trônes Wood in July 1916 during the Battle of the Somme.

John Mather

Robert Mather

Ellis Mather

None of the boys' bodies were ever found and all three are commemorated on Memorials to the Missing; John on the Menin Gate at Ypres, Ellis at Thiepval and Robert at Pozières. The Mather family would be one of three Cheltonian families to lose three sons to the war.

By the end of the month as the German advance continued towards Amiens, the increasing necessity for rear-guard actions was so acute that even cavalry units, flushed with their success and élan at Cambrai, were pressed into the line as infantry. Richard Percival-Maxwell (Christowe, 1912) was a young subaltern with the 16th Lancers. Like Minden, he too was a rugby player being in the XV the year before. On leaving College, he entered the Royal Military College at Sandhurst and received his commission as a

---

[324] Supplement to *The London Gazette*, 28th June 1917, page 6391.

second lieutenant in the 16th Lancers on 15th August 1914.[325] Richard remained on the Western Front for the next three years, and though promoted to lieutenant in March 1916, much of this time was spent fighting as dismounted troops as the requirement for cavalry rarely presented itself. He was killed in action on 30th March; the unit war diary recording the confused nature of the fighting.

> Rushed up to position of readiness on west slope of hill near big wood north of MOREUIL. 16th, 4th, and Canadian Cav Bde attacked and occupied wood. About 12 noon D Sqn was sent to reinforce 4th Hussars. A Squadron was sent to fill gap made by 4th Hussars retiring. C Squadron was sent to reinforce A Squadron. A general attack was then ordered to be made by the infantry consisting of a 100 and ourselves consisting of A Squadron, C Squadron and 4th Hussars. The eastern edge of the wood was cleared but C Squadron and the 4th were held up by MG fire. The regiment was relieved at 10pm and went back to THENNES where it remained standing to all night. Casualties: Capt Allen wounded, Lts Maxwell and Wodehouse killed.[326]

Charles Campbell, France 1914

Another member of the 16th Lancers was Charles Campbell (PBH, 1892), though of a more senior generation to Richard. Charles arrived at College from Eton in May 1889, aged 15. An outstanding sportsman, he played cricket for the XI for his last two years and for the rugby XV in 1892; he was also Captain of the Rifle Club. Opting to follow his father into a military career he went directly to the Sandhurst and was commissioned as a second lieutenant in the 16th Lancers on 13th February 1895. With training complete, almost immediately active service came thick and fast for Charles: the North West Frontier including the Tirah expedition (1897- 1898) and then the South African War (1900-1901). From December 1901 he was

---

[325] *The London Gazette*, 14th August 1914, page 6400.
[326] The National Archives, WO 95/1134, War Diary of the 16th Lancers 1918.

attached to the New Zealand Defence Force for five years. Consequently, by the outbreak of the war Charles was an experienced and well-decorated soldier, serving with his regiment as a major.

On 5th October 1915, he was promoted as a temporary brigadier general to command the 5th Cavalry Brigade, a post he retained throughout the hard fighting on the Somme in 1916 and then at Arras and Cambrai the following year. He was seriously wounded on 21st March 1918 and evacuated to England but died 10 days later from complications at 17 Park Lane, London. Besides his many campaign medals and clasps, Charles' long and prominent service was also recognised with his appointment as a Companion of the Most Distinguished Order of Saint Michael and Saint George in the 1917 New Year's Honours List and then, in the King's Birthday Honours list in June 1918, Companion of the Most Honourable Order of the Bath; an honour he received posthumously. Sadly for the Campbell family, this marked the end of two very bright army careers; as recorded previously, Charles' younger brother Duncan was killed in action at Messines in 1917, having gallantly won the Military Cross.

The first of the German spring offensives, *Operation Michael*, ran out of steam near Villers Bretonneux just seven miles from Amiens in the opening week of April. By this time, 23 Old Cheltonians had been killed in action during the assault. Despite advancing over 40 miles, the German Second and 18th Armies had not delivered their anticipated 'knock out' blow to the BEF. Both sides had suffered casualties of over 250,000, though for the Germans the more acute and greater loss was that of their best storm troopers: the damage would prove irrevocable. Furthermore, with their supply lines over-extended, the Germans made the capture of allied supply dumps a significant, albeit secondary, objective. However, seeing how well the allies were equipped and supplied only served to degrade the morale of the German assault troops. Many instances of German soldiers refusing to obey their officers were recorded, as troops preferred to imbibe captured wine and liberate British provisions which their own logistical chain could not match or supply in either quality or quantity.[327]

Following Waves

Within four days of *Operation Michael* reaching its high-mark just short of Amiens, a second wave of German attacks crashed onto the British front line further north. Focussed this time against the British First and Second Armies on the Franco-Belgian border, *Operation Georgette* had the important logistical hub of Hazebrouck as its primary objective.[328] A day later, on 10th April, a second push by the German Fourth Army launched yet another

---

[327] D Stevenson, *1914-1918: The History of the First World War*, Penguin Books, London (2004) 2012, pages 411-412.

[328] This German assault was initially called *Operation George*, but General Ludendorff reduced its size and scale as German forces were increasingly stretched on the Western Front, not least engaging in three other attacks against the French and American forces in Champagne. It was thus renamed *Operation Georgette*, reflecting its diminished size and scope.

assault against the British Fifth Army holding Messines Ridge. This put significant political and strategic pressure on both the British High Command and the war cabinet. The security of the Channel ports, and therefore the entire logistical tail for the BEF was placed in jeopardy. Consequently, on Thursday 11th April, Douglas Haig issued a '*Special Order of the Day*':

> There is no course open to us but to fight it out. Every position must be held to the last man: there must be no retirement. With our backs to the wall and believing in the justice of our cause each one of us must fight on to the end. The safety of our homes and the freedom of mankind alike depend upon the conduct of each one of us at this critical moment.[329]

The final German dice had been rolled and for 20 days, German troops slogged their way slowly forward, while all the time the BEF's resolve and defences stiffened, and German momentum crumbled. It was noticeable to British intelligence officers interrogating German prisoners that the German attack consisted largely of trench 'garrison' troops rather than the trained storm troopers which had enjoyed so much initial success further south in Picardy. Nevertheless, for the British it remained a case of 'backs to the wall'.

James Forbes-Robertson (Day Boy, 1902) was in command of the 1st Battalion, Border Regiment struggling to hold the line near Vieux Berquin, near Estaires, after the Germans had overrun the old 1915 British positions at Neuve Chapelle and Festubert. In his early days, he lived close to College and grew up in the family home at Langton Lodge in Charlton Kings. After leaving College, James and brother Kenneth sought careers as infantry officers, Kenneth being commissioned into Seaforth Highlanders and James into the Border Regiment. Kenneth was sadly killed early in the war, leading a reconnaissance party in Ploegsteert Wood in October 1914. James had seen a great deal of action from the start of the war, and, although wounded twice, appeared to live somewhat of a charmed life. Serving in Gallipoli, he was wounded in the shoulder in May 1915, but within five weeks had returned to the battalion as a company commander. After the withdrawal from the peninsula, he returned to England; promoted to major some four months later, he arrived in France on 15th June 1916 as the second in command of the 1st Battalion, Newfoundland Regiment. His task was to train the Canadians and prepare them for their part in the attack on the Somme. Engaged in staff duties in Louvencourt on the fateful morning of 1st July, James was not involved in the calamity that ensued: the battalion went over the top at Beaumont Hamel and was almost annihilated, only 68 of 780 men answering roll call on 2nd July. By the end of November, he was appointed as the reconstituted battalion's commanding officer and awarded the first of his bravery awards; the Military Cross gazetted on 1st January 1917.

---

[329] For a full analysis of the German spring offensive see D Stevenson, *With Our Backs to the Wall: Victory and Defeat in 1918* Penguin, London (2012) pages 30-111; the text of Haig's Special Order is on page 73.

James Forbes-Robertson VC, standing centre with his Newfoundlanders

For subsequent fighting near Monchy-le-Preux on 14th April 1917, he was awarded the Distinguished Service Order:

> For conspicuous gallantry and devotion to duty when in command of his battalion during an enemy attack. He collected all the men he could find and, taking up a position on the outskirts of the village brought the hostile advance to an end by his fire. He undoubtedly saved a very critical situation by his promptness, bravery and example.[330]

James relinquished command of the Newfoundlanders in August 1917 to command the 16th Battalion, Middlesex Regiment which he took into action at Cambrai that November. He received a Bar to his Distinguished Service Order for his part in the fighting:

> For conspicuous gallantry and devotion to duty. He led his battalion with great dash and determination in a successful attack. Later, during continual enemy attacks, though he was wounded in the eye and unable to see, he was led about by an orderly among his men in the front line, encouraging and inspiring them by his magnificent example of courage and determination.[331]

---

[330] *The London Gazette*, 15th June 1917.
[331] *The London Gazette*, 24th August 1918.

The following February, James was given his third battalion command, and one of which he must have felt immense pride; to command the regiment into which he was first commissioned some 14 years earlier – 1st Battalion, Border Regiment.

Now fighting for every inch of ground as *Operation Georgette* pressed forward, James played a pivotal and heroic role in stemming the German advance on his part of the line near Vieux Berquin, for which he was awarded the Victoria Cross:

> For most conspicuous bravery whilst commanding his battalion during the heavy fighting. (near Vieux Berquin, France) Through his quick judgment, resource, untiring energy and magnificent example, Lt.-Col. Forbes-Robertson on four separate occasions saved the line from breaking and averted a situation which might have had the most serious and far-reaching results.
>
> On the first occasion, when troops in front were falling back, he made a rapid reconnaissance on horse-back, in full view of the enemy, under heavy machine-gun and close range shell fire. He then organised and, still mounted, led a counter-attack which was completely successful in re-establishing our line. When his horse was shot under him he continued on foot. Later on the same day, when troops to the left of his line were giving way, he went to that flank and checked and steadied the line, inspiring confidence by his splendid coolness and disregard of personal danger. His horse was wounded three times and he was thrown five times.
>
> The following day, when the troops on both his flanks were forced to retire, he formed a post at battalion headquarters and with his battalion still held his ground, thereby covering the retreat of troops on his flanks. Under the heaviest fire this gallant officer fearlessly exposed himself when collecting parties, organising and encouraging.
>
> On a subsequent occasion, when troops were retiring on his left and the condition of things on his right were obscure, he again saved the situation by his magnificent example and cool judgment. Losing a second horse, he continued alone on foot until he had established a line to which his own troops could withdraw and so conform to the general situation.[332]

James, swiftly promoted to brigadier general, went on to command the first 87th Brigade for a short period, before taking the reins of the 155th Infantry Brigade until October 1918. With the Armistice approaching, James reverted back to the command of his beloved Border Regiment, and surviving the war, took the battalion into Bonn in Germany as part of the Army of the Rhine. James's Victoria Cross marked the last of six such awards won by Old Cheltonians during the Great War.

---

[332] *The London Gazette*, 22nd May 1918, page 6057.

1918 – THE YEAR OF TURNING TIDES

Fighting with the West Riding Regiment, Patrick Henderson (Newick, 1917), one of the 1916 rugby XV, was seriously wounded in action on 15th April 1918, the unhappy circumstances of which the battalion's war diary suggests:

> The battalion moved forward to the canal bank, (proceeding via BERENCHON) preliminary to making a joint attack with the WARWICKS on PACOUT WOOD. At 6pm the Bttn commenced to cross the bridge, PONT LEVIS, to get into position to attack the wood from the west, the WARWICKS attacking it from the SOUTH and SE. The operation was not a success.[333]

During the attack, Patrick was hit by pieces of shrapnel from a shell burst as he crossed the canal bridge, causing serious injuries to his upper right arm and right thigh, with the added complication of a compound fracture to his humerus. He was immediately evacuated to a field ambulance in the rear and then to England, but in the process his wounds became badly septic. The infection and associated fever grew steadily worse, and the medics could do little to stem his high temperature of 105° and an accelerated heart rate of 132. Patrick's condition worsened: he died at Netley Hospital in Southampton on 2nd May; he was just 19 and less than a year out of College. Two other of his rugby side were killed later in the year: Lionel Maby was killed at Moeuvres on 12th September, and two weeks later, Noel Russell died of wounds at No 23 Casualty Clearing Station near Buissy.

During the months of May and June 1918, the Germans embarked on further waves of attack against the British, French and American divisions further south. *Operation Blücher* was launched on 27th May aimed towards the River Marne with Château-Thierry as a primary objective. In its way, however, was the small village of Guyencourt where the 1st Battalion, Wiltshire Regiment, temporarily under French command, were holding positions in the battle zone. Owen Desages (Day Boy, 1908), whose elder brother Wilfred had been killed just two months previously, was one of the battalion's company commanders. Owen, no doubt influenced by his father's teaching career at College, was teaching English in France when war broke out. He returned home as war gripped that country and enlisted at Cheltenham on 28th April 1915 as a private in the 18th Battalion, Royal Fusiliers, a volunteer 'pals' battalion made up from the Public Schools and University Men's Force. Once the battalion arrived in France in November 1915, Owen's linguistic skills were quickly recognised and he served for over a year in the intelligence section before being transferred back to England for commissioning in May 1917. Owen was appointed to the Wiltshires on 29th January 1918 and was quickly promoted to temporary captain. The battalion reoccupied the line in front of Guyencourt on Sunday 26th May following a church parade. Suddenly, early the following morning, it was facing the full force of the next German onslaught. The battalion war diary recorded that 'At 1am the enemy starts a heavy gas bombardment which lasts until 5am, when he

---

[333] The National Archives, WO 95/1481/3, Unit War Diary of 2nd Battalion, Duke of Wellington's (West Riding Regiment), January 1918 to June 1919.

commenced to attack'.[334] In the confusion which enveloped them due to the momentum of the attack, the battalion withdrew in small groups as best they could after the Brigade ordered a retirement, but when a roll call was finally taken Owen was missing, and reported as such to his parents by telegram dated 8th June. Following enquiries from his family as to his fate, Captain J F Arnott, a fellow officer in the battalion who was taken prisoner in this action, reported:

> He was severely wounded in the abdomen and a doctor gave no hope of his recovery.[335]

Another brother officer, Lieutenant H C Reid, corroborated the account:

> Desages was pretty badly wounded, and captured.[336]

Owen's personal file records that many of the officers reported missing and taken prisoner that day were doctors in the Royal Army Medical Corps, suggesting that they had stayed to tend the wounded as the remainder retired. His body, like that of brother Wilfred, was never recovered and Owen is commemorated on the Soissons Memorial to the Missing. The loss of both brothers within eight weeks of each other was weighty enough grief to bear on its own. But being so closely connected to the College community, not simply as Old Cheltonians but especially through the long and dedicated teaching service of their father, would have cast an even longer shadow of sorrow.

Operation Blücher was wound down by Ludendorff on 6th June, strangled once again by overextended supply lines, troop fatigue and robust rearguard action by Allied battalions. Three days later *Operation Gneisenau* followed to the west of the River Oise on a front between Noyon and Montdidier. Both attacks enjoyed immediate initial success, gaining significant ground in the opening days. However, such stunning early progress only conspired to form protrusions in the German front line which became ever more susceptible to flanking counter-attacks, exacerbating the increasing difficulty in maintaining logistical support. The result was that early German momentum was quickly checked and by 11th June, the attacking options for the German army had all but run out.

While the Germans attacked further south in France, they made every effort to hold their gains in the British sectors, often resorting to frequent defensive barrages of gas shells to debilitate and limit any retaliatory action. Sydney Trevenen and his battery were located near Bethune and witnessed such bombardments:

> May 20th. Between 2 and 3am the Huns shelled the crossroads where we sleep, his first round landing on the road just outside our front door. Decidedly unpleasant even though we were in the cellar. The front system between the canal and Hinges inclusive was

---

[334] The National Archives, WO 95/2243, War Diary of 1st Wiltshire Regiment, dated 1918.
[335] The National Archives, WO 339/123106, Personal Record of Captain OL Desages.
[336] Ibid.

plastered with gas shells at dawn with the result that the Infantry had about 700 casualties, all eye cases. Lt Nash and his two signallers were also gassed. The rest of the day passed quietly. Lt Everett came up to the guns.

May 21st. Hostile artillery was more active on our back areas today. About 10.20am we had to leave our mess for a time. Padres Harvey and Davies blew in for lunch. Since we became a silent battery, from 9pm Lts Champneys and Durbin went down to the WL for three days, Lt Everett to Btty HQ leaving myself and Williams at the guns. Just after we had finished dinner the Boche commenced a harassing fire and we again had to withdraw. We practically sweltered all day even when we weren't moving about. Bethune is still burning and has been for the last three days.

May 23rd. I took Colonel Stubbs of the 2nd Suffolks up to the OP this afternoon, the light was perfect but unfortunately it was far too windy to register. Very quiet all day and the evening as well.[337]

This was the last entry that Sydney would make in his pocket book diary. Two days later, the Germans again saturated his gun and wagon lines with gas shells and Sydney was overcome by the deadly fumes. He was swiftly evacuated to No 1 British Red Cross (Duchess of Westminster) Hospital at Le Touquet, where, despite the best efforts and treatment of the medics, his condition slowly worsened. His mother, Jessie, was waiting for news back in the family home in Christchurch Road, Cheltenham, when an ominous telegram arrived on 11th June. Expressing condolence, it reported that Sydney had died the previous day from septic broncho-pneumonia induced by gas poisoning. He was buried in the military cemetery at Etaples later that day. But when his marker was replaced after the Armistice with a now familiar CWGC headstone, so prevalent across the fields of Picardy, Artois and Flanders, his original wooden battlefield grave marker was returned to England and still hangs in St Stephen's Church, Cheltenham; an enduring memorial to a brave soldier and Old Cheltonian.

Sydney Trevenen's Battlefield Cross from France

[337] Cheltenham College Archives, Diaries of Captain Sydney Trevenen, MC.

Wings

Simultaneously both the Royal Flying Corps and the Royal Navy Air Service continued their operations, though being increasingly hard pressed by the advancing German forces which necessitated withdrawal to new airfields on a frequent basis. As well as this acute pressure on the Western Front, the air services still had to maintain operations in England for home defence and for maritime reconnaissance against the continued U-boat threat. Just as the German spring offensives were launched, arguably in the middle of the most critical phase of the First World War, the British embarked on a reorganisation of its air arms. On 1st April 1918, not lost on more observant sceptics as being April Fool's Day, the Royal Air Force was born and continued to secure the legacy of its two illustrious forbears, becoming an established and essential component of Britain's combat power. With the final phases of the war reaching their boiling point, demand for pilots to establish and maintain air superiority over the battlefields and campaign theatres across the world was vital. Training programmes were accelerated and flying courses were pared to the bare minimum of flying hours for students, and all to get larger numbers of pilots rapidly to the front-line squadrons established to meet the growing operational requirement. The production line output was finally beginning to satisfy with aircraft that could match and beat the technical capability of the German Air Force.[338] For example, aircraft production had risen from 50 aircraft per month in the first weeks of the war to 2,668 per month by 1918, an outstanding industrial effort that far exceeded the combat losses and inadvertent wastage.[339] One consequence of accelerated training was that the rate of flying accidents increased; Old Cheltonians regrettably were not immune to becoming casualties in such circumstances. With engine and airframe reliability still worrying issues in the aircraft types used for training, accidents occurred to veteran and novice aviators alike.

Samuel Saunderson (Cheltondale, 1901) was very much in the former category. Arriving from St Andrew's Preparatory School in Eastbourne, where he played in the cricket XI, Samuel left College in December 1901. Briefly holding a commission as a second lieutenant in the 3rd Battalion, Royal Dublin Fusiliers from 1903 for three years, he subsequently held a reserve commitment to service for any national emergency. Consequently, at the outbreak of war, he volunteered for service and was recommissioned into the North Irish Horse. However, perhaps owing to his engineering background and eye for the future, he requested secondment to the RFC at the beginning of 1915. Between March and June, he attended various courses of flying instruction being awarded his pilot's brevet or 'wings' and the Royal Aero Club certificate (No 1446) having trained on the Maurice Farman biplane at the military flying school at Farnborough on 24th April. With operational training complete, he was appointed as a flying officer to No 17 Squadron on 28th July 1915. By October he had demonstrated sufficient competence and experience to be made a flight commander. The

---

[338] For further reading and research, see A.G. Lee., *No Parachute: A Classic Account of War in the Air in WW1*, Grub Street, London, 2013 [1968].
[339] H. Jones, *The War in the Air: Being the Story of the Part Played in the Great War by the Royal Air Force*, Naval and Military Press, Uckfield, and IWM, (1937), page 155.

following month, Samuel embarked for Egypt with the squadron, where it began reconnaissance flights over enemy lines in Sinai and flew in support of troops engaging the Turkish army in the Western Desert. After three months of operational flying, as clearly an above average pilot, he returned to England to become a flying instructor in a number of flying training squadrons while also employed on Home Defence operations. Gaining considerable experience of night flying in the process, it was not surprising that he was selected to join No 131 Squadron at Shawbury on 9th April 1918. The squadron had only formed four weeks before and was training up as a night bombing squadron, equipped with the luckless and unreliable DH 9 aircraft. Due to poor performance and erratic serviceability of this aircraft's *Adriatic* engine, the squadron disbanded in August without becoming operational, Samuel returning to No 9 Depot Training Station at Shawbury. As a major flying training and aircraft repair unit, his skill and expertise both as an instructor and test pilot were in high demand. On 22nd April 1918, he was flying in a DH6 two-seater with Captain Norman Victor Harrison as the trainee pilot, when the machine crashed into the ground from a vertical dive at the aerodrome, killing both men. The reason for the crash was never fully established, but Samuel was buried nearby in the peaceful setting of St Mary's churchyard. The loss of such experienced pilots in flying accidents was a cause of concern and considerable dilemma as suitable replacements were hard to find without stealing talent from front-line squadrons. On the other hand, the flying training system had to continue without reduction in student throughput, otherwise battle casualties could not be replaced to the necessary extent.

Nestling in the folds of the Wiltshire farmland, just north of the A4 between Marlborough and Chippenham, lies the site of the former First World War airfield at Yatesbury. Although still occasionally used 100 years later by local microlight enthusiasts, in 1918 it was a buzzing hive of aerial activity. Located there was No 13 Training School, whose senior instructor and wing examiner was Douglas Gabell. As previously noted, Douglas had flown operationally with No 4 Squadron during 1917 over the Western Front and was recovering in England from his broken wrist. Meanwhile, the War Office was putting his flying skill and combat expertise to good use. Though still only 20 years of age, he was posted as a senior pilot to Yatesbury, where elementary and refresher flying training was conducted, and flew with many students and qualified pilots. Several of these were Old Cheltonians, such as John Chamberlin (Newick, 1916). John had left College aged 16 and applied for a commission in the RFC in 1917. His application accepted, John was commissioned as a temporary second lieutenant (on probation) on 30th March 1918 and posted to Yatesbury to start his flying training.[340] Just four weeks later on St George's Day, he was killed in a flying accident on one of his first solo flights. He was taken home and buried near his parents' home in Mylor, Cornwall, another victim, perhaps, of the deadly combination of insufficient training hours and inexperience.

Later that summer, John Tanner (Day Boy and OJ, 1911) was another victim of a flying accident. The son of Reverend Maurice Tanner, the housemaster of Christowe, he was

[340] Supplement of *The London Gazette*, 1st May 1918, page 5271.

educated initially at the Junior School. John went on to Marlborough and gained a place at Keble College Oxford but deferred his entry for war service in the RNAS. Commissioned on 14th February 1916, John gained his Royal Aero Club certificate (No.3088) and pilot's brevet on 3rd June at the Royal Navy's flying school at Chingford, Essex. As a flight sub-lieutenant, he then commenced his operational training which proved eventful. On 30th August, when setting off on a coastal patrol, he suffered an engine failure on take-off from RNAS Scarborough and crashed in his two-seat BE2c (Serial No. 1120). While he and his crewman survived, the aircraft was deemed irreparable and written off. Nevertheless, John was assessed as a good pilot and converted on to the Sopwith Pup, a fighter and scout aircraft, and was posted to No 9 Naval Squadron. By mid-1917, he was flying regular offensive patrols over the Western Front, an activity which again proved eventful. On 7th July flying with 'C' Flight, on his second flight of the day, he was wounded (fractured jaw and abrasions) following a combat patrol in his 'Pup' (Serial No. N6264). The formation, led by Lieutenant Hervey, the 'C' flight commander collectively engaged and downed a German two-seater aircraft near Haynecourt, and returned towards the squadron's airfield at Izel le Hameau in the early evening. At 6.15pm and being short of fuel John began a glide towards the airfield and when overhead initiated a spin descent from about 1,500 feet. Due to the low altitude, John did not fully recover the aircraft and it crashed onto the airfield. The aircraft was a total write off, but he luckily survived the wreckage with minor injuries and a distinctly bruised professional pride. Early in 1918 John was posted back to England for instructor duties with No 56 Depot Training Squadron at Cranwell, being transferred to the Royal Air Force as a captain after the merger on 1st April 1918. Five months later, he was killed when his Avro 504K (Serial No. D2002) crashed while instructing Lieutenant E G Arnott, who, though badly injured, survived. John was buried in the churchyard at Eversley in Hampshire; he was just 21 years of age.

George Delmar-Williamson

The short flying career of George Delmar-Williamson (Day Boy, 1915) was equally interesting. He was the only son of Frederick and Emily Delmar-Williamson whose family had resided in Cheltenham at 8 Lansdown Place for some time. Frederick, a renowned composer and baritone in both the town and the West End in London, sent George to the College where he became a lance corporal in the College's Officer Training Corps and, like many of his peers, was determined to join the army at the earliest opportunity. He was another who left College aged 16, and while awaiting acceptance into Sandhurst, studied for three months for the entrance exam with a private tutor; Mr A Cole of Radcliff House, 22 College Road, Clifton. He was commissioned and gazetted as a second lieutenant on 26th October 1916 into the Black Watch, despite the medical board observing, rather ironically, that he was short-sighted.[341]

---

[341] Supplement to *The London Gazette*, 26th October 1916, page 10407.

He spent little time with the regiment, however, as he elected to undertake pilot training which he conducted at the Vendôme flying school in France. Awarded his 'wings', George was then attached as a pilot to No 21 Squadron flying RE8 aircraft on artillery observation and contact patrol sorties over Belgium.

The flying weather on 31st July 1917 was poor, with rain falling for most of the day and a cloud base that seldom rose above 1,000 feet. George flew that day, one of nine sorties undertaken by the squadron, and all conducted at very low level to harass enemy troops, transport, and to bomb aerodromes. Given the need to fly under the low cloud to remain visual with the ground and their targets, the aircraft were heavily fired at by enemy rifles and machine guns. George's aircraft was hit in several places and was brought down in flames and crashed on the lines. Shaken but otherwise unscathed, he escaped the wreckage and was taken back to the aerodrome. Just nine days later, he had another serious air incident which further affected his nerves and flying confidence. When flying RE8 (Serial No A/3594) on 9th August 1917 from an airfield near Poperinghe, George suffered an engine malfunction during take-off:

> On taking off at 5.30am, 9/8/17, undercarriage struck top of RE hangar, machine turned over and crashed. Pilot uninjured, observer thrown out and died on admission to hospital.[342]

Although the observer Captain Cutler was killed, George was far from unharmed. He suffered serious concussion, being unconscious for some 30 minutes after the crash, and post-traumatic shock set in. George was invalided back to the UK for tests and observation. His father Frederick, naturally concerned about the welfare of his only son, wrote to the War Office on 19th August:

> Dear Sir
>
> I have written to the Secretary of the Air Board regarding the case of my son 2nd Lieut Geo F Delmar-Williamson, RFC who was sent home from France on 14 days special leave to recover from an accident which occurred on the 9th inst and in which his observer was killed. He has sustained severe mental shock. Previous to this he was brought down in flames on the 31st July. I was obliged to put him under the charge of Capt Braine-Hartwell, RAMC who has given me a certificate to the effect that at present he is totally unfit even to fly for some 3 to 6 months. I have enclosed this certificate in my letter to the Secretary. I should be much obliged if you would give the matter your kind and immediate attention as his leave expires on the 27th. My son is just 18½ years of age. Thanking you in anticipation of your kind attention to the matter, Yours faithfully, F Delmar-Williamson.[343]

---

[342] The National Archives, WO 339/78270, Personal Record of Lieutenant GF Delmar-Williamson.
[343] Ibid.

The letter did the trick. At a medical board held on 31st August, the army doctors confirmed that George was 'tremulous with exaggeration of all deep reflexes' and recommended an extended period of rest.

George was a qualified and combat-experienced pilot, too valuable to be left idle at home or returned to the infantry, especially at a time when the BEF needed every pilot to support the fighting at Cambrai in late 1917 and then against the German offensive in the following spring. For George to regain his confidence, two things needed to be addressed: his nerves and his short-sightedness. Accordingly, he was posted to No 13 Training Squadron as a supernumerary officer for refresher flying in the more benign skies above Wiltshire while getting used to the new set of flying goggles specifically made for him by the service opticians to rectify his eyesight. More importantly, he was posted to the very unit where Douglas Gabell, a contemporary at College, was serving as the examining officer. Whether this was a happy coincidence or had been by design a piece of masterly pastoral planning, the fact that the two pilots were of similar age, had families living in the same town, and had shared a common education together, made George's recovery all the more likely. His refresher flying continued at Yatesbury and by 18th March 1918 he had resumed flying the RE8, an aircraft quite familiar to him from his time on No 21 Squadron, having by then a total of 180 hours flown. However, the RE8 was not an easy aeroplane to fly and had some disturbing characteristics. Referred to in rhyming slang as the 'Harry Tate', after the popular music hall comic of the time, the aircraft was not very popular with its crews and some of its characteristics were far from amusing. Particularly, the RE8 gave little notice or indication of the stalling point and, if in a turn, could quickly flick into a spin. Experienced crews tended to keep a wary eye on the airspeed and fly somewhat faster than the aircraft handling notes suggested. More worryingly, at higher airspeeds the wing tips had a fatal tendency of collapsing, causing immediate catastrophic failure of the rest of the airframe.

By 12th July, George was making good progress. He had taken to his new goggles which not only improved his all-round vision, but also helped to alleviate feelings of motion sickness to which he had previously been prone. Equally, his flying was improving under Douglas Gabell's skilful and encouraging instruction. On that bright and sunny summer's day, the pair took off from Yatesbury in RE8 (Serial No C2236) to conduct a navigation exercise and headed off to the west. Ten minutes later, close to Chippenham, the airframe collapsed on them and the aircraft plummeted to the ground. The two young Old Cheltonian pilots were killed.

Douglas was buried in the gentle setting of St Lawrence's churchyard in Swindon village by his father who was rector there at the time, and George was taken back to Cheltenham, being similarly laid to rest with full military honours at St Peter's Church, Leckhampton; a peaceful end to two short lives, both though lived to the full in the shadow of war.

One other young aviator had a short but notable career. Grahame Heath (Newick, 1916) left College at the age of 17. With a passionate interest in flying and aeronautics, he worked

Wreckage of Gabell's and Delmar-Williamson's RE8

as an apprentice aeroplane fitter while waiting for entry into the Royal Naval Air Service. Commencing officer training at Greenwich on 28th October 1917, he moved to Vendôme for basic flying training on 10th December, and then to Cranwell for applied flying training the following March. By the time he graduated on 24th April, he had only had some nine hours and 36 minutes dual, a remarkably small amount of flying instruction, despite having over 40 hours in his log book. Having been a probationary flight officer with the RNAS, he was commissioned into the RAF as a second lieutenant on 24th April.[344] Although Grahame was assessed as an average officer, his flying ability was deemed 'First Class' and he was graded 'a very good pilot'. Due to his inherent flying skills, he was seconded to HMS *Furious*, a battle cruiser that had been recommissioned in May 1918 into one of the first aircraft carriers. Initially, the ship had her forward gun turret removed and a short flight deck added in its place, thus requiring pilots to manoeuvre around the superstructure in order to land. Later, with the removal of her aft turrets, the flight deck was extended in length to some 600' for its onboard squadron of Sopwith Camels. Grahame quickly got to grips with operating from a carrier, and on Wednesday 19th June, he was launched from the ship to intercept two German aircraft which had started bombing a task force operating in the North Sea. Scoring hits on the enemy aircraft's radiator and engine, he managed to shoot one down which ditched in the sea otherwise undamaged but neither the aircraft nor its crew could be recovered due to the threat from enemy submarines.[345] Grahame was mentioned in despatches for this action, but sadly

---

[344] *The London Gazette*, 11th June 1918, page 6937.
[345] FF49c seaplanes (Serial No 1796) based at Friedrichshafen on Lake Constance and being flown by Leutnant der Reserve Wenke.

posthumously, as he was killed on 20th August in a flying accident at Turnhouse whilst flying Sopwith Camel (E4414) with the Fleet Practice Squadron.[346] He was buried in Birmingham, close to the family home in Moseley, just three months before his 19th birthday.

If these flying accidents appeared to be yet another gloomy tragedy of the war, despite the mirage of relative peace and tranquillity of the rural idyll setting in England, the first few hints of fairer weather were starting to register on the Allies' military barometer as higher pressure on the German army began to build. As spring gave way to early summer, across the Channel two notable events signalled the change. By the end of June 1918, all the German offensives against the BEF had been called off in the face of hardening resistance and the inability of the German artillery to move forward to support the gains made by the infantry, a serious constraint that had plagued all attacking enterprise so far throughout the war. The second key factor which restricted German forward movement was the increasingly effective use of air power to locate enemy gun batteries and neutralise them either through counter battery fire or by aerial bombing.

The Changing Tide

The contributions of her Dominion forces had made a huge impact on Britain's combat effectiveness from the time the Indian Army divisions first held the line in the trenches on the Western Front in 1914. This crucial involvement continued throughout the war; famously in Gallipoli with the Australian and New Zealand army corps, on the Somme with the South Africans at Delville Wood and the Australians, again, at Pozières, and then the consistently capable Canadians at Ypres, Vimy Ridge and Passchendaele. Yet, arguably, the seminal fortnight of the war occurred during the defence of the small town of Villers Bretonneux, which straddled the main route to Amiens and the coast. Three Australian infantry brigades amongst others halted the German westward advance. But the spectacular Australian counter-attack on the night of 24th/25th April, despite being considerably outnumbered, pushed the Germans back, and recaptured the town which was to remain in Allied hands for the rest of the war. At the vanguard of this action could be found the 51st Australian Battalion.

Ronald Cox (Southwood, 1900) left College aged 16 and emigrated to Australia. He was farming in Baandee, Western Australia when he enlisted into the 11th Infantry Battalion, the first battalion to be recruited in Western Australia as part of the Australian Imperial Force's 2nd reinforcement. After brief training, Ronald embarked on board HMAT *Itonus* on 22nd February 1915 and sailed from Freemantle to Egypt for additional and more intensive training near Gaza. Ronald fought with the battalion in Gallipoli, including the Battle of Lone Pine. When the Peninsula was evacuated, 11th Battalion was split up so that combat hardened veterans could be distributed throughout the new battalions being

[346] Supplement to *The London Gazette*, 21st September 1918, page 11258, 'For valuable services rendered'.

formed in Egypt. As part of this process, Ronald joined the 51st Infantry Battalion in March 1916 and sailed for Europe, arriving on 12th June. Ronald fought with the battalion at Mouquet Farm during the BEF's Somme offensive, and at Messines and Polygon Wood the following year. Ronald was killed in action during the 51st Battalion's legendary counter-attack at Villers Bretonneux. When he died, he was 34 years of age and, though still a private, had experienced some of the most famous and bitter battles of the war. The reputation of the Australian Imperial Force as well-trained and highly effective infantry brigades was hard earned and fully justified, and Ronald had contributed to it over three years of hard fighting. His body was never found, and he is commemorated on the memorial to the Missing at Villers Bretonneux.

The Canadian Corps had a similar reputation. After their stunning but hard-won successes during 1917, the Canadians too had forged an enviable reputation for dogged determination and combat capability as a separate but coordinated fighting entity. As we saw previously, Old Cheltonians also contributed in the ranks of the Canadian Expeditionary Force. Anthony Bredon (Newick, 1903) left College aged 17 and returned home to Scarborough where his father was an established surgeon in the East Riding of Yorkshire. Living in a comfortable home environment, Anthony began work as a clerk in a local solicitor's firm run by William Drawbridge. After five years of working and growing up in East Yorkshire, Anthony sought change (and possibly excitement) emigrating in 1910 to Canada where he quickly found work as a clerk in Alberta. He volunteered for the 49th Battalion, Edmonton Regiment on 4th January 1915, undergoing training at Valcartier Camp, the home of the Canadian Expeditionary Force in Quebec. Basic training complete, the battalion sailed for England in June 1915, reaching France at the beginning of October. Having fought and proved itself near Ypres that autumn, Anthony's division was moved to the Somme, but in action near Flers in September 1916 Anthony was seriously wounded and spent several weeks at the 8th Stationary Hospital in Wimereux before being evacuated back to England to convalesce. He rejoined the battalion in November 1917 which, having wintered in the Ypres sector, was redeployed to the Amiens sector where it took part in the rearguard action against *Operation Michael* during the German spring offensive. By the beginning of August 1918, however, Anthony's battalion was readying itself for the forthcoming Allied offensive: its objective was the stubbornly held village of Monchy-le-Preux, the costly crucible of many a British battalion the year before.

A further significant factor was the attack by the American Expeditionary Force on 28th May when the US 1st Division captured the town of Cantigny, southeast of Amiens. Small though this attack was, it symbolised a growing Allied numerical and logistical advantage and added to the weight of evidence that the tide was finally turning in the Allies' favour. Small tactical, localised reversals in German military fortunes began to occur on an increasingly frequent basis. By the beginning of August, the orchestration of a combined arms approach, where artillery, tanks and aircraft worked in concert with the infantry, had been tested and proved. All of the resources of manpower and mechanisation were in place for a full and durable Allied assault at scale. Moreover, the army and corps commanders had learned from previous painful experience and their tactics and strategies had evolved into a more flexible and inventive set of options. In the face of stubborn German strongpoints, as experienced on the Somme, at Arras and Passchendaele, rather than throw more battalions and brigades at such choke points, they were simply to be by-passed, surrounded and eventually 'mopped up'. Furthermore, command and communications had also been improved with the increased use of wireless to feed a valuable flow of information back to commanders. With over 580 tanks and armoured vehicles in close support of the infantry, and with 800 ground attack aircraft to strafe and weaken defences ahead, the momentum of advance could be maintained until, of course, they reached and breached the Hindenburg Line. But the key element would be that of surprise.

In the early hours of 8th August, the first fingers of daylight revealed a relative quiet and misty setting just to the east of Amiens. At 4.20am, 2,050 Allied guns opened a sudden and ferocious barrage on the German front line and pre-registered targets. The BEF, spearheaded by the Canadian and Australian Corps rolled forward behind a creeping barrage supported by 500 tanks. By the end of the day, the Allied forces had advanced up to seven miles in places, destroyed over 400 German guns and taken nearly 15,000 prisoners. The readiness of some German troops to throw down their arms and surrender suggested that their morale was close to breaking point. Indeed, General Ludendorff writing later dubbed events of 8th August as the 'black day' of the German Army during the war.[347] More importantly for the attacking force, the casualty list of 9,000 was only 30% that of the defending Germans. Sadly, one of that number was Colin Donald (Cheltondale, 1915). He had left College for 11 months of private tutoring under Reverend Carlton in Leominster to prepare him for entry into Sandhurst, to which he applied on 7th October 1916 aged 17. He was subsequently gazetted as a second lieutenant in the Seaforth Highlanders on 20th December 1917 joining the 2nd Battalion at the Front.[348] Just before first light on 8th August 1918 to the north of Arras, the battalion conducted a reconnaissance in force near the Turbeaute River and, after initial probing patrols, had penetrated the German line without opposition, finding at first the enemy positions unoccupied.

> At 5am on the 8th the advance was continued for 200 yards no opposition was encountered. Sniping and MG fire was then opened on our patrols and progress became very slow as the bttn on our right were held up. It was thought enemy were not holding position on the QUENTIN ROAD in strength and a further reconnaissance in force was decided upon by the local commander. Progress was resumed.[349]

---

[347] E Ludendorff, *Ludendorff's Own Story August 1914-November 1918 the Great War from the siege of Liege to the signing of the Armistice as viewed from the Grand headquarters of the German Army*, Volume 2 Harper and Brothers, London (1920), page 326.
[348] Supplement to *The London Gazette*, 20th December 1917, page 13337.
[349] The National Archives, WO 95/1483, Unit War Diary for the 2nd Seaforth Highlanders, August 1918.

During the advance, the battalion gained their objectives beyond the St Quentin road, capturing five machine guns and taking 24 prisoners in the process. However, for the remainder of the day the Germans counter-barraged relentlessly as the battalion pushed forward, their positions coming under increasingly heavy machine gun and sniper fire. Colin was one of the battalion's casualties, killed in action while leading his platoon forward.

The general advance pushed towards the old defences of the Hindenburg Lines, rapidly being rejuvenated and strengthened by the Germans. A fortnight after Colin's final action, three other Old Cheltonians were killed on the same day. During the early morning of 24th August, Frank Powell-Ackroyd (Cheltondale, 1915) was killed while attached to the 9th Battalion, King's Own Yorkshire Light Infantry during the 64th Infantry Brigade's advance on Grandcourt, the small ruined village nestling in the Ancre valley below Thiepval. The objective of the advance was to retake the ground, so dearly won during the Battle of the Somme two years earlier, yet so quickly lost during the German spring offensive. The Brigade war diary describes the events:

> The left attacking Battalion was the 1st East Yorkshire Regiment, and the right attacking Battalion was the 9th K.O.Y.L.I. The Brigade Reserve was the 15th D.L.I., who formed up about 300 yards in rear of the front Battalions.
>
> An artillery barrage had been arranged, but alterations in plan cancelled this. About the time of the attack, 11.30 p.m., a few shells were fired, but they did not have much effect. The 9th K.O.Y.L.I. dealt with the dug-outs in the ravines running out of Battery Valley over the side of the hill, and then formed up for the next advance. The Support and Reserve Company 1st East Yorkshire Regiment were sent to mop up the village of Grandcourt, which they quickly overran, capturing four field guns, 20 machine guns, and over 100 prisoners, About 1 a.m. a further advance was made by the remainder of the 1st E. Yorkshire Regiment and the 9th K.O.Y.L.I., and after advancing about three-quarters of a mile attacked across Boom Ravine, where little resistance was met.
>
> As dawn was breaking on the morning of the 24th August, the Durham's and the 9th K.O.Y.L.I. advanced in small parties up the hill, but here it was evident that we were up against resistance once more, but our task was accomplished. The enemy rearguards opened out an annihilating machine gun fire, and the Brigade was hurried into a position of all-round defence, for it was evident that the Brigade (or such portion as was on the hill) was surrounded, but intact, in the enemy position. The men held shell holes, and dare not stand up. The enemy made several small counter-attacks, but at great cost in lives to himself.
>
> About 10.30 a.m. Capt. Spicer, the Brigade Major, after an affair with a German sentry, managed to get away, passed Grandcourt and informed the 1st E. Yorkshire Regiment of the position, found a horse and rode to 21st Division Advanced H.Q. at Mailly-

Maillet, where he explained the situation. The report was confirmed by aeroplane reconnaissance. These 'planes dropped messages on our little hill promising speedy assistance. The Brigade was in a rough circle round the hill, but in no formation as regards units.

During the enemy shelling early in the morning the Brigade suffered far more heavily than in the attack. At noon on the 24th August there was a sudden quiet; the sun had got up and was very hot, the mists had lifted from the river below and dissipated, and away to the north the advanced troops could be seen advancing on Miraumont.[350]

Frank was buried in the cemetery at Grandcourt the following day after the village had been secured.

Later that same morning, Douglas Collier (Newick, 1916) was killed flying with No 56 Squadron on a low-level raid near Barastre, some 15 miles east of Grandcourt. After leaving College aged 16, he worked at the Royal Aircraft Factory, Farnborough, until old enough to apply for a commission. In mid-September Douglas received his call-up papers and, after enlistment and attestation into the RFC at Farnborough he commenced pilot training. Following the award of his 'wings' in February 1918 and promotion to second lieutenant, he was posted to the squadron based at Valheureux in France to fly the SE5a, one of the war's most capable 'scout' aircraft. Sadly, on that morning's attack sortie Douglas's aircraft (Serial No D6121) was seen to fall out of control, crashing behind enemy lines.

Finally, that evening, Bruce Jameson (Day Boy, 1910) was killed in a German bombing raid on his airfield at Bertangles just to the north of Amiens. Bruce had transferred from the infantry to the RFC to become an observer on No 87 Squadron. Recovering from a bout of scarlet fever in England, he successfully reapplied for pilot training at No 5 School of Military Aeronautics at Denham, an opportunity which he clearly embraced as he also acted as an assistant instructor: his previous operational flying experience evidently gave him a distinct advantage over, and much value to offer, his class mates. Once awarded his 'wings' Bruce was posted to No 48 Squadron at Bertangles operating Bristol Fighters, under the command of Major Keith Park, later famous as air officer commanding No 11 Group during the Battle of Britain. That evening, a concert party was being held by the squadron in one of the airfield's hangars. It was a bright moonlit night when at 9pm the drone of approaching aero engines grew louder. Minutes later, five German Gotha bombers from *Schlachtstaffel 16* began to attack the airfield, scoring a direct hit on the middle hangar which lit up the airfield making it an easy target for the other attackers. The Germans continued to bomb the aerodrome for a further 15 minutes destroying the squadron's hangar in which were six Bristol Fighters, all fully fuelled and armed with 25lb bombs. Bruce was one of four squadron personnel to be killed that evening.

---

[350] The National Archives, WO 95/2160/5, 64th Infantry Brigade: Headquarters, dated 1st July 1918 – 31st March 1919.

Three days later, Guy Handley (Boyne House, 1899) was killed whilst leading No 3 Company of the 2nd Battalion, Coldstream Guards into action against German defensive positions at St Leger just north of Bapaume. Guy had experienced a full and interesting life after leaving College where he had been in the top academic stream. Commissioned in 1900 as a second lieutenant in the Royal Field Artillery, Guy resigned from the army in 1902 for colonial service abroad, joining the Nigerian Civil Service as a native commissioner. When war broke out in 1914, he was acting as an assistant police officer and for 18 months saw active military service in the Cameroons against German colonial forces, being mentioned in despatches and earning the West African Frontier Medal.

Guy Handley MC

Returning to England, Guy was recommissioned into the York and Lancaster Regiment and quickly made a temporary captain, with his seniority backdated to November 1914.[351] He won the Military Cross during the Battle of the Somme:

> For conspicuous gallantry in action. He led his men with great courage and determination. Later, although wounded, he remained at his post, consolidated the position, and repulsed an enemy attack.[352]

Attached the following year to the King's Own Yorkshire Light Infantry, Guy won a Bar to his Military Cross:

> For conspicuous gallantry and devotion to duty. During an attack he showed a splendid example in steadying the men under heavy hostile barrage prior to the assault. He visited the whole battalion front and reorganised the men, remaining in command in the captured line for three days in succession, and by his personal example and utter disregard of danger inspiring all ranks to fresh efforts. His gallantry made possible the consolidation of a difficult position.[353]

Guy was transferred once again, this time attached to the Coldstream Guards in December 1917 and though still a lieutenant he assumed the duties of a company commander. At 7am on 27th August, the 2nd Battalion led the 1st Guards Brigade in launching an attack on an important system of German trenches concentrated on a small area to the east of the village at St Leger. The enemy position was taken that day, but the battalion lost 10 officers and 314 men. Guy's illustrious war had come to an abrupt end.

The following day, Anthony Bredon was killed in action as the 49th Canadian Infantry captured the small and shattered village of Pelves to the north east of Monchy-le Preux. His

---

[351] Supplement to *The London Gazette*, 23rd October 1915, page 10479.
[352] Supplement to *The London Gazette*, 25th November 1916, page 11536.
[353] Supplement to *The London Gazette*, 16th August 1917, page 8355.

The remains of the village of St Leger, 1918

body was hastily buried in a nearby shell hole as the battalion moved forward to its next objective, but fortunately the grave location was properly recorded. When the fighting in the area moved on eastwards and a degree of peace and quiet descended once again onto this rural area, so appallingly battered and scarred from two years of bitter fighting, Anthony's body was found, reinterred from his battlefield grave to the formal setting and tranquillity of Gourock Trench cemetery near Tilloy les Mofflanies. His elder brother Alexander (Newick, 1904), who had also fought in the war as a captain in the Royal West Kent Regiment fighting in Mesopotamia, would come to the cemetery once he had returned from the Middle East after the Armistice to pay his final respects to a brave brother.

Over the next 10 weeks from the start of September to the Armistice, in the fighting referred to as 'the last hundred days', the Allied advance to, and then beyond, the Hindenburg Line continued remorselessly, claiming the lives of 29 Old Cheltonians. Sadly this number included Auriol Lowry, killed in action at Arleux, east of Arras on 23rd September. A gallant and inspirational leader and commanding officer, his unit war diary simply records that:

> Lieut Col AEE Lowry, DSO, MC, was killed in action by a machine gun bullet whilst visiting the outposts.[354]

[354] The National Archives, WO 95/1714, Unit War Diary of the 2nd West Yorkshire Regiment September 1918.

He was a pipe smoker and unusually carried an automatic pistol on his person while in the trenches (rather than the issued Webley revolver), and one can easily imagine the inspiration such a confident and highly decorated character gave to the soldiers under his command.

Another young and remarkable Old Cheltonian to be killed in these final weeks was Edward Matthey (Currie, 1917). He had left College prematurely in July 1917 aged just 17 and, having been a private in the OTC, was keen to serve. He applied for entry into the RNAS as a pilot, being strongly recommended by Reverend Reginald Waterfield, the College's head. From February 1918 he underwent his initial officer training at Greenwich Naval College, but as his training spanned the formation of the Royal Air Force on 1st April, Edward was actually commissioned as an acting second lieutenant (on probation) and sent to RAF Uxbridge to start his flying ground training before going on to the Central Flying School at Upavon to learn to fly. He clearly took to flying quickly and did well being assessed as A1 standard, the highest grade of pilot ability. Accordingly, Edward was selected to become a fighter pilot. On 19th August he went to No 33 Fighter School at RAF Bircham Newton, and following conversion training on Sopwith Camels was put into No 5 Pilot Pool, eventually being posted on 16th September to No 204 Squadron based at Heule (near Courtrai) in Belgium. Just two weeks later, at 3.20pm on the misty afternoon of 3rd October, he took off eastward in company with 21 other Sopwith Camels for an offensive patrol in the Thourout-Roulers area. It was cloudy over the lines with poor visibility and, having climbed above the cloud, no enemy aircraft were seen. But soon after, while diving back down through the clouds, he collided over Ramscapelle at 12,000 feet with another Camel of the same patrol flown by Captain Charles Hickey, a Canadian pilot and ace with a Distinguished Flying Cross and Bar. Both pilots were killed. Edward was one of the youngest pilots to be killed in the war, aged 18: Charles was only 21. The young pilots were buried beside each other at Coxyde cemetery in Belgium.

A similar fate befell Richard Bingham (Cheltondale, 1915).[355] He was serving with No 209 Squadron based at the airfield at Poulainville near Amiens. At 1pm on 8th October, Richard took off in Sopwith Camel (Serial No H7278) for a low level patrol in company with another Camel (Serial No E4423), flown by Captain Dudley Allen, an experienced aviator on the squadron who was leading the pair of fighters. At about 3pm the two aircraft collided to the west of Bourlon, near Cambrai: again, both pilots were killed and buried beside each other in Triangle Cemetery near where they fell. In this first era of aerial combat, where aircrew fought in open cockpits in temperatures well below freezing without any survival aids such as parachutes and at higher altitudes where the insidious but debilitating, disorienting effects of hypoxia were ever present, one can only honour their dedication, sense of duty and, for too many, their sacrifice.

As the Allied forces began pushing the German army inexorably back towards the Hindenburg Line, key towns, most of which now lay shattered by four years of war, were

---

[355] Richard was the seventh and youngest son of Lord and Lady Clanmorris of Bangor Castle, and the only one of the six brothers to serve during the war who was killed, with Commander (later Rear Admiral) Barry Bingham winning the Victoria Cross at Jutland.

recaptured one after the other. Albert was retaken on 22nd August, an operation during which John Peyton (Christowe, 1911), a pre-war schoolteacher, was killed. A lieutenant serving with the 7th Battalion, Norfolk Regiment, John was with the battalion in the trenches at Ville sur Ancre, just south of Albert, when his brigade prepared to attack, keeping up a constant fire with Lewis guns to allow the approach of their supporting tanks to go unheard. At 4.50am the Norfolks went forward with the brigade and the advance was successful. Sadly, John was killed early in the action, the second and last son of the family to be killed in the war. John's younger brother Montegu, who had been schooled at Lancing College, had died at Ypres in 1917.

A week later, Bapaume was recaptured, followed by Peronne on 1st September. St Quentin finally fell to the Allies four weeks later as the BEF began to puncture the Hindenburg Line over a broad front between Cambrai and St Quentin, until finally it ruptured fully on 6th October. Hugh Morgan (Boyne House, 1909) was killed in action at Sancourt, to the north west of Cambrai serving with the 31st Canadian Infantry (Alberta). Having been commissioned from the ranks, in which he had been awarded the Military Medal, Hugh was leading his platoon when killed by shellfire. He is buried at Sains-Les-Marquion British Cemetery. Also killed at Sancourt later that day was Vivian Pemberton (Christowe, 1913). Originally serving with 7th Battalion, Royal Munster Fusiliers, Vivian had transferred to the Royal Garrison Artillery in January 1915 to join his twin brother, Alexander (Christowe, 1911). Vivian was commanding a battery of heavy guns of the 216th Siege Company, and had recently been awarded the Military Cross:

> For conspicuous gallantry and devotion to duty. When the enemy had broken through he kept his guns in action until the last possible moment, and when forced to withdraw them organised his men so that they kept up a steady rifle fire on the enemy. His coolness and courage saved a most critical situation.[356]

Alexander survived the war and was also awarded the Military Cross for his bravery in the final operations of the Mesopotamian campaign:

> For conspicuous gallantry and devotion to duty. He commanded his battery boldly and skilfully while his commanding officer was acting as the forward observation officer. He anticipated orders with judgement, affording close and effective support at a critical moment. He exposed himself fearlessly, and continued to engage the enemy's infantry at close range, though hotly opposed by enemy artillery.[357]

Sadly, Vivian's death was the second that the family had to bear as their elder brother, Oswald (Christowe, 1907), had been killed leading an attack at Festubert in December 1914. As the Allied advance rolled remorselessly eastwards, previous battlefields, where so

---

[356] Supplement to *The Edinburgh Gazette*, 29th July 1918, page 2705.
[357] Supplement to *The London Gazette*, 11th January 1919, page 638.

many Old Cheltonians had been killed in earlier years, were fought over once again. At Le Cateau, where Douglas Reynolds had so bravely saved the guns and earned his Victoria Cross during the long withdrawal to the Marne in 1914, two other Old Cheltonians were now to fall within a month of the Armistice. Charles Barton (Christowe, 1909) who had first fought in Gallipoli (earning the Military Cross for gallantry during the landing at Suvla Bay), and then in Salonika, later still in Palestine.[358] Now on the Western Front in October 1918 with the 6th Battalion, Royal Inniskilling Fusiliers, Charles' 'C' company consisted of just two other officers and 72 other ranks representing less than 50% of its established strength. The battalion was ordered to attack the brickworks south of Le Cateau and began their advance on the evening of 17th October as a heavy mist began to develop, continuing the attack into the early hours of the following day. Owing no doubt to the poor visibility, neither their allocated tank support materialised nor could they be supported by ground attack aircraft, both by then customary and critical factors in the tactics employed by the BEF. Consequently, 'C' Company suffered high casualties: Charles and his two young subalterns were killed.

A week later and within a mile of Charles' last action, Herbert Young (Day Boy and OJ, 1899) also died, killed instantaneously by shellfire while encouraging his battalion, the 11th Sherwood Foresters, and moving his headquarters forward to keep in touch with the advance.[359] Herbert served with distinction in the Second Boer War, and was thus an experienced officer by the time the war broke out. By February 1916, Herbert was given command of the 7th Battalion, a position he held until the end of November 1917. After a long stint of command during the action on the Somme in 1916 and at Messines the following year; he was awarded the Distinguished Service Order in January 1917. During the evening of 25th October 1918, and just 17 days before the Armistice, as the advance pushed on towards Mons, Herbert's battalion was involved in heavy fighting:

> The Battalion moved forward into FONTAINE au BOIS into billets, as support for 13th DLI and 9th Yorks Regt. FONTAINE AU BOIS was shelled by the enemy also the road leading up to it from LE CATEAU. Casualties: Lt Col HN Young DSO killed (by shell), Captain BW Bird MC wounded. At 1700 hrs Lt Col HN YOUNG DSO, CO of the Battalion, was killed by shell fire, and the Adjutant, Captain BW BIRD MC wounded whilst coming to his new HQ in FONTAINE AU BOIS along the POMMEREIL – FONTAINE AU BOIS road. Death was instantaneous and his body was brought back to POMMEREIL.[360]

Herbert was buried by the battalion the following day in the small village cemetery at Pommereil.

---

[358] Supplement to *The London Gazette*, 2nd February 1916, page 1337.
[359] The 'Sherwood Foresters' is the popular and accepted term given to battalions of the Nottinghamshire and Derbyshire Regiment.
[360] The National Archives, WO 95/2247/5, War Diary of the 11th Battalion, Sherwood Foresters, September 1918 to February 1919.

During the last two weeks before the Armistice, the Allies' advance through Northern France and Belgium became unstoppable, not least as the German will to fight on was rapidly evaporating. Lille was liberated on 17th October, the same day the Belgians captured the important port of Ostend. The sailors of the German High Seas Fleet mutinied at the end of October and refused to put to sea, and on the Western Front, the Canadians took back Valenciennes on 2nd November. Serving with them was Greville Shaw (Day Boy, 1909), the elder brother of Giles (Day Boy, 1913), who had been killed at Arras the year before. Greville had flirted with a military career at Woolwich in the Royal Engineers, but decided to emigrate to Canada, working in Ottowa. He enlisted in October 1915 and was offered a commission as a captain in the Canadian engineers. Serving on the Western Front, he was mentioned in despatches for his excellent work and devotion to duty. Now in the final week of the war, Greville was in command of the 2nd Canadian Anti-Tank Company. The problem was that no one knew where the German tanks were. With enemy dispositions so uncertain, and without the benefit of any aerial reconnaissance due to bad weather, he decided to go out himself to reconnoitre. At 2pm on the afternoon of 3rd November, Greville borrowed a motor bike and set off from his positions to make a reconnaissance of the forward roads in St Saulve, barely five miles from Mons. He did not return and was reported missing to the 4th Brigade's Chief Engineer at 11.00pm that evening. Search parties were sent out the following day and he was found in Onnaing. He had apparently ridden into German lines and was mortally wounded by both rifle and shellfire. The Germans had carried him back to a field dressing station nearby where he died of his wounds.

DEADLY VIRUS AND LAST POSTS

From June 1918 a different sinister shadow took form and began to loom increasingly large as the Armistice approached. Spanish influenza, an airborne virus, began in military camps in United States in the winter of 1917 and by June the following year it had rapidly spread. The conditions of wartime service and deprivation greatly encouraged its propagation as malnourishment, poor hygiene and inadequate sanitary conditions prevailed. Its spread was further exacerbated by the overcrowded conditions in billets, trenches and troop trains, at dressing stations and in the base medical camps and hospitals.[361] Furthermore, as the virus seemed to be more aggressive against the stronger human immune systems, it had an increased effect on young male adults, the same individuals serving in all the belligerent armies. Not only were they fighting in a cold and wet outdoor environment, but also their physical condition was so sorely strained and weakened by their battlefield conditions, arduous service and onerous duties. The first Old Cheltonian to succumb to influenza was William Poulett (Cheltondale, 1898). As the son of the Right Honourable William Poulett, the 6th Earl Poulett, he was known by the courtesy title of Viscount Hinton, as recorded in the College Register, until the death of his father in 1899 when he inherited the earldom.

Having gone up to Trinity Hall, Cambridge from College, William held a commission from May 1903 with various territorial units, including the Highland Light Infantry and later the Warwickshire Royal Horse Artillery, and by November 1915 was a captain. William died on 11th July 1918, struck down by the virus, at Saltburn in Yorkshire.

Over the following weeks the number of influenza cases erupted, and, given the nature of the virus even the sturdiest of metabolisms and constitutions was not spared. Arthur du Boulay (Southwood, 1897) was one such example. Attending College from his family home of Murchmont, Parabola Road, Cheltenham, he had enjoyed a full and athletic school life. Not just a College prefect, Arthur was also an excellent cricketer, playing in the XI of 1895 and 1896, finally captaining the team in 1897. When war was declared in 1914, his division was mobilised and Arthur, now an experienced Royal Engineer, was promoted to captain and appointed to his new role of assistant quartermaster general to the Division. However, by November 1915, Arthur arrived on the Western Front in France where he remained for the next three years, seeing action at the Battle of the Somme in 1916. He was mentioned in despatches three times over this period of fighting and promoted to major. In June 1917, he was promoted again, this time to brevet lieutenant colonel serving on the Corps staff for which he was mentioned in despatches twice more. His performance and contribution were recognised even more illustriously when he was awarded the Distinguished Service Order in the 1918 Birthday Honours List that June. However, while serving on the staff of the Third Army as its assistant quartermaster general, he fell ill during the opening week of October as the flu epidemic began rampaging through the ranks, and he died on 25th October. He was buried in the Fillièvres British Cemetery south-west of Arras. Even after his death, as bureaucracy struggled to keep pace with events, his outstanding contribution continued to be recognised, with a further mention in despatches once more after his death. Arthur was posthumously awarded the Order of Leopold II with Palm, and the Croix de Guerre.

---

[361] Dr Marianne Dyer, UK medical director for Shell International, has responsibility for dealing with global pandemics and has provided the following explanatory précis. The outbreak of Spanish Flu in 1918-1920 was one of the world's most serious pandemics of infectious disease killing approximately 50-100 million people worldwide which equates to 3-6% of the world's population. The first cases appeared in Europe in Brest, France in August 1918. The virus was particularly virulent and easily transmitted with an infection rate of up to 50%. Flu pandemics occur in waves and flu viruses mutate and adapt as they spread. With Spanish flu, by the second wave, the flu virus had mutated into its most deadly form and this caused the major peak of deaths in late 1918. Those who had caught the milder first wave were immune showing that it was the same virus.

The virus mainly attacked healthy young adults rather than the old, young or vulnerable and had a very high mortality with an estimated 10% to 20% of those who were infected dying. It is thought that it was particularly deadly in young adults due to the immune system in these relatively healthy people having a severe over-reaction to the virus causing a 'Cytokine Storm'. This severe reaction is devastating to the tissues of the body, particularly the lungs' leading to respiratory failure. The weaker immune systems found in the old, young and vulnerable are less able to have such an extreme response and hence were not affected as much.

The circumstances of the war itself was an additional factor in the spread and severity of the disease. Factors such as the close proximity of soldiers, overcrowding of camps and hospitals, the lack of isolation of infected cases and the frequent movement of large numbers of troops is very likely to have influenced the spread internationally and within the theatre of the war. In addition, malnourishment, exposure to chemical gases, poor hygiene, fatigue and poor general health promoted an increased individual susceptibility to further complications such as secondary bacterial superinfection leading to pneumonia and sepsis in an era when antibiotics had yet to be discovered.

The epidemic was indifferent in the selection of its victims and even the hardiest of souls became infected. Dallas Moor, who had so bravely won his Victoria Cross at Gallipoli on 24th July 1915, aged 18, continued to prove his gallantry over the following three years, being awarded the Military Cross and Bar, and also being wounded in the upper left arm by a rifle bullet at Monchy-le-Preux on 22nd December 1917. After convalescing in England, he returned to France and was appointed as aide de camp to the general officer commanding the 30th Division in March 1918. In the same week that Arthur du Boulay died from its grip, its shadow passed on to Dallas. He died on 3rd November from pneumonia, just a week before the Armistice, after contracting influenza at No 3 Canadian Casualty Clearing Station at Mouvaux, France.

Other infections, such as diphtheria, also affected weary warriors fighting towards the war's finish. Spread in much the same way as influenza, a diphtheria infection is caused by a bacterial covering in the back of the throat, which can lead to difficulty in breathing, heart failure, paralysis, and therefore death. In 1918, Richard Britten (Newick, 1894) was deputy director of remounts for the Fifth Army, an important role for an army whose war horses were invaluable to its combat effectiveness. Richard's equine experience, gained on the family farm in Great Billing, was therefore of great importance to his tasks with the army. However, it came with some downsides. Having been appointed as a remount officer in France from January 1915 at No 1 Base Remount Depot, Rouen for six months, he was transferred to No 2 Base Remount Depot at Le Havre where in 1916 he was kicked in the leg by a horse, suffering serious contusions, no doubt considered an occupational hazard. By July 1918, he was appointed deputy assistant director of remounts for the Fifth Army, but within four weeks he became seriously ill and died of diphtheria and acute tonsillitis at No 54 Casualty Clearing Station at Aire in France on 18th August. As these deadly infections spread quickly and universally, especially the influenza epidemic which is estimated to have claimed some 100 million lives across the globe, they rather compounded the effect and circumstances of the final wartime casualties.

The last civilian Old Cheltonian to be killed in the war was Charles Johnston (Christowe, 1893). In his final year at College Charles rowed for the VIII, then went out to South Africa in May 1894, aged 18. Later he worked for the British South African Company producing grain for the empire's commodity markets. He became a government agent working as the chief organiser for the Ministry of Food in London, directed by fellow Old Cheltonian Sir Arthur Lee, both president of the College Council and the Minister for Agriculture and Fisheries. Charles was drowned whilst en route back to South Africa aboard the SS *Hirano Maru* which was torpedoed and sunk on 4th October 1918 by German submarine *UB 91* off the coast of Ireland during a violent storm. The foul weather and the presence of the submarine hindered the rescue attempts of the escorting US destroyer *Sterett* and a total of 292 lives including many children were lost.

The last Old Cheltonian to be killed in the Middle East during the war was Richard Evans (Newick, 1891) who died in Palestine. After College, he trained as a solicitor while holding a militia commission in the 1st Battalion, Welsh Regiment. Later serving in the

South African War with distinction: he was mentioned in despatches and was awarded the Queen's Medal with five operational clasps. By the outbreak of war, he was a major with the 4th Battalion, Welsh Regiment, and was posted at his own request to Alexandria in December 1916, joining the front-line unit, the 1/4th Battalion, Welsh Regiment. Richard saw action during the three Battles of Gaza and witnessed the capture of Jerusalem, before being mortally wounded near Gaza. He died in Palestine on 13th September 1918 aged 46, and just three weeks after his younger brother, Lawrence, who was educated at Clifton, had been killed during the Battle of Albert back in France. Richard is buried at Gaza War Cemetery, Israel.

Fighting in Mesopotamia continued right up to the Armistice, and Reginald Lynch-Staunton (Hazelwell,1897) was the last Old Cheltonian to die there during the war. He too had served in the South African War in 1900 as a career 'gunner' with the RFA, receiving the Queen's Medal with three clasps. By 1914 he was in command of U Battery, Royal Horse Artillery in India with 7th (Meerut) Division. The Division was sent to France in October 1915, Reginald serving as the artillery brigade major with great distinction for which he was mentioned in despatches and awarded the Distinguished Service Order.[362] At the end of the year he left France for Mesopotamia, and served as brigade major, Royal Artillery in the Tigris Corps, until 15th August 1916 when he was promoted to command 13th Brigade, RFA. Reginald commanded the brigade during the operations on the Hai River and the Shumrar crossing during December 1916, then during the advance and capture of Baghdad the following year. While in action on the night of 26th/27th October 1918, Reginald received a serious bullet wound to the shoulder and was admitted to the Officer's Hospital, Baghdad. After suffering secondary haemorrhaging, he needed immediate surgery on 6th November before he could begin convalescence; his post-operative sickness was relieved apparently with pineapple and champagne. However, the following day, his haemorrhaging started again, probably not aided by the effects of the champagne and any associated thinning of his blood, and the medics immediately initiated emergency intensive care. Sadly, Reginald died that evening at 10.15pm, just four days before the Armistice.

The following day on the Western Front, Harry Perrier (Boyne House, 1916) was killed; the last army Old Cheltonian to die during the war. Leaving College aged 17, he was determined to serve at the earliest opportunity when old enough. Two weeks before his 18th birthday, he enlisted on 26th October 1916 into the Royal Dublin Fusiliers at the Cork Recruiting Centre as a private. His OTC experience ensured rapid promotion to lance corporal, despite being the youngest in his platoon. While undergoing initial training, he also applied for a commission in the Special Reserve of Officers and was successfully posted to No 20 Officer Cadet Battalion at Crookham on 5th May 1917 to commence officer training. Fourteen weeks later on 29th August Harry was commissioned as a second lieutenant and posted to the 2nd Battalion, Royal Dublin Fusiliers.[363] Harry had fought throughout 1918, including an eight-day fighting retreat in March under the weight of the

---

[362] *The London Gazette*, 23rd June 1915.
[363] Supplement to *The London Gazette*, 22nd September 1917, page 9840.

German spring offensive, and then advancing back across the same battlegrounds until the battalion arrived at new positions just south of Maubeuge on the cusp of final victory. Ordered to attack the small village of Floursies on the morning of 8th November the battalion was held up by machine guns, although by the afternoon they had managed to take the village. Harry and four of his men were killed in the attack and were all buried together that evening. He was just one day short of his 20th birthday, and quite ironically, three days later the battalion was almost in the same positions where they had first gone into action in August 1914.

The dubious distinction of being the last Old Cheltonian to die before the Armistice fell to Donald Mackay (Day Boy, 1914) who had left College the same week as Cyril Hillier (from the 1914 cricket XI) in July 1914. Like Cyril, Donald immediately enlisted when war was declared, serving in 19th Battalion, Royal Fusiliers (Public Schools) as a lance corporal before applying for a commission in March 1916. Joining No 4 Officer Cadet Battalion at Oxford Donald was commissioned as a temporary second lieutenant in the Argyll and Sutherland Highlanders on 2nd June but was swiftly transferred to the RFC for pilot training.[364] His first flying tour in France was not without incident: during 'Bloody April' 1917 he was wounded on the 24th when he crashed his aircraft, sustaining a deep scalp wound and concussion. He was invalided back to England the following day for recuperation. When sufficiently recovered he was sent to the RFC at Waddington, and No 57 Training Squadron, for home service and solo currency flying, until declared fit again on 14th September 1917. Returning to France and posted to No 55 Squadron, he flew DH4s on longer-range bombing missions throughout 1918. On 10th November, Donald was the pilot of DH4 (Serial No F5725) engaged on a bombing raid on Cologne with his observer Lieutenant Harry Gompertz. They were regularly crewed together and had been accredited with three aerial victories. However, when over the target and attacking the railway sidings their aircraft received several hits from anti-aircraft fire and Donald was mortally wounded. Struggling to keep the aircraft airborne, they limped back across the border, but control of the aircraft was becoming increasingly difficult. Due to loss of blood, Donald lost consciousness and Harry, fighting with the controls, managed to land the aircraft close to some German infantry positions northwest of Metz to get the quickest medical attention to Donald. Both airmen were immediately made prisoners of war and taken to a German medical facility at Joeuf, France, where early the following morning, Armistice Day, Donald died from his injuries.

Donald was the 667th Old Cheltonian to be killed in the war. Though the fighting was suspended at 11am on 11th November 1918, sadly, the dying was not. A further 35 Old Cheltonians would die or be killed as a result of the Great War.

---

[364] Supplement to *The London Gazette*, 12th June 1916, page 5819.

LIST OF FALLEN
OLD CHELTONIANS
1918

On the following pages (266 to 271) are the names and service details of Old Cheltonians who died in the fifth year of the war.

1918 – LIST OF FALLEN OLD CHELTONIANS

	Died (1918)	**Name**	**Rank**
550	4 January	Hewett H	Captain
551	6 January	Grose WM	Private
552	8 January	Grogan GF	Lieutenant
553	2 March	Townsend REL	Captain
554	3 March	Townsend CC	Colonel
555	6 March	Manley TW	2nd Lieutenant
556	8 March	Knowling FJD	Captain
557	14 March	Cameron JH	Lieutenant
558	17 March	Bolton S	Lieutenant
559	21 March	Cummins FK	Captain
560	21 March	Desages WR	Captain
561	21 March	Festing HW	Lt Colonel
562	21 March	Hughes-Games GB	Private
563	21 March	Lemon VB	Private
564	21 March	Moody TLV	Lieutenant
565	22 March	Rickerby JHE	Captain
566	23 March	Creagh O'M C	Lieutenant
567	23 March	Martin AG	Captain
568	24 March	Cochran HPG	Lt Colonel
569	24 March	Lywood KPG	Captain
570	25 March	Lake NG	Lieutenant
571	25 March	Lowry CJP	Captain
572	26 March	Badcock MF	Captain
573	26 March	Godley GAG	Lieutenant
574	27 March	Holmes TG	2nd Lieutenant
575	27 March	Mather R	2nd Lieutenant
576	28 March	Coghill NH	Lieutenant
577	30 March	Homfray RP	Captain
578	30 March	Percival-Maxwell RN	Lieutenant
579	31 March	Campbell CLK	Brig General
580	2 April	Neame G	Major
581	2 April	O'Keefe MM	Captain
582	4 April	Grieve JR	Major
583	5 April	Mitchell TFW	Private
584	9 April	Thornton GRH	2nd Lieutenant
585	12 April	Conran PWD	Major
586	16 April	Turnly JF	2nd Lieutenant
587	21 April	Dennis C	Private
588	22 April	Armitage FAW	Lt Colonel
589	22 April	Saunderson STB	Captain

1918 – LIST OF FALLEN OLD CHELTONIANS

Unit	Age	Place
No 113 Squadron, RFC	25	Jenin, Palestine
Royal Army Ordnance Corps	37	Kensington, UK
183rd Tunnelling Company, RE	34	Boesinghe, Belgium
16th Middlesex Regiment	44	Gillingham, UK
Royal Artillery (Ordnance Dept)	59	Camberley, UK
School of Aerial Gunnery, RFC	23	Hythe, UK
10th Argyll & Sutherland Highlanders	26	Houthulst, Belgium
5th Light Infantry, IA	29	Fategarh, India
164th Trench Mortar Battery	20	Givenchy, France
6th Connaught Rangers	20	St Emilie, France
2/5th East Lancashire Regiment	34	Hargicourt, France
CO, 15th Durham Light Infantry	35	Epehey, France
36th Machine Gun Corps	27	St Quentin, France
8th (Heavy), Machine Gun Corps	32	Happlincourt, France
1st East Kent Regiment (The Buffs)	21	Lagnicourt, France
2/5th Gloucestershire Regiment	22	Beauvois, France
C Battery, 108th Brigade, RFA	21	Peronne, France
9th Rifle Brigade	35	St Quentin, France
CO, 15th Cheshire Regiment	40	Clery-sur-Somme, France
5th Brigade, Royal Horse Artillery	19	Berlancourt, France
2/5th Gloucestershire Regiment	23	Buverchy, France
att 2nd West Yorkshire Regiment	20	Villers Carbonnel, France
att 9th East Surrey Regiment	22	Rosières, France
15 Div Train, Army Service Corps	20	Arras, France
16th Brigade, Royal Horse Artillery	19	Rosières, France
17th King's (Liverpool) Regiment	25	Folies, France
att Machine Gun Corps	20	Doullens, France
3/7th Worcestershire Regiment	41	Newcastle, UK
16th Lancers	24	Amiens, France
16th Lancers, GOC 5th Cav Brigade	44	London, UK
190th Brigade, Royal Field Artillery	34	Bucquoy, France
48th Brigade, Royal Field Artillery	21	Foreville, France
107th Brigade, Royal Field Artillery	33	Arras, France
13th Royal Fusiliers	22	Bucquoy, France
16th Brigade Royal Garrison Artillery	35	Laventie, France
att 6th Lancashire Fusiliers	32	Estaires, France
9th Machine Gun Corps	19	Wytschaete, Belgium
19th Army Cycling Corps	39	Bohain, Germany
CO, 1st West Yorkshire Regiment	34	Gonnehem, France
No 131 Squadron, Royal Air Force	32	Shawbury, UK

1918 – LIST OF FALLEN OLD CHELTONIANS

	Died (1918)	Name	Rank
590	23 April	Chamberlin JB	2nd Lieutenant
591	24 April	Cox RAH	Private
592	25 April	Bryce-Smith NI	2nd Lieutenant
593	29 April	Coomber HA	Lieutenant
594	30 April	Radcliffe SR	Major
595	2 May	Henderson PG	2nd Lieutenant
596	9 May	McLean JRG	2nd Lieutenant
597	19 May	James CK	Lt Colonel
598	27 May	Desages OL	Captain
599	5 June	Hornby HL	Captain
600	6 June	Bainbridge-Bell HU	Captain
601	8 June	Forde LW	2nd Lieutenant
602	10 June	Trevenen SV	Captain
603	15 June	Radcliffe FV	Civilian
604	17 June	Quill MD	Captain
605	27 June	Foord EA	Lieutenant
606	5 July	Kay NRW	Lieutenant
607	11 July	(Earl) Poulett WJL	Captain
608	12 July	Delmar-Williamson GF	Lieutenant
609	12 July	Gabell DRC	Captain
610	14 July	Dickson AF	Lieutenant
611	20 July	Wilkinson TWM	Captain
612	31 July	Wedd EPW	Captain
613	1 August	Tanner JC	Captain
614	6 August	Ezra DE	Captain
615	8 August	Donald CGH	2nd Lieutenant
616	18 August	Britten RS	Major
617	20 August	Heath G	Lieutenant
618	22 August	Peyton JAW	Lieutenant
619	24 August	Collier DC	2nd Lieutenant
620	24 August	Powell-Ackroyd FA	2nd Lieutenant
621	24 August	Jameson JB	2nd Lieutenant
622	27 August	Handley GFB	Captain
623	28 August	Bredon AS	Corporal
624	3 September	Torney TFH	Lieutenant
625	12 September	Maby LB	2nd Lieutenant
626	12 September	Martin GCR	Lieutenant
627	13 September	Evans RWP	Major
628	17 September	Samson OM	2nd Lieutenant
629	18 September	Campbell CF	Major

1918 – LIST OF FALLEN OLD CHELTONIANS

Unit	Age	Place
No 13 (Training) Squadron, RAF	18	Yatesbury, UK
51st Battalion, Australian Infantry	34	Villers Bretonneux, France
6th King's Own Scottish Borderers	19	Wytschaete, Belgium
138th Brigade Royal Garrison Artillery	32	Rouen, France
172nd Brigade, Royal Field Artillery	33	Kantara, Egypt
2nd West Riding Regiment	19	Southampton, UK
2nd Argyll & Sutherland Highlanders	19	Ypres, Belgium
CO, 2/7th West Yorkshire Regiment	26	Bucquoy, France
1st Wiltshire Regiment	28	Vendresse, France
8th Royal Inniskilling Fusiliers	23	Brighton, UK
Royal Army Service Corps	51	London, UK
6th Dorsetshire Regiment	19	Beaumont Hamel, France
40th Brigade, Royal Field Artillery	24	Le Touquet, France
French Red Cross Service	32	London, UK
Royal Marine Artillery	22	RN Haslar, UK
No 48 Squadron, Royal Air Force	28	Villers Bretonneaux, France
15th Brigade, Royal Field Artillery	20	Boulogne, France
Warwickshire Royal Horse Artillery	34	Saltburn, UK
No 13 Training Squadron, RAF	19	Yatesbury, UK
No 13 Training Squadron, RAF	20	Yatesbury, UK
34th Poona Horse, IA	27	Kefren, Palestine
2/8th West Yorkshire Regiment	23	Marfaux, France
Royal Army Medical Corps	34	Elverdinghe, Belgium
56th Training Depot Squadron, RAF	21	Cranwell, UK
192nd Btty, Royal Garrison Artillery	33	Monchy, France
2nd Seaforth Highlanders	19	Gonnehem, France
Remount Service	40	Aire, France
Fleet Practice Squadron, RAF	19	Turnhouse, UK
7th Norfolk Regiment	25	Albert, France
No 56 Squadron, Royal Air Force	18	Bapaume, France
9th King's Own Yorkshire Light Infantry	20	Miraucourt, France
No 48 Squadron, Royal Air Force	25	Amiens, France
2nd Coldstream Guards	35	St Leger, France
49th Battalion, Canadian Infantry	30	Pelves, France
13th Royal Welsh Regiment	20	Mazancourt, France
2nd Scots Guards	20	Lagnicourt, France
2nd Sherwood Foresters	24	Le Hague, Holland
4th Royal Welsh Regiment	45	Gaza, Palestine
143rd Btty, Royal Garrison Artillery	37	Driencourt, France
14th Brigade, Royal Field Artillery	23	Coulaincourt, France

1918 – LIST OF FALLEN OLD CHELTONIANS

	Died (1918)	Name	Rank
630	18 September	Fane OE	Major
631	18 September	Popplewell BB	2nd Lieutenant
632	22 September	Carey BC	Captain
633	23 September	Lowry AEE	Lt Colonel
634	25 September	Atkinson FB	2nd Lieutenant
635	27 September	Johns G	Lieutenant
636	27 September	Russell NJG	2nd Lieutenant
637	29 September	Hay DW	Lieutenant
638	1 October	Heywood FK	Lieutenant
639	1 October	Morris WF	Private
640	1 October	Thornhill JE	Lt Colonel
641	1 October	Wood CK	Lieutenant
642	3 October	Matthey SE	2nd Lieutenant
643	4 October	Johnston CMG	Civilian
644	4 October	Sparrow GWS	Captain
645	5 October	Wolstenholme GM	Lieutenant
646	7 October	Morgan HP	Lieutenant
647	7 October	Pemberton VT	Captain
648	8 October	Bingham (Hon) RGA	2nd Lieutenant
649	8 October	Birtwistle N	Lieutenant
650	14 October	Talbot JLP	2nd Lieutenant
651	17 October	Barton CG	Captain
652	22 October	Ley JW	Major
653	22 October	Robinson GM	Private
654	25 October	Du Boulay AH	Lt Colonel
655	25 October	Young HN	Lt Colonel
656	27 October	Swinhoe EA	Major
657	30 October	Sharp FAH	Lieutenant
658	31 October	Bouck-Standen PE	Captain
659	1 November	Rowland JWB	2nd Lieutenant
660	3 November	Shaw GH	Lt Colonel
661	3 November	Moor GRD (VC)	Lieutenant
662	4 November	Birnie GB	Lieutenant
663	7 November	Hornby JH	Lieutenant
664	7 November	Lynch-Staunton RK	Lt Colonel
665	7 November	Prichard-Evans EL	Lieutenant
666	8 November	Perrier HCL	Lieutenant
667	11 November	MacKay DRG	Captain

1918 – LIST OF FALLEN OLD CHELTONIANS

Unit	Age	Place
CO 128th (Heavy) Battery, RGA	31	Peronne, France
Royal Army Service Corps	45	Scarborough, UK
1st Northamptonshire Regiment	20	Maissemy, France
CO, 2nd West Yorkshire Regiment	25	Arleux, France
87th Brigade, Royal Field Artillery	19	Bethune, France
2nd Guards Trench Mortar Battery	20	Cambrai, France
26th Brigade, Royal Field Artillery	19	Buissy, France
att 1st Middlesex Regiment	21	Villers Ghislain, France
No 98 Squadron, Royal Air Force	29	Bapaume, France
att Blandford POW Camp from RAF	50	Blandford, UK
Seaforth Highlanders	38	Gibraltar
West African Frontier Force	27	At sea, off Ireland
No 204 Squadron, Royal Air Force	18	Furnes, Belgium
Ministry of Food	42	At sea, off Ireland
10th Shropshire Light Infantry	42	Aubers, France
9th Yorkshire Regiment	21	Beaurevoir, France
95th Field Company, RE	26	Sancourt, France
216th Siege Company, RGA	24	Sancourt, France
No 209 Squadron, Royal Air Force	22	Bourlon, France
19th Hussars	21	Brancourt, France
1/7th West Yorkshire Regiment	18	Flerbaix, France
6th Royal Inniskilling Fusiliers	28	Le Cateau, France
7th North Staffordshire Regiment	41	Kermansha, Persia
Officer Cadet Battalion	36	Cambridge, UK
Royal Engineers	38	Fillievres, France
CO, 11th Sherwood Foresters	36	Le Cateau, France
Supply and Transport Corps, IA	48	Sailkot, India
39th Brigade, Royal Field Artillery	24	Louvière, France
Ministry of Munitions	26	Bristol, UK
175th Brigade, Royal Field Artillery	19	Preseau, France
2nd Canadian Anti-tank Company	27	St Saulve, France
1st Hampshire Regiment	22	Mouvaux, France
39th Brigade, Royal Field Artillery	19	Rouen, France
94th Field Company, RE	21	Eth, France
Royal Field Artillery	38	Baghdad, Mesopotamia
No 13 Squadron, Royal Air Force	25	Kings Lynn, UK
2nd Royal Dublin Fusiliers	19	Floursies, Belgium
No 55 Squadron, Royal Air Force	23	Joeuf, France

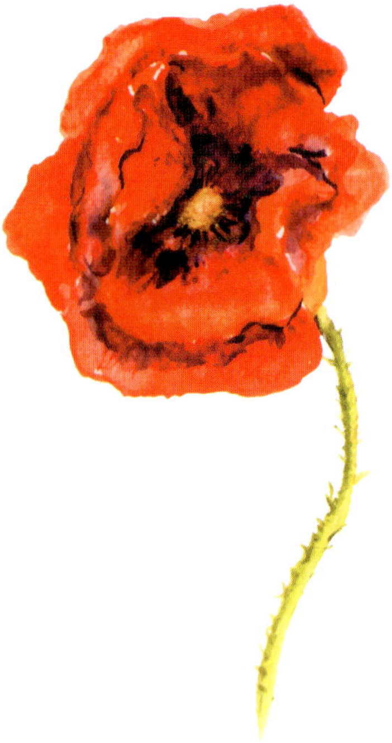

ACTS SIX
ARMISTICE AND BEYOND

Aftermath

It was still dark as a small group of military staff cars quietly arrived in a small forest clearing near Compiègne, some 67 miles north east of Paris, shortly before 5am on 11th November 1918. As the passengers made their way from their cars and into Marshal Ferdinand Foch's personal train, carefully hidden away on a siding and away from prying eyes, everything was still with barely a rustle from the few leaves remaining on the trees. The silence, save that of the quiet crunch of boots on gravel and the odd hushed snippet of conversation, was almost deafening with an overwhelming sense of expectancy and steely determination; it seemed as if the whole world was holding its breath. At 5.12am the first of the six signatories signed the Armistice agreement containing 34 clauses, which committed Germany to cease hostilies, surrender almost all her military materiel, and withdraw her forces on the Western Front immediately to the east of the Rhine.[365] Eight minutes later, the last signature to the document was appended, the pen put down, and the ink carefully blotted. The civilian head of the German delegation, Matthias Erzberger, slowly stood, shook hands with a stern-faced Ferdinand Foch, bowed his head in typical Prussian practice and led his three fellow delegates towards the door. It was done. The ink was dry: and cessation of all hostilities would come into force six hours later at 11am (Paris time). At 5.30am Matthias and the German delegation clambered down from the steps of the carriage, made their way slowly back to their staff cars, and, under the heavy leaden skies that indicated the first hints of a new though still potentially stormy dawn, they departed.

Since Henry Hadley had become the first fatality of the conflict, being shot on the train at Gelsenkirchen just hours before war was declared, a further 671 Old Cheltonians had died as a direct consequence of the conflict. But as the staff cars sped back to their various capitals and headquarters, sadly more Old Cheltonians would be caught in the war's final grip. After all, the Armistice only provided a cessation to hostilities; the peace had yet to be formalised. During the following six-month interlude, there was much associated activity, as the war was not deemed officially over until the Treaty of Versailles was signed on 28th June 1919. Therefore, those who became casualties during this period were included in the final statistics.

Edward Knott (Newick, 1916) is a typical example. Leaving College when he was 17 years of age, he had decided to join the Royal Navy as an aviator at the earliest opportunity, and on 18th March 1917, just a month before his 18th birthday, he was appointed as a probationary Flight Officer in the Royal Naval Air Service (RNAS).

---

[365] Germany was required to surrender 1,700 aircraft, all of her submarine fleet, her capital warships, 5,000 artillery guns, and 25,000 machine guns, as well as the majority of her railway locomotives and rolling stock. Also, Germany was to withdraw her military forces from Africa.

Edward Knott

Four weeks later, Edward arrived at the Royal Navy's Aeroplane School at No 207 Training Depot at Chingford to start his primary flying training. Advanced training then followed at Cranwell from 23rd June to 15th August 1917, where Edward received his 'wings'; his graduation report confirmed he was:

VG pilot. Recommended for active service, Scouts. A good keen officer, Flying Ability: First Class.[366]

Promoted to flight sub lieutenant on 25th July 1917, Edward was posted to No 9 Squadron RNAS, based at Dover flying Sopwith Camels on maritime patrol and anti-Zeppelin duties. The squadron was also detached to the forward operating base at St Pol-sur-Mer near Dunkirk for periods, from where it could also support the infantry fighting in Belgium. On one sortie on 15th September, he and another squadron pilot engaged two German fighters sending them both down out of control. Later, on 20th November the squadron's operations report (No 46) records that he fired about 300 rounds into a company of enemy infantry, killing some and scattering the rest. His personal report from Dunkirk described Edward as a 'G Pilot and officer' and he was strongly recommended for promotion to flight lieutenant, which was granted on 1st January 1918. This coincided with his posting to the air depot in London as ferry pilot transporting new aircraft to the squadrons fighting in France, a role requiring natural flying ability and strong navigational skills which he undertook until the Armistice. With the cessation of hostilities, he was posted to No 1 Communications Squadron at Kenley on 8th December, predominantly employed on special duties, transporting VIPs and government officers to and from the continent, flying to Brussels, for example, on 14th March 1919 and subsequently to Paris on 11th April, supporting the negotiations associated with the Treaty of Versailles. Clearly, high-calibre pilots were needed for such an important role, and Edward, having a first-class flying record (recognised with his award of the Air Force Cross in the 1919 New Year's Honours List) was ideal for the task.[367] On 3rd May, he was detailed to take Air Vice Marshal Sir Frederick Hugh Sykes KCB CMG, the controller of UK Aviation, to Paris for further treaty meetings and discussions. In blustery conditions, Edward took off from Kenley in a DH4 (Serial No D8355), but while in a climbing turn at approximately 50 feet above the runway, his engine seized, the aircraft stalled and crashed onto the airfield. Edward died in the crash but Sir Frederick, although badly shaken, survived the mishap. Edward was just over 20 when he was killed, a remarkably talented pilot who had achieved much in his short flying career. His body was taken home to Sutton Coldfield where he was buried by his family with full and appropriate military honours.

Equally tragic, Edward Gunning (Day Boy, 1906) was killed in a motorbike accident while seconded to No 14 Ordnance Depot. As a captain in the Royal Field Artillery (RFA) and having

---

[366] The National Archives, Air 76/281/29 and ADM 273/12/272, Personal Record of Captain EM Knott, AFC.
[367] Supplement to *The London Gazette*, 1st January 1919, page 79.

been an instructor at the Trench Mortar School, he was an experienced adviser to the Royal Army Ordnance Corps teams disposing of unexploded ordnance. Edward was required to go quickly between the various field teams to supervise operations and to identify the various shells that were being unearthed; the disposal of a shrapnel shell was a relatively simple explosive procedure compared with the clearance of gas shells, that needed very careful and considered handling and storage. On 6th June, while riding his motorbike between inspections, Edward was involved in an accident and suffered a badly fractured skull. Although he was rushed to the base hospital in Calais, Edward died from his injuries that evening.

Such deaths associated with post-Armistice duties were included in official casualty figures, even after the Treaty was signed. Indeed, the Imperial War Graves Commission continued routinely to include other deaths associated with wartime service that occurred after the Armistice in their figures until 1923. This became an enduring and established practice as serious long-term wounds and injuries proved to be fatal. Before the war Raymond Taylor (Cheltondale,1899) was an established London solicitor at Gray's Inn Square in London. Although his family hailed from Bromley, he lived with his wife Harriet and infant son John, at The Dingle, Blenheim Road, St Albans. However, with manpower needed for the army, Raymond was conscripted in late 1916 as a gunner in the Honourable Artillery Company. After training he was sent on active service to France with 2A/B Battery but was badly gassed at St Julien near Ypres during the Battle of Passchendaele in October 1917 and invalided back to England. During his convalescence, Raymond and his family moved back to Birch Cottage, Shortlands, to be near to his parents living in Bromley. His recovery was slow, and the effects of the gas continued to incapacitate him, so much so that he was medically discharged on 10th December 1918 as unfit for military service. He finally succumbed to his illness and died from pulmonary tuberculosis on 12th April 1919, the infection being initiated and aggravated by the gas poisoning some 18 months before. Similarly, Howard Walker (Boyne House, 1907) lived for five years before his injuries became fatal. He had been the senior prefect at College, also playing in the rugby XV in 1906 and 1907. He died on 3rd June 1919 at the RAF's Central Hospital at Finchley from the effects of wounds he received in action in 1914 with the 2nd Battalion, Welsh Regiment.

Other cases of long-term injury attributed to wartime service were also accepted in the official casualty figures. Having been seriously wounded in action, the slow, physical decline of John Moll (Southwood, 1911) presents another poignant story. Educated at the College's Junior School, John was clearly very bright, winning academic scholarships first to College and then to Oxford University, where he read classics at Keble. After the outbreak of war, John was still studying at Oxford but applied for a commission on 25th November 1914 and was gazetted as a second lieutenant in the RFA on 7th December.[368] He served in France in the 21st Divisional Ammunition Column, 95th Brigade, but on 21st June 1916, just before the start of the Battle of the Somme, he received a very serious machine gun bullet wound to his spine that left him paraplegic. Evacuated to England on 8th July from Boulogne, he was nursed in the Empire Hospital in Westminster. Declared permanently unfit for future military service due

---

[368] *The London Gazette*, 8th December 1914, page 10451.

to his paralysis, John resigned his commission on 9th January 1919, but was allowed to retain the honorary rank of lieutenant. However, his condition sadly deteriorated throughout the year and he died from his injury and associated complications at the Empire Hospital on 21st September 1919, six weeks after the Foundation Stone was set in place in the College cloisters. Yet another sad end to a very bright and promising life.

For many serving Old Cheltonians, the squalid conditions they had to endure at the battlefront, coupled to the associated privations of food, comfort and shelter, left many with such weakened physiological constitutions that they were unable to resist the sickness and illnesses contracted by so many at and after the end of the war. Owen Thomas (Cheltondale, 1907) was a fit, athletic young man when at College, a member of the shooting VIII in 1906 and the hockey XI the following year. Commissioned into the Royal Engineers in May 1915, Owen saw active service in Gallipoli, where, however, he contracted a strain of tuberculosis, which worsened progressively. Serving later in France during the summer of 1916, he fell ill again and was deemed medically unfit for active service. He left his unit on 16th July 1916, at the height of the Battle of the Somme and at a time when the British army needed every experienced gunner they had. Yet, so serious was Owen's case, that he was invalided home from France on board the SS *Salta* from Le Havre to Southampton on 24th July with pulmonary tuberculosis of the lungs. He was granted six months' sick leave initially and convalesced in St Leonards-on-Sea. However, no better by November, he applied to the War Office for a special leave of absence abroad in Switzerland, to recuperate having been offered accommodation by the British Red Cross Society through the good offices of Lady Georgina, the Countess of Dudley. His case was supported by Dr J Kincaid Etlinger, the medical superintendent of the Pinewood Sanatorium in Wokingham, and by Lady Georgina herself, who endorsed his case by writing to the War Office on 30th November. His sick leave was extended until 24th May 1917 with permission to travel to Switzerland granted by the War Office providing that: 'Plain clothes must be worn when embarking and on-board ship and in Switzerland.'[369] Once in Switzerland, where it was thought that the clear air would benefit his lungs, Owen convalesced at the Alexandra Hotel in Arosa, accompanied by his wife, Jessica, and under the care of Dr Amrein, the head physician at the Altein-Arosa Sanatorium. But by May, with his leave close to expiring, his condition had not improved. So, he wrote again to the War Office on 6th May, personally supported by Lady Georgina, requesting a further six months' sick leave reporting that, *'my wife has written this for me as I am not able to write many letters'*. The War Office approved this further extension, but, given his long-term illness and his doctor's rather pessimistic prognosis, Owen was asked to relinquish his commission, which he did on 10th December 1917, although he was granted the honorary rank of second lieutenant. On 3rd March 1919, after a long and gallant struggle with his illness, Owen died of pulmonary tuberculosis complicated by tuberculosis of the intestine contracted in Gallipoli, and, importantly for the lawyers, whilst he was subject to Military Law. As his last day of active service was not within three years of his date of death, Jessica was forced into a dispute with the post-Armistice authorities in a protracted and unsupportive exchange of letters

---

[369] The National Archives, War Office Letter, WO 142835/1(A.G.4c), dated 2nd December 1916.

regarding widow's benefits and pensions. It must have been hard enough for Jessica to witness the slow decline and death of her once muscular and energetic husband, without the soul-destroying battle with officialdom that would no doubt have intruded unsympathetically on her personal sorrow.

James Dearden (Day Boy, 1913) survived much hard fighting throughout the war from 1914 onwards, being awarded the Distinguished Service Order, the Military Cross and Bar, and mentioned in despatches on three separate occasions. Having been wounded twice in two earlier actions he was back on duty at the Front in France when on 26th August 1918, he reported sick with suspected pulmonary tuberculosis, 'having been feeling ill for about a fortnight and coughing up blood' as reported by his medical officer. He was quickly evacuated back to England to recover and spent the next year at various sanatoria to convalesce. But his condition slowly but steadily deteriorated and his last assessment at his nursing home in Bournemouth reported that 'there are signs of extensive mischief in both lungs, and his evening temperature is often over 100'. Wanting to be discharged from the sanatorium and be allowed to live his last few months at home, he finally succumbed to his injuries and died there at Mostar, Queens Road, Cheltenham on 6th October 1919 with his cousin by his bedside. His death certificate gave three causes of death; shell gas poisoning, pulmonary tuberculosis, and tubercular meningitis. He was buried at St Peter's Church in Leckhampton, close to College and his boyhood memories. He was only 23 years of age.

JAMES FERRAND DEARDEN,
D.S.O., M.C. (2 Bars)
Captain, Royal Fusiliers,
Died at Cheltenham, of illness contracted on Active Service, 6th October, 1919, Age 23.

James Dearden DSO MC

Although the Armistice brought a cessation to hostilities between the major belligerents and signatory nations, more local warfare in peripheral regions of the world that were attributions to the wider strategic struggle continued after 1918. These regions included Egypt, the North West Frontier, Russia (where bitter post-revolution fighting between the Red and White Russian armies continued) and Ireland, as the republican war against Britain gained momentum towards final independence in 1922. In each of these secondary conflict areas, all of them associated consequences of the Great War, Old Cheltonians served and died.

During 1919 in Egypt, Albert Hazel (Boyne House, 1895) was serving overseas in a civilian capacity in the Egyptian Civil Service. He had won the Silver Mathematics Medal in 1893 before leaving College with a scholarship to Hertford College, Oxford where he gained a double first in mathematics. Throughout the War he was attached to the General Headquarters in Cairo as a civilian adviser. His contribution was clearly significant and noteworthy, as he was mentioned by General Allenby in his commander-in-chief's despatches and awarded an OBE.[370] Albert became responsible for recruiting native labour, holding the honorary rank of lieutenant colonel and for this work was awarded the CBE, albeit posthumously, in June 1919. During the civil unrest regarding Egyptian independence from British authority that followed the Armistice, there was considerable hostility towards British officials, and Albert was killed

---

[370] See *The London Gazette* of 16th and 7th January 1918 respectively.

by a sniper while performing his civil/military duties near Deirut. He was buried at the Cairo War Memorial cemetery where his grave is recorded by the Commonwealth War Graves Commission using his honorary rank. His wife Marie, and their two small children, then made the long, lonely journey back to their home in Wolverhampton.

In 1919 Waziristan, on the North West Frontier between India and Afghanistan, was riven by crisis as fiercely independent Mahsud, Waziri and Baluchi tribesman, sensing British military weakness and preoccupation with fighting the Great War, had sensed advantage and launched raids attempting to gain control in the administered regions. British forces, in a portent of what would recur nearly a century later, were therefore sent to quell the unrest. Reginald Wallace-Copland (Southwood, 1913) was killed in action on 16th July 1919 at Fort Sandeman, now the town of Zhob, leading a relief force making its way to support the besieged British garrison.

Reginald Wallace-Copland

In a letter dated 20th July to his father from Reginald's commanding officer at Fort Sandeman in Baluchistan, Reginald's final moments were described:

Dear Sir,

You will before have received the sad news of your son's death in action on 16th instant. As his Commanding Officer I offer you my heartfelt sympathy in your great loss, but hope that the gallant way in which he met his death will do much to lessen your grief. Your son, Captain [Wallace-] Copland, was commanding an escort that had been sent out to bring in a convoy of stores etc to Fort Sandeman. About eight miles out the column met with a band of 1,600 Waziris. This was about 4pm, and a desperate fight for the position barring the road ensued. Eye witnesses tell me that Captain Copland behaved in a most gallant manner, repeatedly gathering his men together and leading them in an endeavour to capture the position. During one of these attacks he was shot at close quarters through the head. Death was instantaneous. He had a desperate task, but never faltered, and met his death like a true soldier.

He is greatly missed in a Battalion in which he was a great favourite with officers and men alike.

Yours very truly, (Signed) A.B.R. PEARSE.[371]

Reginald is commemorated on the Delhi Memorial (India Gate), as is Percy Mottram (Day Boy, 1900). A soldier from 1900, Percy had fought in the South African War, receiving the

[371] *The Cheltonian,* 1920, page 394.

Queen's Medal with three clasps, and then through the Great War firstly with the Cheshire Regiment, before being transferred to the 109th Infantry Battalion of the Indian Army. He was killed in action at Manjhi in Waziristan on 6th October 1919 fighting against a localised Pashtun uprising. Four months later, on 10th February 1920, Thomas Catterson-Smith (Boyne House, 1906) died of wounds in Rawalpindi. As a young career officer in the Indian Army, he was awarded the Royal Humane Society Bronze Medal for attempting to save the life of an Indian soldier from the Indus river, and later served with the 12th Pioneers seeing active service in Mesopotamia. As a captain, he won the Distinguished Service Order for operations in Afghanistan and Waziristan:

> For gallantry at Pioneer Piquet, on 21st December 1919. Owing to the retirement of the covering party, his working party was suddenly attacked in force and surrounded. By his coolness, sound leadership, and example, he inspired his men and repulsed five assaults. Though twice wounded he remained in control, and did not withdraw his command till all ammunition had been expended.[372]

Owing to the severity of his wounds received at Pioneer Picquet, Thomas remained in a critical condition; he sadly died at Rawalpindi Hospital and was buried in the British cemetery.

Nine days earlier, Francis Prichard (Southwood, 1906) died from typhus whilst on operations with British Military Mission in Novorossiysk, South Russia. The mission was part of a multi-national effort supporting the anti-Bolshevik White forces in their struggle against emergent communism. His is an interesting story as he spent much of the Great War interned in Holland. A scholar at College, Francis decided to follow a military career and gained immediate entry to the Royal Military Academy at Woolwich and was commissioned as a subaltern in the Royal Garrison Artillery on 29th July 1908.[373]

After serving in Mauritius, he was seconded to the fledgling Royal Flying Corps and conducted flying training at the Bristol Flying School gaining his Aviator's Certificate (No 733) and

Francis Prichard

'wings' on 10th February 1914, almost six months before the war broke out. He went on to the Central Flying School at Upavon for further training, before being promoted to captain in October. He was therefore one of the earlier aviators in the war, becoming particularly adept in artillery cooperation and observation, skills that would become essential as the war progressed. On 2nd June 1915 while based at Oxelaere near Cassel with No 8 Squadron he was flying as an observer in BE 2c (Serial No 1653) on a strategic reconnaissance deep into enemy-occupied Belgium to determine the quantities of German rolling stock in stations and sidings. Just north of Bruges his aircraft suffered a loss of

---

[372] *The London Gazette*, 27th November 1920.
[373] *The London Gazette*, 21st August 1908, page 6147.

pressure in the gravity tank with only two gallons of fuel left. His pilot Captain Arthur Gaye force landed in the sand dunes in neutral Holland some 400 yards from the frontier. They attempted to destroy the aircraft to avoid it falling into enemy hands but failed as so little petrol was left. Arrested by the Dutch police, Francis and Arthur were interned in Holland for the next three and a half years. After being repatriated in 1918, he was deployed as part of the British Military Mission in South Russia and the Caucasus. His death on 1st February 1920 at Novorossiysk was due to a rapid onset of typhus. This was attributed to his weakened physical condition, deemed to be a consequence of his military service and extended internment during the war.

Not dissimilar was the case of Charles Elliott (Day Boy, 1888). Another career soldier, Charles had served as a field engineer in the 1903 Tibet Expedition, serving at the action at Niani, the operations in and around Gyantse and the march to Lhasa. His exemplary active service overseas from July 1915 was finally recognised with his award of the Distinguished Service Order on 1st January 1917; he had also been mentioned in despatches on four occasions. On 3rd June 1919, Charles was made a Companion of the Most Distinguished Order of St Michael and St George. Just eight weeks later he was suddenly taken ill when serving as an acting brigadier, whilst immersed in providing facilities for the British forces deployed to the North West Frontier. Charles' personal file contains a memorandum dated 9th January 1920 from the assistant quartermaster general in Rawalpindi, Major R Luppard, to the chief royal engineer, which depicts the workload Charles was under:

> There is no doubt that the late Lieut Col Elliott was suffering from overwork and his weak state was owing to his devotion to duty in the unusual heat and urgent calls on him through war demands, especially to the preparation of the several war Hospitals necessary in this station.[374]

Charles died from cholera at the 19th British General Hospital in Rawalpindi where he was buried in the British War Cemetery. Such a tragedy after the Armistice would have been even more acutely felt by his family back in England, as his younger brother, Reginald had been killed leading his company in an attack at Festubert in 1914.

Perhaps a little less prominent and decorated, though equally deserving of tribute, is Walter Sidebottom (Leconfield, 1902). The younger son of a wealthy cotton trader, Walter grew up in Cheshire with his brother Robert, who on leaving College joined the army. Walter, however, went on to study forestry management at the Royal Indian Engineering College in Egham.[375]

Walter appears to have been somewhat of a 'free spirit', as over the next 15 years, he undertook a distinct amount of travelling overseas, although whether this was concerned with the family's cotton business or for his business interests is unclear. In 1909, for

---

[374] The National Archives, WO 374/22412, Personal File of Lieutenant Colonel CA Elliott.
[375] The site, close to the RAF Runneymede Memorial, later became the Runneymede Campus of Brunel University.

example, Walter visited China and the United States, returning to Liverpool on Cunard's RMS *Coronia* on 16th May.[376] Three years later, he travelled to Hong Kong, returning to visit San Francisco and Vancouver via Hawaii aboard the SS *Nile*. Brother Robert died early in the war, killed in action at Le Cateau in 1914. Walter eventually joined the army in February 1916 at the recruiting office in Knutsford, close to the family home in Alderley Edge, and a month before conscripted service came into force. Enlisted in the 4th Dragoon Guards, as Trooper Sidebottom, he served in France from June 1916, fighting throughout the Battle of the Somme until he was sent home to England for training at Officer Cadet School. However, for some reason he was not commissioned and was returned to the 5th General Base Depot in Rouen at the beginning of February 1917. Perhaps he found depot life boring or was a little too nonconformist in a disciplined military environment and was clearly incompatible with wartime military service, as he soon learned. Five weeks later, he was confined to camp for seven days and forfeited three days pay for being absent from stables and failing to attend guard mounting parade. On 9th April he was awarded 10 days confinement to camp and forfeited seven days pay for being absent from duty for 36 hours. Barely a month later, Walter absented himself again for 26 hours and was awarded seven days' Field Punishment No 1, on the completion of which he was posted to the 7th Dragoon Guards in the field. He settled quickly back into the routines and activity of his regiment as he was promoted to corporal soon afterwards. Just before the start of the German spring offensive the following year, he was seriously wounded by shell fire on 4th April, and the next day he was taken to No 2 Surgical Hospital at Abbeville to have the injuries to his left leg, left arm, right knee, and his head treated. But the severity of his injuries warranted immediate evacuation to England, and on 6th April Walter was put on a hospital ship and transported to the Eastern General Hospital, Cambridge for further treatment, nursing and convalescence. However, his wounds became infected and, with the onset of sharp chest pains, the doctors diagnosed pleurisy. There then followed a slow decline in his condition. On 29th November he was discharged from the army as no longer fit for military service, returning home to Alderley Edge where his health continued to deteriorate. Walter eventually died over two years later, on 9th January 1921, from the infection and subsequent illness that was precipitated by his injuries from action on the Western Front. Strangely, his record of service and associated details of death were not recorded in either the College Register or the Imperial War Graves Commission records.

Walter Sidebottom at College

Walter was by no means the only such anomaly. Edmund Marsden (Day Boy, 1905), another Old Cheltonian career soldier and Sandhurst graduate, had been appointed to the Indian Staff Corps in 1901. He served on the Tibet Expedition in 1903-04, receiving

---

[376] *RMS Coronia* was the ship that sent the first warnings of icebergs to *RMS Titanic* on 14th April 1912. She later served as a troopship during the First World War.

the campaign medal with clasp. He was also a good cricketer and played two first class matches for Gloucestershire in 1909, the same year he was promoted to captain and attached to the 64th Pioneers. Edmund remained in India but was deployed to Burma to support the military police quelling local tribal disturbances. He died of malarial fever while serving as the transport officer on construction and defensive duties at Mytkyina, Burma on 26th May 1915 during the Kachin Uprising. However, these operations and the deaths incurred undertaking them, were not initially considered by the government of the day to be associated with, or attributed to, the First World War. Thus, the contributions, injuries and deaths of the participants in these actions in Burma were for decades overlooked and largely forgotten. However, information collected later by the Commonwealth War Graves Commission formed a case for Captain Edmund Marsden, 64th Pioneers, Indian Army, to be classified as a war casualty. The case, which was submitted in 2006, was accepted by the Ministry of Defence and Edmund is remembered fittingly alongside the 701 other Old Cheltonians to fall in the Great War.

The final Old Cheltonian to die as a consequence of the war was John Wogan-Browne (Hazelwell, 1914).

He was in the same year and House as the young Cyril Hillier, the skilful cricketer from the 1914 XI whose account featured at the start of this narrative. While Cyril joined the infantry at the outbreak of the war, John chose the Royal Artillery, first in France during 1915 and subsequently in Salonika from November 1915 to April 1919. After a short spell in Egypt, first as the adjutant of two artillery units and lastly as the aide de camp of the general officer commanding, he returned home and was detached to Ireland as part of the increasing number of British security forces garrisoned there to counter growing Irish republicanism. The Irish Republican Army had been a constant thorn in the side of the British government ever since the Easter Rising in 1916, when republican volunteers began their short insurrection seeking the opportunity for driving their independence agenda forward, while political and strategic focus and attention in Britain remained fixed on the war against Germany. By 1922, John was stationed with his battery in Kildare, close to his parents' home at Keredern. Being somewhat of a local man, he was well known and popular amongst the local community irrespective of class or politics. John became one of the war's last victims. A memorandum on his personal file records that:

John Wogan-Browne at College

On the 10th Feb 1922, a lieutenant of the 48th Battery, RFA, Kildare received a cheque of £135 from his Commanding Officer for the weekly payment of men of their Battery. He cashed the cheque at the (Hibernian) Bank, about 500 yards distant from the barracks, but when returning he was attacked by armed civilians who shot him dead and stole the money.[377]

Another statement noted that the civilians escaped in a motor car, and that John was unarmed as relations between the civilian population and military had been very peaceful. Four civilians were later arrested for his murder but then released without charge as no one would give evidence against them. No doubt the element of fear and retribution played heavily on the community as there was deeply-felt sympathy for the family throughout the county. At midday on Tuesday, 14th February 1922, after a Requiem Mass held in his honour, John was buried at Naas Cemetery, within sight of the Wicklow Mountains, with full military honours. His coffin carried slowly by gun carriage was draped in the Union Flag on which his service cap and officer's sword were placed. John's death marked another significant final chapter; as the only son, the family name and the estate at Keredern, which for generations had been at the centre of county affairs, passed into history.

Brothers in Arms

Of over 3,540 Old Cheltonians that served during the war, many fathers, sons and brothers served together and some, such as the Winterbothams and the Lowrys, even saw action alongside each other in the same battalions. In certain families, up to seven of their menfolk went to war. Sadly, 38 sets of brothers died during the war, including three cases where three brothers were killed, with devastating effects on the families concerned. The grief and anguish of these families is unimaginable as, in many cases, the bodies of their loved ones simply disappeared, and there was no grave on which to focus the process of grieving. Arthur and Ethel Mather, for example, lost three of their seven sons all of whom were educated at College as day boys, growing up in the town in Parabola Road. John was killed at Ypres in 1915, Ellis on the Somme the following year, and Robert during the German spring offensive in 1918. None of their bodies was found: all three are commemorated on different memorials to the missing. Their other sons thankfully survived: William, a pre-war farmer in South Africa, was a corporal in the Hussars; Horace, a qualified doctor, served in the Royal Army Medical Corps; Oswald was a career soldier in the Indian Army and fought in Mesopotamia; and finally, Charles was in the North West Frontier Police in Canada where he remained on duty throughout the war years.

As recounted earlier, William and Annie Lowry lost three sons, all killed in action; their eldest son William, during 1915 in Gallipoli, and then both Cyril and Auriol in 1918 fighting in France. Only Auriol's body was found and gently laid to rest in the peaceful cemetery at Neuville St Vaast.

---

[377] The National Archives, WO 339/43238, Personal File of Lieutenant JH Wogan-Browne.

William Grieve   James Grieve at College, standing second right   Charles Grieve

Finally, William and Margaret Grieve had two sons killed before the Armistice; William at Ypres in February 1915 and James at Arras in April 1918.

When later widowed, Margaret had only her sons' medals to treasure alongside the many touching letters of condolence she had received from their comrades; in just one such example, James' commanding officer wrote:

> I am writing to let you know how very much we all feel the loss of Major Grieve. I have known him for a long time, during which he served under me, and during which time he has done brilliant work.
>
> He was killed by a German shell while giving orders to his battery on 4th April. He always showed the greatest courage and disregard for danger in carrying out his duty, and set a fine example to his officers and men, who had the greatest regard and respect for him.
>
> I remember well on one occasion he registered his battery east of Trônes Wood, on the Somme, in 1916, laying out his map and taking angles to get a datum point, under heavy fire, perfectly cool all the time, for which I am glad to say he got his Military Cross.[378]

For William and Margaret their personal anguish was not over with the signing of the Armistice. Although their eldest son, Charles, survived the war seeing more than his share of action with 2nd Battalion, Cameron Highlanders and later as a brigade major, he was killed accidentally on 20th September 1920 while stationed in the British garrison in Cork as part of the security forces. To lose any family member to war is tragic enough, but for families who lost three sons, the grief and sorrow is simply indescribable.

Other families had mixed wartime experiences. Although Richard Bingham (Cheltondale, 1915) was killed in action near Cambrai in 1918 when flying with No 209 Squadron, the Royal

---

[378] *Old Androvian News*, 2018 edition, page 4.

Air Force, his elder brother George (Cheltondale, 1912) served in the Royal Welch Fusiliers and survived. Furthermore, three other brothers, who were educated elsewhere, also survived; brother Edward winning the Victoria Cross at Jutland in 1916. A similar family story applies to the Grogan family. Brigadier Edward Grogan served during the war and survived. He had sent his two sons by his second marriage to College, Gerald leaving in 1901 and James in 1908. Both were killed during the war at Ypres in 1918 and in Gallipoli in 1915 respectively. However, they had three half-brothers by Edward's first marriage, all of whom survived, with George, the eldest of the five, and also a brigadier, winning the Victoria Cross in May 1918. Other families managed to navigate through the dreadful experience of war relatively unscathed. The Shelmerdine family, three brothers and their two cousins, all survived the war having all been college prefects and renowned sportsmen when at school; their long family association with College and Newick House spans well over a century.

After the Armistice, as Old Cheltonians returned from the war to renew relationships and restart their lives and professions at home, many households had conspicuous and painful gaps at the dinner table. Often, it was the mothers who bore the burden of adjusting their families to post-war realities, family remembrance and sorrow. Perhaps this offers a fitting perspective with which to close this narrative. Amy Cousins was mother to Brian and Harry Coomber (Cheltondale, 1905 and 1902) and remarried after their father's untimely death, before the boys went to College. Harry was the eldest of the two brothers and had emigrated to start ranching at Kootenay Lake, Canada. When war was declared he enlisted as a private in the 7th Battalion (British Columbia Regiment), becoming a member of the first contingent of the Canadian Expeditionary Force. Shortly after his arrival in England he applied for a commission in the Royal Garrison Artillery and, after officer and gunnery training, was gazetted as a second lieutenant on 28th December 1915. After two years of continual operations on the Western Front, Harry was awarded the Military Cross in July 1918 for his bravery during the German spring offensive earlier in April:

> For conspicuous gallantry and devotion to duty. This officer directed the withdrawal of guns, in full daylight, under heavy shell fire, and with enemy aeroplanes flying at 100 feet plastering them with machine gun fire. Two guns were got clear, with six wagonloads of stores and ammunition, two men and two horses being wounded, and he only left when all available wagons had been sent away.[379]

Seriously wounded in this action Harry was taken to the Base Hospital at Rouen where he subsequently died on 29th April 1918, his award being made posthumously. His mother Amy wrote to the War Office, dated 8th November 1921:

> I beg to apply for, as I have not yet received, the medals of my son Lt Harry Alan Coomber MC who died of wounds on 29th April 1918. My son was a Lieutenant, Kent Heavy Battery RGA, attached to the 138th Heavy Battery RGA at the time of his

---

[379] Supplement to *The London Gazette*, 26th July 1918, page 8789.

death. He came over with the first Canadian Expeditionary Force and served as a private in the 7th British Columbia Regiment, arriving in this country in September 1914 and going to France in February 1915 and being wounded for the first time in June 1916. I applied to the Canadian authorities in respect of the medals on a card forwarded by them to me, but they say that as my son was holding a commission in the Imperial Service at the time of his death, application for the British War and Victory Medals should be made to you. I would be obliged if you would acknowledge and if you will inform me what medals my son was entitled to, and when I am likely to receive them.

I am, your obedient servant, Amy F Cousins.[380]

Clearly, Amy was aware that Harry had been awarded the Military Cross posthumously, and perhaps when finally she received his medals she looked on them with mixed emotion, undoubtedly with great sadness but also with immense pride.

Harry was just one of this remarkable generation of Old Cheltonians, whose striking testimony in these pages epitomises the ethos of their schooldays, when courage, teamwork, friendship and service were inculcated in these men from a very early age. Their indomitable endurance and determination remain a shining example of unselfish service to the many Cheltonians, boys and girls, that follow in their footsteps. In our modern era of globalisation and the digital world it may be regarded as unfashionable to comment on such feelings of duty, stoicism, altruism and patriotism. Yet, these personal attributes leave an indelible mark on history, a standard for successors to match, and a rich legacy to treasure.

Legacy

In the spring term of 1919, relief that the fighting had ended was palpable at College. Thoughts naturally turned to the human costs that this dreadful conflict had incurred and the legacies it might leave. *The Cheltonian* magazine at the beginning of that year recorded the sentiment and perspective:

> At last, after thirteen terms of war, we have returned to school if not in peace-time at least with a cessation of fighting. There are, we are told, only five boys left who were in the Senior Department in that July of 1914, which ended our old summer world of exams and cricket and all the rest of it. And all of us who fill Chapel this term, are just about the same in number as those other Cheltenham boys who will not return to it again, from France or Belgium or the East. If the new world is to be made a happier place, we shall have paid our full share of the price in making it so.

[380] The National Archives, WO 374/15263, Personal Record of Lieutenant HA Coomber MC.

Of all the schools, colleges and universities whose alumni went to war after August 1914, the legacy of the Great War generation of Old Cheltonians is exhibited in almost unparalleled fashion. Their collective distinction has been recognised in several unique ways, which collectively leave a lasting example for the many other Cheltonians to follow.

The nucleus of these tributes at College is the Chapel. The Foundation Stone in the Memorial Cloisters, laid on 4th July 1919 by Lord Lee of Fareham, reads 'In Memory of Six Hundred and Seventy Five Old Cheltonians who gave their lives in the Great War 1914-1919'. Since then, the main West Door has ceased to be used as the regular entrance to chapel and access since is usually made through the Cloisters. Above the Stone is a long shelf where a wreath of crimson poppies has been placed on every subsequent Remembrance Day since the Armistice. With Chapel remaining a focal point for the pastoral and moral well-being of College, and a perpetual and constituent part in its daily routine, successive generations of students and staff have passed this tribute several times each week during term time and they continue to do so. Immediately after the Memorial Cloisters were completed, the custom whereby pupils were expected to pay their respects to their fallen forbears by remaining silent and removing their hands from their pockets was quickly adopted. It remains encouraged today. In so doing, one hundred years after the Armistice, the Cheltonian community remains faithful to the dignified and moving words written by Reverend Reginald Waterfield, the principal of the College throughout the war years, and inscribed above the window in the Cloisters:

> You that would enter here to worship God,
> Think of your brothers who before you trod
> These walks and ways, and did not grudge to give
> Their lives in war that you in peace might live.
> Ask for a heart to follow in the way
> Of sacrifice and duty. Pass and pray.

Within the Chapel itself, a surprisingly large space that can accommodate the entire population of students and staff while retaining a peaceful atmosphere for prayer and reflection, one's eye is quickly attracted to the individual shining brass plaques, not just a memorial for each of the Old Cheltonians that fell during the Great War, but also for those who subsequently died from injuries and illnesses associated with the conflict.[381]

Memorial Plaques in College Chapel

---

[381] The anticipated figure for the College's student population for Autumn 2018 was expected to be in the region of 720. There are also brass plaques in the Chapel commemorating 55 Old Cheltonians who were killed in the South African War. The 363 Old Cheltonians who were killed in the Second World War are commemorated in the Dining Hall, the original chapel, alongside the previous Sovereign's Colours presented to the College.

The College's first Sovereign's Colours

The number of individual plaques in Chapel well exceeds the 675 Old Cheltonians enumerated on the Foundation Stone as more individual cases came to light after its initial consecration. Even a century on, further research at The National Archives has revealed yet another eight Old Cheltonians whose deaths were a consequence of service during the war; their tribute plaques have now been placed in the Chapel alongside those of their former school friends and comrades. Now the total has reached 702; a figure that is to have its own permanent place of record and honour. Set in stone beside the Cloisters in the rose garden it will provide a most appropriate and peaceful setting, in the sunshine looking out on to College Field.

On the morning of Saturday, 23rd July 1921, the College's Corps of Drums marched on to College Field from under the shadows of the Chapel. Followed by the entire Officers' Training Corps, the drums and bugles thumped out a quick march; boots, brasses and bayonets glinting in the summer sunshine. The contingent came to a smart halt abeam the old Victorian gymnasium (now referred to as 'Lower Gym'), right turned, and dressed off to the right. The officers took post, and when all was set, arms (rifles) were ordered, and the parade was stood at ease.[382] An air of hush, mixed with reverential expectancy, descended on the gathering, with only the odd charabanc spluttering its way along Sandford

[382] When the command 'Order Arms' was given by the parade commander, rifles were brought from the shoulder to the ground and held upright.

The Colours – Presentation Parade

Road breaking the calm. On the sharp words of command, the contingent came to attention with guardsman-like precision as members of the reviewing party arrived and took their positions. In pride of place and guest of honour was Lieutenant General Michael Willoughby, who at 88 years of age was still an active member of the College Council and the last survivor of the very first intake of students to enter College in 1841. To him fell the great honour and privilege of presenting the two new Royal Colours to the College with the gracious permission of His Majesty the King and with the approval and sanction of the Army Council.[383]

In his short address, General Willoughby stressed the three core principles, displayed by Old Cheltonians on active service since the school's foundation, that had underpinned the granting and Royal Assent of such a prestigious and unprecedented distinction; duty, devotion and discipline.

With the formal presentation complete, the contingent proudly marched off with its two new Colours at the head of the parade, swaying gamely together to the bugle tune and drumbeat.

Over its history, Old Cheltonians have won 14 Victoria Crosses (six of which were during the First World War) alongside a plethora of other awards for gallantry and distinguished military service. For such a record of military contribution to the nation's defence, it was

[383] The Sovereign's Colour, based on the Union Flag, and the College's Colour.

The College Memorial at the National Arboretum

the first English non-military school to be presented with Sovereign and College Colours; the only other school to be similarly honoured later was Eton. These colours are paraded by the Combined Cadet Force each year, with new colours being presented to the College periodically; the last by the Princess Royal in 2000. These colours are the focus of the College's annual remembrance events and are paraded on other special occasions. For example, on the evening of 8th May 2004 at the Menin Gate in Ypres, as the haunting bugle notes of the Last Post echoed across the old battlefields where so many Old Cheltonians still lie, the College Colours, accompanied by a cadet Colour Guard, were dipped in silent but moving tribute in honour of their forbears who fell 90 years before. The following day in St George's Church, the College memorial to the Old Cheltonians who gave their lives in the conflict was rededicated.

On 7th October 2012, The Right Reverend James Longstaff, the Bishop of Rochester, consecrated a stone of remembrance in the National Memorial Arboretum at Alrewas in Staffordshire. It reads:

> To the memory of former pupils from Cheltenham College who have served in wars and campaigns since 1841.

Cheltenham College was the first school to have its own memorial at the National Memorial Arboretum.

Depicting an open book waiting to be read, the stone is symbolic of the story of over 6,000 Old Cheltonians that have served in the nation's military forces, and at the heart of which lies the loss of the 702 from the First World War. Portraying this central theme is a lectern board beside the memorial outlining the College's significant military history. It was generously and most fittingly donated by Doctor Bridget Jepson, the niece of Desmond Scott (Hazelwell, 1914), killed in action in 1916 at Pozières serving with 54th Battery, 39th Brigade, RFA; he was 19 years of age and barely two years out of school.

In addition to these significant physical symbols of collegial heritage, perhaps there is one further, even more important, legacy which acts as a subliminal compass to successive cohorts of College students. The honest values that the Old Cheltonians of the First World War held, including those of service, duty and altruism, are aspirational ideals that continue to resonate. They represent the sum of all the individual motivations, attributes and contributions of every Old Cheltonian who has served in the armed forces, but especially those who fought in the First World War, that manifests itself today in the various symbols of legacy. To follow in their footsteps, with the development, encouragement and sustainment of a positive and constructive attitude, is perhaps the most substantial legacy of all.

This gently concealed but powerfully applied ethos is one that future Cheltonians can embrace and instil not only in themselves, but also in their families and communities. The distinction which the Old Cheltonian contingent of the First World War bequeathed to successive generations of alumni, though it may have been equalled, has rarely been surpassed. To borrow from the text of the Memorial Scroll, issued on behalf of King George V and sent to every family who had lost one of its members to the war, perhaps the following adaption is most appropriate to close these chapters, and encapsulates the purpose of this volume:

> These whom this book commemorates were numbered among those who, at the call of King and Country, left all that was dear to them, endured hardness, and finally passed out of the sight of men by the path of duty and self-sacrifice, giving up their own lives that others might live in freedom.
>
> Let those who come after see to it that their names be not forgotten.

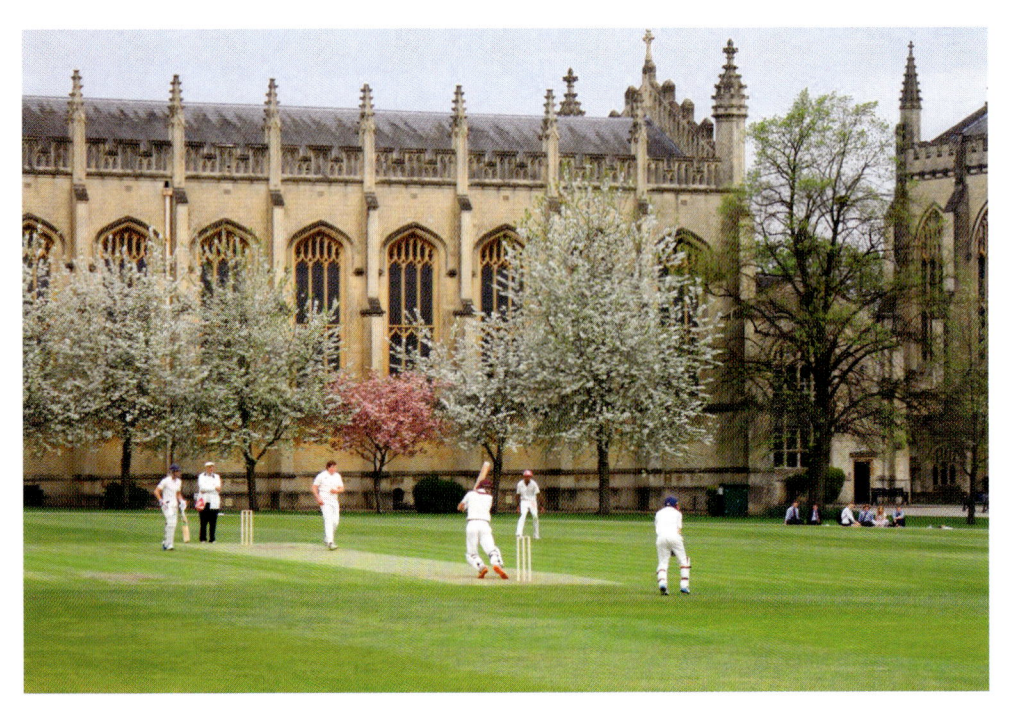

College Cricket in perpetuity (courtesy of John Jamieson-Black)

LIST OF FALLEN OLD CHELTONIANS: ARMISTICE AND BEYOND

On the following pages (294 to 295) are the names and service details of Old Cheltonians who died after Armistice Day.

ARMISTICE AND BEYOND – LIST OF FALLEN OLD CHELTONIANS

	Died	Name	Rank
668	14 November 1918	Scott LB	Lt Colonel
669	19 November 1918	Ferguson JCM	Captain
670	30 November 1918	Winter WO	Major
671	5 December 1918	Stuart CM	Cadet Gunner
672	9 December 1918	Davy JE	Major
673	18 December 1918	Dickinson HC	Lt Colonel
674	12 February 1919	Growse RH	Major
675	16 February 1919	Lascelles RH	Lt Colonel
676	2 March 1919	Longden AH	Captain
677	4 March 1919	Thomas OR	Lieutenant
678	15 March 1919	Fuller JS	Captain
679	25 March 1919	Hazel AW	Lt Colonel
680	26 March 1919	Reeves SR	Major
681	12 April 1919	Taylor RS	Gunner
682	3 May 1919	Knott EM	Captain
683	10 May 1919	Down CB	Major
684	12 May 1919	Inglis AMcC	Major
685	3 June 1919	Walker HN	Lt Colonel
686	10 June 1919	Gunning EGR	Captain
687	16 July 1919	Wallace-Copland R	Captain
688	15 August 1919	Elliott CA	Brigadier
689	26 August 1919	Geddes JG	Brigadier
690	20 September 1919	Percy-Smith V	Captain
691	21 September 1919	Moll JA	2nd Lieutenant
692	6 October 1919	Dearden JF	Captain
693	6 October 1919	Mottram PJ McQ	Captain
694	19 October 1919	Nixon ALE	Captain
695	1 February 1920	Prichard FH	Captain
696	10 February 1920	Catterson-Smith TMO	Captain
697	21 March 1920	Chesney HF	Colonel
698	2 August 1920	Lucas MH	Lt Colonel
699	22 September 1920	Grieve CC	Major
700	9 January 1921	Sidebottam W	Corporal
701	27 February 1921	Lee HW	Sergeant Major
702	10 February 1922	Wogan-Browne JH	Lieutenant

Unit	Age	Place
Royal Army Ordnance Corps	55	Le Havre, France
2nd Bedfordshire Regiment	30	Rouen, France
No 5 Railway Survey, RE	27	Douai, France
Officer Cadet Battalion, RFA	18	Brighton, UK
266th Brigade, Royal Field Artillery	29	Taranto, Italy
att King's African Rifles	34	Dar-es-Salaam, Africa
Royal Army Service Corps	31	Duren, Germany
Royal Horse Artillery	38	London, UK
5th Sherwood Foresters	38	Rugeley, UK
11th Division Signal Company, RE	29	Leysin, Switzerland
177th Brigade, Royal Field Artillery	23	Hong Kong
Egyptian Recruiting Service	42	Deirut, Egypt
Royal Garrison Artillery	41	Calcutta, India
Honourable Artillery Company	35	Shortlands, UK
No 1 Comms Squadron, RAF	20	Kenley, UK
40th Battery, Royal Garrison Artillery	36	Catterick, UK
att 6th Tank Corps, (Heavy MGC)	34	Cheltenham, UK
2nd Welch Regiment and RAF	30	Finchley, UK
Royal Field Artillery	28	Zeninghem, France
1st Gurkha Rifles	24	Sandeman, Baluchistan
Chief Royal Engineer, Waziristan	48	Rawalpindi, India
Chief Royal Artillery, IV Corps	55	Shoreham, UK
14th Royal Scots and RAF	42	Bombay, India
95th Brigade, Royal Field Artillery	27	Westminster, UK
2nd Royal Fusiliers	23	Cheltenham, UK
att 109th Indian Infantry	35	Manhji, Waziristan
Royal Army Service Corps	30	Seddlescombe, UK
No 8 Squadron, RFC	31	Novorossiysk, Russia
att 3/34th Sikh Pioneers	33	Rawalpindi, India
Royal Engineers	61	Exmouth, UK
37th Lancers	38	Shiraz, Persia
2nd Cameron Highlanders	38	Cork, Ireland
7th Dragoon Guards	37	Alderley Edge, UK
28th Australian Infantry	45	Freemantle, Australia
36th Brigade, Royal Field Artillery	35	Kildare, Ireland

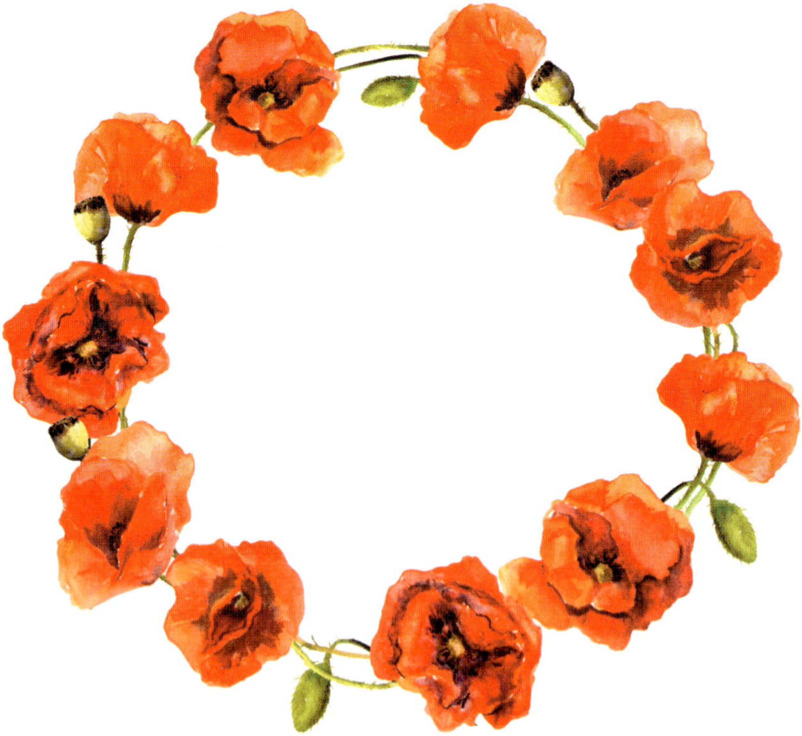

EPILOGUE

Memorialisation
by Catherine Long

As Old Cheltonians and their families began rebuilding their lives after the cessation of hostilities alongside many millions of their fellow citizens, individual responses to war began to shape the post-war nation. For those returning from war, many had to learn to reintegrate into society, making fresh efforts to earn a living and in many cases support a family, while wartime service offered them a sense of pride and a tangible connection to the Allied victory then being celebrated. From female munitions workers to men in the armed services, citizens who had taken up the mantle of supporting the war effort were now promised a 'land fit for heroes'. For many of those who had lost loved ones during the war, the Armistice prompted bitter-sweet feelings. With life on the Home Front no longer dislocated by the war, families had to rebuild their lives without brothers, fathers or sons – often while adapting to the care requirements of the wounded.

Individual response to loss is as varied as human nature. However, for centuries, the loss of a loved one in conflict has been marked by erecting a war memorial. As a tangible connection either naming or representing an individual's toil and sacrifice, war memorials are sometimes the only physical place of mourning. If a loved one's body was lost or buried in a far-flung land, a war memorial can provide an inextricable connection between community and the deceased. This in turn offers a focal point for commemoration, to mark and remind of loss. War memorials have been erected in memory of men and women who gave their lives in conflict throughout the ages. From the Seven Years War to the Battle of Waterloo, names were rarely included on war memorials, with the exception of privately commissioned tributes to an individual. When included on a regimental memorial, or one commemorating larger engagements or battles, names were largely limited to officers. This practice continued when commemorating individuals who served and died in the Anglo-Boer Wars.

The nature of total war is to focus the entire nation on warfare, calling upon its citizens to support the war effort fully through actions, contribution and service. The First World War marked the first time Britain was involved in this type of conflict. Britons could not avoid awareness of events and developments, with film newsreels shown in cinemas nationwide while newspapers provided daily commentary, updates and, increasingly ominously, casualty lists. Unlike the relatively remote and limited conflict in South Africa at the turn of the 20th Century, the shadow of conflict and the call to arms during the First World War covered every city, town and hamlet in Britain.

EPILOGUE

The most distinctive change ushered in by the First World War was the shift away from an army comprising solely of professional soldiers. As civilian men left their homes to become soldiers, sailors and airmen, volunteering at first but conscripted later, their communities had to adjust to their absence as breadwinners, employers and workers. Although most returned, millions of lives were dislocated by the loss of a loved one in active service.

The mark of this loss on the British landscape began to be noticed in 1915. A new phenomenon of street shrines began to emerge. In the form of a roll of honour, the names of those who had left to serve their country were added to each list. When news of an individual's death was delivered home, their name was marked with a cross, or similar symbol, representing that they had passed away. Street shrines tied those in a community to the names of those who had died fighting for them. Often near or within church grounds, religious symbolism was drawn upon and the 'supreme sacrifice for God, King and Country' was emphasised. This was often in an effort to justify an individual's death for the greater good and for a cause greater than the sum of its parts. At College during the early war years, such memorialisation was manifested in *The Cheltonian* magazine which identified the fallen Old Cheltonians in the many obituaries published on a regular basis.

As the war continued, individual memorials were also erected and dedicated. From a window or plaque in a church remembering the son of the local gentry to academic scholarships named after a fallen old boy, commemorative practice was heightened.

Recorded in *The Cheltonian* in June 1917 was the independent war memorial stained-glass windows in College Chapel:

> When Harold Rolleston Stables, O.C., had fallen in action in November, 1914, his sisters expressed a wish to fill one of the Chapel windows with stained glass as a memorial to their brother. Two years later, Mrs James Winterbotham offered another window as a joint memorial to her husband, who… died in March, 1914, and of their youngest son, Cyril William Winterbotham, O.C., who was killed in action in August, 1916.

This desire for an outward expression of pride and remembrance of two Old Cheltonians, Harold Rolleston Stables (Day Boy, 1905) and Cyril Winterbotham (Day Boy, 1906) demonstrates the significance of place and community for those left bereft by the war. Through these windows, Harold and Cyril would be inextricably, irreversibly and eternally united with College, associated with those individuals who would sit in Chapel for generations to come. The memorials sit alongside windows depicting the merits of Faith, Hope, Charity, Temperance, Justice, Fortitude, Wisdom and Truth. By placing the names of these two Old Cheltonians alongside the vivid depictions of Christian virtues, the explicit message is the association between their deeds and actions and the values they championed.

A symbol to represent every Old Cheltonian's contribution to the First World War was also sought. *The Cheltonian* began the debate in June 1917:

> It is surely time that we started our preparations for a War Memorial. Most other schools have already got their schemes arranged, and the time seems ripe for us to do so also… We cannot venture to forecast what the eventual plan will be but it will probably be divided into two parts, first the endowment of scholarships for the sons of fallen officers and secondly the erection of some building which will stand as an outward and visible sign of our pride in the fallen.

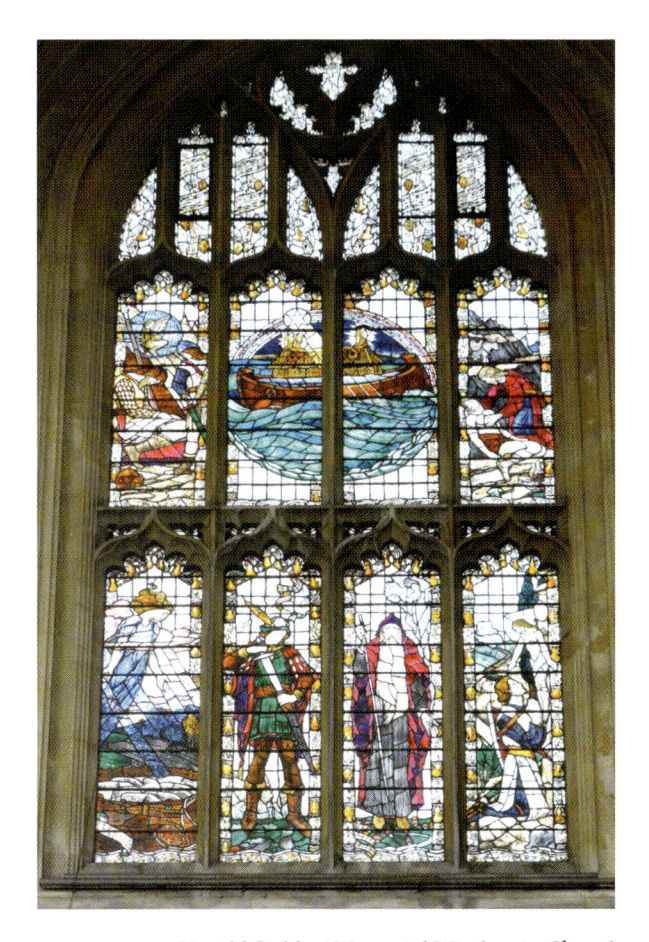

Harold Stables' Memorial Window in Chapel

Whilst the war was still being fought, the nation's communities developed and recognised the need to organise a method of commemoration of those who had served in the conflict, especially those who had died. As previously intimated, Sir Arthur Lee (Leconfield, 1886 and president of the College Council) felt strongly that after the war the College community might become preoccupied by 're-construction, the revolution of society and… not in a mood to do justice to these pious tasks.' Whilst plans were yet to be formed, the dilemma between a memorial of utilitarian benefit to the community versus a structure of aesthetic appeal and symbolism was debated by schools, churches and civic societies across Britain. College was no different.

> For some time past the building of Cloisters from the quadrangle to the Chapel has, we know, been in the minds of the authorities. But we are inclined to favour an idea suggested… namely the building of a Concert Hall… such a building would be much more useful than Cloisters, however beautiful the latter might be.

However, what the College community was in agreement about was the notion that a memorial *had to* be erected. Consequently, the Cheltenham College War Memorial Fund was established on 9th January 1918, with the purpose of erecting a fitting memorial and applying the surplus to the College Endowment Fund. A provision anticipated by the Endowment Fund was the support of provision of education at College for sons of Old Cheltonians who had died in the war. The ambition of ensuring descendants of Old Cheltonians education was upheld was maintained as a core principle. Sir Arthur Lee articulated the thought that:

> our pious duty, that we owe not merely to our old school but to ourselves, to see that there is no Old Cheltonian who has laid down his life for his country who shall have no memorial and who shall have perished as though he had never been.

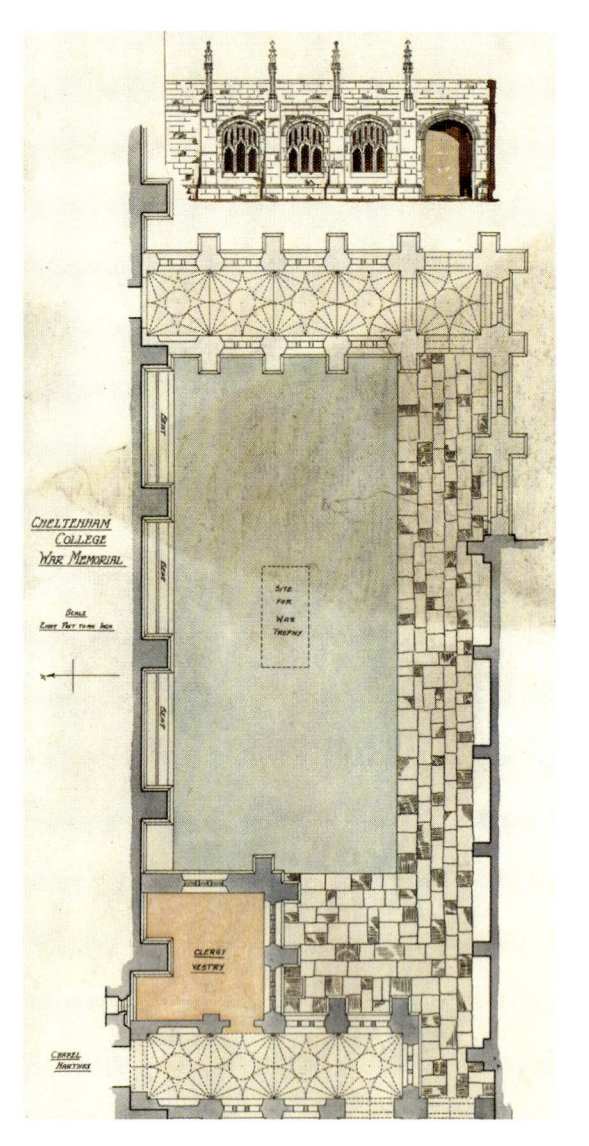

The plan for the Memorial Cloisters

This ambition was echoed by the sentiments of his school colleague Sir Alfred Mond (Cheltondale, 1886) who expressed his desire for 'a visible and beautiful sign which will symbolise to all the boys for all time the fact that men have bravely died for their country and for their Empire.' Sir Alfred was totally committed to preserving the memory of all those who fell. Not only the first chairman of the Imperial War Museum, he also approached Edwin Lutyens to design a national monument to mark the signing of the Peace Treaty in 1919, resulting in the design and commission of the Cenotaph. This simple but moving monument in Whitehall remains the eternal focal point of national commemoration and remembrance.

EPILOGUE

The balance between the desire of College for both utilitarian and architectural expressions of gratitude to the fallen was achieved by plans:

> to erect a double Cloister connecting the new Chapel with the "Little Modern" and to affix to the walls thereof suitable tablets forming a complete Roll of Honour. This Cloister… would not only constitute a beautiful and appropriate shrine, but would greatly add to the architectural setting and unity of the College buildings, besides being a much needed convenience in wet weather.

In addition, scholarships were to be instituted for sons of fallen Old Cheltonians. Any surplus was to be applied to the Endowment Fund in support of the upkeep and development of College. Donations were called upon, and a list of donors and amounts was published regularly in *The Cheltonian*.

For some, this was an opportunity to gift funds, with the act itself explicitly in memory of a loved one. Names followed by 'in memory of …' are common in the records. In December 1918 *The Cheltonian* recorded…

> Mr R. M. Wolstenholme and Mrs Girardot have each given £1,000 to the College to endow a scholarship in memory respectively of George Mellor Wolstenholme, M.C. [Military Cross], Lieutenant, Yorkshire Regiment, who was killed in action on the 5th October, 1918, and of Paul Chancourt Girardot, Second Lieutenant, Oxford and Bucks Light Infantry, who was killed in action on the 16th September, 1914. These scholarships will be awarded triennially.

At 2.30pm on Friday 4th July 1919 the foundation stone of the Cloister war memorial was laid by Sir Arthur Lee, the man who so vocally supported planning of a war memorial from 1917. At the time of the ceremony, total funds subscribed for war memorial purposes was almost £30,117. In 1917, Sir Arthur had stressed the purpose of College's war memorial:

> It is not the mere fact of their deaths that we wish to record. What we wish to record and to make live for all time is what they died for, and how they died, and we do that not merely as a tribute to them and to their kin, but in order that future generations of Cheltenham boys may be inspired and steeled if need be to emulate their example.

College Echoes is a continuation of that pledge, an epitaph to remember the 702 individuals who died in war service as exactly that – individuals. Each man had hopes and dreams, ambitions for the future and his own personal story. This book acts as a tribute: to the men they were, the men they became, and the men they could have been. Lest we forget.

Epilogue

Remembrance

It is entirely fitting, in this centenary year commemorating the signing of the Armistice, that the concluding comments and perspectives on the ultimate sacrifice made by 702 Old Cheltonians (OC) is offered by today's cohort of staff and students. They appropriately echo the principles and values held by the Great War generation of OCs as depicted in the many stories and vignettes captured in this book. Over the four-year centenary period, every Third Form pupil selected an OC to research, and in so doing remember. As more information of the lives and the circumstances of the fallen OCs was explored and uncovered, a subliminal feeling of 'ownership' of a subject OC by his student investigator began to develop, and in some cases was closely, almost protectively, held. This process developed into a silent yet perceptible 'communion of spirit' that even after one hundred years still appears undiminished, as the following contemporary testimonies illustrate.

Jo Doidge-Harrison joined the College teaching staff in 2007 and has been Head of History since 2011. She undertook the first exploratory trips looking for the graves and memorials of Great War OCs from 2013 onwards. As centenary commemorations began in earnest, she supervised Third Form volunteers as an activity group from January 2014, who acted as the 'pathfinders' for subsequent visits of remembrance to Gallipoli and the Western Front.[384]

> Having visited somewhere around 450 of our 702 fallen, I have been lucky to see some stunning sites of remembrance, ranging from Beach Cemetery in Gallipoli, below the forbidding Nek and Chunuk Bair, to the quintessentially English churchyard of St. Michael's, Brimpsfield, where the vicar's third son, Major Denne, cricketer and O.C., rests by the main Cheltenham to Cirencester road. However, perhaps one of the most memorable sites was a very 'ordinary' little cemetery, Guards Cemetery, at Windy Corner, Cuinchy, tucked away in the fields east of Béthune. This was one of our earliest visits in search of College's "intolerably nameless names". Philip Elliott applied to Sandhurst in May 1913, was commissioned in August 1914, only to

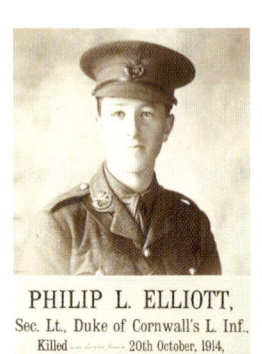

PHILIP L. ELLIOTT,
Sec. Lt., Duke of Cornwall's L. Inf.,
Killed — 20th October, 1914,
Age 18.

Philip Elliot and his gravestone

---

[384] Besides allowing the visiting groups to visit the various graves and memorials and remember the fallen OCs, these battlefields visits also provided a unique experience of the history and topography where the fighting took place. This experience was significantly enhanced by the presence of two expert battlefield guides who accompanied the groups; Tony Eden on the Western Front and Erdem Kesili in Gallipoli. Their respective in-depth explanations of the circumstances of the fighting in which the OCs were embroiled brought essential context to every location visited, thus underpinning the impact of each visit.

EPILOGUE

be killed in October, aged just 18. Every single officer from the brigade's three front platoons was either killed and wounded with Philip, as they held the line under heavy attack between Lorgie and Le Transloy. I visited Windy Corner with Philip's Memorial Album image firmly in mind: grinning, he looked carefree and very similar to any one of my Sixth Formers. At his headstone, we found a poppy with a card, blurry in the rain, inscribed: "In memory of Philip, my great-uncle, with respect". It made a huge impression: this smiling 18-year-old, whom I'd felt so connected to, was somehow somebody else's great-uncle, and, more importantly still, not forgotten.

Richard Moore, College Master, on the Somme

Richard Moore taught History and Politics at College between 2008 and 2016 and has led many battlefields trips, possessing a keen eye for the story behind the headstone. He was driver and chief cemetery interpreter on a series of early recces of Flanders, which enabled us to build subsequent pupil trips entirely around the Old Cheltonians.

On a sunny late afternoon in October 2013, the journey to visit and remember the OCs who fell in the Great War began. Armed with a carefully resourced spreadsheet of names and locations, Second Lieutenant Forbes of the RA was to be the formal start of the journey. Bethune was the town, and we sought a public cemetery: surely nothing could be easier?! Having now spent a number of

Remembrance. (Mr Dan Evans with Charlie Meecham-Jones, Oscar Bromage-Henry, Felix Watson-Smyth and Tommy Ladds)

303

EPILOGUE

Noel Edmund Forbes

NOEL EDMUND FORBES
Sec. Lt., Royal Field Artillery (Special Reserve).
Died of Wounds nr. Richebourg L'Avoué, France,
12th May, 1915, Age 20.

years researching and locating OCs in France, Belgium, England and Gallipoli, my mind always turns to the first found, and Noel Forbes. The Commonwealth War Graves Commission and the serried ranks of the fallen are carved in simple yet powerful Portland stone, the headstones formed up as on a parade square somewhere before embarkation in 1914, ready to serve King and Country. This conventional image was however far removed from what we found in Bethune, and this was a significant moment in learning how to hunt these young men down. Locating Noel was the challenge that prepared us for the task at hand and set the tone – and one in which we were not to be deterred. In this instance, it was after several blind alleys, a stroll around a park, the wrong church, and several about-turns in the car that we found him. As we strolled through the austere, gravelled, Catholic cemetery, the scale of the task in hand and what the CWGC have achieved brought the act of remembrance and the sacrifice of the fallen into context.

Without doubt Forbes occupies that very corner of a foreign field that Rupert Brooke so pertinently referred to. It was the start of an incredible journey that took us to many of the more conventional and exceptionally beautiful resting places of all of the OCs; but the stark loneliness of Forbes was what struck me. When was he last visited? Had anyone taken the time to find him? The OC project began as an attempt to visit young men such as Forbes and to say 'thank you' to those who lay in such innocuous resting places, but without doubt, not forgotten. *Floreat Cheltonia.*

Richard left the Common Room at College to now teach at Blundell's School in Somerset.

Sam Hamilton, currently studying history in the Upper Sixth, was one of the original members of the dedicated research team plotting and logging OC burial sites via the Commonwealth War Graves Commission website. Sam with other fellow researchers also visited the Old Cheltonians buried at St. Peter's Church, Leckhampton.

Data on the Old Cheltonians was primarily collected through use of the Commonwealth War Graves Commission website, which we formatted into spreadsheets listing among

Richard Coxwell-Rogers – Marker and Plaque.

other criteria the birth, rank, accolades, service and final resting place of each soldier. It was an exciting challenge in uncovering the past of our school, but also of our own national history; a war about which we had already learned so much and were keen to discover more, outside of lessons. Cataloguing the lives and achievements of our Cheltonians was subsequently an education in itself as to the sheer scale of the war's reach, its length, and the sacrifice that occurred within it. As we progressed further, there became a tangible sense of reconnecting with 'our own', of re-establishing forgotten memories of long-lost 'friends'. This was especially the case when we, as a group, travelled to St. Peter's Church in Leckhampton and successfully found the gravestones of some of our OCs; having that physical contact with the fallen, who were once Cheltenham schoolboys like us, and contributing in whatever measure we can towards their remembrance, remains an affecting memory and a significant moment in our shared school lives.

Noni Stuckey, a very recent Old Cheltonian, took History A Level and is currently undergoing officer selection for Sandhurst, considering possibly pursuing an eventual career in army education.

She served in the CCF, winning the 2016 Sword of Honour, and was one of the Upper Sixth on the 2015 Gallipoli trip, travelling alongside Lower Sixth and Fifth Formers, to ensure that every single OC on the peninsula was found and remembered.

The Gallipoli Campaign remains cemented in memory as one of the most infamous campaigns of the Great War. Cheltenham College's trip to Gallipoli in 2015 proved to be even more moving than expected. The memorials themselves were in immaculate condition, with the rows of glowing white marble bringing home just quite how much death this coastline witnessed. The beauty of the landscape and its pristine waters contrasted with its gruesome past. Finding an OC's memorial would bring a mixture of emotions; a combination of pride and grief. These were boys who had listened to sermons in our chapel and eaten tea in our dining hall. Personally, it was the messages written on the memorial by a mother or father left grieving that moved me the most. The military rank juxtaposed with the word 'son' reminded us all of the impact this campaign had both abroad and at home. It was a truly incredible experience.

Remembrance. (Henry Johnson, Noni Stuckey and Tommy Maddinson)

EPILOGUE

Remembrance. (Tommy and Charlotte Maddinson's tribute)

Charles Thomas

Tommy Maddinson is currently in the Upper Sixth and hoping to read History at university.

His sister Charlotte, currently in the Fifth Form, produced the work on Lieutenant Colonel Charles Thomas that Tommy subsequently laid, with poppies, at Embarkation Pier Cemetery, on the Gallipoli peninsula.

In October 2015, I visited the Gallipoli peninsula with College to pay my respects to O.C. Charles Earnest Thomas, whom my younger sister had researched for her Third Form project. Thomas is buried at Embarkation Pier cemetery, close to the sea at Anzac Cove. It's a quiet and secluded spot, surrounded by trees. At the cemetery, I reflected upon Thomas' sacrifice. He died leading a group of stretcher bearers up a hill in a brave effort to save wounded men in the front line. For me, knowing the story behind the name made my visit to the cemetery that extra bit special. My sister and I are proud to have played a small part in honouring the memory of Cheltonians who served in the First World War.

Felix Watson-Smyth is currently studying History in the Lower Sixth. He found 'his' Old Cheltonian, Gerald Gloster, at Tyne Cot, a markedly different resting place, in terms of scale, to that of his great-great-uncle, Teddy, who we also visited on the same tour in 2014.

Teddy lies with his men of the Coldstream Guards at Mory Street, St. Leger, France.

Remembrance. (Felix Watson-Smyth)

Gerald Gloster

I found researching and visiting the war memorials very shocking but worthwhile. A memory that has stuck with me is the horror of the number of gravestones. Placing my plaque for Gerald Gloster was a truly fulfilling experience. I was happy that I was able to deliver my plaque personally to Tyne Cot as it gave me a real sense of achievement, especially as we are both Boyceites.[385] The thought of someone like Gerald leaving school at sixteen to go and fight is hard to swallow. Visiting the battlefields was one of the most memorable experiences of my life, and one which has definitely had a lasting impact on me and the way I think about world wars.

[385] The term 'Boyceites' refers to all who were educated at Cheltenham College in Christowe House.

EPILOGUE

Charlie Meecham-Jones is intending to read History at either Oxford or Cambridge once he completes Sixth Form. He too was part of our inaugural OC-focussed trip, and at the Loos Memorial the pupils commented that, in tandem with visiting Vimy Ridge, they got a real sense of the strategic aims for this region in 1915.

> Finding out about the life of Charles Cobbold, the OC I was investigating, was fascinating and provided a personal side to visiting the memorial at Loos. Searching through the vast numbers of names on the walls also added an insight into the scale of the battle in which Charles fought. In addition to this, learning about Loos and the use of gas there increased my understanding of the horrors that Charles faced. The site of the memorial seemed strange as well as it was difficult to imagine a battle happening there. Finding information about Charles' school and personal life also made me look at the First World War from a different perspective and meant that there was a larger connection between the person I had been researching and the name at the memorial.

Charles Cobbold

Arras Memorial to the Missing, with Cheltonian plaques

As a committed Sixth Form rugby player and lead in 2018's College musical, *West Side Story*, Angus Thomson is a typical Cheltonian all-rounder. He had to be 'dragged' from the Arras Memorial to the Missing having kept the entire bus waiting, so determined was he to find and honour 'his' Old Cheltonian in 2014.

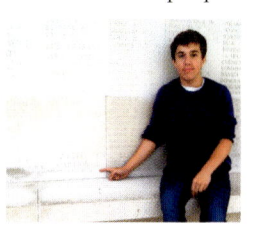

Remembrance. (Angus Thomson)

> Wilfred Desages served as a private for two years in the 6th King's Liverpool Regiment before joining the London Regiment. His body went missing, but it is believed that he was killed in Harcourt, France, in 1918. One of his officers stated: 'I was captured on 21st March, poor old Desages (my captain) was killed immediately on my right.' He is commemorated in Bays 9-10 at Arras. After many hours of research in my first year at College, I was struck by the large number of commemorated OCs at Arras. This compelled me to research Wilfred and Arras itself. Naturally I came to the Battle of Arras. I loved to read about the network of tunnels in which the British used to hide and surprise the Germans. Seeing Wilfred's name, the tunnels and learning more about this particular battle opened my eyes not only to the harshness of it, but also to an understanding that

Wilfred Desages

EPILOGUE

Remembrance.
(Caitlin Brister and Victoria Brain)

tunnel warfare was a prevalent use of warfare in World War One, even if hidden, and the tactics and logistics needed to execute said warfare were incredibly complicated.

Caitlin Brister is an up-and-coming historian, currently in the Fourth Form. Both she and Victoria Brain researched Second Lieutenant William Grieve (whose grandson is the Right Honourable Dominic Grieve Q.C. M.P., another historian and former Attorney General). William's son (and Dominic's father, also named William Percy) was born just five weeks after his father was killed near Ypres.

William Grieve at College

William Grieve was the youngest son of Margaret Grieve who had two children before him, Charles and James. After Sandhurst, and studying medicine at Edinburgh University, William became a foreign correspondent in Buenos Aires, returning to England to be married to Dorothy in July 1914, just before enlisting for the war. They had a son in 1915 who was named after his father, but unfortunately William never saw his son, because William was killed in action at Ypres on the 16th February 1915, just five weeks before the birth. I had the opportunity to go to Ypres to see William Grieve's name and to put down a memorial for him. It was a proud moment for Cheltenham College to pay respect to Old Cheltonians that fought for our safety. Whilst I was visiting the great Menin Gate I felt a sense of sadness; however, I was also proud that I was going to the same school that men risked their lives to protect. Furthermore, I felt a personal connection with William Grieve because of how much I knew about him and the research I had done into his short life.

Remembrance.
(Charles Hellens)

Charles Hellens won a prize for asking the best, and the most number of, questions on our 2016 trip to the battlefields on the old Western Front. He is currently in the Fourth Form and left his plaque at the Lochnagar Crater, where the huge mine explosion was the signal for Captain George Cope to advance through La Boisselle toward the German lines at 7.28am on 1st July 1916. George's body was never recovered: he is commemorated on the Thiepval Memorial to the Missing.

Charles also laid a second plaque, recognising Captain Elliott Crooke, one of four brothers who fought in the war, who also died fighting at La Boisselle, three days later.

EPILOGUE

I visited the battlefield of La Boisselle on the 23rd October 2016 as part of the First World War Battlefields Trip where we saw the graveyards and battlegrounds of two of the war's most famous battles: The Somme (1916) & Passchendaele (1917). I had researched an Old Cheltonian named George Cope who had left school in 1914 aged 16 to join the Northumberland Fusiliers and had been involved in the opening day of the Somme Offensive on the 1st July. Apart from the 30m deep crater that was left by the Royal Engineers on the 1st July, I found it hard to imagine that such a harrowing battle could have ever graced the placid fields that now grew there. However, whilst I toured the memorial by the crater, I thought about how George Cope would have felt, fighting in a place that much resembled the Cotswold countryside of his youth. Seeing the place in which he fell made me feel both sombre about the lives of boys, like George (raised in a similar fashion to myself) who died too soon, as well as reassured that, despite the cacophony of the German artillery and machine guns that destroyed both earth and man, the last thing he would have seen was a land that resembled his home.

George Cope

Freya Haddon began her research work on Captain Minden Badcock MC in 2017 and completed it in 2018, during the first academic year of our new girls' house, College Lawn, her new house at College. By extraordinary consequence, Minden had lived with his parents Francis (who worked in the Indian Civil Service) and Adele, at No.1 College Lawn during his time at College, where he had been a College prefect and a member of the College rugby XV. Minden left College in July 1914, and, when war was declared just three weeks later, immediately joined the army and went to war. He never returned. Now his old family residence is the home for the latest generation of Cheltonians who have not forgotten him, as Freya's elegantly recorded feelings portray:

Remembrance.
(Freya Haddon outside the Badcocks' former residence, now her College House.)

> I found it was such a nice experience to find out about people who came to our school, were educated like us, and then where they lived – and passed away. It was so special. The fact that Minden was from College Lawn made it fit that bit more personally for us; that he lived in the house where we now live made it feel that he was even closer to us than the other Cheltonians were. There was a sense he was in our family in a way. I have become really interested in my own family history, and

EPILOGUE

we have our own archive at home. My great-grandfather Percy Haddon served in the navy in the First World War and was on HMS *Warrior* at the Battle of Jutland. I have read his diary. I love World Wars One and Two. It is so strange to think that only a hundred years ago all these people were risking their lives, for the world we have now.

Thus, these final telling and current testimonies draw to a most appropriate close an astonishing story about a truly remarkable generation of Old Cheltonians, whose 'echoes' are still apparent through the daily bustle and hubbub of today's Cheltonians as they pass through their education at College and march forwards in their lives. Through their many youthful and exuberant activities, these 'echoes' continue to be heard on College Field, along the College Cloisters, but most loudly in the Chapel.

Remembrance.
Cheltonians remember at Cape Helles, Gallipoli.

Floreat Cheltonia!

CHELTENHAM – TOO

by Patrick Stevens OC (Boyne House, 1971)

Floreat Cheltonia! Passed generations sigh,
As sunbeams through the Chapel's panes
Make tribute plaques shine high.
Seven Hundred and Two the final count of black and cerise tie.

Lest we forget those hundred years? 'Not so!' the Forms retort.
To Flanders Fields and the Dardanelles
Where forbears bravely fought,
One crusade made, one Last Post played, one common spirit sought.

And what of legacy you ask? No more to count the cost.
Our Sovereign's Colour boldly won by our generation lost.
Successive cohorts, boys and girls, their energies embossed
With bright and upbeat attitudes; life's hardships safely crossed

BIBLIOGRAPHY

ARCHIVES

School archives:
Cheltenham College Archives, *1914-1918*.
Old Cheltonian Register, *1841-1927*.
St Andrew's Prep, Eastbourne, *Old Androvian Archives*.
Temple Grove, Magazine, *1914-1935*.

Other archives:
Hansard, Volume 68.
Imperial War Museum Archives, London.
Public Record Office, The National Archives, Kew, London:
WO 338 Officers' Services, First World War.
WO 339 Officers' Services, First World War.
WO 372 Service Medal and Awards Index, First World War.
WO 374 Officers' Services, First World War.
ADM 196 Officers' Service Records, Series III.
ADM 273 Royal Naval Air Service: Registers of Officers' Services.
ADM 317 Royal Navy Volunteer Reserve: Records of Service, First World War.
ADM 337 Royal Navy Volunteer Reserve: Records of Service, First World War.
AIR 27 Operations Record Books of Squadrons, *1911-c1960*.
AIR 76 Royal Air Force Officers' Service Records, *1918-1919*.
WO 76   Records of Officers' Services.
WO 95   First World War and Army of Occupation War Diaries.
Regimental Archives, Norton Barracks, Worcester.
Reichsarchiv, Berlin.

Supplements:
Referenced supplements of *The Birmingham Gazette*.
Referenced supplements of *The British Medical Journal*.
Referenced supplements of *The Daily Telegraph*.
Referenced supplements of *Guy's Hospital Reports, Vol. LXX, Hospital Gazette*.
Referenced supplements of *The London Gazette*.
Referenced supplements of *The Morning Post*.
Referenced supplements of *The Stockport Advertiser*.
Referenced supplements of *The Timaru Herald*.
Referenced supplements of *The Times*.
Referenced supplements of *The Toronto Star*.

Papers

Changboo Kang. *The British Infantry Officer on the Western Front in the First World War*, (PhD Thesis, University of Birmingham, June 2007).

Command Paper. *Report of the Committee appointed to consider the Education and Training of Officers of the Army*, (Akers-Douglas Report), (Cd 982,1902).

Command Paper. *Report of the Military Education Committee – Minutes of Evidence*, (Cd. 983, 1902).

Morton, A. *Sandhurst and the First World War: The Royal Military College 1902-1918*, (Sandhurst Occasional Paper, No 17, RMA Central Library, 2014).

Sheffield, G. *Officer-Man Relations, Morale and Discipline in the British Army, 1902-1922*, (PhD Thesis, Kings College London, 1994).

Journals

Englander and Osborne, '*Jack, Tommy and Henry Dubb: The Armed Forces and the Working Class*', Historical Journal, Volume 21, No 3, 1978.

Online

The Canadian Letters and Images Project, The Taylor Bury Collection of Letters (on line), Department of History, Vancouver Island University, at www.canadian letters.ca/collections/war/468/collection/20545 accessed 23 April 2018.

First World War letters posted on Clifton RFC website, www.cliftonrfchistory.co.uk/memorial/WW1/fayle.htm, accessed 23 April 2018.

Bibliography

Baker, C. *The Truce, The Day the War Stopped*, (Stroud, Amberley Publishing, 2014).

Barnes, A. *The Story of the 2/5th Battalion Gloucestershire Regiment, 1914 – 1918*, (Gloucester, The Crypt House Press, 1930).

Baynes, J. *Morale – A Study of Men and Courage*, (London, Cassell, 1967).

Beckett, I, and Simpson, K. *A Nation in Arms; The British Army in the First World War*, (Barnsley, Pen and Sword, 2004).

Bell, M. *Sevenoaks War Memorial: The Men Remembered*, (Stroud, Amberley Publishing, 2014).

Bet-El, I. *Conscripts; Lost Legions of the Great War*, (Stroud, Sutton, 1999).

Bidwell, S. *Modern Warfare: A Study of Men, Weapons and Theories*, (London, Allen Lane, 1973).

Blundon, E. *Undertones of War*, (London: Penguin, 2010 [1928]).

BIBLIOGRAPHY

Bourne, J.M. 'British Generals in World War One', in G.D. Sheffield, ed., *Leadership and Command: The Anglo-American Experience since 1861*, (London: Brassey's, 2002 [1996]).

Bowman, T and Connelly, M. *The Edwardian Army; Recruiting, Training and Deploying the British Army, 1902-14*, (Oxford, Oxford University Press, 2012).

Bowyer, C. (Ed) *Royal Flying Corps Communiqués, 1917-1918*, (London, Grub Street, 1998).

Brendon, V. *Prep School Children; A Class apart over Two Centuries*, (London, Continuum, 2009).

Buchan, J. *Francis and Riversdale Grenfell*, (London, Nelson, 1920).

Buckley, T. *The Iliad of Homer*, (London, George Bell and Sons, 1876).

Carpenter, A. *The Blocking of Zeebrugge*, (London, Jenkins, 1924).

Cassar, G. *Kitchener: Architect of Victory*, (London, Kimber, 1977).

Cassar, G. *Trial by Gas: The British Army at the Second Battle of Ypres* (Nebraska, Potomac Books, 2014).

Clark, C. *The Sleepwalkers: How Europe went to War in 1914*, (London, Penguin Books, 2012).

Clark, A. *The Donkeys*, (London, Hutchinson, 1961).

Clayton, A. *Paths of Glory; The French Army 1914-18*, (London: Cassell, 2003).

Clutterbuck, L. *Bond of Sacrifice, Volume 1*, (London, Anglo-African Publishing, 1915).

Clutterbuck, L. *Bond of Sacrifice, Volume 2*, (London, Anglo-African Publishing, 1915).

Corrigan, G. *Mud, Blood and Poppycock*, (London, Cassell, 2003).

Costello, R. *Black Tommies: British Soldiers of African Descent in the First World War*, (Liverpool, University Press, 2015).

Dewey, P. *War and Progress; Britain 1914-45* (London: Longman, 1997).

Edmonds, C. *A Subaltern's War*, (London: Mott, 1984 [1929]).

Ellis, J. *Eye-deep in Hell*, (Baltimore, John Hopkins University Press, 1989 [1977]).

Farndale, M. *Western Front 1914–18. History of the Royal Regiment of Artillery*. (London, Royal Artillery Institution, 1986).

Ferguson, N. *The Pity of War*, (London, Penguin, 1999).

Gilbert, M. *Prep Schools; An Anthology*, (London, Murray, 1991).

Gilbert, M. *The Somme; Heroism and Horror in the First World War*, (New York, Henry Holt, 2006).

Goold Walker, G. *The Honourable Artillery Company, 1537-1947*, (Aldershot, Gale and Polden, 1954).

Graves, R. *Goodbye to All That*, (London, Penguin, 1960 [1929]).

Griffith, P. *British Fighting Methods in the Great War*, (Abingdon, Cass, 1996).

Grogan, G. *A Drop in Infinity*, (London, John Lane, 1915).

Grogan, G. *William Pollok, and Other Tales*, (London, John Lane, 1919).

Grogan, G. *Poems*, (London, Whitefriars Press, 1925).

Hall, D. *Muscular Christianity; Embodying the Victorian Age*, (Cambridge, Cambridge University Press, 1994).

Hamilton, I. *When I was a Boy*, (London, Faber and Faber, 1939).

Harries-Jenkins, G. *The Army in Victorian Society*, (London, Routledge & Kegan Paul, 1977).

Hart, P. *Bloody April: Slaughter in the Skies over Arras, 1917*. (London Weidenfeld & Nicolson, 2005).

Hart, P. *The Great War 1914-1918,* (London, Profile Limited, 2014).

Holmes, R. *Tommy – The British Soldier on the Western Front 1914-1918*, (London, HarperCollins, 2004).

Holroyd. J. *The Great War Illustrated; 1915*, (Barnsley, Pen and Sword, and Longford, W. 2015).

Jackson, R. *Britain's Greatest Aircraft*. (Barnsley, Pen and Sword, 2007).

James, L. *The Rise and Fall of the British Empire*, (London, Abacus, 1994).

Jeffery, K. *Field Marshal Sir Henry Wilson: A Political Soldier*, (Oxford, Oxford University Press, 2006).

Jenkins, P. *The Great and Holy War*, (New York, HarperCollins, 2015).

Jones, H. *War in the Air, Volume 2*, (Oxford, Clarendon Press, 1928).

Jones, S. *Stemming the Tide; Officers and leadership in the British Expeditionary Force 1914,* (Solihull, Helion, 2013).

Laffin, J. *British Butchers and Bunglers of World War One*, (Stroud, Sutton, 1988).

Lee, A. *No Parachute*, (London, Grub Street, [1968] (2013).

Lewis-Stempel, J. *Six Weeks; The Short and Gallant Life of the British Officer in the First World War*, (London, Orion, 2011).

Liddle, P. (Ed). *Passchendaele in Perspective*, (Barnsley, Leo Cooper/Pen & Sword, 1997).

Ludendorff, E. *Ludendorff's Own Story August 1914-November 1918 the Great War from the siege of Liege to the signing of the Armistice as viewed from the Grand headquarters of the German Army, Volume 2*, (London, Harper and Brothers, London,1920).

McCartney, H. *Citizen Soldiers: The Liverpool Territorials in the First World War,* (Cambridge, Cambridge University Press, 2005).

McPhail, H. *Sassoon and Graves: On the Trail of the Poets of the Great War,* and Guest, P. (Barnsley, Pen and Sword, 2001).

Mitchinson, K. *Gentlemen and Officers*, (London, IWM, 1994).

Montgomery, B. *The Memoirs of Field Marshal The Viscount Montgomery of Alamein KG*, (London, Collins Books, 1958).

Moore-Bick, C. *Playing the Game; The Junior Infantry Officer on the Western Front 1914-18*, (Solihull, Helion, 2011).

Morrow, J. *The Great War in the Air*, (Washington, Smithsonian Institution Press, 1993).

Meyer, J. *Men of War; Masculinity and the First World War in Britain*, (Basingstoke, Palgrave Macmillan, 2009).

Newman, S. *With the Patricia's in Flanders 1914-1918*, (Saanich, BC, Bellewaerde House Publishing, 2000).

Osborn, E. *The Muse in Arms: A Collection of War Poems, for the Most Part Written in the Field of Action, by Seamen, Soldiers, and Flying Men Who Are Serving, or Have Served, in the Great War,* (New York, Frederick A Stokes Company, 1917).

Page, T. *The Aeneid of Virgil,* (London, Macmillan, 1894).

Palazzo, A. *Seeking Victory on the Western Front,* (Lincoln, University of Nebraska Press, 2000).

Parker, P. *The Old Lie; The Great War and the Public School Ethos,* (London, Constable, 1987).

Patch, H and van Emden, R. *The Last Fighting Tommy,* (London, Bloomsbury, 2009).

Philpott, W. *Attrition, Fighting the First World War,* (London, Little Brown, 2014).

Prior, R. *Command on the Western Front: The Military Career of Sir Henry Rawlinson 1914-1918,* (Barnsley, Pen and Sword, 2004).

Renshaw, A. (Ed) *Wisden on the Great War: The Lives of Cricket's Fallen 1914-1918,* (London, Bloomsbury, 2014).

Roper, M. *The Secret Battle: Emotional Survival in the Great War,* (Manchester, Manchester University Press, 2009).

Roynon, G. (Ed), *War Diaries, A Chaplain at War: The Great War Diaries of Kenneth Best,* (London, Simon and Schuster, 2011).

Scott, A. *Sixty Squadron RAF; A History of the Squadron from its Formation,* (Uckfield, Naval and Military Press, 2015).

Searle, G. *A New England? Peace and War 1886-1918,* (Oxford, Oxford University Press, 2004).

Seldon, A, and Walsh D. *Public Schools and the Great War; The Generation Lost,* (Barnsley, Pen and Sword, 2013).

Sheffield, G. *Leadership in the Trenches. Officer-Man Relations, Morale and Discipline in the British Army in the Era of the First World War,* (New York, Palgrave, 2000).

Sheffield, G. *Forgotten Victory – The First World War: Myths and Realities,* (London, Headline, 2001).

Sheffield, G. *Command and Morale; The British Army on the Western Front 1914-1918,* (Barnsley, Praetorian Press, 2014).

Sheffield, G. and Todman, D. *Command and Control; The British Army's Experience 1914-18,* (Stroud, Spellmount, 2007).

Simkins, P. *The First World War: The Western Front 1914-1916,* (Oxford, Osprey. 2002)

Simkins, P. *World War 1: 1914-1918 The Western Front,* (Godalming, Colour Library Books, 1992).

Simkins, P. *From the Somme to Victory; The British Army's Experience on the Western Front 1916-1917,* (Barnsley, Praetorian, 2014).

Snape, M. *God and the British Soldier: Religion and the British Army in the First and Second World Wars,* (Abingdon, Routledge, 2005).

Spiers, E. *Haldane: An Army Reformer,* (Edinburgh, Edinburgh University Press, 1980).

Stevenson, D. *1914-1918: The History of the First World War,* (London, Penguin Books, London [2004] 2012).

BIBLIOGRAPHY

Stevenson, D. *With Our Backs to the Wall: Victory and Defeat in 1918*, (London, Penguin, London, 2012).

Strachan, H. *The First World War*, (London, Simon & Schuster, 2003).

Travers, T. *The Killing Ground: The British Army, the Western Front and the Emergence of Modern War 1900-1918*, (Barnsley, Leo Cooper. 2003)[1987].

Van Emden, R. *The Soldier's War: The Great War through Veterans' Eyes,* (London, Bloomsbury, 2010).

Watson, A. *Enduring the Great War: Combat, Morale and Collapse in the German and British Armies, 1914-1918,* (Cambridge: Cambridge University Press, 2008).

Whitton, F. *The History of the Prince of Wales's Leinster Regiment-Volume 2,* (Aldershot, Gale and Polden, 1924).

Wilson, H. *With the Flag to Pretoria: A History of the Boer War 1899-1900, Volumes 1 and 2,* (London, Harmsworth, 1900).

Winter, D. *Death's Men: Soldiers of the Great War,* (London: Penguin, 1978).

# IMAGE SOURCES

Page no.	Source
x	College Chapel Interior, Cheltenham College Gallery.
2	College Chapel Exterior, Cheltenham College Gallery.
3	College Cricket, circa 1914, Stevens Private Collection.
4	Cheltenham College Cricket XI team photo, 1914; Cheltenham College Archives.
5	Cyril A. H. Hillier (d. 1915), War Memorial volume, Cheltenham College Archives.
5	Hubert du Boulay (d. 1916), War Memorial volume, Cheltenham College Archives.
5	Norman Birtwistle (d. 1918), War Memorial volume, Cheltenham College Archives.
7	Cheltenham College Chapel Cloisters and Memorial Stone, Cheltenham College Archives.
12	Alan Robertson (d. 1914), War Memorial volume, Cheltenham College Archives.
13	HMS *Aboukir* leaving Malta, circa 1912, courtesy IWM.
14	Glendower Gilliat (d. 1914), War Memorial volume, Cheltenham College Archives.
14	Reginald Gilliat (d. 1915), War Memorial volume, Cheltenham College Archives.
16	Teignmouth Melvill (d. 1879), Cheltenham College Archives.
17	Frederick Coplestone (d. 1915), War Memorial volume, Cheltenham College Archives.
17	HM Submarine, *D2*, courtesy IWM.
18	Kenneth Brooke-Murray (d. 1916), War Memorial volume, Cheltenham College Archives.
22	Henry Hadley (d. 1914), Cheltenham College Archives.
23	Douglas Reynolds (d. 1916), Cheltenham College Archives.
31	HMS *Bulwark*, entering Chatham, courtesy IWM.
33	Philip Neame (d. 1978), Cheltenham College Archives.
35	Cheltenham College in Winter, E Burrows, 1899, Stevens Private Collection.
48	The Western Front, Winter 1914-15, courtesy of Sir Hew Strachan and Simon and Schuster UK Ltd.
57	Thomas Brooks with the Leicestershire Yeomanry, Cheltenham College Archives.
49	Ernest Taylor (d. 1916), War Memorial volume, Cheltenham College Archives.
61	Henry Reed (d. 1915), Cheltenham College Archives.
62	Isaac Woodiwiss (d. 1915), War Memorial volume, Cheltenham College Archives.
63	Morane Parasol Aeroplane and crew, courtesy RAF Museum.
66	Maurice Shaw, née Schwabe (d. 1915), Cheltenham College Archives.
70	The V Beach Landing, sketch by Guy Geddes, courtesy IWM.
71	The Gallipoli Peninsula, courtesy IWM.
73	George H. Pownall (d. 1915), War Memorial volume, Cheltenham College Archives.
74	Edward Boyle (d. 1967), Cheltenham College Archives.
77	Dallas Moor (d. 1918), War Memorial volume, Cheltenham College Archives.
77	Montague Proctor-Beauchamp, Cheltenham College Archives.
78	The 5th Norfolk Officers, courtesy IWM.
84	The Ottoman Empire, courtesy of Sir Hew Strachan and Simon and Schuster UK Ltd.
87	Kenneth Markham-Rose (d. 1915), War Memorial volume, Cheltenham College Archives.
88	The College Common Room, circa 1895, Cheltenham College Archives.
111	Edward Disney (d. 1916), War Memorial volume, Cheltenham College Archives.
113	Battle lines North and South of the Somme, Cheltenham College Archives.
114	Last Will and Testament, courtesy TNA.

IMAGE SOURCES

128	The Albert Medal, for gallantry, open source.
131	Walter North, Cheltenham College Archives.
133	Trench Map, Map 57D SE4 Ovillers, The Somme Offensive 1916, G.H Smith & Son.
135	Charles Pigg (d. 1960, Assistant Master 1909–1940; Treasurer and secretary for the Cheltonian Society 1945-1960), Cheltenham College Archives.
139	Arthur Apperly (d. 1916), War Memorial volume, Cheltenham College Archives.
139	Cyril W. Winterbotham (d. 1916), War Memorial volume, Cheltenham College Archives.
140	Cartoon in the Fifth Glo'ster Gazette, circa 1916, courtesy Soldiers of Gloucestershire Museum.
142	James P. Winterbotham (d. 1925), 1896-1902, Cheltenham College Archives.
149	George Bidie (d. 1916), War Memorial volume, Cheltenham College Archives.
149	FE 2B aeroplane and crew, courtesy RAF Museum.
150	Francis Tuke (d. 1916), War Memorial volume, Cheltenham College Archives.
152	Reverend Reginald Waterfield (d. 1919, Principal of Cheltenham College 1899-1919), Cheltenham College Archives.
166	College XI 1916, Cheltenham College Archives.
173	Africa in 1914, Courtesy of Sir Hew Strachan and Simon and Schuster UK Ltd.
174	Frederick Booth (d. 1960), Cheltenham College Archives.
177	Sydney Trevenen (d. 1918), War Memorial volume, Cheltenham College Archives.
178	Richard Wilkinson, Cheltenham College Archives.
183	Douglas Gabell (d. 1918), War Memorial volume, Cheltenham College Archives.
184	Nieuport 17 Scout Aeroplane, courtesy RAF Museum.
184	Challoner Caffyn (d. 1917), War Memorial volume, Cheltenham College Archives.
185	No 59 Sqn Record, James Stuart's last flight, courtesy RAF Museum.
193	No 65 Sqn aircrew at Wyton, courtesy RAF Museum.
194	RMS *Arcadian*, open source.
195	Charles Garstang (d. 1917), War Memorial volume, Cheltenham College Archives.
196	*SS Gartness* (commissioned as the *SS Charles T Jones* in 1890), open source.
201	Marshall Featherstone, Cheltenham College Archives.
204	Noel Saw (d. 1917), War Memorial volume, Cheltenham College Archives.
219	Sir Arthur Lee (d. 1947), Cheltenham College Archives.
222	Harold Hewett (d. 1918), War Memorial volume, Cheltenham College Archives.
223	The wreckage, courtesy RAF Museum.
224	Reverend Percy Hattersley-Smith (d. 1918, Assistant Master 1869-1913), Cheltenham College Archives.
232	Cyril Lowry (d. 1918), War Memorial volume, Cheltenham College Archives.
232	Auriol Lowry (d. 1918), War Memorial volume, Cheltenham College Archives.
232	William Lowry (d. 1915), War Memorial volume, Cheltenham College Archives.
233	Minden Badcock (d. 1918), War Memorial volume, Cheltenham College Archives.
233	1, College Lawn, Cheltonian Home and House, Cheltenham College Gallery.
235	John Mather (d. 1915), War Memorial volume, Cheltenham College Archives.
235	Robert Mather (d. 1918), War Memorial volume, Cheltenham College Archives.
235	Ellis Mather (d. 1916), War Memorial volume, Cheltenham College Archives.
236	Charles Campbell, France 1914, courtesy IWM.
239	James Forbes-Robertson VC, courtesy The Border Regiment Museum.
243	Sydney Trevenen's Battlefield Cross from France, Cheltenham College Gallery.
246	George Delmar-Williamson (d. 1918), War Memorial volume, Cheltenham College Archives.
249	Wreckage of Gabell and Delmar-Williamson's RE 8, courtesy RAF Museum.
255	Guy Handley (d. 1918), War Memorial volume, Cheltenham College Archives.
256	The remains of the village of St Leger, 1918, courtesy IWM.

IMAGE SOURCES

274	Edward Knott (d. 1919), War Memorial volume, Cheltenham College Archives.
277	James Dearden (d. 1919), War Memorial volume, Cheltenham College Archives.
278	Reginald Wallace-Copland (d. 1919), War Memorial volume, Cheltenham College Archives.
279	Francis Prichard (d. 1920), War Memorial volume, Cheltenham College Archives.
281	Walter Sidebottom (d. 1921), Cheltenham College Archives.
282	John Wogan-Browne (d. 1922), 1911, Cheltenham College Archives.
284	William Grieve (d. 1915), War Memorial volume, Cheltenham College Archives.
284	James Grieve (d. 1918), Cheltondale 2nd XI, 1990, Cheltenham College Archives.
284	Charles Grieve (d. 1920), Cheltondale House Group photo, 1898; Cheltenham College Archives.
287	Memorial Plaques in College Chapel, Cheltenham College Gallery.
288	Presentation of the Cheltenham College Royal Colours, 1921, Cheltenham College Archives.
289	Cheltenham College Officers Training Corps Royal Colours Presentation Parade, 1921, Cheltenham College Archives.
290	College Memorial at the National Arboretum, Cheltenham College Gallery.
292	College Cricket in perpetuity (courtesy of John Jamieson-Black), Cheltenham College Gallery.
299	Harold Stables – Memorial Window in Chapel, Cheltenham College Gallery.
300	The plan for the Memorial Cloisters, Cheltenham College Archives.
302	Philip Elliot and his gravestone, Cheltenham College Gallery.
303	Richard Moore, College Master, on the Somme, Cheltenham College Gallery.
303	Remembrance. (Mr Dan Evans with Charlie Meecham-Jones, Oscar Bromage-Henry, Felix Watson-Smyth and Tommy Ladds), Cheltenham College Gallery.
304	Noel Edmund Forbes, Cheltenham College Archives.
304	Richard Coxwell-Rogers – Marker and Plaque, Cheltenham College Gallery.
305	Remembrance. (Henry Johnson, Noni Stuckey and Tommy Maddinson), Cheltenham College Gallery.
306	Remembrance. (Tommy and Charlotte Maddinson's tribute), Cheltenham College Gallery.
306	Charles Thomas (d. 1915), War Memorial volume, Cheltenham College Archives.
306	Remembrance. (Felix Watson-Smyth), Cheltenham College Gallery.
306	Gerald Gloster (d. 1917), War Memorial volume, Cheltenham College Archives.
307	Charles Cobbold (d. 1915), War Memorial volume, Cheltenham College Archives.
307	Arras Memorial to the Missing, with Cheltonian plaques, Cheltenham College Gallery.
307	Remembrance. (Angus Thomson), Cheltenham College Gallery.
307	Wilfred Desages (d. 1918), War Memorial volume, Cheltenham College Archives.
308	Remembrance. (Caitlin Brister and Victoria Brain), Cheltenham College Gallery.
308	William Grieve (d. 1915), Cheltondale XI hockey team, 1904, Cheltenham College Archives.
308	Remembrance. (Charles Hellens), Cheltenham College Gallery.
309	George Cope (d. 1916), War Memorial volume, Cheltenham College Archives.
309	Remembrance. (Freya Haddon outside the Badcocks' former residence, now her College House.), Cheltenham College Gallery.
310	Remembrance. Cheltonians remember at Cape Helles, Gallipoli, Cheltenham College Gallery.
311	Approved Design of the College Crest, Cheltenham College Archives.

INDEX

A

Abbott, GD	40
Abelson, EG	145, 162
Abraham, GWP	216
Adams, EC	65, 104
Adams, HI	132, 158
Adams-Mathieson, HFR	216
Aikenhead, R	98
Aldin, DC	156
Allaway, TR	158
Allen, GM	148, 160
Allen, RAS	98
Allen, T	96
American Expeditionary Force, US 1st Division	251
Apperly, AL	139, 160
Arbuthnot, ADS	126, 156
Armitage, FAW	266
Armstrong, GP	102
Armstrong, MRL	156
Astlay, AGL	212
Atkinson, FB	270
Atlay, HW	98
Attree, FHWT	100
Australian Imperial Force	
11th Infantry Battalion	250
51st Infantry Battalion	251
9th Australian Light Horse	21, 79
Ayrton, FJ	75, 102

B

Badcock, MF	233, 234, 266, 309
Baghot de la Bere, CJ	160
Baillie, G	40
Bainbridge-Bell, HU	268
Baines, AFCT	194, 212
Baines, HPB	212
Balders, AW	106
Banks, P d'A	98
Bannerman, OWE	58, 96
Barnes, GG	158
Barnes, J	162
Barton, CG	259, 270
Bayley, GB	40
Beadon BHE	102
Beale, RA	212
Bedfordshire Regiment, 2nd Battalion	170
Bell-Irving, K	216
Bertram, RG de la V	160
Best, TAD	216
Betjemen, Sir John	1
Bewicke, CG	137, 158
Bidie, GMV	148, 158
Bingen, CM	156
Bingham (Hon), RGA	270, 284
Birch, H	125, 156
Birch-Reynardson, EV	106
Bird, FC	96
Bird, K	80
Birnie, GB	270
Birtwistle, N	5, 270
Biscoe, AJ	96
Biscoe, FCF	100
Bishop, A	22
Blagrove, RC	102
Blakeway, NC	117, 156
Blest, MA	91, 106
Bligh, FA	104
Blomfield, CGM	100
Blood, B	104
Boileau, FRF	15, 38
Bolton, S	266
Bond, FHB	20, 100
Booth, FC (VC)	173, 174
Boothby, EB	158
Border Regiment,	
1st Battalion	238
2nd Battalion	52
Bottomley, HR	100
Bouck-Standen, PE	270
Bourgoyne-Wallace, DB	83, 96
Bowen, GES	214
Boyd, TC	214
Boyle, E (VC)	73, 74
Bradley, S	100
Bradshaw-Isherwood, FE	55, 98
Brain, V	308
Braithwaite, HL	158
Bramwell, CG	102

INDEX

Bredon, A	256	Princess Patricia's Light Infantry	202
Bredon, AS	251, 255, 268	2nd Canadian Anti-Tank Company	260
Bren, HAH	160	Mounted Rifles,	
Bridgeman, HHO	214	1st (Saskatchewan) Battalion	49, 67
Brister, C	308	No 5 Canadian General Hospital	127
Britten, RS	262, 268	Capel-Davies, JR	212
Bromage-Henry, O	303	Cardew, EB	104
Brooks, TE	56, 58, 100	Cardew, JH	216
		Carew, RT	171, 212
Brooke-Murray, KA	18, 147, 160	Carey, BC	270
		Carnegy, RL	102
Brooke-Taylor, AC	100	Caruth, JG	104
Brooke-Taylor, G	4	Catterson-Smith, TMO	279, 294
Brown, HW	38	Central Flying School, Upavon	189, 279
Browne, CNF	100	Chads, HC	47, 96
Browne, MC	145, 162	Chadwick, FJ	85, 98
Bruce, E	199	Chamberlin, JB	245, 268
Bryce-Smith, NI	268	Champion de Crestigny, CN	38, 121
Buckley, EM	102	Chard, RAF	158
Bullock, TEG	212	Cheetham, AH	162
Bush, JS deL	189, 216	Cheshire Regiment,	
Butler, LG	143, 160	1st Battalion	192
Buist, K	96	2nd Battalion	65
Byrde, E	22	Chesney, HF	294
		Chichester, Major General A	152
C		Clarke, HC	156
Caffyn, CHM	184, 212	Clayhills, G	40
Cameron, DA	216	Clayton, WJ	98
Cameron, JH	266	Clerk, RV	102
The Cameronians (Scottish Rifles),		Coates, GWT	52
10th Battalion	189	Cobbold, CA	104, 120, 307
Cameron Highlanders,			
1st Battalion	116	Cochran, HPG	266
2nd Battalion	284	Cockshott, FW	212
Campbell, AB	216	Coghill, NH	266
Campbell, CH	116, 156	Cohen, GH	100, 209
Campbell, CF	270	Cohen, J	208
Campbell, CLK	236, 266	Cohen, S	209
Campbell, DDH	198, 214	Coker, JC	38
Campbell, JD	38	Coldstream Guards, 2nd Battalion	255
Campbell, IP	98, 119	Cole-Hamilton, CWE	187, 214
Campbell, WUM	96	Collier, DC	254, 268
Canadian Expeditionary Force		Collingwood-Thompson, E	38
3rd Battalion	203	Collins, PRM	214
7th (British Columbia) Battalion	285	Connaught Rangers,	
31st (Alberta) Infantry Battalion	258	1st Battalion	13, 54
49th (Edmonton) Infantry Battalion	251, 255	2nd Battalion	55
		Conran, PWD	266
98th (Lincoln and Welland) Battalion	203	Conybeare, EB	156
		Conybeare, MHC	96

INDEX

Coomber, B	285	Desages, WR	19, 227, 241, 266, 307
Coomber, HA	268, 285		
Cooper, R	20,		
Cooper, SG	20, 104	Devonshire Regiment,	
Cope, GE	132, 158, 308, 309	2nd Battalion	86
		9th (Service) Battalion	134
Coplestone, F	17, 20, 29, 30, 42, 73,	Dick, JC	98
		Dickinson, GB	98
		Dickinson, HC	294
Cowan, RC	40	Dickinson, RS	104
Cox, RAH	250, 268	Dickinson, WV	216
Coxwell-Rogers, N	5	Dickson, AF	199, 268
Coxwell-Rogers, RH	102	Dickson, AG	214
Crane, CE	38	Dickson, WH	199, 214
Crawford, E	100	Dighton, LP	21, 198, 214
Crawford, JC	19, 160		
Crawshay, M	40	Disney, EO	45, 111, 156
Creagh, O'MC	229, 266		
Creed, CO	100	Doherty-Holwell, RV	168, 212
Crichton, HR	171, 212	Doidge-Harrison, J	v, 302
Crofton, EVM	214	Donald, CGH	252, 268
Crooke, EH	158	Dorsetshire Regiment,	
Crooke, HN	19, 162	1st Battalion	115, 117
Culley, GMG	160	2nd Battalion	86, 105
Cummins, FK	266	5th Battalion	81, 102
Cummins, HJ	102	Dove, EH	212
Cunningham, CA	102	Down, CB	294
Cutfield, H	96	Dragoon Guards,	
		4th	6, 281
D		7th	281
Damiano, WH	158	Drysdale, HD	104
Darnell, CV	186, 212	Du Boulay, AH	5, 261, 270
Dashwood, LA	100		
Daubeney, GHJ	104	Du Boulay, HLH	5, 160
Davidson, GL	158	Dunlop, GM	70
Davidson, RIM	40	Dunsterville, GE	40
Davis, AH	125, 156	Durand, RHM	158
Davy, JE	294	Durham, E	42
Dawe, RHO'N	160	Dyer AE	191
Deakin, CG	156	Dyer, F	192
Dearden, JF	277, 294	Dyer, HA	191, 216
De Lautour, HA	214	Dyer, L	192
Delmar-Williamson, GF	246, 247, 248, 268		
		E	
Denne, WH	170, 212	Edwards, C O'R	106
Dennis, C	266	Elliot, RWS	40
Denroche-Smith, AJ	38	Elliot, WCA	158
Desages, G	227,	Elliott, CA	280, 294
Desages, OL	19, 227, 241, 268	Elliott, PL	38, 302
		Elmslie, KW	40
Desages, P	227	Elwes, RHLC	21, 40

INDEX

Essex Regiment, 10th Battalion	115	Gabell, I	183
Evans, D	303	Gabell, R	183
Evans, HTP	160	Gard'ner, BGC	98
Evans, RWP	262, 268	Gharwal Rifles, 39th Battalion	91, 107
Evatt, GRK	40	Garnett, PN	27
Eyre, SHR	212	Garrett, RD	203, 216
Ezra, DE	268	Garstang, CH	195, 214
		Garstang, W	195
F		Gatacre, EG	156
Fairburn, AH	100	Geddes, AD	98
Fairtlough, FH	65, 104	Geddes, JG	294
Fane, OE	270	Geoghegan, JR	40
Fawcett, BJA	212	Gilliatt, CGP	13, 14, 17, 24, 25, 38
Featherstone, MB	201, 216		
Fenton, GR	38		
Ferguson, JCM	294	Gilliatt, RHC	13, 14, 54, 55, 98
Ferris, SBC	98		
Festing, HW	266		
Fifth Glo'ster Gazette	140	Girardot, PC	38
Findlay, JT	102	Glenny, HQ	40
Finke, RF	98	Gloster, GCE	216, 306
Finnimore, A	150	Gloucestershire Regiment,	
Finnimore, DK	150, 214	1/5th Battalion	139
Fisher, CEH	102	2/5th Battalion	230
Fitzgerald, J	151	7th (Service) Battalion	151
Fleming, JH	104	Godley, GAG	266
Flint, RB	96	Goodeve, L	102
Floyd, HM	70, 100	Gordon, CG	38
Foord, EA	268	Gore, ACE StG	102
Footner, HE	158	Gore, GR	42
Forbes, FR	19, 104	Gosset, RF	160
Forbes NE	19, 100, 304	Gransmore, R	104
		Grant, H deB	104
Forbes-Robertson, A	124, 156	Grant, IAW	212
Forbes-Robertson, H	124	Grantham, HF	102
Forbes-Robertson, J (VC)	238, 239, 240	Greatwood, H	216
		Gregory, HW	216
Forbes-Robertson, K	40, 238	Gresson, JE	100
Forbes-Semphill, RA	100	Grieve, CC	20, 284, 294
Forde, LW	268		
Fort, L	96	Grieve, JR	20, 266, 284
Foster, ACH	38		
Frankland, RCC	70, 102	Grieve, WP	20, 96, 284, 308
Frankland, THC	70, 98		
Fuller, JS	294	Griffith, RV de B	96
Furse, GA	38	Grogan, EG	220
		Grogan, GF	266
G		Grogan, JC	74 100, 220
Gabell, C	183		
Gabell, DRC	183, 245, 248, 268	Grose, WM	220, 266
		Growse, RH	294

324

INDEX

Gudgeon, FG	75 102	HMNZT *Star of India*	80
Gulland, AF	214	HMS *Aboukir*	9, 12, 13, 28
Gunning, EGR	274, 294	HMS *Arethusa*	45, 111
		HMS *Britannia*	16, 73, 88
H			
Haddon, F	309	HMS *Bulwark*	30
Hadley, H	22, 23, 38, 273	HMS *Cressy*	28
Haig, Field Marshal Sir Douglas	109, 127, 238	HMS *Egmont*	73
		HMS *Endymion*	29
Hall, AH	162	HMS *Formidable*	45, 47, 111
Hamilton, JW	100		
Hamilton, S	304	HMS *Furious*	249
Hampshire Regiment,		HMS *Hawke*	16, 29
2nd Battalion	76	HMS *Hogue*	28
Handley, GFB	255, 268	HMS *Implacable*	89
Harding, JM	40	HMS *Lark*	89
Harington, Major General Sir CH	153, 165	HMS *Lord Nelson*	73
Harington, WG	216	HMS *Onyx*	73
Harries-Jones, LA	158	HMS *Pegasus*	89
Hart, AC	98	HMT *Alaunia*	125
Harvey, KW	104	HS *Kildonan Castle*	113
Harvey-James, AK	212	HS *Soudan*	113
Hattersley-Smith, GA	88, 89, 104	HS *St Patrick*	227
		Hodson, C	151
Hattersley-Smith, J	88	Hodson, F	151
Hattersley-Smith, Percy	87, 88, 224	Hodson, G	151
		Hodson, HB	98
Hawkins, AE	216	Hodson, R	151
Hay, DW	270	Hodson, T	151
Hazel, AW	277, 294	Holmes, FL	40
Heath, G	248, 268	Holmes, TG	266
Hellens, C	308	Homfray, RP	266
Henderson, PG	166, 241, 268	Honourable Artillery Company,	
		1st Battalion	220
Herbert, JG	160	Hope-Johnstone, HM	214
Hewett, GE	96	Hope-Johnstone, WGT	40
Hewett, H	222, 266	Hore, CO	156
Heywood, FK	270	Hornby, HL	268
Highland Light Infantry,		Hornby, JH	270
12th Battalion	105	Hospitals,	
Hillier, CAH	5, 19, 22, 34, 47, 49, 264	No 1 British Red Cross, Le Touquet	243
		No 2 Surgical, Abbeville	281
Hind, ACS	86, 98	No 7 Stationary, Boulogne	148
Hirst, CP	134, 158	No 8 Stationary, Wimereux	251
HM Submarine *D2*	17, 20, 29, 30	No 8 General, Le Havre	146
		No 14 General, Boulogne	232
HM Submarine *E14*	74	No 16 General, Le Treport	53
HMAT *Itonus*	250	No 19 British General, Rawalpindi	280
HMAT *Karoo*	79	Royal Naval Hospital, Bighi, Malta	113

INDEX

Hough, JEC	190, 216
Hovenden, AL	214
Howe, GFT	98
Hughes-Games, GB	266
Humphreys, DF	100
Hunt, JCM	160

I

Ievers, OG	156
Inglis, A McC	294
Iohnson, EF	216
Isherwood, FEB	98

J

James CK	268
James, EG	160
James, GM	40
Jameson, JB	268
Jamieson, GA	156
Jenkins, RA	156
Jeune, H StH	214
Johns, G	270
Johnson, H	305
Johnston, CMcG	262, 270
Jollie, FOH	98
Jones, VHS	214
Joseph, WGA	212
Jowitt, TL	102

K

Kay, NRW	268
Kellett, RHV	160
Kenworthy, D	60
Ker, AM	38
Ker, CH	38
Kerr, HG	214
Kerr, HRG	42
Kershaw, SR	214
King's African Rifles, 1st Battalion	27
King's (Liverpool) Regiment,	
1st Battalion	131
1/5th Battalion	208
1/6th Battalion	19, 227
17th Battalion	234
King's Own Scottish Borderers,	
1st Battalion	74, 207
King's Own Yorkshire Light	
Infantry, 9th Battalion	253
Knott, EM	273, 274, 294
Knowling, FJD	266
Knox, AR	212
Kuhn, AE	100

L

Ladds, T	303
Lake, NG	230, 266
Lambert, FC	156
Lancashire Fusiliers, 2nd Battalion	23, 132
Lancers,	
15th	58, 97
16th	235, 236
Landale, JR	112, 126, 156
Lanyon, WM	98
Lascelles, RH	294
Laverton, FK	190, 216
Layng, GRS	160
Lee, CS	91 106
Lee, Sir Arthur (Lord Fareham)	6, 10, 219, 287, 299, 301
Lee, HN	42
Lee, HW	294
Legard, GB	40
Leicestershire Yeomanry	56, 57
Leicestershire Regiment,	
6th Battalion	220
Leinster Regiment,	
5th Battalion	54
Lemon, VB	266
Leslie, RFWF	81, 102
Leslie-Smith, K	5
Lewin, FH	90
Ley, JW	270
Littledale, AC	100
Littleton, CFH	214
Livock, G	5
Llewellyn, HA	126, 158
Lloyd, FCA	104
Lloyd, GA	96
Loch, AAF	158
Lock, H	30
Lockley, REH	104
Lodwick, JT	91
London Regiment,	
1/14th (London Scottish) Battalion	26, 199
1/24th (The Queen's) Battalion	228
28th (Artists Rifles) Battalion	201
Long, C	v, 297
Longden, AH	294

INDEX

Longstaff, Right Reverend J	291	Maddinson, T	305, 306
Louis, AG	160	Mahratta Light Infantry,	
Lousada, BC	14, 55, 58	110th Battalion	86
		Manley, JD	38
Lousada, C	14,	Manley, TW	223, 266
Lousada, EA	14, 25, 26, 58	Mansel, JL	42
		Mansfield, CJ	156
Lousada, W	14, 58	Marker, TM	216
Lowndes, EW	100	Markham-Rose, K	87, 98
Lowry, AEE	231, 256, 270, 283	Marsden, E	100, 281, 294
Lowry, CJP	231, 266, 283	Marten, HH	102
		Martin AG	266
Lowry, WAH	100, 232, 283	Martin, GCR	268
		Mason, AEK	156
Lowther, TB	100	Mather, E	158, 234, 235, 283
Loyal North Lancashire Regiment, 4th Battalion	199	Mather, JK	96, 235, 283
Loye, RP	171, 212		
Lucas, CM	158	Mather, R	234, 235, 266, 283
Lucas, MH	294		
Lyall, CG	38	Matthey, EG	132, 158
Lynch-Staunton, RK	263, 270	Matthey, SE	257, 270
Lywood, KPG	266	Maude, CCW	21, 79, 102

M

		Maxwell, J	102
Maby, LB	165, 241, 268	Maxwell, JMcC	156
		Mayne, AB	216
MacBryan, EC	121, 158	McCammon, TVP	214
Macdonald, DR	16, 29	McCormick, JG	100
Macdonnell, AC	64	McGregor, DG	26, 27, 40
Macdonnell, HC	63, 100		
MacFadyen, ND	98	McKay, HM	40
MacGeough-Bond, RS	201, 214	McKay, WE	26, 27
Machine Gun Corps,		McLean, JRG	268
16th Company	204	Meecham-Jones, C	303, 307
27th Company	177	Meikle, WRD	207, 216
190th Company	145	Meire, WHG	104
MacKay, DRG	264, 270	Melvill, T (VC)	15, 16
MacKenzie, CL	38	Meyricke, RJC	112, 156
MacKenzie, FO	83, 96	Middlesex Regiment,	
Mackinnon, N	128	16th (Public Schools) Battalion	125, 230, 239
Mackinnon, RF	160		
Macleod, AR	98	Mills, HV	214
Macleod, GC	266	Mitchell, TFW	266
MacNeece, JDG	158, 168	Moll, JA	275, 294
MacNeece, JFD	167	Molson, EE	54, 96
MacNeece, WF	167	Momber, EMF	214
MacPherson, J	132, 158	Mond, Sir Alfred	300
Macrae, FL	104	Monkton, MH	102
Maddinson, C	306	Montagnon, BC	203, 216

INDEX

Montgomery, AS	126, 158
Montgomery, B (Field Marshal, of Alamein)	25
Monmouthshire Regiment,	
1/2nd Battalion	22, 34, 47, 61
3rd Battalion	58
Moody, TLV	266
Moor, GRD (VC)	76, 77, 262, 270
Moore, RCD	216
Moore, JO'H	42
Moore, R	303
Moores, CG	42
Morgan, HP	258, 216
Morgan, WD	104
Morris, WF	270
Morse, GTH	38
Mortimore, OJ	86, 104
Moss, EH	104
Mottram, PJMcQ	278, 294
Murray, GR	162

N

Neame, G	266
Neame, GT	134 158
Neame, P (VC)	33
Nesbitt, MS	23, 38
Newfoundland Regiment,	
1st Battalion	238
Newton, VF	143, 160
New Zealand Expeditionary Force, 2nd Battalion	198
Nicholson, BH	214
Nigerian Regiment, 2nd Battalion	27
Nix, PK	30, 42
Nixon, ALE	294
Nixon, GF	40
Noel, FM	216
Norfolk Regiment,	
1/5th Battalion	77, 78
7th Battalion	258
9th Battalion	89
Norman, SS	42
North, WBG	130, 156
Northumberland Fusiliers,	
20th (Tyneside Scottish) Battalion	132
Norton, LG	38
Notts and Derby Regiment,	
1/7th (Sherwood Foresters) Battalion	134
11th (Sherwood Foresters) Battalion	259
Noyes, RE	104

O

O'Callaghan, D McK M	96
Odling, ERM	96
Officer Cadet Battalions,	
No 4 Oxford	264
No 5, Trinity College, Cambridge	166
No 20, Crookham	263
O'Keefe, MM	266
Oldham, LWS	102
Onslow, BW	102
Orlebar, RE	47, 96
Osborne, MG	96
Osmaston, OCH	216
Owen, NM	38
Owen, RM	158
Oxfordshire and Buckinghamshire Light Infantry	
1st Battalion	125
3rd Battalion	125

P

Page, RB	40
Parsons, KTJ	196, 214
Patrick, DB	158
Payne, JO	98
Peel, AR	27, 28
Peel, CM	98
Peile, JSC	214
Pemberton, A	258
Pemberton, O	42, 258
Pemberton, VT	258, 270
Percival-Maxwell, RN	235, 266
Percy-Smith, V	294
Perrier, HCL	263, 270
Persse, CdeBG	102
Peyton, JAW	258, 268
Phibbs, WGB	40
Philpot, G	160
Pigg, C	22, 135
Popplewell, BB	270
Pottinger, ROB	100
Poulet (Earl), WJL	260, 268
Powell-Ackroyd, FA	253, 268
Pownall, GH	73, 98
Prendergast, CR	156
Prichard, FH	279, 294
Prichard-Evans, EL	270
Proctor-Beauchamp, MBG	77, 102

INDEX

Punjabis,
    66th Battalion — 86, 106
    69th Battalion — 171
Purdey, MS — 156
Purdon, TO — 160
Pym, WP — 169, 212

Q
Quill, MD — 268

R
Radcliffe, FV — 268
Radcliffe, JF — 115, 156
Radcliffe, SR — 268
Rainey, EF — 158
Rajputs, 7th Battalion — 83
Ramsay, N — 40
Ramsbottom, R — 158
Rawlinson, LH — 98
Raymond, EWH — 100
Rayner, NR — 187, 214
Reed, HWT — 22, 61, 98
Reeves, SR — 294
Reeves, VCM — 156
Regiment of Foot, 24th — 15
Reid, FH — 60, 100
Reid, JG — 160
Reilly, AST — 171, 212
Reilly, RA — 40
Renny, GM — 212
Reynolds, D (VC) — 23, 115, 156, 170, 259
Richardson, GSt J — 162
Rickerby, JHE — 230, 266
Rimington, ECW — 65, 104
Riordan, H de B — 100
Ripley, CR — 40
RMS *Arcadian*, — 194
RMS *Coronia*, — 281
RMS *Lusitania*, — 45, 66
Roberts, A — 81, 102
Roberts, AD — 189, 216
Roberts, RJ — 216
Robertson, ADC — 9, 12, 28, 38
Robinson, AT — 214
Robinson, DGM — 100
Robinson, GM — 270
Robinson, HA — 156

Rohde, JH — 40
Rolph, CC — 104
Rome, HC — 42
Rowland, JWB — 270
Royal Air Force,
    No 1 Communications Squadron, Kenley — 274
    No 48 Squadron — 254
    No 55 Squadron — 264
    No 56 Squadron — 254
    No 131 Squadron — 245
    No 204 Squadron — 257
    No 209 Squadron — 257, 284
    No 5 (Military Aeronautics) School, Denham — 254
    No 13 Training School, Yatesbury — 245, 248
    No 33 Fighter School, Bircham Newton — 257
    No 9 Depot Training Station, Shawbury — 245
    No 56 Depot Training Squadron, Cranwell — 246
Royal Berkshire Regiment,
    2nd Battalion — 52
Royal Dublin Fusiliers,
    1st Battalion — 70, 72
    2nd Battalion — 263
Royal Engineers, 183rd
    Tunnelling Company — 220
Royal Field Artillery,
    37th Battery — 24
    51st Battery — 168
    108th Brigade — 229
    112th Brigade — 198
    296th Brigade — 198
Royal Flying Corps,
    No 3 Squadron — 62, 167
    No 4 Squadron — 245
    No 5 Squadron — 64
    No 8 Squadron — 279
    No 11 squadron — 148
    No 15 Squadron — 148
    No 17 Squadron — 244
    No 21 Squadron — 247
    No 25 Squadron — 186
    No 41 Squadron — 189
    No 43 Squadron — 149
    No 53 Squadron — 170
    No 56 (Reserve Training) Squadron — 187
    No 57 Squadron — 187

INDEX

No 59 Squadron	185
No 60 Squadron	184
No 65 Squadron	193
No 67 Squadron	222
No 87 Squadron	254
No 113 Squadron	222
No 10 Training Squadron	189
No 57 Training Squadron	264
No 1 School of Aerial Gunnery, Hythe	223
No 5 School of Military Aeronautics, Denham	254
No 3 School of Aerial Gunnery, New Romney	190
No 5 Training School, Castle Bromwich	187
Royal Fusiliers,	
6th (Reserve) Battalion	134
12th (Service) Battalion	171
16th (Reserve) Battalion	75
18th (1st Public Schools) Battalion	19, 241
19th (2nd Public Schools) Battalion	264
Royal Inniskilling Fusiliers,	
5th Battalion	127
6th Battalion	259
Royal Garrison Artillery,	
57th Siege Battery	60
216th Siege Battery	258
Royal Marine Light Infantry,	
1st Battalion	145
Royal Munster Fusiliers,	
7th Battalion	258
Royal Naval Air Service,	
No 1 Squadron	190
No 9 Squadron	246, A6
No 207 Training Depot, Chingford	190, A6
Fleet Practice Squadron	250
Royal Scots,	
1st Battalion	148
2nd Battalion	187
Royal Sussex Regiment, 2nd Battalion	14
Royal Warwickshire Regiment,	
1st Battalion,	13, 24, 25
Royal Welch Fusiliers, 15th Battalion	177
Royal West Surrey Regiment,	
8th (Service) Battalion	65
Russell, NJG	165, 241, 216

S

Sackville-Cresswell, AE	96
Saltren-Willett, AJ	216
Samson, OM	268
Sanders, AA	96
Sanger, J	5
Sarsfield, WS	38
Saunders, AH	52, 96
Saunders, AHR	125, 156
Saunderson, STB	244, 266
Saw, NHW	204, 216
Saward, HD	54, 96
Scots Guards, 2nd Battalion	165
Scott, AH	214
Scott, D	160, 291
Scott, LB	294
Seaforth Highlanders,	
2nd Battalion	252
1/4th Battalion	116
Sharp, FAH	270
Sharp, FL	160
Shaw, Giles H	212, 260
Shaw, Greville H	260, 270
Shaw, RP	106
Shaw (Schwabe), MS	66, 104
Shelmerdine, GO	165
Shewell, PG	104
Shubrick, RB	98
Shurey, C	158
Sidebottom, RY	23, 38
Sidebottom, W	125, 171, 280, 281, 294
Silk, NG	102
Sim, BV	98
Simpson, FWH	169, 212
Smith, EP	98
Smith, JB	214
Smith PL	104
Soames, WN	156
Solomon, LI	212
Sorby, CMC	58
Somerset Light Infantry,	
1st Battalion	60, 189
South Wales Borderers,	
8th (Service) Battalion	126
Sparrow, BC	52, 96
Sparrow, GWS	270
SS *Caledonia*	18
SS *City of Edinburgh*	19

INDEX

SS *Gartness*	195, 196	Thomas-O'Donel, G O'DF	102
SS *Hirano Maru*	262	Thompson, IFR	212
SS *Nile*	281	Thompson, RWHEDF	104
SS *Persia*	91	Thomson, A	307
SS *River Clyde*	69, 76	Thomson, HGA	212
SS *Salta*	276	Thornhill, JE	270
SS *Winifredian*	26	Thornton, GRH	266
St Hill, FH	160	Thornton, LN	158
Stables, HR	40, 298	Thursby, AD	96
Stainforth, RT	38	Tindall, EV	38
Stansfeld, HA	32, 42	Tindall, RF	104
Stanuell, CM	38	Torney, TFH	268
Steinman, BP	156	Torrie, TGJ	162
Stewart, AD	189, 216	Tosswill, WR	160
Stewart, B	156	Townsend, CC	266
Stirling, WD	40	Townsend, GJ	89, 106
Stock, JLW	214	Townsend, REL	266
Stock, JMT	162	Trevenen, S	176, 177, 182, 200, 206, 220, 226, 227, 228, 242, 243, 268
Stokes, TF	212		
Stotherd, SB	104		
Stuart, CM	294		
Stuart, JM,	185, 212		
Stuckey, N	305		
Sulivan, HE	202, 216	Trimmer, WC	158
Swales, GM	216	Tuke, FH	9, 150, 158
Sweet-Escott, LW	104		
Swiney, ERR	91, 106	Turnbull, HVC	40
Swinhoe, EA	270	Turner, CRS	158
Sykes, GW	100	Turner, GP	158
		Turner, HG	96
T		Turner, HS	106
Talbot, JLP	270	Turnly, JF	266
Tandy, AMS	38	Tyler, AH	40
Tanner, JA	214		
Tanner, JC	245, 268	**U**	
Tannett-Walker, FW	212	Urquhart, EFM	40
Tate, FH	214	USS *Sterett*	262
Tate, WL	96		
Taylor, CM	212	**V**	
Taylor, EM	49, 67, 68, 91, 109, 122, 128, 156	Vanrenan, AS	102
		Vaughan GC	158
		Vaughan, JM	61, 100
		Vicat, FH	208, 216
Taylor, HM	102	Vicat, HJ	38
Taylor, RS	275, 294	Villar, RH	216
Terry, A	209	Vyall, LE	160
Terry, WG	162		
Thomas, BLB	177, 212	**W**	
Thomas, CE	80, 81, 104, 306	Waddell, JD	104
		Wakefield, MS	216
Thomas, OR	276, 294	Walker, HN	275, 294

INDEX

Walker, R	160	Winterbotham, CW	139, 160, 298
Walker-Coren, E	102		
Wallace-Copland, R	278, 294	Winterbotham, J	139,142
Wallis, DB	102	Wise, AVD	214
Walsh, TE	165	Wiseman-Clarke, CFR	156
Walter, B	160	Wogan-Browne, JH	282, 294
Walter, WF	102	Wolstenholme, GM	270, 301
Walters, EC	42	Wood, CK	270
Warren, D	38	Wood, GD	104
Warren-Sweatenham, TEW	96	Wood, RP	160
Waterfield, Reverend Reginald, College Principal	152, 167, 225, 287	Wood-Martin, FW	96
		Wood-Martin, JI	96
		Woodham, CB	102
Waterhouse, R	98	Woodhouse, AJ	40
Watson-Smyth, F	306	Woodhouse, B	216
Webb, EM	98	Woodhouse, GS	104
Webster, JAC	212	Woodiwiss, IN	62, 100
Wedd, EPW	268	Woollatt, CH	160
Wellesley's Rifles, 104th Battalion	85	Woollatt, PR	158
Welsh Regiment,		Woollcombe, JM	212
2nd Battalion	138	Woolstenholme, G	120, 270
1/4th Battalion	263	Worcestershire Regiment,	
Welstead, HM	102	2nd Battalion	135
West, FCB	120, 160	4th Battalion	204
West Yorkshire Regiment,		Worsey, TA	160
2nd Battalion	187, 208, 231	Wrigley, HN	216
		Wythes, CA	98
Whipple, HC	42		
White, LW	38, 121	# Y	
White, GSA	38	York and Lancaster Regiment,	
Whitehead, H	156	1st Battalion	55
Widowfield, G	104	Yorkshire Regiment,	
Wiggin, NH	212	6th (Service) Battalion	82
Wilkinson, RHS	178, 179, 180, 181, 212	Young, HN	259, 270
Wilkinson, TWM	268		
Williams, FT	158		
Williams, RB	160		
Willis, HD	214		
Willis, SA	214		
Willoughby, EC	102		
Willoughby, JG	96		
Willoughby, Lieutenant General M	289		
Wills, JP	21, 196		
Wilson, CR	214		
Wilson, CW	52, 96		
Wilson, SC	22		
Wiltshire Regiment,			
1st Battalion	241		
Winter, WO	294		